In Search of the Forty Days Road

A Desert Dies

Impossible Journey

Shoot to Kill: A Soldier's Journey through Violence

Thesiger: A Biography

The Last of the Bedu: In Search of the Myth

Sahara (*with Kazoyoshi Nomachi*)

Phoenix Rising: The United Arab Emirates, Past, Present and Future (*with Werner Forman*)

LAWRENCE

The Uncrowned King of Arabia

Michael Asher

With colour photographs by
Mariantonietta Peru

VIKING

VIKING

Published by the Penguin Group
Penguin Books Ltd, 27 Wrights Lane, London w8 5tz, England
Penguin Putnam Inc., 375 Hudson Street, New York, New York 10014, USA
Penguin Books Australia Ltd, Ringwood, Victoria, Australia
Penguin Books Canada Ltd, 10 Alcorn Avenue, Toronto, Ontario, Canada m4v 3b2
Penguin Books (NZ) Ltd, Private Bag 102902, NSMC, Auckland, New Zealand

Penguin Books Ltd, Registered Offices: Harmondsworth, Middlesex, England

First published 1998
1 3 5 7 9 10 8 6 4 2

Copyright © Michael Asher, 1998
Colour photographs copyright © Mariantonietta Peru, 1998
Maps copyright © Reg and Marjorie Piggott, 1998
The moral right of the author has been asserted

Set in 11.25/13.75pt Monotype Baskerville
Typeset by Rowland Phototypesetting Limited, Bury St Edmunds, Suffolk
Printed in Great Britain by Clays Ltd, St Ives plc

A CIP catalogue record for this book is available from the British Library

isbn 0–670–87029–3

For Mariantonietta

Arian Hok Buda

'The story I have to tell is one of the most splendid ever given to a man for telling.'

T. E. Lawrence to Vyvyan Richards

'Il faut souffrir pour être content.'

T. E. Lawrence to Charlotte Shaw

CONTENTS

PART THREE: THE MAGICIAN, 1918–1935

LIST OF PLATES

ILLUSTRATION ACKNOWLEDGEMENTS

The author and publishers are grateful to the following for permission to reproduce black and white photographs:

The Lawrence Estate and the Bodleian Library, Oxford, for nos. 1, 2, 3, 42, 43
The Trustees of the Imperial War Museum, London, for nos. 8–20, 22–24, 26–34, 36, 37, 40

The National Trust Photographic Library for no. 4
The Liddell Hart Centre for Military Archives, King's College, London, for nos. 5, 6, 7, 21, 25, 35, 39, 44
St Martin's, Wareham, for no. 46 (both photographs)
The National Portrait Gallery, London, for no. 38
The Visitors of the Ashmolean Museum, Oxford, for no. 41

LIST OF MAPS

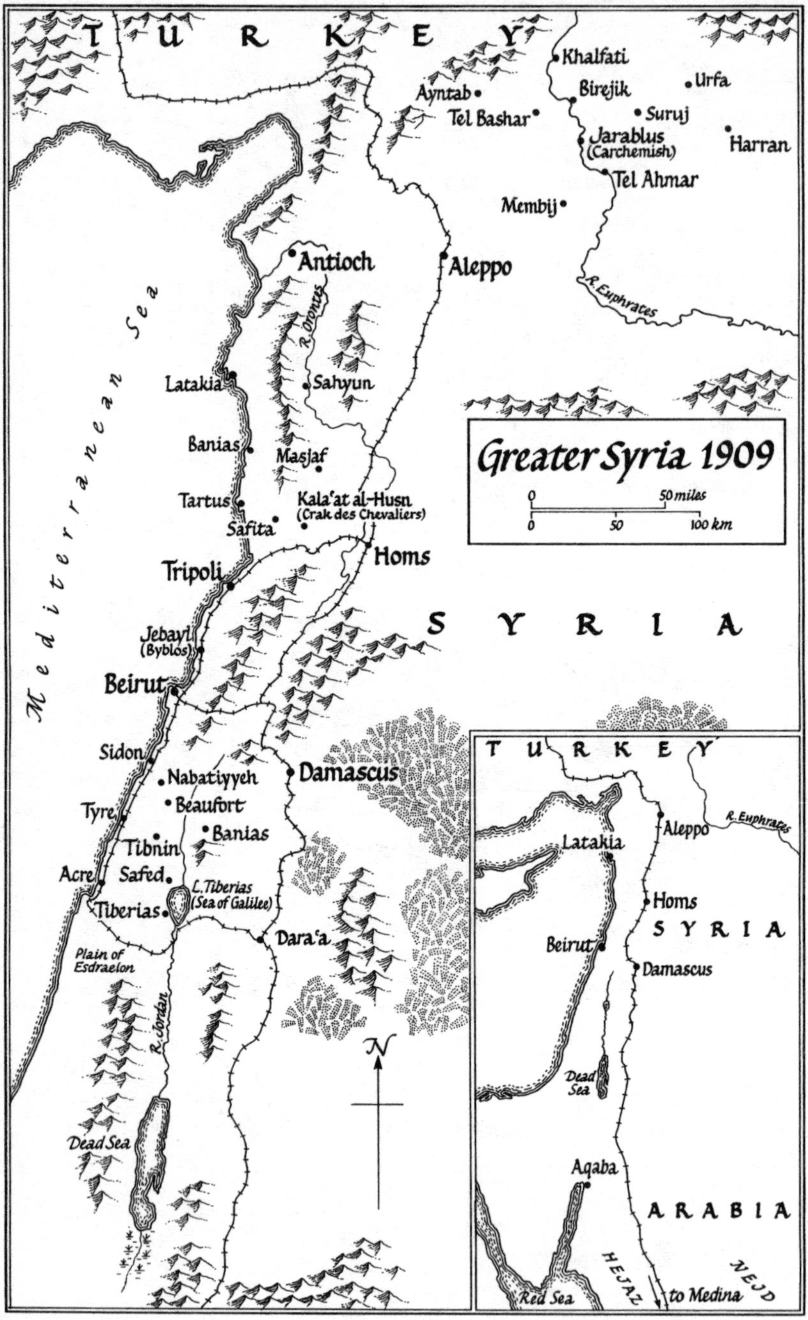

TURKEY
Khalfati
Urfa
Ayntab
Birejik
Suruj
Tel Bashar
Jarablus
(Carchemish)
Harran
Tel Ahmar
Membij
Antioch
Aleppo
R. Euphrates
Mediterranean Sea
R. Orontes
Latakia
Sahyun
Banias
Masjaf
Greater Syria 1909
0
50 miles
0
50
100 km
Tartus
Kala'at al-Husn
(Crak des Chevaliers)
Safita
Homs
Tripoli
SYRIA
Jebayl
(Byblos)
Beirut
Sidon
Nabatiyyeh
Damascus
Beaufort
Tyre
Banias
Tibnin
Acre
Safed
L. Tiberias
(Sea of Galilee)
Tiberias
Dara'a
Plain of
Esdraelon
R. Jordan
N
Dead Sea
TURKEY
Aleppo
R. Euphrates
Latakia
Homs
SYRIA
Beirut
Damascus
Dead Sea
Aqaba
ARABIA
HEJAZ
NEJD
Red Sea
to Medina

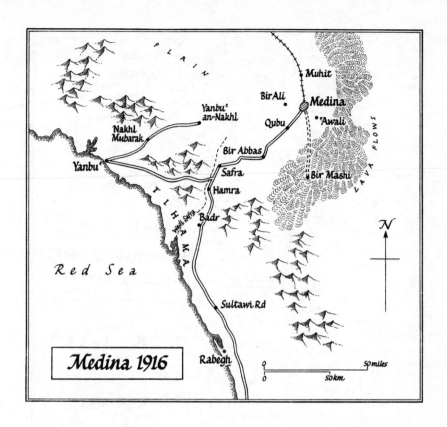

PLAIN

Muhit

Bir Ali   Medina

Yanbuᶜ
an-Nakhl   Qubu   ᶜAwali

Nakhl
Mubarak

Bir Abbas

Yanbuᶜ   Safra   Bir Mashi

Hamra

Wadi Safra   Badr

Red Sea   *T I H A M A*

Sultawi Rd

Medina 1916

Rabegh

LAVA FLOWS

N

0   50 miles
0   50 km

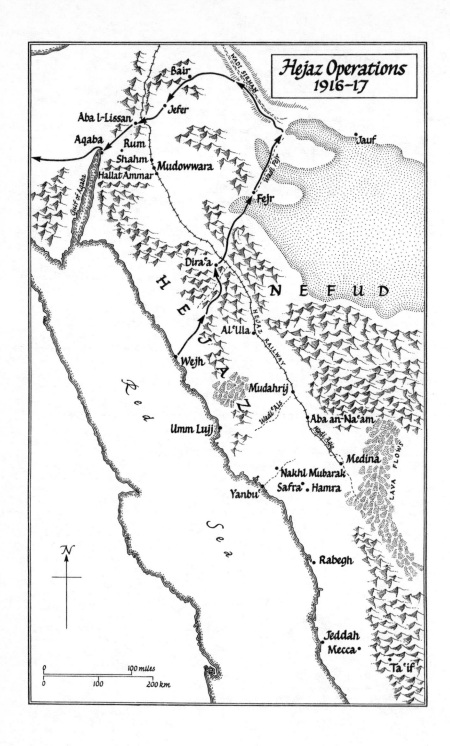

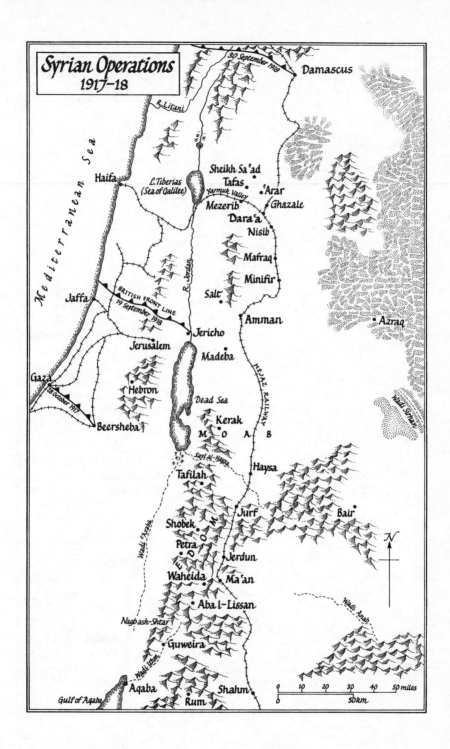

Syrian Operations 1917–18

Damascus

30 September 1918

R. Litani

Haifa

Mediterranean Sea

L. Tiberias (Sea of Galilee)

Sheikh Sa'ad
Tafas
'Arar
Yarmuk Valley
Mezerib
Ghazale
Dara'a
Nisib
Mafraq
Minifir

R. Jordan

Jaffa

BRITISH FRONT LINE
19 September 1918

Salt

Amman

Azraq

Jericho

Jerusalem
Madeba

HEJAZ RAILWAY

Gaza
28 October 1917

Hebron

Dead Sea

Wadi Sirhan

Beersheba

Sayl al-Hasa

Kerak
M O A B

Haysa

Tafilah

Jurf
Bair

Shobek

E D O M

Petra
Jerdun
N

Waheida
Ma'an

Wadi Ghazala

Aba l-Lissan

Wadi Aqab

Nagb ash-Shtar

Guweira

Wadi Itim

Aqaba
Shahm
Gulf of Aqaba
Rum

0 10 20 30 40 50 miles
0 50 km

Introduction:
The Valley of the Moon

On a hot morning in April I climbed a hillside in the Wadi Rum, in Jordan, pausing occasionally to savour the breath of the desert wind which was peeling off the canyons I could see below me, gnarled in ancient orange light. They might have been remnants of some great Martian city warped and buckled by time – indeed, the Bedu of Rum call it the Valley of the Moon and believe that it crashed to earth from the stars. I was looking for a place known as Lawrence's Spring, where T. E. Lawrence – 'Lawrence of Arabia' – had bathed during his sojourns in the wadi in 1917. In my knapsack I carried nothing but an enamel mug and a battered copy of his *Seven Pillars of Wisdom* – a book I had read and re-read over many years. Today, though, it felt as heavy as a millstone. I had just left the tent of some Bedu of the Howaytat – descendants of tribesmen who had actually ridden with Lawrence on his raids – and what they had had to say astonished me. 'Lawrence wasn't the leader of the Arab Revolt,' one of them told me. 'He was just an engineer who knew how to blow up the railway – a dynamite man – that's all he was!' T. E. Lawrence had been a childhood hero for me as for thousands of others, and the words of these Arabs struck an almost blasphemous note in my ears.

It took me only twenty minutes to find what I was looking for: the spring lay in a V-shaped cleft where water plunged down from the head of Rum mountain, thousands of feet above, gurgling into a rock cistern from which ribbles of silver liquid streamed out through shallow pools and luxuriant growths of mint and wild thyme. I filled the mug with water from the cistern and tasted it – it was sweet and deliciously cool. Then I sat down in the shade of the rock wall, opened *Seven Pillars* at the pre-marked page, and began to read: '. . . a rushing noise came from my left,' Lawrence had written, 'by a jutting bastion of a cliff over whose crimson face trailed long, falling runners of green leaves ... on the rock bulge above were clean-cut Nabataean inscriptions and a sunk panel ... and Arab scratchings, some of which were witnesses of forgotten migrations, but my attention was only for the splashing of water in an opening under the shadow of an overlying rock.'[1] I glanced up to find the Nabataean inscriptions and Arab tribal marks, exactly where Lawrence had seen them almost eighty years before. I took in the rushing of the water, the green, fragrant streamers of the wild herbs, and was momentarily stunned by the immediacy of the description. It was as if Lawrence of Arabia, who died eighteen years before I was born, was actually there beside me: I could almost sense his presence, as if he were peering over my shoulder. Glancing back at the page, I had the irrational but powerful feeling that he was speaking directly to me – that he had somehow *known* that I would follow in his footsteps, and had written this especially for me to read at this very moment, on this very day.

I have often experienced such transcendent visions while travelling in the desert. The vastness, the silence, the emptiness, induces a timeless feeling that is almost palpable: I have picked up prehistoric hand-axes lying on the surface, knowing that my hand was the first to touch them since they were discarded by their makers 100,000 years ago. Somehow, in the desert, the human spirit can leap over even such a gap as this. I was certain that Lawrence felt it too, for *Seven Pillars* is permeated by a sense of spiritual awe which is, for me, the essence of human experience in the desert. T. E. Lawrence has affected my life with particular power. Without Lawrence I would probably not have become an Arabic speaker and a camel-rider, would not have covered 16,000 miles by camel, nor made the first ever west–east crossing of the Sahara – a distance of 4,500 miles – nor lived with a traditional Bedu tribe for three years. Without Lawrence I would probably not have served in the Special Air Service Regiment, simply because without Lawrence there would probably never have been an SAS. The words of my Howaytat hosts still burned in my head, and as I sat there I wondered, as so many others had wondered before me, who Lawrence had really been. To his adulators, everything he said or wrote is held up as true, while his critics have gone to extraordinary lengths to prove the reverse. Surely, I thought, eighty years on, it must be possible to attain a more reasonable, more honest, and more balanced view.

For two years, I tracked Lawrence from library to library and thousands of miles across the deserts of the Middle East, some of it by camel and on foot. Occasionally, in unexpected places – in a shaded nook of the Ashmolean, in the gate-tower of Azraq castle, on the ridge at Mudowwara – I felt his presence and heard his voice once more. Sometimes – when I rode across Sinai, or climbed the Hafira pass – I felt he was simply a few steps ahead, laughing at me, and that if I hurried fast I could catch him up. My quest for Lawrence acquired the character of a pilgrimage, and I came to see that biography was itself a religious act, a form of ancestor-worship, a re-affirmation, a re-invention of the past. I searched and read and travelled, but the moment I thought I had Lawrence in my grasp, he eluded me, laughing, and appeared somewhere else. In the end, I realized that there was no 'real' Lawrence at all. There was only my own reflection in a glass: Lawrence and I were two facing mirrors reflecting each other to eternity. At last, in those far-off deserts, I finally knew that the observer is part of his subject: and I understood that there could be no definitive Lawrence, but only an infinite number of Lawrentian images, like crystals in the eyes of his beholders. What I discovered was *my* Lawrence and *my* truth, for 'truth' is of more than one kind: the kind which remains static, and the kind which bends and shifts according to the individual and the time.

PART ONE

———

THE WANDERER
1888–1916

1. Apparent Queen Unveiled Her Peerless Light

Early Childhood
1888–96

In 1879, a beautiful young woman called Sarah Lawrence alighted from a ferry at Dublin to begin the great adventure of her life. She was to be governess to the children of a wealthy gentleman called Thomas Chapman, who owned a mansion and a vast estate near Delvin in County Westmeath. Though just eighteen, Sarah was a woman of extraordinary dominance and ability, who had already overcome social barriers which many would have found insurmountable. Born the illegitimate daughter of a Tyneside shipwright named John Lawrence, deserted by her father and orphaned at nine by her own alcoholic mother, she had been brought up by an Episcopal minister and his wife in the highlands of Scotland and the Isle of Skye. In the late Victorian era, when illegitimacy attracted dire social stigma, when the classes were almost as fixed in their orbits as the celestial bodies, she was determined to leap the gulf between deprived working-class orphan and respectable, middle-class housewife. If she could not become a queen or a lady of the manor, she could at least use her power to captivate the heart of a nobleman – and that is precisely what she did.

Thomas Chapman, her employer, had been educated at Eton and Cirencester, the grandson of a baronet and the scion of seven generations of colonial English landlords who had originally been granted land in Kerry under the patronage of Sir Walter Ralegh. He had all the benefits of a privileged birth – education, breeding, a vast estate, an opulent mansion, horses, carriages and servants, and the wealth and leisure with which to enjoy them. Yet he was not a happy man. His wife, Edith, was a shrew who regarded any form of pleasure as sinful – 'the kind of woman', a neighbour later observed, 'who was terribly pious, who would go to church all hours of the day, and then if a wretched kitchen maid got herself into trouble, would cast her out without a character'.[1] Edith's belligerence – which found its most extreme expression in attempts to convert the local Roman Catholic peasants to Protestantism – had become so painful that Thomas could hardly endure her company. When Sarah first appeared on his horizon he was the father of four young daughters and found himself approaching middle age, trapped in marriage to a woman he had long ago ceased to love. Morose, ineffectual, much given to drink, he had abandoned even the pleasures of hunting, shooting and fishing with which most country gentlemen filled their days. Into his dark universe the beautiful Miss Lawrence shot like a comet. She captivated him. As gay and energetic as Edith was ethereal and sour, she was an indomitable organizer. She came to his mansion – South Hill – to take charge of his daughters, but very soon she had taken over the running of the entire household. Thomas was seen to revive visibly whenever she entered the room. Presently – inevitably perhaps – squire and governess fell in love.

It was no rare thing, of course, for a bored Victorian gentleman to dally with an attractive servant-girl. But in an era when the British aristocracy still preserved an almost supernatural reputation, the idea of a gentleman actually forsaking his caste for a liaison with a minion was almost unthinkable. Sarah was aware that she walked a tightrope. She had nothing to offer but herself, and any young girl less determined, or less charismatic, might easily have ended up an unmarried young mother with recourse only to the workhouse – or worse. Her hold over Thomas tightened by degrees, however. In 1885 she became pregnant and left the post of governess at his mansion, to reappear as his mistress in a house in Dublin. It was here, in December 1885, that their first son, Montague Robert – Bob – was born. For a while, Thomas led a double life, commuting between his wife and daughters at South Hill and his mistress and son in Dublin, but soon prudish tongues wagged. The Chapmans' butler once spied Miss Lawrence in a Dublin store and overheard her giving her name as 'Mrs Chapman'. Curious, he followed her to her lodgings, where he saw Thomas Chapman emerge. He rushed to Edith with the news, and she erupted with fury. Thomas was obliged to choose between his privileged but emotionally barren marriage with her, and an unconventional, materially pinched, but fulfilling relationship with Sarah. In choosing Sarah, he made the most courageous decision of his life. Some time in 1887, he left his mansion with its unkempt park of green meadows and Irish yews, forsook his inheritance and his culture for ever, and joined Sarah in Dublin. At her insistence, perhaps, he asked his wife for a divorce. Edith stubbornly refused, and in defiance they decided to elope to Britain, where, together, they could make a new start. They left Ireland by ferry on an evening towards the end of 1887. When they stepped ashore in North Wales the next day, they were no longer Thomas Chapman, landowner, and Sarah Lawrence, governess, but 'Mr and Mrs Thomas Lawrence' – identities they would continue to assume successfully for the rest of their lives.

They could scarcely have chosen a more repressive moment in the entire history of British morals in which to commit themselves to a common-law marriage. Since the end of the relatively liberal eighteenth century, society had been growing ever more puritanical under the influence of the Evangelical Revival – a movement to which, ironically enough, Sarah belonged. The year 1885 marked the climax of the so-called 'Purity Campaign' – a crusade against lax sexual morals which had harnessed powerful Victorian terrors of social chaos and the degeneration of the 'Imperial race'. Sex had become the great taboo, and society was so fanatically leery of anything smacking of bodies or nudity that polite people went so far as to lap the legs of grand pianos in cloth so that they should not be seen 'naked'. The moral code was rigid. Chastity was the ideal, the family was sacrosanct, and 'the fallen woman' who had been 'seduced' was deserving of utter contempt. The pervading *omertà* on all things sexual led to such incredible ignorance at all levels of society that even a learned Oxford physician could be heard to declare that 'nine out of ten women are indifferent to sex or actively dislike it; the tenth, who enjoys it, will always be a harlot'.[2] The dark complement to Victorian prudishness, however, was captured with superb imagination by Robert Louis Stevenson in his novel *The Strange Case of Dr Jekyll and Mr Hyde*, published in 1886. At the height of the purity campaign, London was actually an international centre of prostitution, where there were more brothels than schools. Many of these bordellos were frequented by respectable 'gentlemen', who, by day, were pillars of the establishment. Despite the strict ban on pre-marital sex, many middle- and upper-class boys had their first sexual experience with a female servant living in the same house.

9

These were the Gothic shadows lurking behind the respectable Victorian façade – the dark milieu into which Thomas Edward Lawrence – Ned to the family – came squalling in the early hours of 16 August 1888, the son of unmarried parents who had vanished from one life to recreate themselves in another. He was born in a house called Gorphrwysa at Tremadoc on the coast of North Wales, sufficiently near to the terminus of the Dublin ferry to suggest that the Lawrences had merely settled in the first convenient place. It was characteristic of Lawrence, perhaps, that as a boy he would claim proudly to have shared his birthday with Napoleon Bonaparte, one of the great military minds of the nineteenth century – even though Napoleon had actually been born on the 15th. In later life, having become a world-famous military hero himself, though, he revised his adulation, patronizing Bonaparte as 'a vulgar genius who did things expected by the crowd'.[3]

The fear of exposure which accompanied his parents' elopement allowed them no rest. Within a year of Lawrence's birth they moved again, to Kircudbright on the shores of western Scotland. There followed short-term halts on the Isle of Man and at St Helier in Jersey, and a longer one at Dinard in Brittany – all of them remote from the main centres of polite society in which Thomas Chapman might have been recognized – and during this period two more sons, William and Frank, were born. At last, in spring 1894, there came a turning point. Thomas and Sarah had been together for the best part of a decade, and their assumed identities had remained intact. Moreover, their four sons – educated until then largely by governesses – were growing fast and the eldest would soon need a good school and a more settled life. First they made the heady jump to the English home counties, settling at Fawley on the shores of Southampton Water, and then, in September 1896, came their last and most decisive migration, to Oxford, where, in a spacious semi-detached house at 2 Polstead Road, there arrived after three miscarriages the final addition to the family: Arnold, the fifth son, born in 1900.

Here they had come to stay. The new home was an Englishman's castle – a miniature fortress of red brick, bay windows and castellations, in the best tradition of Victorian Gothic. Had it been part of an older, more established community, the Lawrences might have stood out, but the street dated only from 1890, and was consequently full of displaced people like themselves. No one – in Thomas's lifetime anyway – seems to have suspected their secret, and as children the Lawrence boys were not affected by it. Clearly, Lawrence's illegitimacy was not a direct source of guilt or shame at least until after his character was formed. Yet it mattered desperately to Thomas and Sarah, and their terror that it might be discovered prevented them from entering an active social life. They avoided the prim tea-parties presided over by the widows of college Fellows, whom John Betjeman described as 'the queens of north Oxford society'[4] – perhaps without any great feeling of loss, especially on Sarah's part – and settled into a somewhat introspective and secluded life: 'the family didn't go about much in Oxford,' a neighbour recalled, 'but they had some very true friends. They were always happy [with] a lot of fun and silly jokes, but of course Mrs Lawrence managed them all.'[5]

Within the home, indeed, Sarah Lawrence 'managed them all' with a rod of iron. She was, as a friend later observed, 'an utterly fascinating but rather alarming person', who exercised a relentless, obsessive control over all domestic details.[6] Tiny and trim, with beautiful small hands and feet, she had rich blonde hair, penetrating methylene-blue eyes and a determined set of jaw. Her movements were precise, her speech clear and deliberate, and her bearing dignified. She looked directly at anyone who spoke to her, with a wide-eyed, slightly disarming expression, and she missed nothing. Her observations were acute and her memory prodigious. Her small figure radiated authority. She was frugal in habit, baking her own bread and feeding the family on porridge which was painstakingly prepared and left to cook slowly overnight in a leather haybox packed with straw. In her household there was only one way to do things, and that was Sarah's way. Servants and children argued at their peril. Her kitchen lore was graven in stone: apples were never to be peeled and cored, but wiped, quartered and stewed or baked whole; leftovers must never be thrown away but added to the stockpot. Possessed of an encyclopedic knowledge of plants, she would proclaim the qualities of exotic vegetables such as calabrese and butter-beans, and she was an avid gardener, tirelessly pressing seeds and cuttings on to others, and demanding to know their results with equal gusto. She read widely, spoke decent French, and wrote a fair letter in the same clean copperplate hand with which she kept her punctilious housekeeping accounts. Intelligent, opinionated, bossy, a woman who 'seemed to know about everything' – as one neighbour commented – she was also generous to a fault and capable of great warmth and devotion: to those she liked 'a faithful true friend'.[7] Slightly ill at ease with social superiors, she was decidedly autocratic with everyone else: 'she fitted you into a pattern of the moment as into a delicate and important piece of machinery,' Mrs Kennington commented, 'and there you had no function [but that of] a cog, a tappet or a lever – as she wished, so you were. You felt the forces arrayed against you so vast should you protest, that I for one never tried . . . I just handed my will completely over to her.'[8]

To Sarah the world was either black or white, either right or wrong – there was no room for discussion, no margin for debate. The only yardstick of morality was God's ten commandments, the only authority the Bible. It is hardly surprising that the fundamentalist doctrine of the Evangelical Movement should have appealed to her. Her own venial sin of adultery with Thomas was a burden she would carry with her to the grave, yet her mantra 'God hates the sin, but loves the sinner' reminded her that redemption was possible. She glimpsed a path to redemption through the children of her sinful union, and made it her duty to rear them as immaculate soldiers for Christ. She found encouragement in Canon A. W. D. Christopher, Rector of St Aldate's church in Pembroke Square, Oxford. It may well have been partly to join the Canon's flock that the Lawrences had moved to Oxford in the first place, for they had heard him preach at Ryde on the Isle of Wight while living at Fawley, and had been struck by the message of love he proclaimed.

The Canon was regarded as a saintly old man. Almost eighty years old when the Lawrences first knew him, he was renowned both for his gentleness and his enthusiasm, and for the vitality which took him out in all weathers and at any time of the night to visit the sick and the aged. Christopher's brand of fundamentalism had developed as a reaction to the increasingly self-critical views of the Anglican High Church which, he believed, had led to the disenchantment of the poorer classes. He advocated a clear assertion of Christian principles, the literal interpretation of the Bible, and a return to the extreme orthodoxy of traditional English Protestantism. It is unlikely that the Lawrences confessed their secret to him, but it is certain that he became a very dear and influential figure in their lives. They were regular members of St Aldate's congregation and Thomas sat on the church council, partly because of his generous donations to the collection box. Christopher was vice-president of the Church Missionary Society, and immensely proud that St Aldate's had provided a crop of missionaries from among its own curates. Both Bob and Ned Lawrence were to become Sunday School teachers at St Aldate's and officers in the St Aldate's section of the Boys' Brigade. It was Sarah's highest ambition that they too would become missionaries, and thus redeem the unholy circumstances of their birth.

By the time they reached Oxford, Sarah had long ago parted Thomas from the bottle and, as Sir Basil Blackwell later commented, the Lawrences had a reputation as 'punctilious, church-going and water-drinking' folk even by the strict standards of the day.[9] Thomas's religious convictions provided him with a degree of spiritual comfort, and he would read to the boys from a well-thumbed and annotated Bible before school every morning, and lead the domestic prayers at home on Sundays. A tall, bearded, retiring man, he made little impression on outsiders: 'He was always friendly and charming,' said Mrs Ballard, whose son often played with the Lawrence boys. 'But it was Mrs Lawrence who was the leading spirit . . . I said to my boy once, "you talk a lot about Ma Lawrence but you don't even [mention] Pa Lawrence." He replied, "Oh yes, he's just Mrs Lawrence's husband!"' [10] Diffident, shy, seeming to feel out of place in the genteel surroundings of Oxford, he rarely expressed his feelings. Some thought him distinguished-looking, others remembered him as a cadaverous figure on whom the clothes flapped like a scarecrow. Some believed him eccentric, idealist, or just plain barmy. Lawrence later painted a romantic picture of his father as a man 'on the large scale, tolerant, experienced, grand, rash, humoursome . . . naturally lord-like', who, before having been 'tamed' by Sarah, had been 'a spend-thrift, a sportsman, a hard rider and drinker'.[11] Thomas was a gentleman by profession and, despite his somewhat reduced circumstances, never needed to work. He spent his days pursuing interests such as photography, cycling, carpentry, or the study of church architecture, and occasionally yachting or potting pheasant and snipe in the New Forest, where he had taken out a shooting licence. He had plenty of spare time on his hands to teach these skills to his sons, and as a result Lawrence's photography became technically accomplished even before he left school. Like his father, he became a devoted cyclist and water-man, a carpenter of sorts, an expert on medieval architecture, and a crack pistol shot. Thomas enjoyed the company of his sons, playing word-games with them, leafing through boys' magazines, taking them on outings to hunt for fossils or to explore medieval ruins. But his influence was far less profound than Sarah's. Their characters were so much in contrast that Lawrence was later to blame their 'discordant natures' for the demons that haunted him.[12] In fact, there is little evidence of discord. By all accounts, indeed, their relationship was affectionate and the domestic atmosphere a harmonious one. Thomas's reserved nature seems to have complemented Sarah's more fiery spirit: peace-loving and gentle, he had consummate skills in tact, diplomacy and tolerance to impart. Lawrence's picture of his 'hard riding, hard-drinking' younger days, though, was highly idealized. Thomas was essentially a submissive man, clearly dominated by Sarah, and, subconsciously, Lawrence despised his lack of authority. He would search for more powerful father-figures throughout his life, writing to one of them, Lord Trenchard, in 1928, 'If my father had been as big as you the world would not have had spare ears for my freakish doings.'[13] Beside Sarah, Thomas remains a shadowy figure, a reformed drinker whittling out his days, 'just sitting in his chair and smoking and perhaps reading a book', as Mrs Ballard recalled.[14]

It was, nevertheless, Thomas's income upon which the family depended. Shortly before his second son's birth in 1888, he had signed an agreement handing over his estates in Ireland to the care of his younger brother Francis, in return for an annuity of £200. Lawrence later claimed that his parents lived in near poverty, a fiction taken up with righteous conviction by his biographer Basil Liddell Hart. In fact, with other capital, income and inheritances, the family may have had an income of up to £600 per year. This placed them fairly high up in the social scale of the day, for in 1903–4 the population of Great Britain amounted to 43 million, of whom only 5 million lived on an income of more than £160 per year. The 3 million persons with incomes of between £160 and £400 per year were described as 'comfortably off', while those with over £700 were said to be 'rich'. Though for most of Lawrence's childhood the family did not fit into this latter category, they were able to employ one or two servants and to enjoy expensive holidays every year. Lawrence's trip to Syria in

1909, for instance, cost over £100 – a good annual wage for most Britons of the era. By any other standards than the very highest, their financial circumstances were extremely happy ones.

Lawrence said later that he regarded his father as a friend rather than a figure of authority, suggesting an equality unusual in father–son relationships of the time. In fact, Thomas was too gentle and imaginative to administer corporal punishment to his sons, and left this task to the more resolute Sarah – an inversion of the generally accepted Victorian ethos. Reared strictly by her puritan foster-parents, she had imbibed the Biblical adage, 'Spare the rod and spoil the child; but he who loves him chastens him betimes',[15] and would administer severe thrashings to the boys' bare buttocks for disobedience, wilfulness or dishonesty, convinced that in doing so she was perpetuating God's will. According to the Evangelical canon, babies were born not innocent, but tainted with the sins of their forefathers: the children of adulterous parents were likely to develop a premature sensuality themselves.[16] As the boys grew up, Sarah exercised a hawk-like vigilance for the appearance of such sensual traits, ready to nip them in the bud with a sound thrashing. She stood guard over her brood with the possessive greed of one who has known abandonment, distrusting women as dishonest schemers: 'she never wanted any of the sons to marry,' Mrs Ballard said. 'In fact, when Arnie [the youngest son] was engaged he wrote and asked me to break it to [his] mother.'[17]

Sarah's need to control and dominate her world was blind, desperate and beyond reason. Her omnipotent, omniscient exterior actually concealed a fathomless rage of doubt and pain within. Victoria Ocampo, who knew her in old age, sensed that she was a woman seething with violent passions kept tight in the straitjacket of her unbending determination. Her childhood deprivation had left her with a chronic fear of abandonment and a massive emotional vacuum, which she could fill only by draining energy, attention and reassurance from her husband and children and anyone else who came within her reach. Bob – kind, solicitous, prudish – was the first to succumb to her insatiable demand for love and attention and never managed to escape it. He adopted her fundamentalist religious philosophy, did not marry, and remained attached to her for the rest of his life. Of all her sons, he was the only one who fulfilled her ambitions, becoming a medical missionary in China, where he was joined by Sarah herself after

Thomas's death in 1919. Ocampo, who visited Sarah in the 1950s, found her confined to her bedroom by a broken leg, with Bob, himself an elderly man, occupying the room immediately below. Whenever she banged on the floor with her stick, Bob would scurry upstairs like a servant – an arrangement, Ocampo noted with amusement, that Sarah referred to as 'convenient'.

As a child, Ned developed a terror of Sarah discovering his feelings: 'If she knew, they would be damaged, violated, no longer mine,' he later wrote.[18] Unlike Bob, his disposition was prickly, and any pressure applied to him was likely to meet resistance. Even his teachers at school felt an instinctive recoil if they tried to push him in a way he did not wish to go. Given Sarah's character, a clash of personalities was inevitable: 'No trust ever existed between my mother and myself,' he wrote later. 'Each of us jealously guarded his or her own individuality, whenever we came together.'[19] He and Sarah were mirror-images, attracted to each other but repelled by their sameness. He was sensitive to her wishes and anxious to please her, but intensely aware that if he lifted his emotional shield, she would get in and devour his independence, just as she had devoured Bob's. Though he was not her favourite son, she had great expectations of him, and for her he had to be perfect: brave, noble, strong, hard-working, honest, respectful, obedient and loving – a white knight, *sans peur et sans reproche*. Arnie revealed that it was Ned who received the lion's share of Sarah's beatings, and felt that his life had been permanently injured by her. Though Bob and Will were never beaten, and Arnie required only one dose, Ned's more dogged obstinacy occasioned frequent repetition. Beneath the Biblical justifications, there lay a simple power-struggle.[20] Bob was never whipped because he offered no resistance: he and his mother were 'at one'. Ned provoked her determination to 'break his will'. She did not succeed. In fact, she only strengthened his resolve, as with every blow he became more and more determined never to give in. He became detached from the pain and from the body which sustained punishment, but the will he developed to such an immense degree of strength became a monster with a life of its own – a serpent which would eventually suffocate his creative power. His character – no less than his elder brother's – was ultimately to be defined by Sarah. The two elder Lawrence boys were predisposed to react to her demands in ways that were diametrically opposite – Bob by total surrender, Ned by total resistance – and both were scarred by the experience. 'I know Ned had a real struggle to achieve spiritual – let alone physical – freedom,' Celandine Kennington wrote. 'He and his mother were better friends apart. When together for more than a short time [he] was constantly forced to refight his battles for mental freedom.'[21] Arnie – twelve years younger than Ned – had a similarly traumatic struggle to free himself from Sarah's grip, but eventually succeeded by choosing a third way: he simply 'took no notice of her'. Of the three sons who survived the war, he was the only one to marry, have a child, and lead a 'conventional' life.

In his later life, Lawrence paid a man named John Bruce to flog him at intervals over a period of thirteen years, and invented a complex farrago of lies to explain why such treatment was necessary. Bruce disclosed that Lawrence experienced orgasm as a result of some of these beatings. It is possible that this behaviour might have been initiated by horrific experiences during the war. On the other hand, there are clear traces of Lawrence's masochism in his early interest in self-punishment and self-denial. As an adolescent he would fast, go without sleep, deny himself pleasure, and continually push himself on long and arduous walks and bicycle rides. He would even dive through the ice into the frozen river Cherwell on chilling winter nights. It seems likely that any trauma Lawrence suffered in the war only intensified a capacity for masochism which had been part of him since his earliest days – a capacity which emerged through his relationship with Sarah. The intolerable conflict of attraction and repulsion he experienced could only be resolved by physical punishment. Severe beatings could not make the sexual feeling go away, but they could atone for the forbidden desire. Pain thus became a means of release. As he grew up, he developed a terror of the feelings he associated with the sexual act, and was compelled to diminish his anxiety by intentionally bringing about the situation he feared: instead of fleeing *away* from the threat, he fled *towards* it: 'When a thing is inevitable,' he advised Charlotte Shaw years later, 'provoke it as instantly and as fully as possible.'[22] His position was like that of the little girl who was obliged by her mother to take showers in cold water, and who, terrified by the prospect, would open the tap prior to shower-time and expose herself to the numbing water for a few moments. This act served to relieve the girl's anxiety. She did not derive pleasure from the pain itself, but from the relief of tension it provided. All his life, Lawrence was utterly terrified of pain: 'pain of the slightest had been my obsession and secret terror since I was a boy,' he later wrote.[23] His brother Arnie confirmed that his fear of pain was abnormal.[24] By inflicting punishment on himself – by diving into freezing water, fasting, resisting sleep, pushing himself to the limits of physical endurance – he was able to preview what he most feared, and gain a kind of mastery over it. Lawrence may even have subconsciously provoked the violent clashes with his mother, in his compulsive 'flight forwards'.

It was not only physically, but also psychically that Lawrence felt himself threatened. His mother would probe constantly into his inner-most feelings, giving him a lifelong hatred of what he called 'families and inquisitions'. He chose to protect himself against this psychical threat by emotional withdrawal – by assuming an aloofness which extended from his mother to almost every other person with whom he came into contact. Even when he was quite small he seemed to remain aloof from the ring of children, and had some unfathomable sense of sadness about him. His schoolmasters noticed that he was silent, self-possessed and inscrutable, and gave a hint of a latent power, just out of reach.[25] As a young man he was difficult to know, unobtrusive, cheerful, even jocular in moments, but extremely reserved about himself. Ernest Altounyan would write that he was simply 'impersonal': 'someone cleaving through life, propelled by an almost noiseless engine'.[26] His need to protect his spiritual independence would emerge throughout his life in an obsession with images of siege warfare, of attack and defence: 'I think I'm afraid of letting her get, ever so little, inside the circle of my integrity,' he wrote of his mother, 'and she is always hammering and sapping to come in . . . I always felt she was laying siege to me and would conquer if I left a chink unguarded.'[27] This image of his self as a circle or citadel of integrity recurs repeatedly. Even as a boy, he would tell his brothers an endless tale about the defence of a tower by warlike dolls against hordes of barbarous enemies,[28] and the motif appears again in the study of crusader castles in Britain, France and Syria to which he devoted much of his youth, and which led to the thesis he presented for his degree. Cyril 'Scroggs' Beeson, who accompanied him on some of his trips around castles in France, noted that his interest was not primarily in military history but in the hearts and minds of the designers, and the extent to which history had tested their intentions. It was upon the military knowledge acquired from this study of castles that he would later found his theory of guerrilla war. So it was that the pattern forged in the dark recesses of his childhood struggle would one day spill out into the light as the strategy he would wield to brilliant success in the Arab Revolt.

Nietzsche – whom Lawrence much admired – wrote that every profound spirit requires a mask: the mask Lawrence wore was one of paradox. His aloofness concealed a craving for the attention of others, for fame and distinction, which he despised and could not allow himself to show. Aloofness was a barrier he created against the outside world, a means of preventing anyone from coming too close. He was able to relax his guard only with those who were younger or socially inferior, and though, in later life, he formed relationships with the great and famous, he confessed to John Bruce – a poorly educated man from a working-class background – that most of these high and mighty folk 'could not be trusted'. It was an aspect of his masochistic nature that he felt himself undeserving of love, and it was terror of failure which prevented him from opening himself. He found another way to attract people, using his aloofness as a tool for drawing attention by offering tantalizing glimpses and wrapping himself in an intriguing cloak of mystery. In short, as Sir Harold Nicolson coldly, but correctly, declared, 'he discovered early that mystery was news'.[29] At school and college he was regarded by his peers as a pronounced eccentric, and would intrigue others by such idiosyncrasies as riding his bicycle uphill and walking down, by sitting through prescribed dinners in hall without eating, by adopting odd diets, by going out at night and sleeping during the day, by refusing to play organized games, or by fasting on Christmas Day when everyone else was feasting. This exaggerated form of atten-tion-seeking was the shadow side of Lawrence's aloofness, and the social aspect of his masochism. He was like the woman from the provincial town who wanted to attend the opera in the capital wearing fine jewels and her most expensive evening dress. Ashamed of her desire for ostentation, though, she actually attended the opera in a plain dress, and as a result was the only woman in the audience not wearing evening clothes. She became the focus of attention by 'reverse exhibitionism' – not because of her finery but through her conspicuous lack of it. Lawrence's tendency to cycle uphill and walk down has its parallel in the masochistic folk hero Till Eulenspiegel, who felt happy when toiling uphill and sad when coming down.

Soon, Lawrence learned to shroud everything he did in ritual and romance, a technique he found remarkably successful and which he sharpened into the most effective blade in his armoury. He learned to manipulate others with his aura of mystery, to lay false trails, to concoct endless mazes of riddle and conundrum. He learned to intrigue those who interested him by what he called 'whimsical perversity' or 'misplaced earnestness', whetting their curiosity and then rushing off abruptly, hoping the object of his attention would pursue, 'wish[ing] to know whom that odd creature was'.[30] Few could resist Lawrence's 'whimsicalities', and his jokes and buffooneries, his sudden flashes of brilliance or impish roguery gave him an almost infallible ability to charm, allure and seduce. Basil Liddell Hart, one of his most ardent admirers, summed up the quality most succinctly when he likened Lawrence to 'a woman who wears a veil while exposing the bosom'.[31] Though Liddell Hart put Lawrence's exhibitionism down to vanity, in fact it was 'reverse exhibitionism': his wish was less to display his beauty and cleverness to the world than to demonstrate his ugliness, suffering and humiliation. Far from being 'in love with himself', Lawrence would write that he despised the 'self' he could hear and see.[32]

2. Dominus Illuminatio Mea

Schooldays
1896–1905

Though Oxford had been changing slowly for half a century before the Lawrences arrived in 1896, it remained a city which moved at the pace of the horse-drawn era. The man who was shortly to transform it into a centre of the motor industry, Lord Nuffield, was then plain Mr William Henry Morris – a cycle-maker with dreams, and a shop in the High – and the city remained, as Jan Morris has put it, 'a kind of elfin workshop, full of respectable craftsmen tapping away in back-alleys . . . and weavers' looms . . . clack[ing] in Magdalen Grove'.[1] A few colleges already had their own motor cars, but the most ponderous vehicles commonly to be found in Oxford streets were the drays of Hall's or Morrell's Breweries. Horse-drawn trams – there were nineteen of them by 1910 – were required to keep to a sedate eight miles per hour, and their drivers were given instructions to 'slow down for a herd of cattle, and to stop completely at the approach of a flock of sheep'. It was a dignified, unhurried Oxford – a place of gas-lit houses, of college barges, private fire-brigades, hansom cabs and coaches-and-four: a town where milkmen still carried their churns in handcarts from St Aldate's dairy, where the University Clerks still weighed butter in the covered market opposite Jesus College, where boys wore plus-fours and winged shirt-collars, where girls rode bicycles in pinafore-dresses like Tenniel's Alice in Wonderland, and where demure young women in ankle-length skirts and straw bonnets played a round of stately tennis on the University parks.

I travelled to Oxford to see if I could recapture something of the atmosphere in which T. E. Lawrence grew up, and to taste the vision of Britain he was to carry with him to the deserts of the East. Though the drays are gone, and the horse-drawn trams have long since been replaced by diesel-powered double-deckers, I found that much of turn-of-the century Oxford remains. I stood outside No. 2 Polstead Road – now a slightly seedy building with overflowing rubbish bins and rusty Morris Minors parked in a concrete yard – straining over the decades to hear the voices of the four eldest Lawrence boys, Bob, Ned, Will and Frank, as they set off to school each morning in that long, bright Indian summer of Old England before the Great War changed the world for ever. I walked down Woodstock Road towards the city centre, holding in my mind a vivid image of the boys riding their bicycles, in single file, in strict order of seniority, wearing the blue and white striped Breton jerseys which were almost a family uniform. There were massed may trees in bloom in the gardens, and horse chestnuts budding cream and pink, the hedgerows scented with hawthorn and alder. I passed the same massive stone villas with granite steps and ornate porticoes they would have seen, the same mansions of yellow limestone in stands of spruce and pine, and the same churches spanning a thousand years of history, from G. E. Street's High Victorian Gothic prayer-hall of St Philip and St James in Walton Manor, to the crusty Anglo-Saxon bulwark of St Michael's in the Cornmarket. I passed the same corner shops and terraced cottages, the same pubs with double-barrelled names like the Horse and Jockey and the Eagle and Child, the same austere Elizabethan façades of Balliol and St John's. I turned right before the Saxon Tower and walked west along George Street, towards the Boys' High School on the corner of New Inn Hall street. The building was still there, but it was no longer a school, neither did it face St George's church as it had done in Lawrence's day: the church was gone, replaced by the less elegant ABC cinema. It was an impressively solid Victorian edifice, however, with its arches and ecclesiastical window, flanked by sculpted Latin mottoes: *Dominus Illuminatio Mea* and *Fortis Est Veritas*.

Lawrence spent ten years at this school, and while a student there dreamed of freeing the Arabs from the shackles of the Ottoman Turks: 'I fancied to sum up in my own life,' he wrote, 'that new Asia which inexorable time was slowly bringing upon us. The Arabs made a chivalrous appeal to my young instinct and while still at the High School in Oxford, already I thought to make them into a nation.'[2] This might seem an extraordinary premonition for a schoolboy who had never set foot in the East, yet Lawrence was acquainted with the geography, history and ethnology of the Arab lands long before he arrived there. Daily study of the Bible had made the deserts and mountains of Midian, Moab, Edom, Judah and other places almost as familiar to him as the streets of Oxford, and a remarkable little volume entitled *Helps to the Study of the Bible* provided him with up-to-date details. Between its modest covers he found surveys of the Holy Land, lists of topographical features connected with the Gospels, indices of biblical plants, flowers, mammals, reptiles, birds and fishes in their English, Latin, Hebrew and occasionally their Arabic names. As a youth he chose as school prizes two books on the history of Egypt, and later he obtained Henry Layard's works on the excavation of ancient Nineveh. These were no stilted academic reports, but thrilling adventures which epitomized the Victorian view of the East as a place of mystery and exoticism, where fabulous cities lay buried under desert sands prowled by wandering Bedu tribes. In Layard, Lawrence discovered all the elements the East should possess: the bizarre, the sensuous, the alluring. It was an irresistible picture, and throughout his youth he was aware of the East as a parallel world, a dimension to which, in future, he might find the chance to escape.

Meanwhile, though, there was the more prosaic business of school to be attended to. Lawrence looked back on his schooldays as a time of misery, yet he proved to be a remarkably quick learner, outpacing Bob, from whose lessons he had picked up reading and writing early, as many young siblings do. He had a precocious ability with language, and knew colloquial French from his time in Brittany, as well as some Latin, which the boys had been taught by a private tutor in preparation for school. He had a retentive memory and became an unusually fast reader, able, according to his own testimony, to assimilate the core of any book within half an hour. He won two prizes during the years 1896 and 1903, and in 1904 took the Vth Form prize for Divinity, despite claiming to have left the paper unfinished so that Bob, who was still in the Vth Form, might gain first place. In the same year, he was listed eightieth in the Junior Section of the Oxford Locals examinations. Yet despite his apparent success, school did not interest him, for it did not teach him the kind of thing he wanted to know: he later wrote that it had been 'an irrelevant and time-wasting nuisance, which I hated and contemned'.[3]

One reason for this may have been that at school Lawrence felt himself a misfit among his peers. From his schooldays onwards he developed a sense of oddity which he never quite lost: '. . . the oddness must be bone deep,' he wrote years later. 'At Oxford I was odd . . . In officers' messes, too, I've lived about as merrily as the last-hooked fish choking out its life in a boat-load of trippers.'[4] As a youth Lawrence often saw himself as a giant trapped in a dwarf's body, and his smallness and unimpressive appearance would colour his self-concept throughout his life. In later years 'big' would become his favourite accolade to those he admired, and even to works of art and literature he appreciated. Although he claimed to despise organized games simply because they had rules and results, it was actually a sense of physical inadequacy which led him to reject them. 'Never compete in anything' became his personal motto, so impressing his youngest brother that Arnie admitted years later to having been embarrassed when Ned asked him how he had done in a race.[5] Though his brothers paid lip-service to his non-competitive whim out of deference, their physical qualities overshadowed his. Will – only sixteen months younger and often compared with him – was tall, athletic, and a paragon of classical excellence. The athletic ability which later brought Will a half-blue at St John's College was surpassed by that of his younger brother Frank, who won the Challenge Cup for Athletics while at the High School, and was three times school gymnastics champion as well as captain of football and vice-captain of cricket. Lawrence, who would later mutter darkly about the 'sinful misery' of games, was affronted at this apparent break in 'family tradition'. Actually the motto 'never compete' was an aspect of Lawrence's paradoxical mask which hid a nature so extremely competitive that he could not even bear to hear someone else praised without feeling diminished. Yet so low was his self-esteem that if he was directly praised he would dismiss it as undeserved. His rejection of the norms of middle-class society was an aspect of his reverse exhibitionism, and his refusal to take part in organized sport was his most overt expression of that rejection. It is perhaps difficult to conceive now that in the late Victorian–Edwardian era sporting prowess was close to Godliness, and the qualities sport was supposed to engender – 'true grit', 'fair play', 'good form', 'team spirit' and 'decency' – were closely tied up with the mythology of Empire. It was seriously believed in many quarters that Britain actually owed her Empire to her sport, and that the battles which had made her great had first been won 'on the playing-fields of Eton'. The purity campaign of the late nineteenth century had led to a shift in the concept of manliness, away from moral strength to physical strength, and away from moral integrity to sexual abstention. One authority of the time defined masculinity as 'the duty of patriotism; the moral and physical beauty of athleticism; the salutary effects of Spartan habits and discipline; the cultivation of all that is masculine and the expulsion of all that is effeminate, un-English and excessively intellectual'.[6]

For much of his life, Lawrence idealized masculinity because he knew that he was not conventionally masculine himself, in spite of his great physical strength. Though many have testified that he was stronger than most people of his size and weight, his appearance as a youth gave no impression of it, and his apparent sensitivity over the issue suggests that it bothered him. In a letter to his mother from France in 1906, there is a hint of defensiveness in his insistence: 'people here say I'm much thinner than Bob, but stronger. Still Bob's fatness is much better than muscle in their eyes, except for Mme. Chaignon, who got a shock when she saw my biceps while bathing. She thinks I'm Hercules.'[7] During his march through Syria in 1909 he boasted of walking 120 miles in five days, then added: 'Bob or Will will laugh . . . but not if they had to do it staggering and stumbling over these ghastly roads.'[8] In the several accounts we have of Lawrence's physical fights, he invariably seems to have come off the worse – once, at school, sustaining a broken leg. He would later tell Liddell Hart that he disapproved of hand-to-hand fighting: 'when combats came to the physical, bare hand against hand,' he would write, 'I was finished.'[9] The words 'boyish' and even 'girlish', which crop up with surprising frequency in descriptions of him until his last years, suggest an almost androgynous figure. As a twelve-year-old, Lawrence possessed a sensitivity rare in adolescent boys. He would delight in taking charge of baby Arnie, sometimes bathing him in an iron bath, wheeling him in his pram to the football field where his 'manly' classmates were engaged in 'masculine' sport. When the three-year-old Arnie conceived a terror of the statues in the Ashmolean Museum, Lawrence carved a face on a stone and made him smash it with a hammer to exorcize his fears. The strategy was not only effective – for Arnie later became Professor of Archaeology at Cambridge, and wrote a celebrated book on classical sculpture – but it also displayed as astonishing degree of empathy. Arnie believed that this special facility Lawrence had for seeing through the eyes of others stemmed from an inner lack of confidence, and described how he would take on the characteristics of anyone he had just seen or was about to see. Paradoxically, this shape-shifting responsiveness was one of Lawrence's great strengths, and the quality which would later set him apart from the rigid, authoritarian generals of the war as a truly great, if unconventional leader.

Lawrence's sensitive traits grew out of the deep imprint of his mother's personality. Beneath his aloofness, he had a great capacity for friendship with both men and women. His most profound ties would be with other men, and according to Arnie, these friendships 'were comparable in intensity to sexual love, for which he made them a substitute'.[10] While still at school, he made friends with an older man called Leonard Green, then an undergraduate at St John's College, and took great pride in flouting college rules to visit him in his rooms. Together they dreamed of printing fine books, and of living together in a windmill on a headland washed by the sea. Green, an aspiring poet, belonged to a secret homosexual order called the Chaeronea and to a circle of poets, artists and novelists known later as the Uranians, whose inspiration was the 'innocence and sensuality of young boys'. A prominent member of the Chaeronea was the poet Laurence Housman, six of whose books were found in Lawrence's personal library after his death, together with three homoerotic works by F. W. Rolfe, another member of the Uranians, whom Lawrence may have known personally while at school. Green was himself a Uranian poet, whose work Lawrence admired enough to tell him in 1910 that though he was unlikely to find a publisher he should not adulterate his verse by developing 'a sense of sin or anything prurient'.[11] Lawrence was to include the work of two more Uranian poets in his own anthology which appeared in the 1920s, and listed Henry Scott Tuke, a Uranian artist, as one of his three favourite painters. He may have met Tuke while a schoolboy at Oxford, and even modelled for him, for Tuke was a friend of Charles Bell, Art Curator at the Ashmolean Museum, who was an early mentor of Lawrence's. Bell himself certainly had interests in common with the Uranians. Though they idealized homosexual love – especially that between an adult male and a young boy: often a boy of lower social class – they rarely practised it. Many were respectable churchmen, and in any case, the first decade of the twentieth century was a mean time for homosexuals. The shadow of Oscar

Wilde, sent to prison for his dabblings with telegraph boys in 1895, still loomed menacingly over the Edwardian literati. Lawrence's relationship with Leonard Green was almost certainly platonic. That he shared at least some of the sentiments of the Uranians as a youth, though, was later suggested by Arnie, who would write that he was 'impressed often with the physical beauty and animal grace of the young, particularly the young male, in uncivilised countries'.[12]

Though Lawrence despised women in their sexual role, he was able to form closer relationships with some women than most heterosexual men are capable of. He felt at home with older women of 'the good-wife-and-mother type',[13] and Clare Sydney Smith – who fell into this category – wrote that he 'was able to have a deep friendship *for* a woman – myself – based on the closest ties of sympathy and understanding but containing none of the elements normally associated with love. No effort on his part was needed to do this. His presence was . . . hardly a physical one and he never seemed to be aware of oneself physically'[14] (*my italics*). Mrs Smith's husband, Sydney, must also have been aware that Lawrence presented no sexual challenge, for when someone suggested that he and Clare might be having an affair, Smith's reaction was to throw back his head and roar with laughter.[15] Lawrence's great struggle in childhood was to extricate himself from his mother's smothering clutches, and afterwards he remained frigid towards women, especially those who were possessive or impulsive. He could happily consort with women like Clare Sydney Smith who sent him no sexual signals and behaved 'like a man', but the moment he detected any sexual advance his psychical barriers would snap shut. He would talk to a woman as if she was another man, and if she refused to do the same he would run away. Women's bodies did not attract him: 'I take no pleasure in women,' he would write. 'I have never thought twice or even once of the shape of a woman, but men's bodies, in repose or in movement – specially the former, appeal to me directly and very generally.'

Lawrence was a rebel against convention by instinct, but his sense of history was profound. He was fond of declaring that 'the world stopped in 1500 with the coming of printing and gunpowder', and affected to despise the Renaissance with its reason and humanism. He became fascinated by the medieval world as a boy, and this interest quickly became a passion which eclipsed his school work. He would cycle to churches in and around Oxford, taking brass-rubbings of medieval priests and knights in armour, and by the time he was fifteen had acquired a fine collection of rubbings from all over the south-east of England, which decorated the brothers' shared bedroom at 2 Polstead Road. Cyril 'Scroggs' Beeson recalled making his first rubbing under Lawrence's direction at Wytham in October 1904: '. . . from that date onwards,' Scroggs wrote, '. . . we made excursions by cycle to nearly every village in the three counties and to many places farther afield.'[16] Lawrence pursued his interest with thoroughness, experimenting with different techniques, eliciting advice from the tradesmen who supplied the paper and 'heelballs' used to make the rubbings. He scoured libraries and museums for information about the knights, priests and ladies whose effigies he rubbed, and soon acquired a detailed knowledge of medieval costume and armour. He became obsessed with the devices of heraldry and collected heraldic terms: gules, blazons, flanches, mascles, octofoyles and bars sinister, rolling them richly off his tongue with the relish of a wordsmith. He would compile long scrolls of coats of arms, painting in the escutcheons and the armorial bearings in the correct colours with punctilious care. He lost himself in romantic literature: Tennyson's Arthurian cycle *Idylls of the King* gave way to authentic medieval fare such as the Finnish epic *Kalevala* and the thirteenth-century *chanson* of the Charlemagne cycle, *Huon de Bordeaux.* His search for brasses and relics assumed almost the proportions of a sacred quest itself, and while other youths were out watching girls at St Giles's Fair or at the festivities of Eights Week, Lawrence could be found scouring local crypts and churches. He spared no reverence for consecrated ground, though, and honed his powers of persuasion in dealing with caretakers – once, memorably, when he and Beeson were caught emerging from the crypt of St Cross church with armfuls of human bones. Theo Chaundy, another schoolfriend, remembered his 'sinister' chuckle as he once happily smashed his way to a brass through some obstructing pews. It was E. M. Forster who pointed out the parallel between Lawrence's quest for brass-rubbings and his later archaeological adventures in the East, noting that the brasses were later transformed into ancient ruins, and the truculent guardians metamorphosed into savage Bedu tribes.

Lawrence's interest in the medieval was essentially an attempt to escape from the circumstances of his life, and to cock a snook at the conventions of the bourgeois social landscape, behind which lay his uncertain relationship with Sarah. The feelings of inferiority and shame that relationship generated contributed to the painful shyness which was noticed by almost everyone who met him. He confessed that he was 'abnormally shy' . . . 'ashamed of my awkwardness, of my physical envelope, and my solitary unlikeness which made me no companion, but an acquaintance, complete, angular, uncomfortable as a crystal'.[17] Yet he had no real need to feel odd or solitary at school. Despite his shyness and his rejection of games he was not unpopular: his awkwardness was largely in his own mind. In fact, he did play cricket for the school at least once, entered swimming and cycling races, led paper-chases and joined enthusiastically in playground games. He did not lack in personal friendships. As a young boy he had a special friend called John Snow, and from 1903 he and Scroggs Beeson formed an inseparable partnership, becoming famous – almost notorious – for their archaeologizing and brass-rubbing expeditions. Though Lawrence was evidently the dominant partner and the initiator of their schemes, Beeson recalled the 'enduring bond' of their friendship with some affection. Theo Chaundy noted that Lawrence introduced many school-friends, including himself, to the mysteries of brass-rubbing, and since he managed to persuade this future mathematics don to do his algebra for him in the Vth form, Lawrence cannot have lacked charm. A friend from early childhood remembered that he had been 'frightfully bossy' as a six-year-old but had ordered everyone about in a very nice way.[18] Bob Lawrence recalled that although he was the eldest, it was Ned who generally led the brothers in their games. Arnie described him as 'one of the nicest people I've known, perhaps the kindest, certainly the most exhilarating to be with'.[19] Midge Hall, who knew Lawrence both at school and at college, wrote of his schooldays that 'any conception of a solitary, moody schoolboy shunning the company of his fellows is wide of the mark. He was far too whimsical . . . too interesting in his hobbies, ever to be unpopular.'[20] Arnie felt that it was Lawrence's empathy – his ability to reflect what others needed and felt – which made him extraordinarily adept at inspiring others and bringing out the best in them.

Sarah believed that she had been a good mother, and after Lawrence's death painted an idealized picture of family life which was echoed by her 'lieutenant', Bob: 'We had a very happy childhood,' he wrote, 'which was never marred by a single quarrel between any of us. Our parents were constantly with us, to our great delight and profit, for they shared in our progress, made the home the place of peace it was, planned the future and our education, and were the greatest influence on our lives.'[21] Certainly, Lawrence's childhood was happy in the sense that he did not want for anything material, was successful at school, and was surrounded by friends and loyal brothers of whom he was often the undisputed chief. But under the surface his childhood did not glow with the primary colours Bob's Pre-Raphaelite image suggests. Arnie's description offers a darker insight: 'There was a strong puritanism in the family,' he wrote, 'a spirit of sin, unnaturalness. Hush hush was great. Many subjects were taboo which to the child's mind are not. It perplexed the children, leading to doubts and ultimately to a lack of confidence.'[22] Bob's assurance that Ned enjoyed his school-days hardly squares with Lawrence's own recollection of 'the school fear hanging over one – that haphazardly suspended punishment which made my years between eight and eighteen a misery'.[23] Far from being the 'delight and profit' she might have wished, Sarah destroyed Lawrence's life and made certain that he would never achieve happiness or fulfilment. His need to be an individual and separate from her, loved whether strong or weak, honest or dishonest, right or wrong, was totally subordinated to the needs of her own ravenous soul. She could not help this: in her own mind she was still the terrified little girl who would never know why she had been so heinously abandoned to the whims of the dark universe. It was a wound without salve, and no one whom she loved could be allowed to leave her again – ever. Lawrence was desperate for his mother's love, but he also needed to be regarded as a person in his own right. She loved him dearly, but as an extension of herself, seeing any expression of individuality on his part as a threat. The kind of power she could exert over her sons was terrifying. When Arnie finally made up his mind to marry, he wrote to tell Sarah so from the apparently safe distance of Athens. On the day he had calculated she would receive the letter he awoke in a daze and found he had forgotten where he was. He staggered out into the garden and only pulled himself together with some effort. He knew that Sarah was violently opposed to his marrying, and he felt that her influence had 'absorbed' him even at such a distance. If this was a sample of the psychic forces ranged against Ned, it is hardly surprising that he felt the need to defend his 'circle of integrity'. Often he hated his mother. Often he could not stand even to be in the same room, but he never once let it show. He behaved irreproachably to her, because she was his mother, and he felt he owed it to her to play the dutiful son. His Achilles' heel in the struggle was always his own sense of guilt. He made a great show of joviality and lightheartedness in her presence and practised suppressing his emotions. He talked only about things which pleased him, so that he would appear happy even when he was not. He knew quite well that until he was free from Sarah, he would be unable to let unfold the hero within himself: his great task in life was to escape from her.

Some time in 1905, matters reached a head. That summer, Lawrence had joined his father on a cycling trip around East Anglia, making brass-rubbings, visiting ruins and sending dutiful, if stiff, reports back to Sarah. He enjoyed the expedition, but began the new term at school under a cloud. His name had been put forward for a mathematics scholarship at Oxford University, and maths was a subject which did not interest him. Instead, he wanted to study history. Sarah disapproved, sensing instinctively a move away from her. The matter became contentious: she may have tried her old tactics – bluster, violence, manipulation – but this time it did not work. Lawrence was seventeen years old and Sarah had allowed him no adolescence. He was still tied to her apron strings, and this issue was one which would affect the course of his life. He decided that he must make a final stand. He did not try to fight against her overtly: his upbringing as an Edwardian gentleman precluded that. Instead, he took the only other option open to a smothered adolescent: he ran away from home.

3. *Nothing Which Qualified Him to be an Ordinary Member of Society*

Last Year at School and First Years at University
1906–8

A hundred years earlier he might have run away to sea: instead he joined the army. Within days Lawrence found himself a gunner in the Royal Garrison Artillery on sentry duty at St Just in Cornwall, overlooking the estuary of the Fal. Suddenly, this girlish little pipsqueak with his 'five pound note' voice was rubbing shoulders with rude boys who had grown up in streets far meaner than those of genteel north Oxford. He had long fantasized about serving in the ranks, but in the reality he found much to regret. The men were astonishingly brutal, and every argument ended in either a bloody fist-fight or mass bullying of the party least favoured. They brawled drunkenly all Friday and Saturday night, frightening him with their roughness, and every morning parade saw five or six men with injuries. Lawrence was restless and uncertain, and when he witnessed one of his colleagues smashing up another who had stolen from him, it was the last straw. He disclosed his whereabouts to his father, who came to purchase the discharge of his missing son.

Lawrence later told Liddell Hart that he had served for six months: in other versions it was eight and three. Only one of these figures can be correct, and probably none is, and the ordeal lasted only a matter of days. In January 1906, Lawrence and a boy called H. E. Mather had attempted to paddle a canoe up the flooded Cherwell to Banbury, but had capsized near Islip. Sarah confirmed that in the Easter holidays that year, Ned and Will had tried again. If this is so, then Lawrence's military service cannot have begun much before February or extended much after March 1906. There is no record of a T. E. Lawrence having served in the Artillery in 1905–6, and though he would presumably have taken an assumed name, no long absence was recalled by his school-friends or brothers. He was certainly in Oxford to take the

Senior Locals examinations in May. Many biographers have concluded that the episode did not take place at all. After Lawrence's death a painting by the Uranian artist Henry Scott Tuke, apparently showing Lawrence in army uniform, was found among his effects and claimed as evidence of his sojourn in Falmouth in 1906. Eric Kennington identified the cap badge in the picture as belonging to the Royal Garrison Artillery – rather remarkably, for it is badly smudged. Tuke was certainly living in Falmouth in 1906, and was fond of using young boys and soldiers as models. Lawrence later told an acquaintance that he had 'often' modelled for Tuke in his youth. Yet Tuke kept a register of his pictures, and this one was clearly recorded as having been painted in 1922 – a year, incidentally, in which Lawrence visited Cornwall. The picture is entitled *Portrait of Gray* and was eventually bought by a man named Gray. How it came into Lawrence's possession is unclear, unless he himself was 'Gray'. Did Lawrence actually meet Tuke in Oxford on a visit to his friend Charles Bell? Was his trip to Cornwall in 1922 made with the object of renewing a friendship he had first made as a seventeen-year-old gunner? As in so much of Lawrence's life, all that can be said for certain about his early enlistment in the Royal Garrison Artillery is that his account of it is not the whole truth.

Lawrence confessed later that the sense of inadequacy he felt with other men led him to compensate with what he called 'elaboration – the vice of amateurs'. In a world of bigger, more athletic, more physically powerful boys, his skills of 'elaboration' were a protective mechanism which gave him an aura of being much more than he appeared. Though he was capable of building a sustained edifice of falsehood, as he was later to do with John Bruce, his tendency was less to fabricate than to inflate the prosaic into something of an altogether more heroic order. His grand gesture of rebellion in running away to the army was spoiled by a quick and ignominious retreat, yet Lawrence salvaged his defeat by turning it into a darkly romantic tale – notably a tale involving elements of violence, suffering and degradation about which he fantasized. Fantasy, exaggeration, and distortion are tools of masochism, and one expression of Lawrence's masochism was a running fantasy of self-degradation, of being bound for life to servitude as a 'beast' in the ranks, of working among the outcasts of many nations on the docks at Port Said: 'There seemed a certainty in degradation,' he wrote, 'a final safety. Man could rise to any height, but there was an animal level beneath which he could not fall.'[1] One early discovery he made about human beings was that almost everyone – even the erudite – will believe what they want to believe, and most want to believe the romantic rather than the prosaic. This was a great revelation to Lawrence, and it enabled him to hone his skills as a bluffer to the highest degree. 'A reputation as a classical scholar is easily gained,' he would boast to his mother from Beirut, having dropped a quote from Theocritus he had just acquired into the conversation, while visiting the American College.[2] As a young intelligence officer he would report with delight that 'The War Office people are very easily to be deceived into a respect for special knowledge loudly declared.' Lawrence's 'lily gilding' was precisely that, for often he had no real reason to 'elaborate'. Take two letters, for instance, both written in 1912, concerning the purchase of some camel-bells Lawrence later had on display at his house. The first, dated 18 February, is to James Elroy Flecker, the second, dated 20 March, is to his mother:

> Today there came through the bazaar a *long caravan of 100 mules* of Baghdad, marching . . . to the boom of two huge iron bells swinging under the belly of the foremost . . . I went and bought the bells . . . And I marched home triumphant making the sound of a caravan from Baghdad . . .[3]

> You will like my camel bells: *I met a camel caravan* coming swinging down the spice market in Aleppo to the booming of two huge iron cylinders under the belly of the foremost: and I stopped the line and bought the bells and walked back to the hotel making a noise like a caravan from Baghdad.[4]

The animals were either mules or camels, and at least one of the accounts is untrue: it is hardly likely that Lawrence could have forgotten in the space of a month what kind of animals they were. One might ask, 'What does it matter if they were mules or camels?' and this is precisely the point: whether they were mules or camels is supremely unimportant, and there is no conceivable motive for lying. One can only conclude that either Lawrence enjoyed misleading others, or he had a very uncommon conception of the truth. Indeed, his attitude to fact would be well demonstrated years later, when he advised Robert Graves that the best way of hiding the truth was by making mystifying, contradictory or misleading statements.[5] Working with the Arabs during the war, he would admit that he did not tell the whole truth either to them or to his British masters, but designed a version of reality which suited himself. He would write that he himself often could not tell where his 'leg-pulling' began or ended, confess to having lied even in his official dispatches and reports, and would add: 'I must have had some tendency, some aptitude, for deceit, or I would not have deceived men so well.'[6] Ronald Storrs, who worked closely with him in Cairo during the war, would say that he could be 'reckless in speech, irresponsible, misleading, tiresome, exasperating, maddening, *stating as facts things which he knew nobody could or would accept* – a street Arab as well as an Arab of Arabia'.[7]

His quick withdrawal from the Artillery in 1906 may have shattered his own illusion that he was the 'hard man' he craved to be, yet in another sense the gambit had been eminently successful. Sarah no longer tried to force her will on him, no longer had recourse to the stick. Any freedom he felt himself to possess in the following years began the moment he showed his mother that he was capable of separating himself from her. Long afterwards he wrote that seventeen was the age at which he found himself.[8] The incident had disturbed the family's smooth running, but the respectable façade had to be maintained for the world. On his return the waves closed over him swiftly, and the episode was hushed up. In exchange for his silence, he got his wish to have his name put forward for a history scholarship, and sat the Senior Locals examinations that summer with a more peaceful mind.

He was also allowed to make the cycling tour around the Côtes du Nord in France that he had long been planning with his friend Scroggs Beeson. To this end he ordered a new bicycle from the Morris Company – a specially designed lightweight model with racing drop-handlebars and a unique three-speed gear, which, he liked to say afterwards, had been made by Lord Nuffield's own hands when he was just plain Mr William Henry Morris. Cycling was a relatively new phenomenon at the turn of the century. Though the rear chain-driven bicycle with pneumatic tyres had been invented before 1895, it remained an expensive luxury item until 1900, when it was first mass-produced. Thomas Lawrence had been an enthusiast even in the early 1890s when the family lived at Dinard in Brittany, and Ned had acquired his first bike as a schoolboy in 1901. Whether his special racing model of 1906 was actually made by Lord Nuffield's own hands remains unknown. It is a typically Lawrentian story, and Nuffield emphatically denied it, though since he is known to have made bicycles in Oxford High Street until 1908, it is at least theoretically possible. Whatever the case, there is no more poignant symbol of Lawrence's youth than his racing bicycle, which was later remembered vividly by his friends, almost as if it had been an extension of himself. Edward Leeds recalled how it would vanish surely and swiftly up the road, 'almost before one had turned one's back', while Vyvyan Richards remembered with pleasure how the machine would 'slide silently into the Iffley Road after midnight'. Lawrence was to make eight cycling trips to France and to cover several thousands of miles on this machine.

He left England on a ferry bound for St Malo on 3 August 1906, in expansive mood. The examinations were over at last, he was away from his mother, and the brave new world seemed full of light. There was an appropriately magnificent sunset, and Lawrence stood on deck for hours, letting long stanzas of romantic poetry wash through his head, and taking in the glory of the moon reflected in the waters. Leaving England again more than twenty years later, he would remember this night as a dream of delight: the beginning of his voluntary travels.[9] He was to remain in the Côtes du Nord for a month and cover the best part of 600 miles by bicycle, travelling with Beeson in a long figure of eight around the north-east of the region, staying in modest hotels and lingering among great cathedrals, churches and the ruins of ancient châteaux. The delight he experienced in escape is reflected in his letters home, and towards the end of his holiday he described the glories of the Breton coast to his mother in a stream of verse from Keats and Shelley, concluding with a subliminal message to Sarah, that it was all so wonderful 'because there was no-one else there'. This letter evidently reflects a near rapturous mood, for Lawrence was generally happier extolling the virtues of man-made objects than the beauties of nature. His letters contain descriptions of architecture and church interiors which sometimes run for pages, and though they were written principally for his own future reference they were also a barrier to real emotion, which – apart from some superficial expressions of familial affection – these letters lack almost totally. In this sense, Lawrence's 1906 letters are a perfect showcase of his profound aloofness from his family, from the mother who believed they should have no secrets from each other. If Sarah must know everything, Ned felt, then he would tell her all, but instead of the expressions of warmth she hungered for, he would give her only dry stones. While human passions could be wild and unpredictable, architecture was a triumph of human order, a successful fusion of the conscious and the unconscious, a symbol of the human ability to transform matter. He would later assert – more than half seriously – that there could be no true creative work into which the hands did not enter, and would become convinced that the human mind was expressed most com-pletely in the manipulation of material, whether stone, clay, wood, cloth, skin or steel: by contrast with frail human flesh, human artefacts seemed solid and enduring. Another impulse behind these endless descriptions, though, was the sheer compulsion to describe. It is as if the things Lawrence saw and heard had no objective existence unless he described them to someone else. He admitted years later that his writing practice had been to put down more and more exactly what he had seen and felt. His talent for description became both his strength and his weakness as a writer: his sense of detail was photographic, but his skills were episodic and lacked economy and continuity. George Bernard Shaw would later conclude that Lawrence was 'one of the greatest descriptive writers in English literature',[10] while Francis Yeats-Brown would add that his 'itch for description . . . developed into a mania'.[11]

The main business of the tour, however, was medieval castles, and the jewel of them all was Tonquedoc, a thirteenth-century Norman château standing on a hill overlooking the wooded valley of the Guer. Lawrence and Beeson reached the ruins after riding from Lannion on the eve of Lawrence's eighteenth birthday and spent four hours exploring them in idyllic sunshine. As he examined the castle, tower by tower, stone by stone, Lawrence found himself playing out a mental game of attack and defence – placing himself in the position of the besieged: '. . . the place would have been impossible to enter,' he decided triumphantly. 'An enemy would have had to make two bridges before he could reach the door. The drop to the ground was about 40 feet . . .'[12] He declared that Tonquedoc was the best castle he had ever seen, and felt he had somehow lessened its glory by describing it. He had brought no camera with him on this trip, and to Beeson was assigned the task of sketching. The friends enjoyed each other's company, but inevitably they argued. Beeson thought Lawrence needlessly reckless, jumping moats instead of using bridges and clambering up walls full of loose stones. He guessed that this was not boldness so much as bravado, and this was confirmed once when he noticed Lawrence's legs quaking in fear as he struggled to climb some perilous rocks, and offered his hand only to have it brushed aside indignantly. Beeson was an enthusiastic naturalist, and noted that Lawrence was unusual in having not even the normal schoolboy's interest in natural history. This grew, perhaps, from a subconscious disgust he felt for the idea of reproduction, which would become more apparent in his later life, when he would regard the word 'animal' as a term of abuse, conjuring up the 'beastly' instincts of the unconscious mind. Of all things in the world, he wrote later, it was 'animal spirits' that he feared most.[13] Lawrence nursed a grudge against Beeson for being 'such an ass' in slowing the pace of their cycling, but the truth may be that Beeson lacked Lawrence's special three-speed gears, whose superiority he demonstrated proudly once on the flat sands at Erquy by covering a measured half-kilometre in thirty seconds. Even this remarkable speed did not satisfy him, though, and he dropped hints in a letter to his family about the efficacy of a motorcycle.

After Beeson left on 19 August, Lawrence stayed on for another two weeks, and shortly before leaving received the anxiously awaited results of the Locals examinations. They were excellent. He had come thirteenth out of more than 4,500 candidates, and had collected first place in English and third in religious knowledge. His place in Oxford University seemed assured, yet the result did not satisfy him: '. . . on the whole,' he wrote, '[it is] not as good as I'd hoped.'[14] Such dissatisfaction would haunt him throughout his life. No matter to what heights he scaled, it would never seem good enough for the perfectionist soul within: 'It does not seem to me,' he would write, '. . . as though anything I've ever done was quite well enough done. That is an aching, unsatisfied feeling and ends up by making me wish I hadn't done anything.'[15] This was evidently true of the 1906 cycling tour. Lawrence had covered 600 miles, and had even ridden 114 miles from Dinard to Fougères and back on one of the hottest days of the year. Yet this was not good enough. On returning to Oxford, he told Scroggs Beeson that he had continued the tour alone, 'eager to set his own pace', and presented such 'glowing descriptions of what was to be seen in Normandy and the Loire Valley' that Beeson was stimulated to meet him there the following year. But Lawrence's letters make clear that he never went near Normandy or the Loire Valley in 1906, spending the two weeks after Beeson left him based at Dinard, where – apart from occasional excursions – he went bathing almost every day.

That autumn, while Lawrence and Beeson worked for their 'Re-positions' – the Oxford University entrance examination – several major building projects were taking place in the city, particularly in Cornmarket Street, at various university colleges, and in the High. Lawrence, ever alert to the possibility of archaeological treasures, would make a round of these sites almost daily, slipping the labourers a few pennies to preserve their finds. After months of persistence, he and Beeson had assembled a superb collection of pottery, glazed ware, bottles, pipes, coins and tokens, and though it was disappointingly modern for Lawrence's taste – dating mainly from the sixteenth and seventeenth centuries – it was interesting enough to present to the Ashmolean Museum, where Lawrence had already made the acquaint-ance of the junior Assistant Keeper, Leonard Woolley. Woolley, who would come to know Lawrence better than most in the pre-war era, was then twenty-five, and had recently graduated from New College. He was just embarking on the career which would bring him a knighthood in recognition of his brilliant work as an archaeologist. A kind, energetic and sensitive man, Woolley was one of the few who never succumbed to the spell of Lawrence's later fame, and confessed that though he had found the young Lawrence charming, even talented, he had not recognized in him any special 'genius'. He characterized their early acquaintance in Oxford as 'slight'. The Ashmolean's Art Curator, Charles Bell, took a greater interest in Lawrence, however, and soon accepted him at the museum as an unofficial acolyte. He gave him odd jobs such as sorting out collections of brass-rubbings and pottery, and Lawrence quickly became more familiar with the medieval collection than the museum's own staff.

Meanwhile, he applied for a scholarship at St John's College – where his elder brother Bob was already studying medicine – but was unsuccessful. The following January, though, he succeeded in obtain-ing a Meyricke Exhibition at Jesus College – available to him because of the accident of his Welsh birth – which provided £50 for the study of Modern History. Jesus was very much a Welsh college, and during Easter 1907 he felt compelled to make a cycling tour of Wales – which he had never seen – to acquaint himself with his country of birth. His letters home from this tour show a new fluency, a factor Lawrence may have owed to John Ruskin, whose book *The Stones of Venice* he had read the previous year. Ruskin, a poet, was one of the founders of the Victorian Gothic Revival, and was concerned with the way in which architecture mirrored the human spirit. He believed that the fineness of true medieval Gothic stonework was a consequence of the fact that the workmen of the age had been allowed more freedom of expression than the modern artisan, condemned as he was to be a cypher on the production line. Ruskin's writing, considered a beau ideal of Victorian mannered prose, stimulated Lawrence into imitation: 'I now have some conception of the right way to study architecture,' he wrote on first reading Ruskin, 'and how to draw the truest lessons from it.'[16] One of the most frustrating moments on the trip, though, was when he overheard the young landlady of the Pelican Hotel at Kidwelly discussing him with her family. Few of us would have been able to refrain from listening, perhaps, but Lawrence, whose inner lack of self-image gave him a lifelong craving to know how he appeared to others, strained desperately for every word: 'It really was awfully funny,' he reported, '. . . the family council ended by deciding I would probably "be" something – rather a pointless conclusion I think.'[17]

Lawrence went up Jesus College on 12 October 1907, but he continued to live at Polstead Road for most of his time as an undergraduate, taking rooms for only one term – Trinity 1908 – to comply with college rules. Theo Chaundy, who entered Christ Church in the same year, admitted that he and his peers had been surprised to see Lawrence up for a scholarship – not because of any lack of intellect, but because they doubted that he had the commitment required for an academic life. Lawrence later claimed to have attended no lectures while at Jesus, and to have spent all his time in private reading – often reading which had little connection with his subject. In history, anything after 1500 bored him anyway, and his concept of the Middle Ages was much more the chivalrous world of *Morte d'Arthur* than the down-to-earth one of serfdom and the Plague. L. C. Jane, a rather neurotic but brilliant tutor who coached Lawrence for his Repositions, felt that he was not a scholar by temperament, and observed that the only books he would read were those which were out of the ordinary: books, in other words, which appealed to his sense of self-mystification. Jane noticed Lawrence's aloofness, and his habit of making provocative statements in order to test his personality. Ernest Barker, a history don, believed that Lawrence had chosen to study history simply because it was a hurdle to be jumped, and saw him as a knight girding himself for action. The more observant Midge Hall, who was at Jesus with Lawrence, though, realized that he was, in fact, 'a wanderer for wandering's sake' with no settled purpose other than to escape. Reginald Lane Poole, Lawrence's tutor in medieval history, thought him a romantic, though noted, obversely, that he would begin his essays with some challenging statement – a technique he had acquired from the advice of Sir Charles Oman, whose theories on medieval castles he would one day set out to refute. Once, when Lawrence wrote Poole a note apologizing for missing a tutorial, his tutor riposted with rapier-like wit that it was unimportant since it 'had given him time for an hour's useful work'.

Lawrence played little part in the life of the college, and drew attention to himself by his very solitariness. His refusal to join in sport raised some eyebrows, but he was too subtle to argue the toss with college hearties, preferring to lampoon them by following them through the streets on their way to the sports field or rowing club, making fun of their physical characteristics. There were other abstentions too. He did not smoke, he did not drink, he rarely attended official meals in hall. He explained to one fellow undergraduate, A. G. Prys-Jones, that he did not sit on chairs if he could avoid it and took no breakfast, lunch, tea, dinner, no tobacco or strong drink: '. . . in fact,' said Prys-Jones, 'he did nothing which qualified him to be an ordinary member of society.'[18] Once, he burst into Midge Hall's room with a grotesquely distorted face and began firing a revolver through a window into the Turl below. Hall realized that the shots were blanks, and concluded, probably correctly, that Lawrence was play-acting, though Lawrence claimed to be letting off steam after a marathon forty-five-hour work-session without food or sleep. In Trinity Term 1908 he took rooms in the inner quadrangle of Jesus, overlooking the covered market, and above the college kitchen whose stale cooking smells drifted miasmically through them. Late at night, when everyone else was retiring, Lawrence would come alive, 'like a cat', prowling the dark streets on his bicycle or merely tramping the quadrangles alone. A. T. P. Williams, an undergraduate who would later become Bishop of Winchester, recalled meeting him there often: 'I do not know when he went to bed,' he wrote, 'some nights, I'm pretty sure, not at all, certainly seldom till well on in the small hours.'[19] His sleepless tramping eventually piqued the curiosity of a third-year undergraduate named Vyvyan Richards, who went to investigate the solitary freshman and immediately fell in love with him. Richards, a sharp, angular, sensitive man, was the son of a Welsh inventor and his American wife, who had spent his life gaining distinctions, and sneering at art, history and literature. His fascination with Lawrence took him abruptly into a very different dimension, a world of old things: 'castles, churches, memorial brasses, pottery and books-books-books'.[20] The two young men could not have been more different: Richards, sporty, snobbish, unintellec-tual, critical, orthodox: Lawrence, mercurial, whimsical, unconven-tional, super-cerebral, wrapped up in antiquity and romance – and yet, on their first meeting, Richards would write, 'some deep and quick affection took hold upon us whose vividness stirs me still after thirty years have passed away'.[21] Richards became obsessed with his love for Lawrence, offering him boundless affection, subservience and sacrifice, but his passion went unrequited. Lawrence was not attracted to him, and though he enjoyed his company and was flattered by his attentions, never gave the slightest hint that he understood the nature of his friend's interest. He recognized that Richards was a difficult and complex personality, inclined to be dismissive of what he understood poorly, and with a horror of vulgarity, which he euphemistically referred to as 'professionalism'. He liked Richards's latent artistic talent and enjoyed helping to nurture it, and he could not ignore the tremendous energy Richards sent his way, which he turned to their mutual advantage. He loved Richards's directness and experienced with him an intimacy which he had never known before. Much to Richards's disappointment, though, that intimacy remained chaste. Years later, he claimed that Lawrence was 'sexless', and his conviction that he had 'neither flesh or carnality of any kind' echoes Clare Sydney Smith's view that 'Lawrence's presence was hardly a physical one'. Neither understood that Lawrence was a masochist whose sexual feelings were closely tied up with his fear of pain. Though he preferred men to women and his later writings show a fascination with the idea of homoerotic sex, he had a horror of the reality of physical intimacy, which was directly connected to his early relationship with his mother: 'The disgust of being touched revolted me,' he would write, '. . . perhaps because one . . . terrible struggle in my youth had given me an enduring fear of contact.'[22] He would tell E. M. Forster that he was 'funnily made up sexually', and as regards the homosexual act, would write: 'I couldn't ever do it, I believe: the impulse strong enough to make me touch another creature has not yet been born in me.'[23]

Richards later told Robert Graves that after he had moved to digs outside the college, Lawrence would frequently visit him after midnight, and once, he said, he had asked Richards to join him on a bizarre bathing trip – they would dive through the ice on the frozen Cherwell to find out whether it was thin enough to let them in and out again. Richards dismissed the idea as ridiculously dangerous, but Lawrence went off to do it alone, and repeated it several times later. Richards explained that his friend's pleasure in these strange outings derived partly from the astonishment he saw on the faces of orthodox people such as himself. It is a key observation, for while Lawrence's fasting, dieting, and denial of sleep were expressions of his masochistic nature, they were also aspects of his reverse exhibitionism. If he had been simply 'hardening himself for the ordeal to come' in the classical 'heroic' sense, an audience would have been unnecessary, but Lawrence had no penchant for 'suffering in silence': his ordeal must be witnessed. It was characteristic of him throughout his life, Richards said, to seek some private gallery for his exploits.

Together, Lawrence and Richards explored the world of William Morris, the colossus of Victorian art and design who would influence Lawrence for the rest of his life. It is not clear when Lawrence first became aware of Morris (not to be confused with the industrialist William Henry Morris – Lord Nuffield), but living in north Oxford during the 1890s he could scarcely have avoided hearing about him, since Morris's pomegranate wallpaper designs were *de rigueur* in the houses of university dons. Morris was precisely the kind of polymath that Lawrence would have liked to be: a poet of distinction, novelist, master craftsman, designer, printer and painter who had pioneered the art of brass-rubbing, toured Gothic cathedrals in France in the 1850s, trekked through the cold deserts of Iceland, rediscovered

Malory's classic *Morte d'Arthur*, inspired the Arts and Crafts movement, espoused radical socialism, helped found the Pre-Raphaelite Brotherhood, and set up the famous Kelmscott Press. Morris's inspiration, like Lawrence's, was the medieval period, and his objective was to revive the spirit of individual craftsmanship which he believed the industrial Victorian era had lost. This made him a giant in Lawrence's eyes, for as a youth he was always engaged in some kind of handicraft – if not brass-rubbing, then poker-work, stone-carving, metal-work, wood-carving or even sewing. While Richards admired the diligence with which Lawrence worked at his crafts, he rarely admired the results. Lawrence once showed him an electric lamp he had hammered out of brass, modelled on a Moorish lantern in Holman Hunt's engraving *The Light of the World*. Richards thought the lamp poor, but was more impressed with the griffon-figure Lawrence once carved on the bar of a table in his room. Bob Lawrence wrote that even as a child Ned had a great aptitude for improving and fixing household appliances – an ability Lawrence would later boast of as his 'faculty for making and repairing things'.[24] Though Ned called himself 'a wanderer after sensations and an artist of sorts', Arnie thought his brother more of a craftsman than an artist, and believed he had a craftsman's appreciation of sound work in sound material irrespective of artistic merit.[25] Later, in his writing career, Lawrence would behave as if there were a craftsman's technique to literary expression, which, if it could only be learned, would enable one to create a masterpiece 'by numbers' as it were. He was adept at learning technique, but discovered with some bitterness that great literature lay not in mastering 'tricks', but in the power of creative vision. The truth was that the dominating force in Lawrence's psyche – that supreme will he had built up against the barbarian hordes which were ever hammering and sapping at the frontier of his consciousness – was inimical to creativity. If it kept out maverick emotions it also attenuated the originality of vision those emotions entailed. Lawrence was too controlled, too mechanistic, too rational, ever to be a poet or an artist. The great tragedy of his life was the discovery that creativity was in reality the outpourings of the dark side which he had spent his life trying to suppress.

It was Morris who inspired Lawrence with the idea of setting up a hand-press, for printing seemed the ideal occupation for the kind of artistic dilettante he saw himself becoming in the future. When he thought of a career, he could not tolerate the idea of being pigeon-holed into one profession or another. Moreover, printing seemed to have a mystique about it which appealed to him: 'Printing is not a business but a craft,' he told his mother later. 'We cannot sit down to it for so many hours a day, any more than a picture could be painted on that system.'[26] Like Morris, Lawrence was also attracted by the sensual quality of a well-produced book, not merely the aesthetic appeal of the type-face, but the feel of the paper and the texture of the binding. His letters are full of esoteric references to the merits of vellum or the intricacies of obtaining fine purple from the Levantine murex. While rooms in Hammersmith Mall had been good enough for Morris, however, for Lawrence and Richards only a proper 'medieval hall' would suffice. This notion might have come to them on a pilgrimage they made to a sort of Morris shrine at Broad Campden, where a couple called the Coomeraswamis had converted a fourteenth-century chapel into a house packed with Morris memorabilia, including a copy of the exquisitely bound Kelmscott *Chaucer*: 'the prince of modern printing'. Here they were also privileged to see the actual press Morris had used in his Kelmscott studio, which was still functioning, and Richards took pains to record that their reaction was not merely sentimental: '. . . it was a notable stimulus,' he wrote, 'to the practical enthusiasm which was taking root in our minds. We, too, would print, and would get enough by it, we hoped, to live without bowing to any form of professionalism.'[27] The visit also stimulated Lawrence to read Morris's novel *The Roots of the Mountains*, a fantasy about Gothic mountain tribes who lived communally in halls, slept in 'shut-beds', held 'folk-moots' and fought gallantly in battle. *Roots* led him to other novels: *The Well at the World's End*, *The Wood Beyond the World*, *Sigurd the Volsung* – each transporting him into a fabulous, heroic world. While his feeling for more celebrated authors waxed and waned, his taste for Morris would last all his life: 'I suppose everybody loves one writer unreasonably,' he would tell Charlotte Shaw. 'I'd rather Morris than the world.' 'My reason tells me he isn't a very good writer: but then, he wrote just the stuff I like.'[28] Lawrence thought the idea of a medieval hall more authentically Morris than Morris's own 'Red House' at Upton, and once dragged Richards over to look at a disused stone chapel near Weymouth which he considered buying. It had, said Richards, a 'naked simplicity' which appealed to Lawrence. The Morrisian fantasy – for Morris's 'medieval' was no more truly medieval than Lawrence's – exerted enormous power over him. There is more than a hint of the communal halls of *Roots of the Mountains* in his later attachment to the life of the barrack-room, and as Richards himself pointed out, for Lawrence 'the desert tents of black goats hair were many pillared dark halls too'.[29]

Lawrence's excursions while at Jesus College were not exclusively into the intellectual and aesthetic spheres, however. In the summer of 1908 he asked Richards to join him on a peculiarly urban adventure – the running of the Trill Mill Stream. This is the first image we have of Lawrence the organizer and man of action – a persona he frequently sought to deny in later years. He had always been interested in boating and canoeing, and in his first year at Jesus had discovered references to a medieval watercourse – the Trill Mill Stream – which now passed beneath the city. After some careful local detective work he came to the conclusion that the stream began at the mouth of a sewer near Hythe Bridge, and he determined to discover whether it debouched into the Isis at Folly Bridge as he suspected. Richards was only one of a group of friends he gathered together in three canoes for the adventure, the others being Midge Hall, Theo Chaundy, A. T. P. Williams and H. E. Mather – the water enthusiast with whom Lawrence had made the unsuccessful ascent of the Cherwell in 1906. On the appointed day the canoes were lowered into the sewer at Hythe Bridge, lit with candles and acetylene lamps. The tunnel was very narrow and the young men had just enough room to crouch forward in the canoes with their arms touching the sides. It was no place for the victim of claustrophobia. Lawrence remarked that it would be interesting to see which of their light-sources would expire first as the air became foul, and wondered aloud what the attitude of the incumbent rats would be. 'Anyway,' he said, as the canoes slipped into the darkness, 'there's no room to turn back.'[30] Lawrence was electrified by an exquisite thrill of fear, which had once again prompted him to bravado. Secretly, he was terrified that the water might flow through a grating, in which case the canoes might be stuck, or that a sudden shower outside might raise the water-level and drown them. Fortunately there were no obstacles or hitches of any kind, and Lawrence camouflaged his relief by firing blanks from his pistol under the gutter-gratings to attract the attention of pedestrians above. The canoes shot out into the daylight near Folly Bridge only twenty minutes after setting out.

Since Lawrence was more intent on such extra-curricular activities, or on escape into Morris country, than on his lectures, he was amazingly fortunate that in 1908 the History Examiners introduced the option of presenting a thesis on any question connected with a special subject. Lawrence realized that if he chose 'Military History and Strategy' as his special subject, he could present a thesis on crusader castles which would deploy all his hard-earned knowledge of medieval defensive warfare. In summer 1907 he had made his second cycling tour of France with Beeson, and now, in summer 1908, he decided to make a third tour to look at the crusader castles he had missed, and to glimpse some of the cathedrals which had so inspired William Morris in the 1850s. This would be his most ambitious expedition yet: he would ride all the way across France to the Mediterranean, and this time he would do it alone.

He arrived at Le Havre in mid-July, and battled in violent hailstorms through Gisors to Compiègne, and from there to Provins, near Paris, where he discovered a unique twelfth-century keep and ruined town walls, which almost defied his cerebral game of attack–defence. He wandered around them for hours trying to puzzle out what the designer had intended, and came to the conclusion that they had been built as an experiment: '. . . the keep would have been almost incapable of defence,' he decided, 'yet in spirit it is half a century ahead of its time.'[31] Living on bread, milk, peaches and apricots, he rode into Champagne, where the weather became 'fearfully hot'. His days followed a strict regime: up at dawn, he would reach his castle usually by midday, and investigate it for a couple of hours. In the afternoon he would ride on, reaching his hotel by seven or eight in the evening. The sheer imperative of the journey soon eclipsed even his joy in reaching the castles, though he would occupy his mind in composing whole pages of his projected thesis as he pedalled. The Champagne country was stunningly beautiful and he felt himself filling with energy as he cycled, through cherry-orchards and across sparkling streams, past fields of ripe golden barley and wheat. He watched peasants advancing to the harvest in cohorts, their sickles flashing like swords in the sun, the great wains of hay being drawn by bilious-white oxen. Steadily he made his way south, and by late July he was steering a course beneath the austere volcanic plugs of the Auvergne, past gardens enclosed with massive dry-stone walls, toiling up thousands of feet and consoling himself with the thought that such agony as his was undreamed of in classical times – a combination of the tortures of Sisyphus, who had to roll a great stone endlessly uphill, of Tantalus, who was condemned to grasp at fruit just beyond his reach, and of Theseus, who was forced to remain forever sitting. His reward was a 4,000 foot free-wheel descent into the Rhône valley, so perilous and exciting that he felt sick when he reached the bottom. He rode on through Provence and the lovely but mosquito-infested marshlands of the Camargue, where he contracted his first dose of the malaria which would plague much of his life. At last, he arrived at the lonely, olive-covered mountain of Les Baux, from where he looked down a precipice and far across a plain. Suddenly, as he watched, the sun leapt from behind a cloud, illuminating a silvery shimmer. It was one of the most thrilling moments of his life, and he celebrated it in a way that only an Oxford man of that era would have done, screaming out the words of Xenophon, so loudly that it disturbed the nearby tourists: '*Thalassa! Thalassa!* The Sea! The Sea!'

4. The Sultan Drank Tea as Usual

Young Turks' Revolution
1908

As Lawrence had cycled southwards to the Mediterranean that July, news of a *coup d'état* in Turkey seemed to leap at him out of the headlines. One day the newspapers would confirm that a revolution was taking place, and another they would assure their readers that all was calm, and 'the Sultan drank tea as usual'. On 23 July he wrote to his mother asking desperately for clarification: 'it might well be important,' he said.[1] What was actually taking place was the beginning of the end of the Ottoman Empire, the tottering giant which had dominated the Middle East and eastern Europe for nearly 500 years. On 22 July, a handful of young Turkish officers had taken control of the Ottoman 3rd Army in Europe. On 24 July they offered the Padishah Sultan, 'Abd al-Hamid II, an ultimatum: either grant a constitution or step down. Whichever path he chose, the tyrant's power was effectively at an end.

They called him 'Abdul the Damned', 'The Red Sultan', 'Abdul the Bloody', and for years he had presided over a corrupt and oppressive empire that stretched from the sands of the Sahara to the Persian hills. Behind the grim walls of his Yildiz Palace, surrounded always by a horde of eunuchs, dwarfs, deaf-mute chamberlains and Circassian dancing-girls, the Padishah had run his domain through a vast network of spies and spies-upon-spies connected to him by thousands of miles of telegraph wires. The palace was itself a dark icon of his monumental paranoia, for he rarely ventured beyond its limits, and even within them had constructed a warren of secret passageways whose plan was known only to himself. So unpredictable were 'Abd al-Hamid's rages that even seasoned courtiers were seen to quake in his presence. His food was tasted by a corps of professional poison-snoopers, his cigarettes puffed first by a eunuch, his milk brought in sealed bottles from specially guarded cows. He had secreted thousands of revolvers about the palace, a brace of them above the Imperial bath, and had twice shot dead innocent bystanders who had startled him – one of them rumoured to have been his own daughter. His administration had become such a travesty that his chosen advisers included a circus clown, a bootblack, a Punch and Judy man, the son of one of his cooks, and a slave he had bought on the open market. 'Abdul the Damned' had lost all touch with reality: the Ottoman Empire was rotten to the core, and only the slightest push was required to set it rocking. That push was provided by the keen young firebrands of the CUP – the 'Committee of Union and Progress' – who were mostly army officers trained in the Sultan's own military academies. Their aim was to reduce the Padishah to a figurehead. 'Abd al-Hamid, who believed he could strike back later, decided to granted a constitution, and for almost the first time in living memory, the streets of Stamboul were filled with cheering crowds.

Among those celebrating the Padishah's reduction was the Sharif Hussain ibn 'Ali, a senior member of the Hashemite family of the Hejaz in western Arabia – the Holy Land of Islam. Exiled in Stamboul under close surveillance by the tyrant's spies, the Sharif had never forgiven the Sultan for having ordered the murder of his uncle, who had been stabbed to death brutally in a Jeddah street in 1880. Hussain had continued to scheme and plot against the government, until, in 1893, the Sultan had finally ordered him to Stamboul with all his family – which had then included three small sons. He must have disembarked from his ship with some trepidation, for he was well aware that critics of the Red Sultan were in the habit of finding themselves stitched into a sack and dropped into the Bosphorus on moonless nights. The Sultan had even had his own brother confined to a cell for twenty years. To his surprise, perhaps, Hussain had been allowed to live quietly, and for fifteen years he had wisely bided his time, never losing sight of his determination to return to Arabia as Emir of Mecca. He was much respected by those who met him – opinionated, domineering, determined, but extremely polite. In 1908 he was about fifty-five, a small, hard man with a bushy beard and eyes as wide and cold as a vulture's. He had delicate hands and fine-drawn features which lent him an exquisite air of grace, and he wore his black *jubba* cloak and tight Meccan turban with the simple dignity appropriate to his patrician status. A conservative of the old school who spoke Turkish more readily than he spoke Arabic, he was renowned for his religious scholarship, his knowledge of international affairs, his love of poetry and his encyclopedic knowledge of natural history. His people, the Hashemites, were the most revered family in Islam, able to trace their descent back over thirty-seven generations to the Prophet Mohammad himself, through his daughter Fatima. They were the traditional stewards of Mecca and Medina, the sacred cities of Islam – cities whose possession was of crucial symbolic value to the Sublime Porte. Though Ottoman Sultans had been considered Caliphs or 'Successors' of the Prophet for 200 years, 'Abd al-Hamid had been the first to use the title officially. His empire was crumbling, and he had played the Islamic card in a last desperate attempt to rally the disparate peoples within its borders. He was terrified of internal revolt. In 1888, unrest among the Armenians had provoked a knee-jerk reaction. His armies had moved in and butchered them systematically, men, women and children, village by village, in a resolute attempt to wipe them out. While the Armenians were a Christian minority, however, the Arabs were not only brother Muslims, but comprised almost half the Empire's population – 10½ million out of 22 million, actually outnumbering the 7½ million ethnic Turks. The Sultan decided to court them. He invoked Islamic sentiment, built mosques, endowed Islamic schools, and promoted Arabs to high office. In 1901 he had inaugurated construction of the Hejaz railway, ostensibly to facilitate the *Haj* – the sacred pilgrimage to the two Holy Cities, which every Muslim was enjoined to take at least once in his life. It was not coincidental, of course, that the railway also strengthened his control over these cities, which were a vital part of his Islamic façade. Officially, the Hejaz was run by the senior member of the Hashemite family, who was appointed Emir or Prince of Mecca. By manipulating the rivalries between the three branches of the family whose menfolk were eligible to be Emir – a game so Byzantine in its wheels within wheels as to be almost incomprehensible to anyone outside it – the Sultan had successfully managed to gain hegemony over the post. On taking power, the CUP dismissed the incumbent Emir as corrupt and, after some deliberation, appointed Hussain in his place. The Young Turks wanted in the Hejaz someone who would bow to his masters and preserve the status quo, and Hussain's prudence and respectability over the past decade and a half had convinced the government that he was such a man. It must have struck the Sharif as something of an irony that he, who had been exiled for fifteen years as a dangerous subversive, should now be chosen for his conservatism.

On 3 December 1908, the steamer *Tanta* dropped anchor in Jeddah harbour with Hussain and all his family aboard. The crystal-white tenement houses of the port with their baroque latticework and hidden balconies peeped over the half-ruined sea-gate, where, on the wharf, a crowd of officials and local Arabs had gathered to meet him. From the deck of the *Tanta*, piled high with sea-chests, boxes and furled carpets – the gleanings of fifteen years of exile – the Sharif watched the sunlight flashing off the sails of scores of dhows cutting through the sea towards the ship. They were packed with cheering people from stem to stern: Bedu chieftains, merchant traders, minor dignitaries, court plaintiffs, distant relatives of the Hashemite family – all come to look over their new Emir and ingratiate themselves if possible. Hussain cannot but have suppressed a wry smile. His predecessor had been virtually the toy of the Ottoman Governor – the Vali – who controlled the cities, the army and the courts, and was responsible for budget, taxation, security and defence. In theory, the Emir had responsibility only for the unruly Bedu tribes, who answered to no one. In practice, though, the position was very different. The Turkish administration was regarded as an alien force by most of the indigenous Hejazis, five-sixths of whom were nomadic or semi-nomadic Bedu. That there were ways and means of manipulating the tribes, Hussain had learned almost as a child, for he had been brought up in the court of his uncle – the Emir – in daily contact with Bedu chiefs, and had been well schooled in the art of playing off tribes and factions, of navigating the endless maze of vituperation, vacillation and discussion which had filled the Emir's days. The Turks controlled the cities, but between the cities lay the desert, and there the Bedu ruled. Only the Hejaz railway effectively connected the Ottoman garrisons with the outside world. Hussain had thought a great deal about rebellion as a youth: he had been a party to his uncle's conspiracy to foment a revolt in the Assir – the province immediately to the south of the Hejaz – which had led directly to the Emir's assassination. He was astute enough to be aware of the advantages of courting the British: the Hejaz depended on grain from British India, and the Royal Navy controlled the Red Sea. He admired the British for their straight-dealing and honesty – a refreshing contrast to the Sultan's forked tongue – and his pro-British tendency was well known to the Porte. When Hussain made a visit to the British Embassy in Istanbul not long after his uncle's murder, the Sultan had warned him sharply that he should 'fish in healthier waters'. A secret report made at the same time by a government spy described him as 'wilful and recalcitrant ... with a dangerous capacity for independent thought'; it was just such a capacity which he intended to exercise now to restore the office of Emir of Mecca to its rightful glory.[2] As he stepped upon his native soil on that day in December 1908, the Sharif's dreams ran far beyond the borders of the Hejaz.

When the Prophet Mohammad died in AD 632, he left no male heirs and had made no provision for a 'Successor' or 'Caliph'. For a moment the whole future of Islam hung in the balance. Mohammad had made it clear in his lifetime that he was 'the Seal of the Prophets' – the last in the line of God's apostles which had begun with Father Adam and included Jesus Christ. For some of his followers the very idea of a 'Successor' was thus questionable. Finally, the Muslims had declared in favour of the Prophet's oldest companion, Abu Bakr, initiating a period of rule by the so-called 'Rightly Minded Caliphs', all of whom had been early converts to Islam, none of them related closely to the Prophet. Westerners saw the Caliph as a kind of Muslim 'Pope' – a misconception which continued to be held up to the twentieth century. In fact, the Caliph was not responsible for religious doctrine, which was determined by the *'ulama* – a consensus of learned elders. His function was always that of *defensor fidei* – a role almost parallel to the one played in the Catholic Church by the Holy Roman Emperor in medieval times. In 661 the Caliphate had returned to the Prophet's own line, and the centre of power had shifted from the Hejaz to Damascus in Syria, under the 'Umayyads. Centuries later, the capital was moved again, this time to Baghdad, under the Abbasids, whose most famous scion was Hirun ar-Rashid. The Abbasids were much influenced by Persia, and had long since forsaken their Bedu levies in favour of the Mamluks, a caste of military slaves drawn mainly from the Caucasus. In doing so they had sown the seeds of their own downfall. Inevitably slaves had become masters, and the Caliph had been reduced to a mere puppet whose function was to lend credibility to the Mamluk regime. When the Ottoman Sultan Selim the Grim broke the Mamluk army in Syria in 1516, he found among the prisoners an unimpressive personage called Mutawakkil, who turned out to be the last in the line of Caliphs of direct descent from the Prophet. Though Selim the Grim never adopted the title Caliph, it was taken informally by his son, Sulayman the Magnificent, whose empire stretched from Baghdad to Budapest. The Caliphate had remained in Turkish hands ever since.

If the Caliphate featured in Hussain's thoughts, though, it was subordinate to the furtherance of his own family, in particular his four sons, 'Ali, 'Abdallah, Feisal and Zayd. The last, born in Stamboul to the Sharif's second wife, the Circassian beauty Adlah Hanum, was still a boy. The others were in their twenties, born in the Hejaz but brought up in Turkey as young patricians of the Empire. They had been well educated, spoke Turkish more fluently than Arabic, and knew French and some English. Sophisticated townsmen, to some extent cosmopolitan, multilingual, religious, they were very much Turkish in outlook, and though well versed in court intrigue, they knew little except by hearsay of the desert, the Bedu, black tents and camel-raids. Despite the driving ambitions of the Sharif, it is unlikely that as the young Sharifs went ashore that December they imagined that two of them would end their lives as kings, or that the instrument of their elevation would be a young Oxford undergraduate who had yet to step on Arabian soil, and who had but weeks before stood on a hill at Les Baux thrilling at his first sight of the Mediterranean sea.

5. A Rather Remarkable Young Man

Oxford and Syria
1908–9

Lawrence returned from his tour of France with his head full of the East, Richard the Lionheart and the Crusades. He had even photographed an Arabic inscription on the castle at Montreuil Bellayn – supposed to have been built by Richard – which he believed had never been translated. He had cycled 2,400 miles, lived on milk and fruit, and had come home 'brown as a jap and as thin as paper', enraptured by the idea for his thesis on military architecture: 'Eureka!' he wrote to Scroggs Beeson. 'I've got it at last for a thesis: the transition from the square keep form: really, it is too great for words.'[1]

He had also had a vision of the real Middle Ages as opposed to the Morrisian romantic image of them. In Chartres cathedral, he had been overwhelmed by a sense of space and light – just as William Morris had been fifty years earlier. It was, he wrote, 'a feeling I had never had before . . . as though I had found a path . . . as far as the gates of heaven and had caught a glimpse of the inside, the door being ajar'.[2] Throwing off his Ruskinesque mannerism, Lawrence's genuine ecstasy shines through in this, the most moving of all his pre-war letters, as for the first time he realized that not freedom – as Ruskin believed – but absolute faith had enabled medieval craftsmen to create a masterpiece like Chartres. The world of the medieval mason had been a narrow one, indeed, but he had had certainty: a certain connection with God, a certain knowledge of his place in the cosmos. It was not freedom which the industrial era had lost – for technology was ultimately a liberating force – but certainty. While the Renaissance, which Lawrence so much despised, had introduced rational enlightenment, it had also introduced doubt, which he would later call 'our modern crown of thorns': 'Certainly Chartres is the sight of a lifetime,' he concluded, 'a place truly in which to worship God. The Middle

Ages were truer that way than ourselves, in spite of their narrowness and hardness and ignorance of the truth as we complacently put it: but the truth doesn't matter a straw, if men only believe what they say or are willing to show that they believe something.'[3] It is another of the great paradoxes of Lawrence's life that as a thinking man *par excellence* he was able to see that faith was everything, but was too rational to believe in anything himself. His condemnation of himself as 'insanely rational' was the perfect expression of this paradox. He would come to envy the Arabs, who humbled him by their simple faith. They were, he saw, a people who still inhabited the spiritual certainties of the Middle Ages: 'a people of primary colours', as he put it, 'or rather of black and white, who saw the world always in contour'.[4] By 1908 Lawrence had already begun to lose his faith in Christianity and, according to one story, had lost his job as a Sunday School teacher for reading 'his boys' a story by the disgraced Oscar Wilde. It was Sarah who destroyed his faith for him, just as she destroyed almost everything else in his life: 'she begs us to love her . . .' he wrote to Charlotte Shaw, 'and points us to Christ, in whom, she says, is the only happiness and truth. Not that she finds happiness herself . . . she makes Arnie and me profoundly unhappy. We are so helpless; we feel that we would never give any other human being the pain she gives us, by her impossible demands . . . we cannot turn on love to her . . . like a water-tap; and Christ is not a symbol but a personality, spoiled by the accretions of such believers as herself.'[5] Any vestige of faith he might have had at twenty was certainly gone by the time he wrote: 'I haven't any convictions or disbeliefs – except the one that there is no "is".'[6] His admission later that though he had 'fenced his life with scaffolding of more or less speculative hypotheses' one could 'really know nothing'[7] was entirely in keeping with the Lawrence who told Robert Graves: 'I fall . . . into the nihilism which cannot find, in being, even a false God in which to believe.'[8]

In place of spiritual certainty, Lawrence used intuition – the rational ability to compute how events have come about and where they are heading. It was a quality which gave him an air of prescience, and which Clare Sydney Smith would romanticize as 'the power of foretelling'. Lawrence certainly did not have some magical fortune-telling ability, as Smith envisaged it, for though his intuitions could be staggeringly accurate, they were occasionally dreadfully wrong. Lawrence was adept at selecting and navigating possible paths through the universe, and, as George Lloyd would comment, he had a 'genius for thinking ahead of nine people out of ten'.[9] It was a correct intuition which had told him, long before his latest trip to France, that Crusader castles in Syria would be the inevitable culmination of his planned thesis. It was Charles Bell of the Ashmolean, though, who guided him towards the topic of the pointed arch and vault. It had long been contested as to whether this structure had been adopted from Oriental sources by the Crusaders, or whether the Crusaders themselves had introduced it as an innovation in the East. Lawrence's knowledge of medieval castles in Britain and France qualified him perfectly for such a study: Bell suggested that he should visit Syria and settle the issue once and for all.[10]

Lawrence was now back in his bedroom at Polstead Road, lamenting the loss of his rooms in college and craving a sense of physical separation from the family. He needed 'quietness' for his studies, and he persuaded his parents to build him a small cottage at the bottom of the garden, containing a bedroom and a study, piped water, a fireplace and even a telephone to the house. To insulate it doubly against outside noise, Lawrence hung its walls with Bolton sheeting. Vyvyan Richards would often find him there, lying on the hearthrug by a crackling fire, reading his way through a pile of books, or carefully drawing his own foot. Once, Richards startled him in the act of striding up and down along an odd-looking board with nails banged into it. Lawrence explained that he was practising the art of pacing out distances covertly, which would be essential for his next trip if he wished to avoid being arrested as a spy. There are other intimations that he was readying himself for an expedition to the East during the winter of 1908. In October he had begun reading Charles Doughty's *Arabia Deserta*, the classic work on Arabia and the Bedu, written by the most distinguished desert explorer of the era – a book which Lawrence would later praise as 'a bible of its kind'. Its combination of Chaucerian prose and Elizabethan construction appealed to him enormously, since he recognized that Doughty had deliberately set out to purify the English language in the same way that William Morris had done. For Lawrence, stirring adventures and dramatic experiences were of little use unless they were presented in perfect prose, and for this reason he did not admire Richard Burton – possibly the most interesting Orientalist and explorer of the nineteenth century. He condemned the highly-strung, irascible, formidably talented Burton as 'vulgar' and dismissed his books as being 'written in so difficult an English style as to be unreadable'.[11] Like Morris's novels, *Arabia Deserta* would remain close to his heart for the rest of his life.

In winter 1908, Lawrence joined the newly formed Oxford University Officers' Training Corps as a cadet – an act which astonished his peers. The avowed non-conformist, who refused to play organized games 'because they were organized, because they had rules', was now voluntarily putting on army uniform, bowing to military discipline and meekly taking orders. The truth may be that the OTC appealed to his masochistic fantasy about military life – not quite as satisfying as being a humble Gunner in the Royal Garrison Artillery, perhaps, but a uniform just the same. The Jesus College contingent was a bicycle-mounted signals unit, which gave him opportunities for cycling, and he considered some of the training to be of real value. He later wrote that he had learned to fire a Vickers machine-gun in the OTC, which was of use to him during the Arab Revolt, though he would tell Liddell Hart that his OTC experience was 'negligible' in the sense of teaching him strategy.[12] He did practise pistol-shooting assiduously, however, and in December found an opportunity to test his compass-work when he and Scroggs Beeson marched on a bearing from the top of Cumnor Hurst in a snowstorm, wading freezing streams and breasting snowdrifts until they almost fell into the Isis at Folly Bridge.

This was, in fact, the last day he and Beeson spent in each other's company, for they had outgrown their friendship. Beeson had forsaken archaeology for zoology, his first interest, leaving Lawrence to archaeologize alone. He became even more deeply involved with the Ashmolean in late 1908, and one day, while visiting the medieval collection, he ran into Edward Leeds, a shy young man eight years his senior, who until recently had been serving in the Colonial Service in Malaya. Leeds had just replaced Leonard Woolley as junior Assistant Keeper of the Ashmolean, and he and Lawrence found much in common – not least their shyness. The following January Leeds introduced Lawrence to the museum's new Keeper, David Hogarth – a man who was to exert a profound influence on his life. Hogarth was then forty-five years old, an Orientalist and antiquarian of the classical school, who had tramped Syria, Turkey and Palestine alone with a revolver for company, and who stood no nonsense from the natives. He had written a notable book about his adventures: *A Wandering Scholar in the Levant,* and was an archaeologist of repute who had once run the British School of Archaeology in Athens, and had excavated in Cyprus and in Egypt under the celebrated Flinders Petrie. He spoke French, German, Italian, Greek and Turkish, sat on the committee of the Royal Geographical Society, and had even worked as *Times* correspondent in Crete during the 1897 revolution. Hogarth was the archetypal Edwardian gentleman-Imperialist: chauvinistic, conservative, auto-cratic, almost congenitally hostile to democracy – an aristocrat of the intellect. Patrician in style, cool in temperament, superbly educated at Winchester and Magdalen, he was the eternal dilettante amateur, whose qualities Lawrence would later sum up with the single epithet 'civilized'. Others, less impressed with his combination of physical repugnance and unstymied erudition, thought him a 'highly educated baboon'.[13] Despite his ability, Hogarth never achieved greatness in any one sphere: his talents were too diffuse, and like Lawrence himself, he was too restless to be labelled, always oscillating between the academic and the adventurous, and ultimately leaving his most distin-guished legacy in his recognition of remarkable talent in the person of T. E. Lawrence. To Lawrence he was to become a kind of father-figure, a parent-surrogate who 'was like a reserve, always there behind me; if I got flustered or puzzled'.[14] Moreover, Hogarth was well connected. Unlike Thomas Lawrence, who had necessarily broken ties with every-one of influence and could no longer call on the Old School to assist him, Hogarth knew almost everyone. Edwardian society was no meritocracy, and despite his intellectual and academic gifts, Lawrence realized he required some kind of sponsor in order to 'get on'. He later admitted that he owed Hogarth every good job he had ever had. He was, Lawrence concluded, 'a very wonderful man . . . first of all human, then charitable, then alive . . . the *parent* I could trust, without qualification, to understand what bothered me'[15] (*my italics*). From the beginning, Lawrence recognized what a man like Hogarth could do for him, and set out to win him over.

Hogarth was not much interested in Lawrence's crusader castles. His attitude to any aspect of archaeology unconnected with classical antiquity and the ancient Near East was dismissive. What moved

Hogarth was the Hittites, a mysterious biblical people about whom, before 1870, hardly anything had been known. The story of the Hittites was a curious one. In 1812, the Swiss explorer Johan Lutwig Burckhardt had discovered a stone set in the wall of the bazaar of Hama – a large town in Syria – which appeared to be incised with hieroglyphs. He was unable to examine it in detail because of local hostility, but on first glance he felt that the hieroglyphs were quite unlike ancient Egyptian ones. It was not until 1872 that the Hama stone was inspected closely, and then its hieroglyphs were compared with those discovered on a similar stone in Aleppo, and various other inscriptions found scattered over Asia Minor. By 1876, it was concluded that the script of the lost Hittite civilization had been found. Hogarth had already made several major journeys in search of that civilization, and had returned to Oxford with a collection of Hittite cylinder-seals which was unique of its kind in the world. These seals offered tantalizing insights into the lost culture. Of similar shape to the joint of a finger, and rarely much longer, they were incised with intricately made, sometimes surreal images – bloated plants, spiky animals, insect-like humans. Although referred to as 'seals', they had originally been printing devices which, when dipped in coloured pigments, could be rolled out to produce designs on human skin or clothing for decoration, or on property to signify ownership. Hittite cylinder-seals had no place in Lawrence's medieval fantasy, but he flattered Hogarth by showing an interest in them, and by asking where traces of Hittite civilization were likely to be found. He explained that he was planning a trip around crusader castles in Syria the following summer, but could certainly spare a few days hunting for Hittites. Hogarth, unmoved, tried to dissuade him from the journey. It would be far too hot in summer, he said, for tramping about Syria. When Lawrence persisted, Hogarth advised him to contact Doughty, the expert on Arabian travel. Lawrence wrote, but Doughty's attitude was little more encouraging than Hogarth's had been. He explained, first of all, that he had been no farther north than Damascus, but added, 'In July and August the heat is very severe day and night . . . it is a land of squalor where a European can find evil refreshment. Long daily marches on foot a prudent man who knows the country would I think consider out of the question . . .'[16] If Lawrence really intended visit the East, Doughty commented, he would be well advised to learn Arabic.

Doughty's forebodings filled Lawrence with fear, but the more his betters insisted on the foolishness of the undertaking, the more tightly the screw of his determination was turned. His ride through France in 1908 had been the preparation: the East would provide the backdrop for the knight-errant adventures he craved. He began taking Arabic lessons from a Syrian Protestant clergyman, the Revd Nasar Odeh, and from him acquired a sound framework of grammar and a vocabulary of about 100 words which, he thought, would suffice for road directions, food, accommodation, and money transactions. His parents provided £40 to buy a camera and tripod, and to supplement his photographs he took drawing lessons from E. H. New, an architectural illustrator who, to Lawrence's delight, had recently illustrated a biography of William Morris. Before leaving, he saw Hogarth again, and this time the Master set him a task. Since he would be visiting the region of southern Turkey in which Hogarth had found many of his Hittite cylinder-seals, would Lawrence bring back more seals for the Ashmolean collection? The seals were small and easily transportable. Lawrence now had his quest. To prepare himself practically for local conditions, he memorized long passages from *Arabia Deserta* and read *Practical Hints for Travellers in the Near East* by E. A. Reynolds-Ball. He took Ball's advice and bought a Mauser automatic pistol for protection against footpads. He had a lightweight suit made with many pockets to carry his things, and through Hogarth met Harry Pirie-Gordon, who had travelled in Syria the previous season, and from whom he managed to borrow an annotated map. Meanwhile, his official *iradeh* – a letter of safe-conduct from the Ottoman Government – had been applied for by Sir John Rhys, Principal of Jesus College, through Lord Curzon, Chancellor of Oxford University. On 18 June 1909, with Pirie-Gordon's map stuffed into one pocket and his Baedeker stuffed into another, he stepped aboard SS *Mongolia*, bound for Port Sa'id and, ultimately, Beirut.

Beirut was then one of the most vibrant cities in the Middle East: Lawrence himself characterized it as 'the door to Syria, a chromatic Levantine screen through which . . . foreign influences entered . . .'[17] When I arrived there in his footsteps, ninety years on, however, it was a shell of a place, its famous 'Downtown' quarter reduced to rubble – a maze of shell-shocked buildings without interiors or roofs. Though

the war between Muslims and Christians had long since ceased and
Israeli troops had pulled out of the city, they were still fighting the
Palestinians in southern Lebanon, which made it impossible for me to
follow that part of Lawrence's 1909 route. Instead I had to approach
it indirectly, taking a bus from Cairo to Jerusalem and up the Jordan
valley to Tiberias, on the Sea of Galilee, where I found a room in the
Church of Scotland Hostel. The verandah of my cell-like room looked
into a private beach-garden full of spruce and cypress and old eucalypts.
There were glowering clouds over the lake, a ponderously spinning
carousel casting beams of light on the embroiled waters. Gulls and
shearwaters rose and fell on the waves like paper boats. Lawrence had
found the lake 'very blue and always moving: never quite calm', but
'pretty' rather than 'grand'.[18] He described Tiberias itself as a 'hot and
dirty' town, but found it not altogether unpicturesque: he loved its tiny
port and fishing-boats, and thought its ruined walls 'interesting'. The
walls were still there, but their effect was spoiled by the dozen great
ziggurats of modern hotels which towered over them.

The following day I hired a mountain bike to ride up to Safed, the
highest town in Galilee, where Lawrence had spent a few days. It had
rained in the night. The road along the lakeside through Magdala was
wet and the wheels sprayed a rash of mud over my oilskin jacket. I
climbed painfully above Capernaum, around an endless series of
hairpins, through green meadows full of grey boulders, fat, grazing
cows and elegant white egrets. At Rosh Pinna, the air was thick with
mist and the road darkened by avenues of stone-pines. I halted to
drink coffee at a papershop-cum-café, where a very fat man – the
proprietor of the place – was sitting at a table reading the sports page
of a Hebrew newspaper. He seemed interested in my search for
Lawrence. 'Lawrence was a friend of the Jews,' he told me. 'He believed
in Israel as a National Homeland for us. We will never forget him for
that!' This was essentially true, I thought. Like many Britons of his
day, Lawrence had been excited by the idea of restoring the Jews
to their ancestral homeland after 2,000 years: the British had seen
themselves as secret guardians of time, capable of using their vast
wealth and power to replay history. On his first journey through
Galilee in 1909, indeed, Lawrence had been disappointed to find the
country derelict by comparison with the image he had formed of it
through his biblical study. Instead of the 'polished streets, pillared

houses and rococo baths' he had imagined, he found a place of 'dilapidated Bedu tents, with the people calling to [one] to come in and talk, while miserable curs came snapping at [one's] heels'.[19] There is little trace here of the later Arabophile. He believed that Palestine had been a 'decent' country in Roman times and could be made so again: 'The sooner the Jews farm it all the better,' he wrote. 'Their colonies are bright spots in the desert.'[20]

From Rosh Pinna, I rode up into ice-cold mist which settled over the hills like a blanket, and the pedalling became agony. Headlights loomed out of the fog at regular intervals, like demonic eyes. Occasionally a waft of wind pushed the mist on, and there were momentary glimpses of the country below, a magical, sunlit country of hills and fields. I had never imagined that the road to Safed would ascend so relentlessly for all of its 2,700 feet: at times it seemed that I was pedalling all the way up to heaven. I had been cycling upwards in first gear for almost five solid hours, and my calves were screaming, when the mist suddenly cleared and I saw Safed, a large town spread round the skirts of five or six peaks. As I rode into the centre, rain came bucketing down through the eucalyptus groves. There seemed to be no sign of the crusader castle. I stopped an old man to ask directions. He was friendly enough, but shook his head: 'No English! No Hebrew! No Arabic! Only Yiddish!' he said. Safed was a place of Holocaust survivors and their descendants. Why should they be interested in crusader castles? There was only one history for them. I never did find the castle, but I was content enough with the stunning view I had of Mount Hermon, when the rain peeled back the last skeins of mist.

Lawrence arrived in Safed on the evening of 16 July 1909, exhausted after what he called a 'terrific climb up from the valley and then over undulating country'.[21] He had left Tibnin that morning and halted at noon for a drink at the famous Spring of Kadesh, having in the course of the day marched up and down the height of Mont Blanc: 'Palestine is all like that,' he wrote, '. . . the roads go either up or down all the time . . . and never reach anywhere at all.'[22] There was no hotel in Safed then, but he had found accommodation with the family of an English doctor called Anderson who worked for the Jewish Mission Hospital. The doctor was very kind to his young visitor, and took him to see the castle after dark, but the rigours of the journey were already affecting him, and Lawrence came down with the first of several bouts of malaria which were to dog the entire trek.

He had been walking for just over two weeks, having set out alone from Beirut at the beginning of July. On the first day he had hiked down the coast to Sidon, through mulberry orchards and olive groves. The road had been full of movement: peasants in baggy trousers and fezzes, bristling with rifles, revolvers and cartridge belts, riding horses or driving great trains of camels down to the coastal markets with their harvest. There were camels everywhere, and Lawrence looked at them with interest. He thought their faces 'horrible', but loved the rough tones of the camel-bells which faded as the caravans wound placidly into the haze of sunset. Sidon stood on the tip of a headland and it was satisfyingly medieval – a walled town of alleys so narrow that two men could scarcely pass, and which no wheeled vehicle could enter. From there he had climbed the hills towards Nabatiyyeh, tramping up deep gorges and enjoying the refreshing breeze off the Mediterranean. He passed through hamlets of baked mud houses among patchworks of brown fields, and practised his Arabic with the villagers. For the first time he stayed with Arabs in their own houses, and delighted in learning the social rituals involved. On greeting his host with 'Peace be upon you!' he would be invited inside, where the womenfolk would drag out a heavy quilt for him to sit on. While his host made coffee and plied him with the customary questions, the children would examine his belongings. After tea or coffee, dinner – generally greasy boiled wheat called burghul, and wafer-thin bread – would be presented. There was no talking during the meal, and afterwards, about nine, he would retire with his quilts, either to the verandah or to the roof. The quilts, he discovered, were far too thick for summer nights, and as they were invariably full of fleas anyway, he usually slept on top. He would be up at sunrise, and would join his host at the hearth, and splash a little water over his face for his morning ablutions. After breakfast of bread and sour milk – or fresh milk if he was lucky – he would be on his way. The simplicity of the peasants' lifestyle appealed to him, and evoked the landscape of Malory and Morris. He felt comfortable in the simple houses with their spartan furniture – rush mats, tiny stools, and sleeping quilts which doubled as chairs and which could be packed away in a stepped alcove when not in use. He admired the way in which the house doubled as a byre

– the lower floor for the cattle, sheep, goats, donkeys and horses, the upper one for humans. He approved of the economy of eating with the hands from a communal dish, or of using pieces of bread as a spoon, and appreciated that the Arab way of washing hands – pouring water over them rather than scrubbing them in a basin – was far cleaner than the English method. He also acknowledged the Arabs' sense of hospitality: 'this is a glorious country for wandering in,' he wrote to his father, 'for hospitality is something more than a name . . . there are the common people each one ready to receive one for a night, and allow me to share in their meals: and without thought of payment from a traveller on foot.'[23] Though this was not entirely true, for often his hosts would take money, he clearly found their simple dignity attractive. It was an aesthetic appreciation: some of their ways were quaint, they were pleasant and dignified, but 'very childish and simple of course, and startlingly ignorant'.[24] Lawrence also stayed with foreign missionaries, and expressed high praise for their work in 'civilizing' and 'educating' the natives. In his letters home, he displayed his customary need to bolster self-esteem by revealing his apparent uniqueness: his diet, he said, was that of the natives, and considered 'lunacy' by the expatriates, though his habit of drinking fresh milk was viewed as equally crazy by the Arabs. The natives thought him 'mad' to walk instead of riding, while the foreigners thought him batty to walk round in the heat of the afternoon. He told his mother that he had become 'Arab in habit' yet in the same sentence related proudly how a Frenchman had 'taken him for a compatriot', without apparently being aware of the contradiction. On close reading, the character which emerges from Lawrence's Syrian letters is one who is capable of adapting quickly to a new community, but who essentially belongs to none.

At Nabatiyyeh he found himself carried along in the swirl of a festival, in narrow streets of chaffering crowds, water-sellers, sherbet-sellers, peasants with fresh produce from their gardens, men rushing along with the fly-blown carcasses of sheep or bags of charcoal on their backs. From here he hired a Christian guide called Barak to take him to the castles of Beaufort and Banias, which he thought might be important for his thesis. Beaufort was memorable for its wonderful view: to the west the scintillating blue of the Mediterranean, and to the east – far across the Jordan valley – Mount Hermon, its gorges sparkling with snow. From the castle window he dropped a pebble into the Litani river, 1,600 feet below. To reach Banias – the biblical Caesarea Philippi – Barak took him through the lush green meadows of the Jordan, which seemed almost tropical after the barrenness of the Lebanon range. The village itself was of little interest, but Lawrence discovered there a spring of deliciously cool water in a hidden cave, above which he was delighted to find an ancient Greek inscription dedicated to Pan. Banias castle – built by the Knights Hospitallers in the twelfth century – stood on a spur of Hermon, and Lawrence climbed all over it with enthusiasm. He even had the gall to set fire to the brushwood in the inner court so that he could see it more clearly: 'It must have made a jolly bonfire from a distance,' he wrote.[25] It certainly brought the castle's owner running to see what he was about, though Lawrence reported that he had not objected, since he was now able to enter the courtyard again after twenty years. He set out alone from Hunin, slept at Tibnin and arrived at Safed the following day. Having recovered from his bout of malaria, he made a side-trip to Chastellet on the Jordan, where he had his first taste of the scirocco, the furnace-blast of flint and dust which uncoils off the Arabian desert in summer, giving him a sudden sense of the vast emptiness which lay beyond these homely hills. He descended to the Sea of Galilee, then headed off towards the Mediterranean across the plain of Esdraelon, a vast chequerboard of brown and gold, threaded with red paths like strings, and scattered with nests of black tents, between which great caravans of camels were constantly in motion. Women were winnowing grain on the threshing floors, and now and then he would see clouds of chaff and dust rising above the fields as the peasants reaped or threshed with flails and fans. From the coast at Haifa he passed north into what is today southern Lebanon, trekking through Tyre and Sidon back to Beirut.

After a week of comfort in Beirut's Victoria Hotel, he began the second phase of the journey, which he hoped would take him to Latakia, Antioch and Aleppo. In the first week of August he arrived at Jebayyil, north of Beirut, where he called at the American Mission School, run by a Miss Holmes. Miss Fareedah al-Akle, a teacher at the school, remembered him arriving, dusty and exhausted-looking, 'with a bundle tied to his back'.[26] Miss Akle, who was later to become Lawrence's Arabic instructor, recalled how he had dashed upstairs

after the maid without waiting to be asked in, and how, later, he had
regaled her with tales of the 'adventures and hardships' he had endured
on the trip, with 'many narrow escapes from death' at the hands of
'cruel Kurds and Turks'. Lawrence's avowed preference for 'hardships'
and sleeping out of doors was an aspect of his reverse exhibitionism –
which required public notice – but secretly he much appreciated
comfort, and was blissfully happy to spend a few days at the Mission
in Jebayyil, eating well, bathing, lounging about under 'real green
trees' in the garden, and reading in the extensive library. He was
received at the American Mission in Tripoli a few days later, presumably with an introduction from Miss Holmes. From there it was a
three-day walk to Kala'at al-Husn – the famous Crak des Chevaliers,
where the Turkish Governor or Qaimiqam, far from being 'cruel',
proved exceedingly kind and helpful, indeed 'very comfortable' as
Lawrence himself put it. The Crak was to have a central role in his thesis,
and he lingered there for three days, inspecting and photographing it.
Like Banias, it was a Knights Hospitallers castle – a vast, double-walled
Gormenghast of a fortress standing on a lonely plateau in arid scrub-
land. Lawrence climbed half-way up its moss-covered inner talus barefoot in the sun, his mind ranging over its advantages and drawbacks.
Though he was unable to reach the top, he saw that it would have
presented no difficulty to besiegers with scaling-ladders, but its relatively
gentle incline meant that they could never 'get underneath' the boulders
and burning pitch hurled down on them from the defenders above.
He also noticed with pleasure that the machicolations – the openings
in the masonry through which the defenders threw their projectiles –
were of a kind not known anywhere else in Syria, though they were
known in Europe – suggesting that the Knights Hospitallers had
introduced them as an innovation from the West. Lawrence was
altogether impressed with the Crak, and wrote later that it was 'the
best preserved and most wholly admirable castle in the world'.[27] The
'comfortable' Governor also provided him with an escort to visit the
castle of Safita which stood nearby, and which Lawrence admired for
its Norman keep with original battlements – the like of which, he said,
he had never seen in Europe. Crak, Safita and Sahyun – a castle to
the north, whose slender needle of rock supporting the centre of a
drawbridge Lawrence thought the most sensational thing he had ever
seen in castle building[28] – were the highlights of the tour, and having

seen them, he wrote to his mother: '. . . you may be happy now all my rough work is finished successfully: & my Thesis *I think assured*.'[29]

He left the Governor of the Crak a few days later and set off for the coast, spending the first night sleeping on a threshing-floor with some peasants. The men were threshing their grain, and worked in relays much of the night. When they were all exhausted, they woke Lawrence up and asked him to keep watch with his pistol while they slept, as, they said, there were many thieves about. Lawrence thought it all nonsense, but obliged anyway, only to be told in Tartus the following day that the men had been trying to conceal the extent of their harvest, and that it had not been thieves but landlords they had feared. That there *were* thieves about, though, came home to him strongly, when, near Masyaf, a lone horseman took a pot-shot at him from 200 yards. According to Miss al-Akle, his assailant was 'a huge cruel-looking Turk' whose bullet went wide, whereupon Lawrence had coolly drawn his Mauser pistol and fired a deadly accurate shot which took the skin off the giant's little finger. Petrified by his opponent's supernatural accuracy, the Turk had stood frozen to the spot, while Lawrence had approached and bandaged up the finger, patted him on the back, and sent him off home with half his money. 'It is the story of David and Goliath over again,' Miss al-Akle wrote, 'with the difference that David conquered his enemy with the sword while the weapon which won the day for Lawrence was that of friendliness.'[30] It is a salutary tale, but how much of it is Miss al-Akle's imagination and how much Lawrence's is impossible to say. Lawrence wrote to his mother shortly afterwards that the 'huge, cruel-looking Turk' was simply an 'ass with an old gun' who had shot at him from horseback. Lawrence had promptly shot back, winging the horse, which had bolted wildly. The bandit had managed to get his mount under control, and wheeled round at about 800 yards for another go. Lawrence had put a second round over his head, at which the man had 'made off like a steeple-chaser'. Once again, it seems likely that neither of these reports was the full truth, for while he referred to the incident as 'a joke' there is evidence that in reality he was far less sanguine. He had never been shot at before, and with his abnormal fear of pain, the thought of the bullet – no matter how 'old' – slapping into his flesh cannot have been a pleasant one. In fact, he was shaken enough to report the incident to the local Turkish Governor and sufficiently concerned about a repetition to accept an escort of Turkish troopers, despite knowing that they must hamper his freedom of movement. From this point onwards, Lawrence's confidence took a downward spiral. The fear, the fever, the heat, the hardship – the utter pain of the trek – began to tell on him. His interest in castles waned, as exhaustion, sore feet and malaria took over. He had planned to make a detour to Antioch and remain there several days, but for the first time he dropped one of his major objectives. Though he later claimed to have seen Antioch's town walls from afar, it seems unlikely that he went anywhere near them. His mounted escort only added to the hardship, simply because he refused to ride. Though Lawrence later told Edward Leeds with customary bravado that on the first day he had 'walked them to a standstill', obliging them to return to the starting point to pick up horses, the fact is that once they were mounted, he had to struggle to keep up. The sight of a young Englishman stumping, half-lame, across those hills in the wake of a squadron of horsemen who were supposed to be his escort must indeed have been a bizarre one. No one would have blamed him for riding, but his unrelenting will made it impossible for him to give in. He stalked on on blistered and bruised feet, perhaps cursing the fear which had caused him to report the 'trifling' incident to the Governor in the first place. That last burst of 120 miles in five days almost finished him. When he limped into Aleppo on 6 September, two months after leaving Beirut for the first time, his flesh was pared to the bone, his boots were in tatters and his feet a mass of sores that not even his Nietzschian will could mend. He had sworn that he would walk while others rode, but now he was finished as far as walking went. He had believed that there was no limit to the suffering he could force his body through, but now he had found it. That he had already made a remarkable journey of over 1,000 miles mattered not a jot. It was not good enough. He had failed. He had failed to reach Antioch. He had failed to reach Urfa, and Shobek and Kerak in the Belqa hills. He had failed to obtain Hogarth's Hittite seals. Now, exhausted by overstrain and malaria, he felt that he could not go on.

As he lay in his bath in the Baron's Hotel in Aleppo, he cannot have avoided the conclusion that his own fear had defeated him. Urfa lay 100 miles away across the Euphrates – 200 miles there and back. That would have meant, at best, an eight- or ten-day trek. Frankly, he was not up to it. Very reluctantly, he decided that he would have to play the privileged tourist after all, and hire a carriage with two coachmen at the exorbitant cost to his pocket of £7. He wrote to his mother the next day informing her of his decision, but saying nothing of his exhaustion: for Sarah, he must be the indomitable white knight. He implied only that he was short of time: 'I must make haste,' he wrote. That letter was written on 7 September. What happened to Lawrence between that date and 19 September, when he wrote again from Aleppo, is a mystery.

When Lawrence turned up in Oxford in the middle of October, one week late for term, 'thinned to the bone with privation' – according to Ernest Barker – the camera which had been procured for him at great cost was missing. Though he still had Pirie-Gordon's precious map, it was covered with bloodstains – and thereby hung a tale. Lawrence enthralled his less adventurous but more masculine and sporty colleagues with stories of how, while seeking Hittite seals, he had been attacked by a band of bloodthirsty Kurds who, disappointed that he was not carrying 'treasure' as they supposed, robbed him of all his possessions and beat him to within an inch of death. He had managed to crawl to safety, but having been left penniless, had been obliged to work his passage back to Marseilles on a tramp steamer, earning just enough to pay his fare back to Oxford. His friends were impressed, but, more important, his potential sponsor and mentor, Hogarth, was impressed. The young man had performed his sacred task: he had brought back his thirty Hittite seals for the unique collection at the Ashmolean. Lawrence probably did not tell Hogarth directly that he had risked his life to obtain them, but let the information permeate to its target by circuitous routes. He was already becoming expert at 'massaging the truth' to achieve his goals, and in this case his goal was to attract the attention of Hogarth, who, high on his lofty pedestal, had taken little notice of him until now. No one knows what was said during their first meeting after his return, only that Hogarth told Leeds afterwards: 'That is a rather remarkable young man – he has been in places rarely visited by foreigners.'[31]

Just where *had* Lawrence been during the second and third weeks of September 1909? We last have him writing to his mother that he intended to visit Urfa on 7 September, and that he must 'make haste'. According to his expense-account, though, he had lingered in Aleppo for a week on that occasion – which puts his date of departure as the

13th, at the earliest. We know he was back in Aleppo by the 19th, because he wrote to Edward Leeds on that date from the Hôtel du Parc. The trip to Urfa by carriage generally took three to four days by the most direct route, which ran through the Circassian village of Membij, crossed the Euphrates at Tel Ahmar and passed through Suruj before reaching Urfa, where there existed an important crusader castle. If Lawrence did leave on the 13th, he would have had just enough time to reach Urfa and back by the 19th, assuming he spent one or two days looking at the castle. On 22 September he wrote to his mother, this time from the Baron's Hotel in Aleppo, telling her that his trip to Urfa had been 'delightful' but marred by the fact that his camera had been stolen at Suruj on the way back, when the coachman he had left on watch was asleep. The only other incident he related was that the carriage had been upset by a runaway horse, though he had not been badly hurt. In this letter he seemed keen to return home: he was almost out of money, he was very tired, exhausted by a fourth attack of malaria, and discouraged by the early onset of the rains which had started a few days earlier and which would render further walking impossible. He also mentioned that a report had appeared in the Aleppo newspaper that a 'Mr Edvard Lovance' had been murdered near Ayntab. He noted with amusement that the hotel staff had greeted him like a ghost, and called the report 'an absurd canard', assuring his mother that he had been nowhere near Ayntab, a Turkish town lying sixty miles due north of Aleppo and some eighty miles west of Urfa.

His letter to Leeds, written three days earlier, told a very different story. He had, he wrote, been searching for Hittite seals north of Tel Bashar – a village in the Ayntab district – when a man who had been following him had jumped on him, bitten his hand, pounded him on the head with stones and robbed him. He had recovered the stolen goods, he said, by paying baksheesh, but it had cost him so much effort that he had grown sick of the district and returned to Aleppo. He asked Leeds to keep quiet about the attack for the sake of his parents, but did not mention the trip to Urfa nor the stolen camera. He made no reference to the two coachmen who were supposedly with him, nor the coach. Neither did he express to Leeds any intention of returning home immediately, but declared that he still wanted to seek Kerak and Petra, which lay in the Vilayet of Syria, far away from Aleppo.

Had we only Leeds's letter of 19 September, we would judge that he had been on an entirely different journey from the one described briefly to his mother three days later.

However, he wrote a third letter while in Aleppo. On the 24th, two days after writing to Sarah, and five after his letter to Leeds, he wrote to Sir John Rhys, the principal of Jesus College, explaining that he would miss the first week of term. The letter is a masterpiece of English understatement and a display of stiff upper lip which would hardly have disgraced Lord Nelson. He told Rhys that he had had four attacks of malaria when he had 'only reckoned on two', and had been 'robbed and rather smashed up' only the previous week. It was a combination of these irritating circumstances, he said, which prevented him from carrying out his plans to visit Kerak and Shobek, for by the time he was fit for walking again the rainy season would have begun. Apart from this, though, he told Rhys, his trip had been 'delightful': he had visited three dozen castles out of the fifty on his route, and had secured for Hogarth thirty Hittite seals. He had, he said, travelled 'on foot and alone' all the time and had 'lived as an Arab with the Arabs' and had consequently gained an insight into their way of life that one who had travelled with a caravan would have missed.

It was true that Lawrence had visited thirty-six castles (he would later tell Liddell Hart sixty), and that he had made a remarkable journey, trekking over 1,000 miles through Syria on foot in the height of summer, was undeniable. The rest of the letter to Rhys, however, was lily-gilding. He had not travelled alone all the time – at one point he had employed a guide, and for a major section of the journey he had travelled with a mounted escort. For the last part of the journey – a matter of 'a fortnight', according to his expense account – he had paid current Baedeker rates to hire a carriage and two men to visit Urfa, though the carriage is as conspicuously absent from his letter to Rhys as it is from his note to Leeds. This was hardly 'living as an Arab with the Arabs' in Doughty fashion. In fact he had worn European dress throughout, including the pith-helmet which, as he himself said later, the Arabs regarded with superstitious hatred. He had been the guest of Turkish officials and Western missionaries, had stayed in hotels – good hotels where available – and while he had certainly sojourned on occasions with local Arabs, it was as frequently as not as a paying guest. Since so much was invented, or at least 'exaggerated' in Lawrence's letter to Rhys, why not the story of having been 'smashed up' too? Had Lawrence simply been injured in the coaching accident which he mentioned to his mother, but been too embarrassed to reveal it to Rhys? Certainly it was not true that he had been so badly smashed up that he was unable to walk, as his letter implied. A few days earlier he had told Leeds that he still intended to visit Petra. He had not been injured enough to seek medical treatment; neither, it seems, did he report the incident to the British Consulate in Aleppo. He told Rhys that the thief had been caught within forty-eight hours, and regaled Robert Graves later with an extended yarn about how he had accompanied a large party of Turkish police and volunteers to the bandit's Kurdish village to demand restitution. Yet he seems to have been away from Aleppo for seven days in all: a diversion on foot to the Tel Bashar–Ayntab region – which was not on the direct route to Urfa – with an extra two days' wait for the recovery of his property seems quite out of the question on the grounds of time alone. When he retraced the same journey in 1911, it took him over a month. If he made a diversion in his hired coach, where were the trusty coachmen when he was being attacked? Why does he claim in his expense-sheets to have hired them for 'a fortnight', which would mean that he had left Aleppo even before he had arrived there, on the 6th? Moreover, he clearly bought some of his Hittite seals in Aleppo, for he told Leeds on the 19th that he had only twenty, while by the 24th the number had increased to thirty. If the seals were available so readily in Aleppo, why go to the trouble, expense and effort of visiting Tel Bashar at all? Was the whole story invented merely to ingratiate himself with Hogarth, in whose service, he could claim, he had been 'almost killed'? Why did he choose to write first to Leeds, rather than to his close friends Vyvyan Richards or Leonard Green, unless it was to catch the eye of Hogarth? Lawrence knew that he had not accomplished what he had set out to do: the journey had been too hard, just as Hogarth and Doughty had warned him it would be. He had been too exhausted to complete it on foot. Was the story of the robbery an imaginary expiation of the sin of failure, the first obvious instance of a pattern which would become familiar later, of public success, private failure, expiation by violence? On the other hand, if Lawrence did not visit Tel Bashar, how did he meet 'Ahmad Effendi' – a man who lived in a village near Tel Bashar, to whom he referred in his 1911 diary as being a friend from his earlier visit? Finally, how did he get away with lying to Hogarth, who had been at Tel Bashar only the previous year? It is a conundrum Lawrence would have delighted in bequeathing to his biographers. In the end, we are left with only a series of questions, a cycle of stories, and some tell-tale bloodstains on a map.

1. The author and his son at Lawrence's Spring, Jordan. It was at this spring, known as Shallala to the local Bedu, that Lawrence bathed during his sojourns in the Wadi Rum in 1917. He wrote a moving description of the spring in *The Seven Pillars of Wisdom*.

2. Pharaoh's Island, off Sinai. As a young archaeologist, Lawrence swam out to the island to examine the ruins of the crusader castle (now restored). Known to the crusaders as Ile de Graye, it stands 400 metres off the Egyptian coast, some ten miles south of Aqaba.

3. Ruins of traditional house, Yanbu', Saudi Arabia. Lawrence occupied a house similar to this one while staying in the port of Yanbu' during 1916. Though the Turks advanced towards Yanbu' in December 1916, they turned back in fear of British naval guns, a decision, Lawrence said, which cost them the war.

4. Ruins of mud houses, Hamra village, Saudi Arabia. Often imagined as an encounter in the desert – thanks to David Lean's film – Lawrence and Sharif Feisal actually met first in Hamra, a large village of mud houses surrounded by palm-groves in the Hejaz's fertile Wadi Safra.

5. Aba an-Na'am station, Saudi Arabia. Lawrence's first major engagement with the Turks took place here on 30 March 1917, when Hashemite artillery bombarded the station, setting fire to a wagon whose iron frame can still be seen.

6. Aba an-Na'am bridge. Standing north of the station, this bridge was first dynamited by Dakhilallah al-Qadi of the Juhayna in early March 1917, but had been repaired by the time Lawrence attacked the station on 30 March.

7. Fallen locomotive, Hediyya station, Saudi Arabia. Several of the original locomotives which operated on the Hejaz railway are still to be found in the deserts of the Hejaz. This one was toppled quite recently by Arabs collecting steel track at Hediyya, a key watering-station which Lawrence had targeted in March 1917 before switching to Aba an-Na'am.

8. Hediyya bridge. Solidly built by German architects and Turkish labour between 1902 and 1908, many of the original bridges on the Hejaz railway have survived till the present day. The line was revived briefly in the 1920s, but much of it has been disused ever since.

9. Locomotive, Wayban, Saudi Arabia. This train stands north of Kilometre 1121, where Lawrence mined the railway in early April 1917. Of some fifty-five locomotives – mostly of German or Belgian construction – which operated on the railway in 1914, at least seventeen are estimated to have been put out of action by Lawrence and his colleagues.

10. The King's Well, Jefer, Jordan. The family property of Auda Abu Tayyi, the well was one of several at Jefer blown in by the Turks to prevent Lawrence's advance towards Aqaba in June–July 1917. Though the well had been plugged with earth, it had fortunately not been damaged, and Lawrence's party spent hours digging it out.

11. Guweira plain from the Nagb ash-Shtar pass, Jordan. Lawrence halted to take in this breathtaking sight at dawn on 2 July 1917, just before his patrol engaged a Turkish force at Aba l-Lissan, the major battle in the Aqaba operation. Once Aba l-Lissan was taken, the Arabs were free to descend into the plain and approach Aqaba from the landward.

12. Atwi station, Jordan. Lawrence's patrol attacked Atwi on 27 June 1917 during a side mission on the Aqaba operation, killing two Turks and capturing a flock of sheep. Such pin-prick attacks were intended to confuse the enemy and distract them from the real target: Aqaba.

13. Camel rider, Aqaba, Jordan. Lawrence's patrol rode into Aqaba at 10 a.m. on 6 July 1917, to find the town deserted. It had long since been bombarded by British gunboats, and the population had fled. Lawrence left the same day for Suez, but later claimed falsely to have left on the following day, the 7th, and to have crossed Sinai in forty-nine hours.

14. The pilgrim road, Sinai, Egypt. Lawrence and his escort of eight Howaytat passed through these dunes on 9 July 1917, three days after setting out from Aqaba on their way to the ferry point at ash-Shatt on the Suez Canal. Lawrence's objective on this ride was to take the news of the Hashemite victory at Aqaba to the British GHQ in Cairo, and to establish himself as the principal British officer in the Arab Revolt.

15. A Bedui of the Howaytat today. Neither the largest nor the most 'noble' of Bedu tribes, the Howaytat under their war-leader Auda Abu Tayyi were among the most feared. Notorious as raiders from Damascus to the borders of the Empty Quarter, Lawrence reckoned Auda's men the only Bedu group capable of taking a position by frontal attack.

6. Mr Hogarth is Going Digging

Oxford and Carchemish
1909–11

One day in 1910, some time after Lawrence had returned from Syria, he invited Midge Hall to accompany him on a boating trip on the Isis. He brought with him an attractive girl called Janet Laurie, and asked Hall to take her in a punt, while he tagged along fifty yards behind in his canoe. Hall was astonished by the request and afterwards he demanded what on earth his friend thought he was playing at. 'Getting over the disappointment of letting the other man speak for the girl I adore,' Lawrence told him. 'I don't know.'[1] Hall concluded from this rather confused statement that Lawrence was in love with Janet and had been rejected by her. He had occasionally seen them together and had suspected that a love affair was going on. Later, he asked Janet if she knew of Lawrence's feelings: she knew, she said, but simply couldn't take him seriously as a suitor. Many years later, aged eighty-six, Janet claimed that in 1910 Lawrence had proposed to her, and she had turned him down.

Lawrence had known Janet Laurie from early childhood. While living at Fawley on Southampton Water they had played together, and Janet's father – the steward of a local estate – had frequently gone yachting with Thomas Lawrence. She had been sent to boarding-school in Oxford in 1899, and had remained close to the Lawrences, visiting them often, and even staying in the house at Polstead Road – one of the few women Sarah would allow over the threshold. She became a sort of surrogate sister to the Lawrence boys, and though she returned to Hampshire on her father's death in 1902, she continued to visit. She saw Lawrence frequently during his undergraduate days, and sometimes joined him at home for tea on Sunday afternoons. In 1908, she and her sister had ignored college rules and called on him in his rooms at Jesus, where she had dropped her ladylike mask long enough

75

to shy sugar cubes through the window of a neighbouring don. A lively, warm, mischievous girl with a dominant spirit, about three years older than Lawrence, she regarded him as a bright younger brother. Lawrence enjoyed poking fun at her, daring her to tomboyish acts and challenges, and ragging her if she fell short. One day in 1910, she said, she had been alone with him in the dining-room at Polstead Road when he had suddenly leapt up and held the door shut to prevent the maid from entering. Then, without an embrace or a kiss or a preliminary of any kind, he asked her to be his wife. Janet, who had never nurtured romantic feelings for Lawrence, burst into giggles. Lawrence looked at her resignedly and just said, 'All right.'

This is the only evidence we have that he was ever attracted to a woman, and it seems inconsistent with much that he wrote. It is by no means impossible, of course, that he suddenly felt the species talking powerfully within him, despite everything. Yet in view of the controversy that has raged about Lawrence's sexuality, it seems odd that Janet should have kept the story secret for so long. Several people told Lawrence's authorized biographer Jeremy Wilson that her account was 'exaggerated', and another biographer, Desmond Stewart, pointed out that the story had an 'uncanny resemblance' to the tale of Algernon Swinburne's rejection by 'Boo'. Lawrence revealed much of himself in his letters, but no warm feelings for Janet have come to light.[2] In 1927 he told Charlotte Shaw that his emotional relationship with his mother would prevent him from ever making a woman a mother and the cause of children,[3] and while marriage and being the cause of children are not necessarily the same thing (Mrs Shaw herself was married but childless), Lawrence told Robert Graves that he had never been able to fall in love with anyone, and that as a boy he had never had anything to do with women and had thus acquired the habit of living without them. Though he wrote to Graves later confessing that the former statement had not been entirely true, and that he *had* once been in love, the exception turned out to be someone whom he called 'SA', who he said had inspired his part in the Arab Revolt, and to whom he dedicated his book *Seven Pillars of Wisdom*. It is generally agreed that 'SA' is most likely to have been Salim Ahmad, nicknamed 'Dahoum', a young Arab boy Lawrence grew attached to in pre-war Syria. Lawrence's connections with the Uranians and others are well known, though his homosexual nature does not absolutely preclude the possibility that he might have proposed to Janet Laurie. She was attracted to his more handsome brother Will, and Lawrence may have noticed this and been inspired to compete. If the proposal story is true, then it may be that Janet rejected him because she sensed his fundamental indifference to the female sex.

Whether or not Lawrence felt attracted to Janet Laurie, he bestowed most of his attentions in early 1910 on his thesis. He spent so much time on it, indeed, that he neglected his other subjects – especially his 'special subject', the crusades. He left his revision until the last few weeks of term, mugging up on the facts in three all-night sittings while the exams were actually in progress. The thesis was a tremendous success, and Lawrence achieved a first class honours of such quality that his tutor, Reginald Lane Poole, held a special dinner to celebrate it. Oxford is, of course, as susceptible to personality as any other institution, and while Lawrence's intellect was remarkable, his ability to charm and manipulate his superiors was even more egregious. His attitude to his tutors is summed up in the advice he later gave to his brother Will, who inherited some of them: 'I warn you,' he wrote, 'that [Mr Jane] and Mr. Barker will be an ill-matched pair to *drive*. The only way to *run* them is to keep your own line between & *utilise* such of each as harmonises which is exhausting but very profitable' (*italics mine*).[4] On the surface, he appeared a fiery iconoclast, with what he called his 'knight errant way of tilting at all comers', and Edward Leeds noted 'the fearlessness with which he attacked the views and theories of other writers'.[5] Yet Lawrence's revolt was frequently revolt into style, for he had an uncanny knack of telling those in authority what they most desired to hear. His theory that the major aspects of medieval military architecture had reached the Arabs from the crusaders, rather than vice versa, had an ideological basis which was certain to appeal to Edwardian imperialists, just as the appeal of the Hittites to men like Hogarth stemmed from the fact that they were believed to be of Indo-European stock rather than Semitic, thus proving that 'Europeans' played a part in creating the civilizations of the East. At twenty-one, Lawrence was in full possession of his faculties: the superb memory for facts, the razor-like and confident intuition (occasionally razor-like enough to cut himself), the ability to strike an impressive pose, to juggle fantasy and reality, to charm, seduce, amuse, convince and motivate others, to work devotedly towards a long-projected target, to exercise flexibility in the face of developments, to drive himself on against abnormal fear with unshakeable determination. Lawrence was unconventional, but cannot have appeared to Hogarth and others as anti-establishment. Hogarth himself was a reactionary autocrat who despised lily-livered bureaucracy, and he must have recognized in Lawrence a kindred spirit. Though Lawrence's hero William Morris had dabbled in radical socialism, there is no evidence that at this stage Lawrence had abandoned his parents' staunch conservatism. He sneered at such liberal institutions as the Old Age Pension Act, and the Suffragettes. He detested authority, especially of the rigid and uncongenial kind, but was also fascinated by it. He later wrote that liberality of body and spirit, cleanliness, vigour and good temper could only persist under conditions of common servitude.[6]

Although he had been hoping to return to the East after graduation, no immediate prospect presented itself, and in October he decided to apply for a Fellowship of All Souls College. He failed to gain one of the two places on offer, and instead he registered for a B.Litt. degree in Archaeology, offering a thesis on medieval pottery. Jesus College made him a grant of £50 per year for postgraduate work, and his proposal was accepted on 1 November. The same day he sailed to France for the second time that year, to see the extensive medieval pottery collection at Rouen, where, thanks to a letter of recommendation from the eminent scholar Salomon Reinach, he found himself treated by the museum staff as 'a kind of god'. He carried more exciting prospects than pottery with him on the ferry to Le Havre, though. Some time in October, David Hogarth had sailed for Constantinople to discuss the re-opening of the archaeological site at Carchemish, near Jarablus on the upper Euphrates. Rediscovered by George Smith in 1876, it was an ancient Hittite city mentioned in the Bible, which had subsequently been excavated by the British Museum. In 1881, work on the dig had been abandoned, but now, thirty years later, Hittites had become fashionable again. Hogarth hoped to find at Carchemish the key to ancient Hittite hieroglyphics for which the world was waiting. That September, the Sublime Porte had given the British Museum a *firman* to re-open the dig, but had specified that the work should begin within three months. Hogarth wanted to commence the following February, and had travelled to Turkey to seek a deferment.

As a frequent visitor to the Ashmolean, Lawrence had discovered Hogarth's plans, and asked Edward Leeds casually 'if he knew of any excavations coming up in the Near East'. Leeds told him that he should have spoken sooner – a cuneiformist called R. Campbell-Thompson had already been taken on as Hogarth's assistant for the Carchemish dig. Lawrence suggested that he might go without pay, but Leeds felt that the British Museum would not take him even on those terms. This was a blow, but Lawrence had learned to be persistent. When Hogarth returned at the end of October, he tackled him personally with a request to join the team at Carchemish. He knew that his qualifications could not match those of Campbell-Thompson, yet he trusted that Hogarth had not forgotten how, the previous year, he had been 'rather smashed up' by hostile tribesmen while collecting Hittite seals on his behalf. In fact, his gambit now paid off handsomely. Hogarth leapt at the idea. He told Lawrence that he would not only take him as an extra assistant, but would arrange for him to receive a 'Demyship' or Junior Research Fellowship from Magdalen College which would pay him £100 a year while working on the site. Lawrence could scarcely believe his good fortune. The door to the East had suddenly creaked open: the lands he had dreamed of as a youth now lay before him. At first he had told no one about the arrangement, but while at Rouen in November he could no longer contain his excitement: 'Mr Hogarth is going digging,' he wrote to Leeds exuberantly, 'and I am going out to Syria in a fortnight to make plain the valleys and level the mountains to his feet.'[7] He added with facetious delight that he nurtured only one hope greater than this: that he would enjoy a quieter ferry crossing back to Newhaven than the one he had endured the previous day, when he had been tossed out of his bunk in the middle of the night, on top of another passenger. He had tried to thank the stranger for breaking his fall, he explained, to which the other had answered only, '*Mon Dieu!*': 'I laughed for about half an hour after I got back to bed,' he wrote, 'but I don't think he saw the funny side at all.'[8]

Lawrence, Hogarth and Campbell-Thompson arrived at the village of Jarablus on the afternoon of 11 March 1911, frozen stiff, having forded the Sajur river and battled through a Siberian gale with a caravan of ten camels and eleven pack-horses. They had left Aleppo three days earlier, a week behind schedule, owing to bad weather, for it was the coldest winter in the Near East for forty years. As the caravan wound into the village, the Arabs came swarming out to greet them, and many hands helped the caravaneers to couch the camels and unload the horses. A house belonging to the local liquorice company had been vacated for them, and soon they were out of the biting wind, while a jostling, gabbling crowd of natives cleared out the storehouses, and brought their luggage in piece by piece.

The Carchemish dig lay about three-quarters of a mile away from the village, and consisted of three huge mounds, the largest of which – the central mound – was believed to cover the main Hittite town. George Smith had discovered the site through some sixth sense, for though the town was mentioned in Jeremiah, the biblical account revealed no more than the fact that the city had stood somewhere near the Euphrates – one of the longest rivers in the Near East. Smith, a self-educated engraver, had already been world-famous when he discovered the site, having translated certain texts found in ancient Nineveh which confirmed the biblical story of the Flood. These texts were inscribed in Babylonian-Akkadian cuneiform, a writing system common to many civilizations of the ancient East, so called because its pictograms took the form of cone-shaped wedges which could easily be inscribed by a split reed in wet clay. Cuneiform had been deciphered in 1860, but while the Hittites had used it for their texts, most of their monumental and ritual inscriptions had been in hieroglyphic script which had yet to be deciphered. The secrets of Egyptian hieroglyphs had been unlocked by the Rosetta Stone – an inscription of the same text in three languages – and, as Smith had learned that the city of Carchemish had harboured a colony of foreign hieroglyphers, it was hoped that an excavation there might reveal such a key to ancient Hittite.

Carchemish had been built on the intersection of two waterways, and centred on a 130-foot acropolis which dominated the flat landscape and directly overlooked a major ford on the Euphrates. In spring the waters of the spate would leap and toss, foaming brownly down the maze of channels, and form a stream 1,000 yards wide, which licked around leaf-shaped islands yellow with flowers. On the opposite bank the village of Zamora stood in fields and orchards, set against the backdrop of the Taurus mountains, green in summer but in winter capped white with snow. Carchemish had been a Hittite capital as early as 2500 B C, but its position on the river had given it a strategic importance to invading armies, and it had changed hands many times. Sargon the Assyrian had captured it in 717 B C, and a century later the Assyrians had been defeated there by the Egyptian Pharaoh Necho – an event recorded in the Old Testament. The early excavations had revealed some promising hieroglyphic scripts, but no progress had yet been made in their decipherment. The discovery of the Hittite metropolis at Boghazkoy near Ankara in 1907 had brought the question of hieroglyphics to prominence again, and so it was that Hogarth, Lawrence and Thompson found themselves at Jarablus in 1911.

Work began within two days of their arrival, with a workforce 100 strong which they recruited from Jarablus and the neighbouring villages. While Thompson made a survey of the site, Lawrence marshalled the men, beginning where the previous excavators had left off, and almost at once uncovering a great staircase. The staircase proved to be Roman, however – part of a much later stratum which superimposed the Hittite levels. The great task of the early days was to clear away the Roman detritus in order to get at the more interesting layers, which lay about twenty feet below. Under the supervision of Grigori – a Cypriot overseer Hogarth had imported specially for the task – the men worked with ropes and crowbars, hauling up enormous slabs of Roman concrete, all of them shouting and giving orders at once. Lawrence would be up in the freezing dawn, to breakfast on 'bread like indiarubber sheeting' which was produced by their cook, dragoman and general factotum, Haj Wahid. The Haj was a memorable character. A brawny, powerful townsman from Aleppo, he proved to be honest, faithful and hardworking, but very much given to boasting, especially after plying himself with strong liquor – a habit which he indulged in over-frequently. About forty years old, he was a veteran of the British Consulate in Aleppo, where he had worked as a dragoman, and was said to have once, in a drunken stupor, held up the camel caravans entering the city's Antaki gate by taking pot-shots at the camel-drivers from the roof of his house. Badly beaten in a fight with the five brothers of a woman he had been meeting clandestinely, four of whom – according to the Haj – he had shot down, he had taken refuge from the blood-feud at Jarablus, where he went about his cookery with a revolver stuffed into his belt. Though an admirable cook in his own way, his abilities did not extend to making bread without an oven, and his 'wash leather-like' offerings were only made palatable by copious addition of some of the nine varieties of jam Hogarth had judiciously brought along.

After breakfast, Lawrence and Thompson would stroll down to the site, where the men had begun work at about 5.30 a.m. For the first few weeks they excavated at the base of the stairway, which had not been disturbed by the previous diggers, and where they believed the royal palace to have been. Lawrence found the actual digging 'tremendous fun'. The men generally laboured in teams of four – each team consisting of a pickman, a shoveller and two basketmen, whose job it was to carry the spoil to the river and dump it there. All the men received the same pay, but most wanted the job of pickman, since it was the easiest and the most likely to reveal *antikas* or artefacts. This was a great incentive, for baksheesh was awarded to the man who discovered an *antika*, and the importance of the find was reflected in the amount. The finds actually became more valuable as they neared the river, so that even the basketmen stayed alert for what the pickman and shoveller might have missed. Later, Lawrence displayed his masterly grasp of psychology by introducing a system by which the overseer would fire pistol-shots to announce the finds, the number of shots varying according to the object's importance: a fragment of sculpture might be worth one shot, for instance, while an entire sculpture was valued at seven or eight. The award of pistol-shots came to be regarded as a greater honour than the baksheesh which went with it, for baksheesh was, after all, only money. The finders of *antikas* would argue hotly with the overseers as to how many shots their find was worth, and even come to blows over it. Grown men who had gone days without a single shot fired in their honour were seen to break down in tears. Lawrence soon demonstrated that his forte lay in motivating the workers, and he would often turn the work into a game, pitting pickmen against shovellers and basketmen until the whole team, including himself, was yelling and running about, and a whole day's work might be accomplished in an hour.

From about eight in the morning, streams of women and children wearing shimmering red and blue colours could be seen pouring out of the villages on the water-plains, carrying piles of fresh bread wrapped in checked handkerchiefs and balancing pots of sour milk on their heads. This was the time of day Lawrence relished: the fierce heat had yet to rise, and the men were still fresh enough to chat, sing and play shepherd's pipes. Though predominantly Arab in culture, these Euphrates villagers were a mélange of peoples – Kurd, Circassian, Arab and Turkoman – and they sometimes spoke three or four languages, often compounding sentences from all at once. Lawrence, who had been studying written Arabic with Fareedah al-Akle in Jebayyil prior to meeting Hogarth, found their dialect 'vile' and almost unintelligible. While the men were working, Lawrence and Thompson – who also spoke Arabic – would busy themselves in measuring depths, taking squeezes, copying inscriptions, making sketches and taking photographs. Soon, though, they realized that there was not enough work for the two of them, and decided to work shifts, alternating with periods at the house going over the finds. The men finished work at five, and Lawrence would retire to the house to write up the daily log, compile object-lists, and examine the pottery found during the day, which was his particular charge. His superb memory served him well, and he was able to piece together potsherds almost instantly even when they had been found months apart. He could recall the intricate details of the stratum in which an object had been discovered, even if it was not he himself who had found it. Between 7 and 7.30 p.m. the Haj would produce dinner – a rather limited affair until Hogarth hit on the idea of buying bread from the Turks. Lawrence and his colleagues almost came to grief once when the cook emptied an entire pot of curry powder into the pilaff: 'It was,' said Lawrence, 'like eating peppered flames, and the other two are complaining about their livers!'[9]

His reference to 'the other two' is significant because despite his contentment at Carchemish, it is clear that even here he adopted his self-fashioned mantle of oddness. The continual emphasis in his letters on his uniqueness, his distinction, his greater hardiness, was actually the product of a deep dissatisfaction with himself. While Hogarth's teeth refused to eat the leathery bread, for instance, and Thompson could only just get through it, Lawrence 'flourished'. Lawrence was 'the only one of the three' who got a good night's sleep, due to a special power he had to sleep through anything (though at home he had asked for his cottage to be built because he was unable to stand the noise). It was Lawrence who hung doors, windows and shelves in the house, because he was the 'handiest', and he, apparently, who solved all the practical problems of the dig, with his superior facility for 'fixing and improving things'. This aura of superiority was, of course, assumed – a shell protecting inner frailty – yet some found it disturbing. Ernest Altounyan, who visited Carchemish that year, was one of them. The son of the Armenian doctor who ran Aleppo's hospital, and his Irish wife, Altounyan was a medical undergraduate on vacation from Cambridge when he met Lawrence, and perceived that he was a young man who has 'spun his cocoon but had not yet the assurance which enabled the full-grown man to leave it when required'.[10] Altounyan found the 'frail, pallid, silent youth' snobbish and impossible: 'The shut-up Oxford face,' he wrote, 'the downcast eyes, the soft reluctant speech, courteous, impersonal, were impressive, disturbing, disagreeable.' He thought Lawrence a poseur and commented that his power would have been more constructive had he only 'acknowledged less grudgingly the possibilities of others'.[11] Lawrence was afraid of Altounyan, who was a fluent Arabic-speaker, half-native, half-European, and an educated man like himself, who could see through all his colonial poses and deceptions. He was unable to acknowledge Altounyan's possibilities, simply because deep inside he felt that all men were more 'men' than himself.

Lawrence retained a certain awe of Hogarth, thinking him 'a splendid man' for his vast experience of the East, his ability to converse with equal intelligibility in six languages, and his encyclopedic knowledge. He continually tried to impress him, once, for instance, waking him up on their train journey to Aleppo to see the village of Harosheth, the setting of Deborah's Ode in the Old Testament. Fortunately, Hogarth shared his admiration for the poem, and was delighted: 'That went down very well,' Lawrence wrote home with satisfaction.[12] For his part, Hogarth was suitably convinced of Lawrence's potential as an antiquarian, and thought him technically a better archaeologist than Thompson. Though he wrote later that Lawrence was an 'admirable adjutant', he doubted his ability to drive the work forward. That Lawrence had a certain devil-may-care attitude was noticed also by Leonard Woolley, who was to take Hogarth's place at Carchemish the following season. Woolley wrote that Lawrence was curiously erratic where work was concerned: if he was interested he could be remarkably astute, but if he disliked an object or thought it unimportant he would ignore it. He got on very well with the men, Woolley said, to such an extent that he would sometimes return from another part of the dig to find Lawrence sitting in conference with the Arabs discussing some question of folklore or point of local dialect.[13] Such a fault could not have been levelled at Campbell-Thompson, who had an insular contempt for the natives which enabled him to drive them unhesitatingly – a quality which Hogarth, whose nickname among the Arabs was 'The Angel of Death', appreciated. Lawrence wrote that Thompson was 'pleasant' and 'very good fun' and admired his knowledge of Semitic languages. According to Hogarth they got on excellently, but this was Lawrence's charm working for Hogarth's benefit, for actually he felt a sense of competition with the older man, inwardly mocking his overt displays of physical strength, and the collection of rifles, pistols, swords and fencing equipment he had brought with him to the site.

If Lawrence stood slightly aloof from his English colleagues, he was more at ease with the Arabs, whom he regarded with the paternal benevolence of the autocrat. His relationship with them was not one of equality. It was Alec Kirkbride who later commented that Lawrence was more apt to like those who were his juniors in age and standing, and Lawrence himself later talked much of the satisfaction to be found in living among the lowest strata of society. His first response to the Arabs, though, was aesthetic: they were fine-looking chaps, he thought, though most were thin as rakes, and few were taller than himself. He was fascinated by their culture and set himself the task of learning all about their customs and language. Not only did he learn the names of all the workers, he also quickly assimilated the names of their tribes and families, and the nature of their relationships. Lawrence understood almost instinctively that in the Arab world a man is more than an individual: that his family and kinship ties define him. Soon this knowledge gave him a special standing among the local people, and he was able to use it effectively as a psychological weapon, pointing fun at slack workers by bringing up some skeleton in the family closet. This was not morally defensible but it was an effective style of management, and within months of his arrival Lawrence had become a sort of unofficial arbiter of disputes, sorting out the jealousies between pickmen, shovellers and basketmen, separating members of families with blood-feuds between them, settling fights, castigating the water-boys for falling short, advising a man on the payment of bride-price, bailing another out of prison, and driving away an Armenian tobacco-seller he suspected of trying to buy *antikas*. He even took pride in doctoring their injuries, treating scorpion-stings and dressing cuts they had received from tools or falling rocks. He began to behave and think, in fact, like the model British District Officer in a backwater of the Empire, administering 'his' natives: 'Thompson and I have to be doctors and fathers, & godfathers and best men to all of them,' he wrote.[14] He might have been echoing any decent-minded British colonial official carrying 'the White Man's Burden' when he told his mother: 'Our people are very curious and very simple, and yet with a fund of directness and child-humour about them which is very fine.'[15] Before his eyes, the Arabs had been transformed into noble savages, and while in 1909 he had praised the 'civilizing' influence of foreign missions, he now condemned them for introducing foreign ideas which 'vulgarized' traditional culture. The 'vulgar' educated Arab, worldly-wise and aspiring to power beyond his control, was a threat. Far better the 'noble' traditional Arab who knew his place, who treated him with unselfconscious and forthright respect, and never challenged his right to dominate. Since Lawrence was the one who hired and fired the men, he had absolute power over their fortunes, and there is no doubt he enjoyed that power: 'It is a great thing,' he wrote, 'to be an employer of labour.'[16] He took great pains in choosing the new labourers, and rejected many, not on the grounds that they seemed lazy or incompetent, but because they seemed too solemn or over-polite – that is, because they lacked the child-like simplicity required of the 'noble savage'.[17] Unfortunately, his aesthetic criteria for recruitment did not pay off, for in May there was a serious dispute among the men which was quelled only by sacking no fewer than thirty of them – a good third of the workforce. It was Leonard Woolley who later pointed out that despite Lawrence's paternalistic fondness for the Arabs and their culture, he had no deep personal liking for the men of Jarablus-Carchemish. He had only two friends among them, Woolley said: the local overseer or Hoja, Hammoudi, and the water-boy Salim Ahmad, known by the nickname 'Dahoum'.[18]

Hammoudi, a swashbuckler, proud of his Bedu roots, had lived wildly as a youth and had become embroiled in a number of blood-feuds. Declared an outlaw by the Turks, he had hidden out in the hills for five years, visiting his village only in disguise. An amnesty in 1908 had ended his exile, but he had found life tedious until Hogarth had come along and opened the Carchemish dig. On the site, his keenness had quickly brought him to notice, and Hogarth had earmarked him as overseer. Tall, lean, hatchet-faced, imposing in his long-sleeved astrakhan coat and purple headcloth, he never went to work without his cartridge belt and revolver, and could frequently be heard to declare that if only he had £100, he would buy a good horse and a gun and have done with the sedentary life. 'I'll shoot a man or two,' he would say, 'and take to the hills again, and by God, I should be happier than living within walls like a cow!'[19] If Lawrence's admiration for Hammoudi was marred by the fact that he found him 'a terrible bore conversationally' and as sticky as a limpet, his affection for Dahoum was not similarly hampered. Dahoum first appears in a letter written in June 1911, as a fourteen-year-old donkey-boy who, as part of a trick being played on a Turkish gendarme, is forced to drink Seidlitz powder on pain of being beaten or ridiculed, and declares, in a good impersonation of Crusoe's Man Friday, that the white man's sorcery is 'very dangerous for by it men are changed suddenly into the forms of mares or great apes'.[20] In a letter written a few days later, though, he emerges as an 'interesting character' who could read a little and was more intelligent than the 'rank and file', having expressed a wish to spend the money he was making at Carchemish on attending school in Aleppo, thus becoming the kind of 'vulgar' half-Europeanized Arab that Lawrence disliked. Indeed, Lawrence found himself firmly wedged in an ideological cleft stick over Dahoum, for while he declared grandiosely, 'better a thousand times the Arab untouched', he admitted that the life of the 'Arab untouched' was a 'hideous grind' fit only for the 'low level of village minds'.[21]

Lawrence's letters from this period show the *soi-disant* critic of the Renaissance and the 'age of reason' at his most self-contradictory: he criticized 'foreigners who always come out here to teach whereas they had much better learn',[22] for instance, but concurrently declared with pride that he had taught Dahoum to use his reason as well as his instinct. He told his mother happily that there was as yet no 'foreign influence' in the district, neglecting the obvious powerful influence of two Englishmen: '. . . if only you had seen the ruination caused by French influence, & to a lesser degree by the American,' he wrote, 'you would never wish it extended.'[23] In the case of Dahoum, the colonial itch to improve gained the upper hand, for within a month he was writing to the American Mission School in Jebayyil for books with which to begin his 'education'. These were to be 'Arab' not 'foreign', though Lawrence appeared to notice no inconsistency with his passionate defence of the 'Arab untouched' only a month before. For him it was only the 'touch' of *other* foreigners – particularly the French – which was likely to corrupt: he had no wish, he wrote, to do more for Dahoum than to give the boy a chance to improve himself, which, it might be argued, is precisely what the foreign missions thought they were doing. Lawrence was able to remove himself magically from the equation, because he believed that his influence was entirely benign. This view began with the perfection of the Englishman as its premise. The Arab could never aspire to be an Englishman, but had a duty to be 'good of his type' – to encourage this, Lawrence thought, the Englishman should learn his language, assimilate his customs and admire his traditions: '[catch] the characteristics of the people about him,' as Lawrence put it, 'their speech, their conventions of thought, almost their manner.'[24] Once he had done so, he might 'direct men secretly, guiding them as he would'.[25] Lawrence disdained other colonial styles, particularly that of the French, because, conversely, the Frenchman held himself up as an example to be imitated: rather than learn Arabic, he encouraged the Arab to learn French; rather than learn Arab customs and traditions, he encouraged the Arab to ape his own. The result of Lawrence's style of colonialism would be a people with their own distinct cultural patterns, firmly but covertly under British dominion: the result of the French style, a 'vulgarized' and acculturated people who were unable to attain the heights of the European, but had abandoned all traditions of their own. Lawrence was desperate to avoid such a situation at all costs. He thought Dahoum 'excellent material' for improvement, and later taught him to take photographs on the site, but Woolley found his intelligence decidedly limited, and far outshone by his startling good looks. It was his physical perfection rather than his ability to reason that Lawrence celebrated when, two years later, he made a sculpture of Dahoum naked and set the finished sculpture on the house roof. He may have believed that it was Dahoum's mind that interested him, but in fact he was attracted physically to the boy. Woolley noted obliquely that though Lawrence never admitted feeling affection for anyone, the affection for 'certain people' was 'there and deeply felt'.[26] Quite simply, in Dahoum – Salim Ahmad – S A – Lawrence had found the one great love of his life.

When Hogarth and Grigori left on 20 April, Lawrence compounded his oddness by moving out of the house and sleeping on the site – either on the mound or in a trench – a development which must have struck the Arabs as very strange indeed. Lawrence believed it brought him closer to them, though they themselves would not have dreamed of sleeping anywhere but in their own quarters. The excavation was not proceeding well. It was costing £40 per week, but as yet they had little to show but the odd lion's head, basalt relief, and heaps of pottery: no Hittite inscriptions or hieroglyphic texts had been found. When, in May, having found nothing but a Roman coin, the fragment of a lion's mane and a Byzantine wall foundation for the entire week, they struck solid bedrock, they almost abandoned the diggings then and there. It was under these despairing circumstances that they received a visit from Miss Gertrude Bell, a distinguished Arabist and archaeologist, who had arrived expecting to find Hogarth. Miss Bell belonged to the long British tradition of dominant ladies, who by dint of privileged birth and determination had managed to extrude themselves into a world of men. She was influential, and if she should report back to the British Museum the true state of the excavation, Lawrence feared, it would automatically be closed down. He had already acquired a taste for the lotus-eating life here, and had set his sights on returning for another season. His attitude to Miss Bell was, therefore, understandably defensive. He thought her pleasant enough, but not beautiful 'except with a veil on, perhaps',[27] and at first he found her too captious by half. When she criticized the way the excavations had been carried out, he and Thompson tried to 'squash her with a display of erudition',[28] racing volubly over subjects as disparate as Byzantine architecture, Greek folklore, Anatole France, the construct state in Arabic and the price of riding-camels. After ninety minutes of this onslaught, he said, Miss Bell was happy to have tea, and retreat 'back to her tents', murmuring defeatedly that they had 'done wonders' with the digging.[29] This was Lawrence's account: Miss Bell, seemingly oblivious of any friction, simply added a reginal note to her diary that she had met Thompson and a young man called Lawrence, who, she predicted, was 'going to make a traveller': 'They showed me their diggings and their finds,' she wrote, 'and I spent a pleasant day with them.'[30]

In June, however, Lawrence's worst fears were realized when Thompson received a telegram from Sir Frederick Kenyon, Director of the British Museum, stating that the trustees had been so disappointed with the results of the dig that there would be no second season. There was nothing to be done but to clear up the diggings, glue together those pots which could be glued, and close up the site. In July Thompson and Lawrence moved down the Euphrates to Tel Ahmar to decipher some Hittite cuneiform scripts. From here, Lawrence set off on foot to revisit Urfa and to see Harran, Birejik and Tel Bashar – the region in which he claimed to have been attacked in 1909. Like that excursion, this one also ended in ignominy, when, less than three weeks later, he crept back into Jarablus, spoiling for malaria and dysentery, with festering bites on his hands and his feet in shreds once more. Almost the entire village turned out to greet him, and after an hour's council, Hammoudi brought him bread, fried eggs and yoghourt and left him, mercifully, to eat alone. That night he slept on the roof with a splitting headache, and woke to see the sunrise over the Mesopotamian plain, with high fever. He staggered doggedly off to Carchemish, intending to measure various trenches, but when Hammoudi tagged along to assist Lawrence fell into a blind rage and bellowed at him, sending him away for no apparent reason. Having reached the mound, he promptly fell flat on his back and lay there motionless for seven and a half hours in a cold sweat, with his head bursting. When he finally summoned the effort to get up, he was astonished to find it was three in the afternoon. He lurched towards the trenches with his tape-measure, but some were deep, and he could not trust himself to take any measurements without falling inside. The trek back to Jarablus village was one of the most fearful marathons he had ever endured: it took him two hours to cover the three-quarters of a mile distance. That evening he scrawled letters with a hand so heavy he could hardly hold the pen, and sent a runner with them to Birejik to summon a carriage and invoke the aid of the Governor and the local doctor. Many Arabs, including Dahoum, came in to wish him well, but he was so sick that he could scarcely see them. All the next day he lay prone in the Hoja's house, troubled by spurts of diarrhoea to relieve which he had to hurry outside, once fainting and cutting his cheek badly on a sharp stone. In the evening he was comforted once more by a visit from Dahoum. On the third day there was no sign of the carriage from Birejik, and Lawrence began to fear that the messenger had absconded with his money. Though Hammoudi was taking great pains to make him comfortable, he found himself becoming intolerant of the 'dreadful bore', and was irritated by the way the Hoja seemed to repeat every sentence five or six times, implying that Lawrence's Arabic was poor, and emphasizing his foreign-ness. In his weak condition, Lawrence's Arabic might well have been unintelligible: in fact, he may have owed Hammoudi his life.

While he lay in a half-stupor, the Hoja was fighting a battle with public opinion. His neighbours – almost all of whom had worked on the dig – advised him cold-bloodedly to throw Lawrence out, for if the Englishman were to die, they said, the ex-bandit Hammoudi would certainly be accused of poisoning him for his money, and arrested and imprisoned by the Government. The Hoja dug his heels in, however: to have turned Lawrence out would not only have violated the Muslim code of hospitality, but would also have been a considerable affront to an employer who might possibly offer him a job in the future. Lawrence must have overheard the heated arguments which ensued, for he gave Hammoudi a letter addressed to his father stating that if he should die, the Hoja was not to blame. For three days his life hung by a thread. Dahoum came to visit him each day. Then, on 1 August, there was a slight improvement, and Lawrence managed to drag himself painfully, with long rests, to the river for a much-needed wash. At four o'clock that afternoon the runner arrived back from Birejik without a carriage, saying that the local doctor and the Governor had refused to help. Lawrence was now in dire straits. He was faced with a five-day wait while he sent someone to wire for a carriage from Aleppo, or a ride on horseback to Membij, where there were carriages for hire. He decided to try for Membij, but it was a further two days before he felt strong enough. Just as he was about to set off, Hammoudi turned on him and refused the loan of his horse, without which, he knew, he had no chance of reaching the place. Furious at this sudden and inexplicable reversal in his host's generosity, Lawrence teetered to another part of Jarablus with Dahoum's help, and managed to hire a horse to take him to Tel Ahmar, where he might hitch a lift to Membij. One added problem was that he had no cash to pay for the horse, but the owner generously let him take it on trust on being told that he would change money in the bank at Tel Ahmar and send

Dahoum back with both horse and cash. They travelled by night, under a fair moon, and reached the Euphrates by Tel Ahmar at dawn, to find their way cut off by the swollen Sajur. Dahoum plunged in, swam across, and brought a boat to ferry both Lawrence and horse to the far shore. There, Lawrence managed to change his money at the Syrian Bank, and sent Dahoum off happy with a *metallik* (half a crown) and his neighbour's mount. He lay helpless in a hemp plantation until about mid-morning, when he managed to beg a ride on a wagon bound for Membij. There, after a long agony of bickering with the drivers, he hired a carriage for Aleppo, where he arrived on 5 August, and put himself gratefully to bed in the Baron's Hotel.

The fever came and went, and though he managed to do some shopping in the bazaar with Haj Wahid, and even to quiz local dealers about his camera, stolen in 1909, he frequently felt himself falling into semi-faints. He sat down to dinner once in the Baron's with his head spinning, and only regained his senses long enough to call the diner sitting opposite 'a pig', causing a tremendous uproar. The man was a Greek Jew and his friends wanted Lawrence to apologize, while a group of beefy German railway engineers weighed in on Lawrence's side, and the hotel manager ran around the tables wringing his hands. After three days Lawrence took a train to Damascus, and on the 12th, after another terrible night of fever, he sailed from Beirut. 'Boat very full of people, all Syrians apparently,' he managed to write in his diary. 'Left Beirut 11am. All over.'[31] He had survived the most fascinating and decisive year of his life by the skin of his teeth, but over it was not. All the way from Jarablus he had been nursing a letter from Hogarth saying that the second season at Carchemish was, after all, still under consideration – 'The best news,' Lawrence wrote, 'that I have heard this long time.'[32]

7. The Baron in the Feudal System

Carchemish and Egypt
1911–13

By November Lawrence was back in Jarablus, fully recovered from his illness. Sir Frederick Kenyon of the British Museum had been persuaded to re-open the dig at Carchemish, partly because of the pressure whipped up in the press, much of it by the influential Hogarth. A letter published in *The Times* in late July, entitled 'Vandalism in Upper Syria and Mesopotamia', though, had also played its part, cleverly evoking British chauvinism by suggesting that the stones of ancient Carchemish were to be used as ballast for the German Berlin–Baghdad railway, which was about to reach the Euphrates. Although it was ascribed to an anonymous 'Traveller', this letter was actually the work of Lawrence: his first brilliant attempt to manipulate public opinion to his own advantage by using the establishment media. Kenyon had not only agreed to re-open the site, but had taken on Lawrence as a salaried assistant at 15s. a day. To replace Campbell-Thompson, who had decided to marry, he had appointed Lawrence's old acquaintance, Leonard Woolley, as Director.

The German railway company was much in evidence on Lawrence's return, constructing store-sheds and barracks for their workers in preparation for the wooden trestle bridge they planned to erect. Raff Fontana, the British Consul in Aleppo, had already told them in no uncertain terms that the Carchemish site was British property, and they were not to touch a single stone or blade of grass. The Germans, who had agreed to place the bridge slightly farther to the south, did not know that Fontana's claim was false. Lawrence's task in the district that November was to find out who the land actually *did* belong to, which entailed delving into the government archives at Birejik, with the help of Haj Wahid and a dragoman from the British Consulate in Aleppo. What they discovered was not encouraging. Out of the entire

area of 160 *denums* of land, 120 belonged to a local landowner called
Hassan Agha, while only forty had been purchased on behalf of the
British Museum in 1879. Lawrence guessed that this situation would
lead to problems in due course. His stay was a brief one, however, for
he had made arrangements to work for a short period under Professor
Flinders Petrie in Egypt, to improve his knowledge of archaeological
field methods. He and Haj Wahid left Jarablus by coach on Christmas
Day, 1911, in torrential rain. Crossing a footbridge over the Sajur, the
coach slipped and overturned into the river, submerging one of the
horses, pinning down another, and leaving the third thrashing about
madly. Lawrence and the Haj, who had fortunately been walking
ahead, plunged in to save their belongings, while the driver battled
frantically to pull up the head of the drowning horse. Many of Lawrence's things were carried off, and at one stage the Haj was almost
washed away when he lost his footing and fell headlong into the torrent.
It took two hours to extract the carriage in the freezing rain, and, as
their lunch was well and truly soaked, they dined on a walnut each
and an unlimited supply of muddy water. It was, said Lawrence, 'the
most memorable Christmas I've ever had'.[1]

He joined Petrie at Kafr Ammar, fifty miles up the Nile from Cairo,
in January 1912. Though he had dreamed of Egypt as a boy, he found
the Professor's style too ordered and systematic for his taste, and
disliked the work, which consisted mainly of disinterring heat-
mummified bodies. Petrie, whom Lawrence had met briefly as a
schoolboy at the Ashmolean, was the most distinguished British archaeologist of his day. No patrician Oxford sophisticate of the Hogarth
school, he was a self-trained excavator who had begun as a humble
surveyor without any systematic education, and had used his great
gifts to transform the practice of Egyptology. Before Petrie, Egyptolo-
gists had been little more than glorified treasure-hunters, obsessed with
uncovering temples and carrying off vast statues for museums. Petrie
had been the first to turn his attention to the despised minutiae of
archaeology: the scribble on a potsherd, the fragment of an amulet,
the remains of a ring. His methods of dating included the use of stylistic
degeneration, which later became standard practice. At close quarters
Lawrence found Petrie monumental 'like a cathedral', and he was
amused when, after he had turned up on the site in a blazer and shorts,
the Professor told him bluntly: 'They don't play cricket here.' Lawrence,

who was wearing the same dress he had worn at Carchemish, realized that shorts were considered *infra dig* in Egypt, though the reference to cricket made him chuckle: 'I expect he meant football,' he later wrote.[2] He felt a great sense of admiration for Petrie, but thought him dogmatic and opinionated. He also developed a strong distaste for the Egyptians, who, unlike the Arabs of Jarablus, would not play the colonial game of reassuring the Englishman that they were not diminished by his power. Lawrence found them ugly, dirty, dull and gloomy and 'without the vigour' of the Jarablus men. He could not talk to them with the same 'delicious free intimacy',[3] for either they were surly, reminding him of his status, or else they 'took liberties', ignoring it. Neither of these styles was acceptable to Lawrence, for the Arab was supposed to treat the Englishman with a rough and ready frankness which gave the illusion of equality, without overstepping the mark into disrespect. In Egypt the gulf between the powerful and the powerless was clear to see: in Syria it was comfortably disguised. These prejudices, and the ache to be back with his friends at Carchemish, did nothing to stymie his energy, and Petrie was impressed enough to offer him a salary of £700 to supervise a dig at Bahrein or somewhere else in the Persian Gulf. Lawrence was tempted, but the call of Syria proved too strong, and by the end of February he was back at Carchemish.

Woolley was tied up in Egypt till March, and Lawrence had orders to proceed with the building of an Expedition House as a permanent base. As soon as he reached Jarablus, he recruited twenty-two men and started on the foundations, but the work was halted by the Corporal commanding the Turkish guard which had been posted to the site since Lawrence's last visit. The Corporal inquired politely if he had permission to build a house. Lawrence answered that his sponsors had been given permission and that the local Governor was perfectly aware of it. 'Quite so,' said the Corporal, 'but that Governor is gone.'[4] There was no alternative but to suspend work while the Corporal wired Istanbul for permission, and a fortnight later Lawrence was still waiting for an answer. He travelled to Aleppo to meet Woolley, who arrived on 10 March expecting to find the house ready. He was irate when he discovered that work had not even begun, and whipped off a cable to Kenyon in London, demanding action. There was worse news to follow, however. When Lawrence and Woolley turned up at the site a few days later, and began enrolling workmen, they were told by the same Corporal that work was prohibited. Woolley dispatched a curt letter to the Governor asking him to curb the Corporal's interference, and, confident that he would receive a prompt reply, proceeded to recruit 120 men. The Governor did not even deign to answer Woolley in person. Shortly, the Corporal arrived with a letter stating that the Governor did not know who Woolley was, and that work could under no circumstances commence. 'This was a nasty shock,' Woolley wrote; '. . . to put off the diggings now meant not only a waste of time, but would destroy the men's confidence and respect – an important thing in a country none too civilised.'[5]

Woolley and Lawrence conferred and decided they must confront the Governor, and on 17 March they set off by horse for Birejik, twenty-five miles to the north. They crossed the Euphrates by ferry, and, leaving their mounts at the *khan*, marched briskly up the main street to the government *serail*, standing in the shadows of a twelfth-century castle. Woolley sent in his card to the Governor's office. There was no reply, and after a decent interval, he sent in his card again. Minutes ticked past, and no response came. This was intolerable treatment for respectable British subjects, Woolley felt, and, bursting with righteous indignation, he and Lawrence forced their way into the Governor's office and sat down unceremoniously in front of his desk. As decorously as possible, Woolley inquired why work on the site had been prohibited. The Governor, a corpulent, sly-looking old man with a goatee beard, replied that the *firman* granting permission to excavate at the site was made out to a Mr D. G. Hogarth, and, since neither of the gentlemen in his presence appeared to bear that name, they could not be permitted to start work. Woolley protested that he had letters from Hogarth and the British Museum, but these letters were in English and the Governor waved them aside. He *might* be able to permit work to begin, he said, if the Englishmen were prepared to pay the salary of an unofficial commissaire. Both Woolley and Lawrence then realized that he was fishing for a large bribe. Just what happened next is uncertain. Woolley claimed that he leapt up, drew his pistol, held it to the Turk's head, and threatened to shoot him there and then. It seems more likely, though, that he merely told him that work would proceed whether he liked it or not, upon which the Governor said he would send troops to prevent it.

'I only hope that you will come at the head of your soldiers,' Woolley said. 'Then I shall have the pleasure of shooting you first!'[6]

'So,' said the Turk. 'You would declare war on the Ottoman Empire!'

'Not on the Ottoman Empire,' Woolley replied coolly. 'Only on the Governor of Birejik.'[7]

The Governor realized that his bluff had been called and caved in, declaring that he saw no reason why they could not start the following day, after all. This gunboat diplomacy had a great impact on Lawrence, for all his scorn of 'ruling-race fantasies', and he began to copy his new Director's abrasive manner, just as he had tried to emulate Hogarth's smoothness: 'Woolley is really a most excellent person,' he wrote to Edward Leeds. 'You should have heard him last Sunday, regretting to the Governor of the Province that he was forced to shoot all soldiers who tried to interrupt our work at Carchemish and his sorrow that the first victim would have to be the little [Corporal].'[8]

They returned triumphantly to Carchemish, where their tiny army of workmen had manned the diggings with rifles and pistols to repel the Turks. On seeing the Englishmen riding back jaunty and unharmed, the Arabs cheered enthusiastically and let rip with salvoes of shots. Haj Wahid – whom Woolley had left in charge – put ten rounds from Lawrence's own Mauser through the roof of his tent in glee. The racket drew a troop of German engineers, who rushed down to see what they thought was a battle, only to collide with a cavalcade of horsemen escorting the Governor in person. He had come only to deliver an official apology and to reassure everyone that work could commence, turning a blind eye to the building of the Expedition House, even though Lawrence had not yet received permission from Istanbul. No doubt inspired by his insouciance, Lawrence impudently wired to the capital again suggesting that it would be convenient to have permission to build the house *before* it had actually been completed.

The British had won the first round, but the Governor soon found a way to strike back. For the moment, though, they settled down to build their house, and Lawrence lifted a gloriously coloured and illustrated fifth-century Roman mosaic found in a field a mile away and installed it, piece by piece, as the living-room floor. The Expedition House became the 'medieval hall' he had dreamed about with Richards – a vast structure built round a courtyard, with no fewer than eleven rooms, including a dark-room. Lawrence practised the crafts he had learned as a youth to greater approval than he had received at home. He beat a bath and a firehood out of copper, built a table for the sitting-room, designed two armchairs which he had made for him in Aleppo, constructed basalt pillars and door mouldings, and eventually carved a mock-Hittite lintel over the door. He chose hangings and carpets, and crockery in the form of priceless Hittite pots and drinking-bowls, which he bought in neighbouring villages with Expedition funds, settling his conscience by resolving to let the Museum have anything which survived daily use. Descriptions of Lawrence at this time, indeed, portray him as something of a connoisseur – of carpets, Arab food, coffee, *objets d'art*, and other 'beautiful things . . . to fill one's house with'.[9] Woolley said that the 'evening Lawrence' took on a very different aspect from the wild-haired youth of the day: 'In the evening his hair was very carefully brushed,' he wrote; 'sitting in front of the winter fire reading . . . he would look with his sleek head and air of luxury extraordinarily unlike the Lawrence of the daytime.'[10] The centrepiece of the sitting-room was a William Morris tapestry sent out from Oxford, which became an endless source of amusement to Lawrence. When European visitors arrived, they would invariably pass over the exquisite Arab textiles he had collected, and stand gaping at the Morris. When they inquired in what remote bazaar he had obtained the marvellous stuff, Lawrence would take great delight in replying, 'Oh, you can buy it in Oxford Street for so many shillings a yard!'[11]

Woolley and Lawrence kept open house, and frequently invited the German engineers to dinner in civilized fashion. But though Lawrence's fears about the railway company carting away the ancient stones of Carchemish as railway ballast proved unfounded, he continued to harbour a secret grudge against them. He resented them ostensibly because 'they did not know how to treat Arabs', but actually because they had intruded on his private sphere, and formed an alternative centre of attraction for the natives. Lawrence's skills lay in 'handling' the Arabs, a task he performed by harnessing the British tradition of colonial paternalism, nurtured over centuries. The Germans preferred more Teutonic methods of control, but the end was essentially the same. Although Lawrence genuinely tried to see things from an Arab point of view, and did so more successfully than most, his technique of 'empathy' remained a method of control. He believed the traditional Arabs morally superior to Europeans because they were 'primitive' and therefore 'innocent', but not intellectually so. The reality of his privileged position was stated frankly when he wrote: 'Really this country, for the foreigner, is too glorious for words: one is really the baron in the feudal system.'[12] His sense of rivalry with the Germans was submerged, however, for to begin with they lived in symbiosis. The engineers needed ballast for their railway, and the British needed to get rid of certain heaps of stones they had dumped in the previous season, in order to dig beneath them. It was agreed that the Germans would carry away the British stones, and the British would thus get their dumps moved without cost to themselves. This suited everyone admirably, except the part-owner of the site, Hassan Agha, who felt distinctly hard done by. One morning he strode into the German camp and demanded payment for his stones. The engineers explained that they could not pay and that if he insisted they would go elsewhere for their ballast. Hassan Agha then fled to Birejik to complain to the Governor, who suddenly saw his chance of revenge.

A few days later, a lone horseman arrived in the camp carrying a summons. Lawrence was to appear in an Islamic court accused of having stolen the goods of Hassan Agha – namely the stones – to the value of £30, and sold them to the Germans. The summons was technically illegal, since foreigners were exempt from appearance in an Islamic court, but Lawrence decided to attend the trial as a courtesy, simply because the charge was so absurd. On the appointed day he rode off to Birejik and in the court – part of the government *serail* – he produced two documents: an agreement signed by Hassan Agha relinquishing rights to anything found on the site, and an affidavit signed by the German Chief Engineer, swearing that nothing had been paid for the stones. Lawrence also had with him documents authorizing their work at Carchemish. These papers, he thought, should be enough in themselves to have the case dismissed. He had reckoned without the machinations of the Governor, however, and was shocked when the prosecuting counsel produced six witnesses prepared to swear that the dumps had been paid for. The counsel asked to see all Lawrence's documents and promptly confiscated them, leaving him bureaucratically naked. He arrived back at Carchemish that night far less contented than he had been on his departure. The work continued as before, however, until the Governor ordered the Corporal to post guards on the gate. Woolley managed to sidestep this development by taking the German-employed donkey-men on his own payroll, and having them dump the stones near the German lines.

On the day fixed for the full hearing, Woolley, Lawrence and Haj Wahid, festooned with carbines and revolvers as if on a tribal raid, made for Birejik. To their surprise, they ran into Hassan Agha coming in the opposite direction, who told them that the case had been adjourned. Woolley refused to accept it, envisaging more exasperating delays, and they pressed on to Birejik, where they demanded to see the Governor. Woolley explained that they could not afford to keep halting work on the dig to ride to Birejik, and insisted that the case be heard that day as planned. The Governor seemed friendly and compliant, and neither Lawrence nor Woolley guessed his part in the plot. In the courtroom next door, a crowd had gathered to watch the fun, and a scribe took copious notes. Woolley stood up, announced that he was taking full responsibility for the case, and declared that the prosecution had no witnesses. The prosecuting counsel then asked the court for a week's adjournment to find some, a proposal the judge agreed to at once despite Woolley's violent protests. Woolley was incensed. He refused to recognize the court's jurisdiction and called loudly for the Governor. The judge laughed in his face, and told him that it was the Governor himself who held the papers authorizing work on the site. Only at that moment did Woolley realize what lay behind the conspiracy: 'The trick that had been played on us and the Governor's part in it were now quite clear,' he wrote. 'As long as they had the precious documents . . . I was at his mercy.'[13] Woolley saw that a return to gunboat diplomacy was called for, and drew his pistol, declaring that 'the Judge would not leave the room alive' unless he got his papers back. The judge's sneer froze on his lips, and he sank back into his chair. Woolley told Lawrence to go to the Governor's office next door and demand the papers: 'Woolley kept him in his place,' Lawrence wrote, 'while I went to the [Governor] and pointed out how unpleasant the position of the [Judge] was . . .'[14] Woolley recalled that Lawrence was gone only a few minutes and reappeared brandishing the papers, saying, 'The blighter had them all in his own desk!'[15] When Woolley asked if there had been any trouble, Lawrence answered, 'None', except that the Governor had wanted a copy of Hassan Agha's contract made, 'And could you oblige him with a penny for the stamp!'

The affair was not quite finished, however. In May, when Hogarth arrived to take stock of the situation, he called on the Governor, who tendered his apparently sincere apologies and informed him solicitously 'that he had used his authority to quash a case that should never have been brought'. Evidently this had not been made clear to the procession of soldiers which arrived at the Expedition House the following Sunday with a paper for Woolley's inspection. The paper showed the verdict of the court – 'guilty' – and announced the sentence – payment of £30 plus costs. Woolley's reaction was prompt: 'I tore it into small pieces,' he remembered, 'and the procession went disconsolately back.'[16]

Kenyon's original intention had been to run the dig for only a short season, and as yet only two inscriptions had been unearthed. In May, though, Hogarth announced the wonderful news that an anonymous donor – actually a wealthy businessman named Walter Morrison – had donated £5,000 to support the excavations. The work could now continue indefinitely, and Lawrence decided not to go back to England that summer as he had planned, but to remain on the site to 'keep an eye on the Germans'. A major reason for this change of plan was that Dahoum, whom he had wanted to take back to Oxford with him, had declined the invitation. Lawrence decided to put off his return until after the winter season. The site was closed in June, and he was frankly relieved to see Woolley off from Alexandretta: 'I am my own master again,' he wrote, 'which is a position which speaks for itself and its goodness.'[17] He rested for a few days in Aleppo, then returned to Jarablus, where he now enjoyed complete autonomy. His first move was to install Dahoum in the Expedition House, ostensibly to help Haj Wahid's mother, who worked in the kitchen, but actually to assuage his loneliness. He occupied his time by holding impromptu classes in arithmetic and geography – the itch to improve once more outweighing his admiration for the 'unspoiled Arab'. In geography, he taught his four students that the earth was round, eliciting the predictable question from one of them that if this was the case, how was it that the people on the other side did not fall off? The school soon had to be abandoned, however, when Lawrence went down with yet another dose of malaria, and no sooner had he recovered than Dahoum succumbed, followed by Haj Wahid's wife and his baby son.

The Haj himself later took to his bed with intestinal problems after a drinking bout, and Lawrence doctored them all.

At the end of August, though, he suffered two more spells of malaria, and abandoned his resolution to remain at Jarablus all summer. He moved to Jebayyil on the Mediterranean coast, staying once again with Miss Holmes at the American Mission, where he had been made so welcome previously. This time he took Dahoum with him as his cook and servant. He later told Robert Graves that he and Dahoum had enjoyed a wonderful summer, masquerading as camel-drivers, sailing down the Syrian coast, helping peasants with the harvest, bathing and sight-seeing. In his contemporary letters he described this period as the most glorious summer he had ever had. That they actually passed themselves off as camel-men is doubtful, since Lawrence scarcely knew one end of a camel from the other at this stage, and Dahoum was little better. Certainly, though, Lawrence walked about Jebayyil in native dress, went sight-seeing to the famous Qasr of Ibn Wardan in the Orontes valley, and bathed in the sea with Dahoum almost every day. He was blissful: free at last, alone but for a boy he was devoted to, eating well, sleeping well, reading in the Mission library, and practising his Arabic. All his life he had hidden his feelings for others, repressed his emotions, stood aloof. With Dahoum – a 'savage', still little more than a child – he was able to open up completely as he could not do with anyone of his own age, race and status. With Dahoum, he felt unthreatened. He felt so close to the boy, in fact, that there was no need to play the fool or practise 'whimsicalities'. With Dahoum, he did not feel out of his depth as he did with other, more conventionally 'masculine' men. He felt so absolutely comfortable with him that they were able to sit in silence together for hours, basking in each other's warmth, not needing even to speak. His power over Dahoum was profound, and to the boy he must have appeared almost a wizard from a far-off land, a kind of magical godfather glimpsed only in fairy-tales. The relationship was not and could never be one of equality: socially they were as far apart, almost, as medieval serf and master – at least, this is the way Lawrence himself imagined it: 'Dahoum is very useful now, though a savage,' he wrote later that year; 'however, we are here in the feudal system, which gives the overlord great claims: so that I have no trouble with him.'[18] The boy whom Lawrence had a year previously acclaimed for his ability to read and write remained, in his eyes, a 'savage' whose most appealing qualities were his honesty and strength, and, not least, his ability to wrestle: 'beautifully better than all of his age and size'.[19] It was Dahoum's 'innocence' which Lawrence appreciated most, by which he meant an innocence of the political realities of the world and the vast gulf of culture and economic power that lay between them. Lawrence despised more sophisticated Arabs because they were likely to question the European assumption of authority, which Dahoum, in his 'innocence', did not. In short, Lawrence saw Dahoum as a beautiful boy who was entirely dependent on his own *noblesse oblige* and did not appear to resent it. Here was the perfect romantic subject for the most precious gift that Lawrence, in his omnipotent wizardry, could bestow: freedom – 'the seven pillared worthy house'. Lawrence was utterly in love with this young boy, and for him he felt empowered to shift mountains, to inspire great tides of movement. His poem, most probably dedicated to Dahoum – Salim Ahmad – 'I loved you, so I drew these tides of men into my hands and wrote my will across the sky in stars', must rank as one of the most moving tributes to young love ever written.

It may have been his feeling for Dahoum which prompted him to exchange clothes with him. By slipping into his *dishdasha* he could magically *become* Dahoum, become for a moment the innocent and ignorant 'savage' living close to the earth, become the long-admired craftsman of the medieval era, inhabiting a pre-Renaissance, pre-rational world. Lawrence, whose inner emptiness prompted him to take on the characteristics of others he met, was to spend his life searching for alternative selves. In Dahoum, he discovered his most potent *alter ego* – a persona he could step into and out of as he wished. At last, the obsessions of his youth – the medieval, the Morrisian fantasy – began to coalesce in the overwhelming fascination and delight of being that 'baron in the feudal system', a European in the East: 'I don't think anyone who has tasted the East as I have would give it up half way,' he wrote.[20] His happiness made him oblivious to or uncaring about the scandal he was provoking, especially in the breast of the committed Evangelist Miss Holmes, who had welcomed Lawrence first as a devoted fellow Christian, a member of an Evangelical family, who in 1909 had waxed enthusiastically about the triumphs of her Mission. That shy, earnest, undergraduate of 1909 had metamorphosed before her eyes into a new, more self-assertive man who denounced foreign interference, flaunted his handsome companion, and strutted about wearing native dress. Miss Holmes, who had given up her holiday in the cooler mountains, was unimpressed with his new manner and his dashing young friend. Lawrence later claimed that she had been unable to understand Dahoum's Jarablus dialect – the dialect which he himself had called 'vile', and which in Dahoum's golden mouth had acquired the melodious sound of ancient Greek. It is unlikely, though, that the Near East veteran Miss Holmes could not have communicated with the boy had she wished. Evidently, she did not find Dahoum the 'excellent material' Lawrence had so proudly assured her colleague Miss Rieder he was. Lawrence never stayed at the Mission again, nor did he receive any further letters from Miss Holmes. When he passed through Beirut in February 1913, a visit to Jebayyil was notably absent from his schedule.

Lawrence and Dahoum remained at Jebayyil for three and a half weeks, and would perhaps have stayed longer had he not received an urgent telegram from Haj Wahid, telling him that there was a crisis at Carchemish. The Germans, who had informed Lawrence that they would be suspending work during June, had built an extension railway line to the mound, and were preparing to plunder the stones Lawrence and Woolley had so painstakingly unearthed. Haj Wahid had protested to the Chief Engineer, Contzen, whom Lawrence described as an 'ill-mannered bully'. The Chief told Haj Wahid that Woolley had given him permission, but the Haj knew the value of the stones, and would not budge. He told Contzen that he could not allow work to continue without further orders. Contzen sneered, but the Haj promptly sent a man to Birejik with a telegram for Lawrence in Jebayyil, and the following morning climbed the mound with a rifle and two revolvers and prepared to defend Carchemish. When the railway workforce of about 100 men approached with shovels and picks at the ready, he threatened to put a bullet through the first man to touch the walls of the mound. The workers had no heart for trouble. They simply went and sat down in the shade, until Contzen arrived and began shouting, whereupon the Haj threatened to shoot him, too.

This was the situation when Lawrence arrived in Aleppo. He sent Haj Wahid a telegram to let him know he was on his way, but the Haj replied that he had already resolved to kill Contzen, and in preparation had sent away his wife, downed an entire bottle of whisky, and loaded his rifle. Alarmed, Lawrence sought out Contzen's superior in Aleppo – the Director of the railway – and burst in on him at a dinner party, saying that unless he wired Contzen to desist immediately, the engineer would be a dead man. The Director found this highly amusing. He quickly changed his mind, however, when Lawrence threatened to sign an affidavit in front of the British Consul swearing that the Director had not lifted a finger to defuse the situation. The Director put an electric trolley at Lawrence's disposal, and he arrived at Carchemish the next day to find that Contzen's men were about to pull apart its venerable walls. With the help of the local Minister of Public Instruction, Fuad Bey, he persuaded Contzen to retire and remove his rails. Contzen received a public upbraiding, and the Haj was warmly commended. Woolley returned at the end of September to find peace in the camp.

Work began again, and almost at once they were rewarded by the discovery of a Hittite door-frame with a perfect inscription. Woolley had ordered a light railway to be delivered from Europe, but it had been delayed, and a huge workforce of 200 men was required in consequence. Retaining them proved a headache, for Turkey was now at war in the Balkans and the Porte was recruiting every able-bodied man for the army. The Englishmen used their diplomatic immunity to protect their labourers, however, and gave sanctuary to those fleeing conscription in the Expedition House. Woolley forbade any policemen or soldiers from entering the dig. The ploy was effective, because while the railway camp was decimated, the Carchemish crew lost not a single man. This raised the prestige of the British enormously, and gave them a certain amount of protection against local insurgency, for minorities such as the Kurds and the Armenians were preparing to take advantage of the Balkan war to settle old scores with the Turks. In autumn 1912, Lawrence and Woolley visited Busrawi Agha, chief of the Milli-Kurds, a nomadic folk whose great leader, Ibrahim Pasha, was believed to have been poisoned by the CUP. Busrawi was talking openly of getting rid of the Turkish government once and for all, and the Englishmen learned to their dismay that the Milli-Kurds were planning to ransack Aleppo in revenge for the death of their paramount chief. As autumn turned to winter, news of Turkey's defeats in Bulgaria and the advance of the Bulgarian army towards Istanbul was received with delight by the Kurds and Arabs. Ironically, perhaps, as long as the old Sultan

'Abd al-Hamid II had remained in power as Khalif, these people had remained loyal to the Porte. With the coming of the CUP, though, the old loyalties had been sundered. It cannot have escaped Lawrence's notice that they now regarded Hussain ibn 'Ali, Emir of Mecca, as their religious chief. If the first faint clarion-call of revolt against the Turks sounded at this moment in Lawrence's inner ear, it was drowned out by fears for the safety of the excavations and his countrymen in Aleppo, where, he heard, the Kurds had sent an agent to mark out the best houses for possible plunder. Woolley and Lawrence suspected that one of these might well be the British Consulate.

It was at this troubled time that Lawrence chose to try out his newly acquired skill of disguise in native dress. Though his Arabic was now fluent, he knew that he could never be taken for an Arab – he was too fair in appearance, and his mastery of grammar too poor for a native speaker. But northern Syria was inhabited by many non-Arab peoples, some of whom were fair-skinned and spoke Arabic imperfectly. Lawrence believed he might be able to pass himself off as a member of one of these minorities. Just how good was Lawrence's Arabic? He later tended to be misleadingly modest about his mastery of the language, and even told Robert Graves that he did not know a word of classical (written) Arabic, which differed a great deal from the various spoken dialects. This was untrue: Lawrence had studied written Arabic with Fareedah al-Akle at Jebayyil in 1911, and at least once wrote part of a letter to her in the language. There is also extant a single Arabic letter signed by Lawrence and addressed to Sharif Hussain of Mecca, the language of which, while comprehensible, displays a mixture of dialects and styles. It has been authenticated by Dr Basil Hatim of the School of Arabic Translation and Interpreting at Heriot-Watt University, Edinburgh, as being the work of a non-native speaker, precluding the idea that Lawrence might have dictated it to a scribe. As for Lawrence's colloquial Arabic, that too eventually became a hotch-potch of dialects, mainly Syrian and Hejazi. Lawrence had an excellent vocabulary, but his pronunciation was poor, his grammar 'an adventure' – as he himself admitted – and he spoke with a noticeable English accent. Alec Kirkbride, later one of his colleagues, who had grown up in Egypt and really did speak Arabic 'like a native', commented that Lawrence's accent and pronunciation alone would have marked him as a foreigner. However, Lawrence was game to see whether he could pass as a native, and the opportunity arose near the end of November, when a villager arrived at the dig reporting that a sculpture of a woman riding two lions had been discovered near Khalfati, north of Birejik. Believing that the piece might well be Hittite, Lawrence dressed himself up in local costume and set off with Dahoum to investigate. They found the countryside seething with unrest. Thousands had been conscripted for the army, and whole villages had been depopulated. Kurdish tribesmen were being told by their Aghas to enlist in the Imperial army and then to desert as soon as they were given rifles. The whole district was awash with rumours of marauding bands. The Turkish police were trigger-happy and tense, constantly on the lookout, and no sooner had Lawrence and Dahoum entered Khalfati than they were arrested as suspected deserters by a military patrol. They were kicked downstairs into a filthy dungeon so harshly that Lawrence was badly bruised and Dahoum's ankle sprained. In one version of the story, Lawrence suggested that he was beaten severely enough to be put in hospital. Whatever the case, they managed to escape by offering a bribe, and, abandoning the Hittite find, walked briskly back towards Jarablus. Their way took them through the district of Nizib, where they found the Kurds excited, running about looking for a Christian to kill. Only Lawrence's disguise saved him, and when they reached Nizib village they discovered what lay behind this bizarre behaviour. Two days earlier a horde of armed Kurds, under a chief called Derai, had looted the place and shot dead a Christian Armenian doctor whose fly-blown corpse still lay in the street. In Nizib and Birejik the native Christians were all in hiding.

Despite his bruises, and the alarming knowledge of having been within a hair's breadth of death, Lawrence made his way back to the site with some satisfaction. First, his disguise had worked, and he had been taken for a native peasant. Second, he had gained some exclusive news about the Kurds. Third, and perhaps most important for his own psyche, he had acquired, in his treatment at Khalfati, the elements of a fantasy upon which his masochism could feed. From boyhood, he had nursed a masochistic reverie about the army, a reverie acted out at the age of seventeen, when he had enlisted in the Royal Garrison Artillery. The idea of being a 'deserter' from the army appealed even more strongly to that fantasy: it represented resistance to an overwhelming authority, and provided a justification for the punishment which he enjoyed. He derived no pleasure from the actual beating he had received from the Turks at Khalfati, but the scene, relived and elaborated upon over and over again in his mind, would provide rich material for his imagination in years to come.

8. Peace in Mesopotamia Such as Has Not Been Seen for Generations

Britain and Syria
1913

The Bulgars were turned back at the gates of Stamboul and the threat to Aleppo evaporated, but Lawrence had had his first whiff of revolt, and found it intoxicating: 'As for Turkey, down with the Turks,' he wrote in April 1913. '. . . Their disappearance would mean a chance for the Arabs, who were at any rate once not incapable of good government.'[1] In June, when the excavations closed once again, he finally persuaded Dahoum to come home with him to Oxford. Previously the boy had been chary of accompanying him to a country of which he knew nothing: he had heard stories of Englishmen luring unsuspecting Arabs off to their homes and turning them into tinned meat. Even Hammoudi, the reformed bandit, for all his superior experience, was inclined to believe such tales. Seeing that Dahoum would not consent to come alone, Lawrence made the same offer to Hammoudi, and only a courageous leap of faith made the Hoja accept.

They stayed in the cottage at the bottom of the garden at 2 Polstead Road, and Dahoum's beauty caused a stir among Lawrence's acquaintances, particularly Charles Bell, who commissioned the painter Francis Dodd to make a portrait of him. Dahoum found that he enjoyed being the centre of attention, and once, when Dodd was interrupted at a critical moment by Lawrence's brother Will and some friends, the boy turned to look at them in annoyance. This was just the expression of sultriness the artist had been looking for, and he captured it precisely, leaving Lawrence to rave over the portrait's 'absolute inspiration'.[2] While Hammoudi was pushed off onto Woolley some of the time, Dahoum stayed with Lawrence, lending a hand at the Ashmolean with the unpacking of *antikas* which had come from Carchemish. They were old friends, and it gave him some relief to discover what actually happened to them once they disappeared from the site.

The Arabs found Britain fascinating, but their views were disappointingly rational: '. . . unfortunately,' wrote Lawrence, 'they are too intelligent to be ridiculous about it.'[3] To Dahoum it seemed a fat country, full of fat people, luxuriant, green, wet – a vast garden without villages but with peaceful, populous towns with towering buildings. He found the food rich and plentiful; he stumbled about London on the Underground, enjoyed riding a bicycle up and down Woodstock Road in his *dishdasha*, and once stood in a public lavatory stroking the white-glazed tiles and murmuring 'beautiful, beautiful bricks'.[4] He thought that Syria was a mere flea-bite compared with England, and that the Arabs were too few in comparison with the English ever to count in world politics. Lawrence approved this view: it had been partly to impress these men with the reality of British power and munificence – as opposed to the weakness and corruption of the Turks – that he had brought them here in the first place. As regards his own people, though, his purpose had been to shock: to enhance his reputation as an eccentric Englishman. He was fond of declaring that Dahoum had 'Hittite blood' – a statement which was entirely meaningless in any literal sense, but which virtually established the boy as the *pièce de résistance* of the Hittite collection from Carchemish – a living archaeological exhibit. People came from miles around to photograph the two Arabs in national dress as if they were exotic beasts, and even Woolley conspired in the 'Hittite' fantasy, by claiming that Dahoum's face was reminiscent of some of those found on Hittite sculptures. If he had understood this claim, Dahoum would probably have considered it ludicrous: he was an Arab Fellah who lived on the banks of the Euphrates, and to whom the Hittites meant nothing. To Lawrence and his colleagues, though, he was the epitome of noble savagery: 'The picture of Dahoum still comes back to me,' Edward Leeds wrote; '. . . he seemed too spruce and fine for any menial task – a noble figure.'[5] Neither Leeds nor Lawrence was able to see that they had fallen into the intellectual trap of confusing 'nobility' – a moral quality – with 'beauty' – an aesthetic one. This aesthetic, quasi-zoological objectivism was expressed unselfconsciously by Will Lawrence, who visited Ned in Syria later that year, and wrote of the Bedu that 'the Hoja [Hammoudi] does as a type, but I have seen many *better specimens*'.[6] Lawrence was sensitive to the charge of 'exhibiting monkeys', however, and sought to preserve his Arab friends' dignity by refusing offers of money on their behalf from the numerous people he allowed to photograph them. Hammoudi, for one, was not amused. He did not believe that his dignity was impaired by being so photographed, and for him the practice of honouring a guest with a gift was commonplace. Leeds thought the Arabs 'child-like', and was hugely tickled to hear that when asked what he would like to take home with him, Hammoudi had chosen a water-tap, which he thought would always provide water, and a 'Keep Off the Grass' sign, which seemed to him to have some talismanic power to prevent people from straying where they were not wanted. Only one disquieting moment marred their stay. This was when they encountered an Egyptian called 'Abd al-Ghaffar, who was an undergraduate at St John's and a friend of Will's. They claimed later that he had said to them, 'Soon we will cut the throats of these dogs!' – meaning the British – upon which the two Jarablus men had rushed back to Polstead Road and demanded a gun to shoot him with. Lawrence, who had ordered that they should be kept out of the way of any other Arabs, was irritated by this incident: he despised educated Arabs and he despised Egyptians – what could be worse than an educated Egyptian? Yet the story had a satisfying ring to it – proving the instinctive loyalty of the 'noble' Arab to the European, as opposed to the treachery of the Arab 'corrupted' by education. Lawrence wanted freedom for the Arabs, but for the Egyptians 'freedom' meant liberation not from Turkey, but from Britain, which had annexed their country in 1882.

When the two Arabs returned to Jarablus with Lawrence that August they boasted about their experiences *ad nauseam* to the other labourers, much to the annoyance of the Cypriot overseer Grigori, who was profoundly jealous. For his part, Lawrence became even more proprietorial towards Dahoum than before. Later in the year, when he was visited by a young army officer named Hubert Young – an excellent Arabic speaker who would later fight alongside Lawrence in the Arab Revolt – they sat down to sculpt two gargoyles for the roof of the house. While Young produced the head of a woman, Lawrence made a naked model of Dahoum. Woolley was shocked to find the figure on the roof when he returned. To him, it seemed an obvious declaration of Lawrence's homosexual nature, and he wrote that it was regarded as such by the other Arabs, who were scandalized by the idea. Though Lawrence later delighted in representing homosexuality as a practice casually accepted by the Arabs, this was far from the truth, and very much a product of his wishful thinking. In the European tradition of Orientalism the East was a cultural dumping-ground for those traits European society despised in itself, and the stereotype of the lascivious Arab formed part of this tradition. In fact, homosexuality was neither accepted nor flaunted by the Arabs, and if practised at all was practised discreetly behind closed doors. Though Lawrence's affair with Dahoum was most probably platonic, the naked statue seemed to proclaim otherwise, and much of the reputation that had accrued to him was lost by this heedless but compulsive act.

Lawrence thought of north Syria now as his 'own Arabic country', and his proprietory attitude extended to all 'his' men. He wrote only half jokingly that he would like to become 'The Sheikh' of Jarablus, and when Will visited him in October 1913 he found that his brother was treated as 'a great lord': 'Ned is known by everyone,' he wrote, 'and their enthusiasm over him is quite amusing.'⁷ In Aleppo he had many friends – not only Arabs but also Armenians, Greeks, Kurds and Circassians. His sense of *noblesse oblige* was marked, to the extent that he thought of himself as the local doctor, treating everyday complaints, nursing his friends, dispatching sick villagers to the hospital in Aleppo, and even trying to make arrangements to vaccinate the entire village against cholera when an epidemic broke out in Aleppo in 1912. He also saw himself as an unofficial local magistrate, and was very proud when eighteen Kurdish chiefs turned up at his house to arrange a peace settlement between opposing factions which had been at feud for forty years: '. . . in our house they met on neutral ground,' he wrote, 'and fell upon each other's necks (like a rugger scrum) and kissed. Since then there has been peace in northern Mesopotamia such as has not been seen for generations.'⁸ He was the defender of his people's interests, once threatening to whip a German engineer who had had Dahoum beaten up, and reporting in delight that when the Carchemish dig opened in 1912, almost the entire German workforce abandoned the German camp for the British – even though the railway company paid higher wages. He took this as a personal compliment, but it was actually a triumph for benevolent paternalism: in the German camp the workers were beaten by aggressive Circassian henchmen if they misbehaved, were not allowed to talk to their overseers, and were given no baksheesh.

The atmosphere in the British camp might well have been jollier – though it is a matter of record that there *were* disputes with the workers – but Lawrence's relationship with the Arabs remained essentially one of privilege. He enjoyed the power that being a European in the East gave him. His travels alone and on foot, sometimes in native dress, had enabled him to learn a great deal about the aspirations of the ordinary people, 'to learn the masses' as he put it, and his great sensitivity allowed him to see the world through their eyes more than most Europeans, but ultimately his loyalty lay with the ruling élite, as his remarks about 'the feudal system' make clear. Lawrence claimed that he always found it difficult to deal with people, and loved to portray himself as an eccentric intellectual with his head among exotic objects and ideas. In fact, he emerged from his time at Carchemish highly skilled in man-management.

The most complete expression of Lawrence's romantic view of Arabia and the Arabs at this stage appears in his essay for *Isis* magazine, *The [Qasr] of Ibn Wardani* (actually ibn Wardan), written in 1912. That summer he and Dahoum had visited the Qasr or castle, which had been built by the Emperor Justinian in the sixth century. The building was said to have been constructed with floral scents kneaded into the clay, so that each room had a different smell. Lawrence was led through the ruins by Dahoum, who, sniffing the air, announced: 'This is jessamine, this violet, this rose.' Then, drawing him to an open window, he bade him smell the 'sweetest scent of all' – 'the effortless, empty, eddyless wind of the desert' – which had no taste. 'My Arabs were turning their backs on perfumes and luxuries,' Lawrence wrote, 'to choose the things in which mankind had no share.'[9] The Arabs, Lawrence was pointing out, regarded material civilization as a mere encumbrance which interfered with the real purpose of life. It was a sound philosophical point, and no doubt the idea went down well in pre-war Oxford, but it is as unlikely that Dahoum would have understood Lawrence's romanticism, written from his high pedestal of material well-being, as it is that he actually said the words Lawrence puts into his mouth. The peasants of the Euphrates, struggling for survival, were not given to waxing poetic over the glories of a wind that was more enemy than friend. It is unlikely, too, that Dahoum, who wanted desperately to be able to read and write – presumably so that he could get a better job – would have turned his back on luxuries if they had been available to him. Only they were not, for Lawrence and Woolley forbade their men to use Western products, and would even send them home if they turned up in boots. The Arabs wanted the luxuries the Englishmen enjoyed: the Englishmen were prepared to force them to remain themselves, and thus maintain the romantic vision they admired. The story of Ibn Wardani purports to express the spiritual leanness of the Arabs: in fact it remains a peculiarly Western, peculiarly Orientalist view.

This is not to suggest that some of the Arabs did not like and admire Lawrence tremendously. Hammoudi said years later that from the very beginning Lawrence had been able to outride, outshoot, outwalk and outlast the best of them, and possessed a unique clarity of mind and purpose: '. . . while we would twist and turn with our object far away,' he said, 'he would smile and point out to us what we were after, and make us laugh, ashamed.'[10] Dahoum apparently told Fareedah al-Akle in 1912 that there was nothing the Arabs could do which Lawrence could not do, and that he even excelled the Arabs in doing it: 'he takes such an interest in us and cares for our welfare,' Dahoum said. 'We respect him and greatly admire his courage and bravery: we love him because he loves us and we would lay down our lives for him.'[11] Lawrence's years at Carchemish were the happiest of his life, and by 1913, even the idea of printing with Vyvyan Richards had been dropped. It was, he wrote Richards, a place where one ate the lotus almost every day: 'like a great sport with tangible results at the end of things'.[12] Very soon, though, that idyll was to end, as a great wave of history finally crashed over the world, washing away all innocence.

9. *The Insurance People Have Nailed Me Down*

Sinai, Syria, Britain

1914

At the end of December 1913, Woolley received a telegram from Sir Frederick Kenyon at the British Museum, requesting him and Lawrence to join an officer of the Royal Engineers for an archaeological survey of the Negev and northern Sinai under the aegis of the Palestine Exploration Fund. Its objectives were to trace an ancient caravan route from Palestine to Egypt and identify some of the sites associated with the forty years' wandering of the Children of Israel. Lawrence guessed at once that these objectives were a red herring. The real purpose of the survey was military – an espionage mission inside Ottoman territory. Though Turkey had long been an ally of Britain, the far-sighted Lord Kitchener – British Agent in Egypt – suspected that in the event of a war with Germany the Ottomans would take the German side. Sinai protected the British Empire's jugular – the Suez Canal – and beyond Sinai lay Palestine. It was, Kitchener thought, vital to the future of the canal that the area be thoroughly surveyed.

On 10 January they met the expedition leader, Captain Stewart Newcombe, at Beersheba. Newcombe was nonplussed to find them so young. 'British Museum' had evoked a vision of cobwebby old greybeards with fifteen tons of camp furniture, but instead Woolley and Lawrence travelled light and 'looked about twenty-four and eighteen years of age respectively'.[1] Newcombe decided that his letters had been too deferential and that deference should stop immediately. He dispatched them into the desert with instructions to rendezvous at Qusayma – a desert post across the Egyptian border – in a few days' time, and they promptly disappeared. When they failed to turn up on the appointed day, Newcombe grew worried. He sent a detachment of Egyptian Police Camel Corps looking for them, and the troopers returned having rounded up their camels, but having found no trace of the missing men. The result was wild telephoning back and forth across the border, and a squadron of Turkish border-guards was alerted on the Ottoman side. The local Bedu were suspected of having taken them prisoner and forty tribesmen were arrested as hostages. A day later, though, Woolley, Lawrence and Dahoum arrived at Qusayma, somewhat footsore, and were amazed to discover that the Camel Corps were hunting them. Lawrence explained that the camels had simply gone crazy and rushed off in the night. They had walked to Qadesh Barnea expecting to find the camels there, and had inadvertently taken a path through the hills which no camel could follow: this was why the Camel Corps had not found them: 'It shows how easy it is,' Lawrence wrote, 'in an absolutely deserted country to defy a government.'² It was a lesson he would not forget. They remained at Qadesh Barnea – perhaps once the desert capital of the Children of Israel – for a few days and parted, Woolley for the Dead Sea, Lawrence for Aqaba where he was to meet Newcombe. Five days later he arrived at the head of the escarpment, and saw the Gulf of Aqaba for the first time.

Today, the head of the escarpment stands on the Egypt–Israel border, and in order to reach it you have to make the steep ascent from the Israeli resort of Eilat. Passing through Eilat on my way back to Egypt, I decided to spend a day inspecting the old Pilgrim Road from which Lawrence had first glimpsed the Rift Valley, hiring a mountain bike for the trip, which proved to be an even harder climb than that of Safed – a gradient of one in three and a half, as Lawrence himself recorded. The day was a very hot one, and, certain that there would be some kind of refreshment-stall on the way, I had neglected to bring any water. The road took me through Eilat's 'neighbourhoods' and then up abruptly into a desert of arid rock, marbled abutments of granite, sharp sabre-toothed peaks, broken peduncles, cloven hoofs. I halted breathlessly on a curve to take in the stunning sight of the Gulf of Aqaba, and the great Wadi 'Araba, where the African Rift surfaces from beneath the Red Sea, with its vast walls of cream-coloured limestone and sea-green granite, the perfect, crescent-shaped bay with its fuzz of palm-trees, and the neat crystal-porcelain wedge of Aqaba town lying to one side. I continued, pedalling and sweating, and the day grew hotter and hotter, and my mouth drier and drier. There were no people, no houses up here, nor even any traffic. There were few trees, little vegetation of any kind – just naked flint burning in the sun. At last I came to a signpost which pointed to a fissure in the rock, and read '*Ein Netafim*'. '*Ein*' meant water of some kind, so I turned off the road and bounced for a mile down a stony track, only just stopping myself from plunging over a sheer drop into a ravine of 500 feet. *Ein Netafim*, it seemed, lay under the rock overhang, and to get there you had to climb down a perilous rock chimney. I was already shattered after my pedalling, but thirst was burning in my throat, and I knew I had to get down at any cost. The chimney was slippery and narrow, and I climbed down hand over hand: in places the rock had actually been polished glossy from the passage of people over the years. The wadi bed was clogged with broken blocks – the parings and crumblings of millennia – and the spring was no more than a wet seam where the rock wall touched the valley floor. Someone had made a tiny catch-basin to collect the liquid, which was full of bright green algae and mosquito larvae. I leaned over and scooped it into my mouth, larvae, algae and all: I cannot say that it was the best water I have ever tasted, only that I was so incredibly thirsty that I did not taste it at all. Then I collapsed in the shade of a rock, and listened to the calling and whistling of birds, which seemed deafening. I realized suddenly that this trickle was probably the only water-source in the entire area. I could have kicked myself for neglecting to take water in the desert, but the hardship involved in getting a drink had been, I thought, a salutary and timely lesson in respect. I climbed up the chimney and pushed my bike back to the road. A little farther on I came across a stretch of cobbled track, and a sign which read 'Stop. Border beyond this point.' It struck me that I was on one of the oldest roads in history: the Hyksos shepherd-kings had come this way in their chariots to invade Egypt 4,000 years ago: Cambyses III, King of Persia, had come here with his army in 525 BC and so introduced the camel into North Africa. The present road was hewn and blasted out by Selim the Grim – the Turkish Sultan who had finally smashed Mamluk power in the Middle East – in order to get his artillery up the escarpment during his invasion of Egypt in 1517. Down this road Muslim pilgrims had plodded for centuries on their way to Mecca and Medina, and down this road T. E. Lawrence had come in March 1914, taking just three hours from the plateau to the beach.

*

Eilat's McDonald's now stands amid traffic lights at almost exactly the point where the old Pilgrim Road touches the strand, but in 1914 there was no town called Eilat nor a nation called Israel. Instead of opulent hotels, ice-cream stalls, funfairs and bikini-clad girls lounging on the beach, Lawrence discovered only scrub and sand, a few dom palms, and a score of reed-built fishermen's huts. In Aqaba, a couple of miles further on, he also discovered a disgruntled Newcombe. The local Governor had forbidden any mapping, Newcombe said, and though Lawrence was all for ignoring the order, the following day Newcombe rode twenty miles to receive a phone call from Lord Kitchener in person, who warned him strongly against precipitate action. Lawrence grasped the reason for the ban at once. Aqaba was the only major Turkish port at the head of the Red Sea, and thus of vital significance to any future operations which might take place inland. Automatically, he shifted into his attack-defence mode. Aqaba could be taken from the sea, of course, but any troops there, he saw, would easily have been able to retreat a few miles back to the sweeping mountains which hemmed in the port on both sides. An enemy force making a beach-head at Aqaba would be pinned down and would find it very difficult to advance. The key route to Aqaba was the Wadi Ithm, a great chasm of granite opening to the north-east of the port, so narrow and boulder-blocked in places that even camels could only pass in single file. He who held the Wadi Ithm held the key to Aqaba, Lawrence thought.

Forbidden map-work, Lawrence spent his time scouring the ruins of the ancient citadel of Ayla, where he picked up some sherds of pottery. He tried to hire a boat to take him to Pharaoh's Island – the Crusaders' *Île de Graye* – about ten miles south of Aqaba, where there was a medieval castle. Unfortunately, the boatman he had engaged was immediately arrested by the police, and when Lawrence and Dahoum tried to take the boat out themselves, the police prevented them. Undaunted, Lawrence borrowed three ten-gallon water-drums from Newcombe, and hiked with his camels around the coast to Taba, from where the island lay only 400 yards offshore. He blew air into the tanks, and paddled across using a wooden plank as an oar, towing Dahoum behind him on one tank and his camera on another. Unfortunately, the ruins were not worth the effort, and on his return he was obliged to leave the district under military escort.

Lawrence decided to march north up the Wadi 'Araba to Petra, the ancient Nabataean city carved in solid rock, which he had wanted to reach since his first expedition in Syria in 1909. Photography was forbidden, but despite his escort he managed to get half a dozen photographs by pretending to be suffering from diarrhoea and taking frequent leave. He sent his twelve camels and five camel-men on to Wadi Musa, at the entrance to Petra, and he and Dahoum stalked off fast, managing to lose their military guards in the maze of valleys around Mount Hor. While alone, they discovered a route through the hills which Bedu raiding-parties used when heading for Sinai. Lawrence found Petra itself a feast. Though he had read a great deal about it previously, he was unprepared for the overwhelming effect of the place. It was not the rock-cut tombs and temples which awed him, but the natural beauty of the site, with its marbled colours of red, black and grey, its great cliffs and pinnacles, and its gorge, or *Siq*, like an undersea cavern, abrim with oleanders, ivy and ferns. For once he felt his powers of description inadequate: 'Be assured,' he wrote Edward Leeds, 'that till you have seen it you have not the glimmering of an idea how beautiful a place can be.'[3] Although the rock city was mercifully unmarred by the thousands of visitors who flock through it today, there already existed a tourist camp run by Thomas Cook, and there was a slow trickle of privileged sightseers. From one of them, a Lady Evelyn Cobbold, Lawrence managed to beg the train fare from Ma'an to Damascus, while making a slightly snobbish mental note to have his mother look her up in *Who's Who* to find out 'what' she was.

Ma'an lay only a short distance away across the Belqa hills, and Lawrence sent his baggage caravan on ahead as usual. He was annoyed to find on his arrival that the camels had been impounded by the police for grazing on public pasture, and would not be released until he paid a fine. Lawrence had learned the correct response to such problems at the hands of the firebrand Woolley, and he suddenly snatched a couple of the rifles which the policemen had piled before them and, with the weapons tucked under his arm, marched briskly towards the local Governor's office. The policemen, too cowed to snatch them back, trotted close behind. He confronted the Governor, and demanded that the fine be waived in exchange for the rifles. The Governor was furious, but reluctantly agreed, instructing his men to free the camels, upon which Lawrence cocked a deliciously arrogant verbal snook, saying, 'Please don't trouble yourself. They left the town an hour and a half ago!'[4] He waited at Ma'an two days for a train, grumbling about the inefficiency of the Turkish railway engineers, and finally managed to travel to Damascus third class. He was not to see Ma'an again for three years, and then it would be a distant vision from the desert, as he rode towards Aqaba at the head of a Hashemite force.

Lawrence was glad to be back at Carchemish, and took with him no yearning for the desert. He looked forward instead to the routine of the dig, wanting it to go on and on for years. At last the young man who had wished to spend his life as an artistic dilettante saw himself turning into a 'professional': in his letter to Vyvyan Richards at the end of the previous season he had confessed that ever since he had got to know the East, the idea of settling down at home had faded: '. . . gradually I slipped down,' he wrote, 'until a few months ago when I found myself an ordinary archaeologist. I fought very hard at Oxford . . . to avoid being labelled: but the insurance people have nailed me down now.'[5] However, work could not begin until the end of March since Kenyon had neglected to renew the digging permit, and on the day Lawrence and Woolley arrived back from Aleppo with the permit, there was fighting in the railway camp.

It began when one of the labourers – a Kurd called 'Ali – discovered that his wage for a month's hard labour was only five piastres. The workers were paid eight piastres a day by the German company, but the paymaster had built up a fine racket in docking wages for bread which the labourers did not eat, and for water, which came free from the Euphrates. 'Ali protested that five piastres was not a proper reward for his labour, and when the German paymaster refused to listen, the Kurd dashed the money in his face. The paymaster's Circassian steward promptly knocked him down, and when 'Ali came up with a stone, the steward tried to shoot him. The other Kurds – 150 strong – broke ranks and began hurling stones at the German engineers' office, smashing the windows. The Germans cocked their rifles, and opened up phlegmatically at everyone in sight, wounding five or six Arab workmen who were innocently engrossed in their labours thirty yards away. The Arabs downed tools, drew their pistols and fired back at the common enemy. The besieged engineers telephoned to their camp, and soon a solid phalanx of thirty armed Circassians, Turkish soldiers and fellow engineers swept across the bridge and began shooting from the near side. It was at this point that Lawrence and Woolley, who had run out of their house to find out what was happening, came under fire themselves. Lawrence saw a Circassian guard named Ahmad Zakkari step out about sixty yards away and take deliberate aim at Woolley. Fortunately, the man's aim was bad, and the bullet simply richocheted around his feet. Lawrence sprinted across to the engineers' office to tell the Germans that he and Woolley were not to be shot at. When he arrived back at the mound he was astonished to find that about 300 Kurds and Arabs had climbed it from the back, and were preparing to take the party on the bridge in a suicidal rush. Those who had revolvers were reloading them, and others had picked up crowbars and clubs. Lawrence and Woolley tried to push them back, even knocking some of them down, but soon the Circassian Ahmad Zakkari began shooting again, missing Lawrence but hitting a Kurdish boy he was talking to. This sent the Kurds into a mad frenzy, and it was only with tremendous force of will that the Englishmen managed to prevent them from opening fire. The crisis point had passed, however, and Lawrence and Woolley finally persuaded the men to carry their wounded to the Expedition House. About an hour later the crowd began to disperse into the village. One Kurd had been killed and about twenty men wounded by German fire.

When the British and German Consuls arrived the following day with a detachment of 250 Ottoman soldiers, the camp was calm. The railway company asked Woolley and Lawrence to negotiate a peace settlement on their behalf, through their friend Busrawi Agha of the Milli-Kurds. Lawrence suggested a payment of £80 blood money for the dead man and £40 compensation for the rest. He also recommended sacking the Circassians, replacing the paymaster and another engineer, and installing a dozen Kurds as observers on pay day. These proposals were accepted gladly by both sides, and Busrawi Agha travelled to Aleppo on the safe-conduct of the British Consul, Raff Fontana, to sign the accord there. Woolley and Lawrence had not, however, forgotten Ahmad Zakkari, the Circassian who had deliberately tried to murder them. The Ottoman authorities issued instructions for his arrest, but he had fled into the mountains, and was never found. A few weeks later the excavations closed down. Woolley and Lawrence had already drafted out part of their report on the Negev survey,

The Wilderness of Zin, but some solid research on the background of exploration in the region was required, which could only be provided by libraries in England. Instead of wandering that summer, therefore, Lawrence chose to return to Oxford. He was never to see Dahoum or Carchemish again.

On 11 August, while Lawrence was at Polstead Road, he heard that Britain and Germany were at war. Young men everywhere – including his brothers and former classmates – clamoured to enlist in the forces, but Lawrence held back. Though he would later tell Robert Graves that he had tried to join an Officers' Training Unit, and had been rejected owing to a glut of recruits, he subsequently denied this, confessing to Liddell Hart that he had never tried to enlist. Edward Leeds, with whom he frequently worked at the Ashmolean during late 1914, confirmed that he had not joined the recruiting frenzy: 'My recollection is that he had no doubts about his duty,' Leeds wrote later, '. . . he wanted to do his bit and fretted that he could not do it in the way he thought best . . . but he could bide his time and while waiting could calmly pursue other work and interests.'[6] Lawrence clearly felt that he would be of most value in the Middle East, but Turkey had not yet entered the war on the German side. In anticipation, though, he applied to join the General Staff in Egypt: 'The Egyptian people say they want me but not yet,' he wrote to a friend that September, 'and the War Office won't accept me until the Egyptian WO has finished with me.'[7] Lawrence was particularly vulnerable to tension, and the horrible suspicion that the Ottomans would not enter the war after all weighed on him heavily. If they did not, then the special skills he had acquired over the past five years would be useless to the war effort. There would then be no alternative but to join a combat unit and leave for France. The days of anxious waiting seemed to him interminable, and he wrote of 'the horrible boredom of having nothing to do, & getting news about once a week and all the rumours and theories and anxieties of everybody all round you gets on all our nerves'.[8] When *The Wilderness of Zin* was finished in October, he could stand the waiting no longer, and applied to his mentor David Hogarth to get him a war job. Hogarth was having trouble finding suitable war employment for himself, but managed to insinuate Lawrence into MO4, the Geographical Department of Military Intelligence, whose chief, Colonel Coote Hedley, sat with him on the council of the Royal Geographical Society. Fortunately, Hedley had heard something of Lawrence's ability through Stewart Newcombe, and the Palestine Exploration Fund, and took him on to help put together a large-scale map of Sinai, which existed in sixty-eight sheets in manuscript form. Hedley's instructions to Lawrence were brusque: 'You go down,' he said, 'and see what you can do with the damned thing!'⁹ The fact that Lawrence had seen only a small part of northern Sinai on the Negev survey did not deter him, and the same night he had produced a map six yards square, some of which was accurate, and some of which, he admitted, he invented. Hedley evidently succumbed to Lawrence's apparent omniscience, for when, a few days later, Hogarth inquired if he had found the young man of any use, Hedley replied: 'He's running my entire department for me now.'¹⁰ He might have added that Lawrence *was* the department, since all the other map officers had been sent to France. Lawrence himself was still a civilian, however, and this fact became contentious when he was sent to take some maps to a senior officer, General Rawlinson, who, on seeing the 'little pipsqueak' in mufti, turned apoplectic and roared, 'I want to speak to an officer!'¹¹ Hedley quickly put this right by recommending Lawrence for a commission without even a medical examination. He was soon appointed as a 'Temporary second-lieutenant interpreter', and he bought his uniform off the peg from the Army and Navy Stores the following day.

In February 1914, while Lawrence and Woolley had been wandering about the Negev, Sharif 'Abdallah, second son of Hussain, Emir of Mecca, had arrived in Cairo for a visit to the Egyptian Sultan. He was no longer the inexperienced youth who had landed from the *Tanta* at Jeddah in 1908, but had spent his adolescent years hardening himself to the saddle, riding with Hussain's Bedu levies, and, with his brothers 'Ali and Feisal, carrying out punitive raids against recalcitrant tribes, and fighting in the 'Assir in the name of the Turks. Highly astute, popular among the Arabs, Sharif 'Abdallah was reckoned by many to be the true power in the Hejaz. Now, he was on his way to Istanbul to complain to officials of the Ottoman Government, who had just announced a new system of local administration. Known as the Vilayet system, it was intended to cut out traditional Arab leaders like his father, Hussain, who since 1908 had steadily been gathering power among the Bedu tribes. To install this new system, the Porte was determined to extend the Hejaz railway from its present terminus at Medina to the Emir's seat at Mecca, and a hardline governor named Vehib Bey had already been dispatched from Istanbul with seven battalions of infantry and a regiment of artillery to help carry the job out. If the railway was completed, 'Abdallah knew, it would mean the end of his family's power in the Hejaz for ever.

The Hejaz railway had reached Medina in 1908, the year in which the Hashemites had returned to Mecca, but at that time Sharif Hussain had preferred to travel by ship, partly because Medina had then been under siege by certain Bedu tribes. It was, nevertheless, a triumph of Ottoman imperial vision and German precision engineering, crossing 800 miles of deserts and arid hills which for millennia had lain silent but for the tread of men and pack animals – a steel road, symmetrical, shining and alien. Designed by Meissner Pasha – a German engineer of insuperable drive and genius – it had been laid by a force of almost 6,000 Turkish soldiers, whose blood stained almost every mile of the track. With dogged fortitude, the Turks had swung their hammers, advancing slowly, suffering heat, thirst, hunger, flies and disease. There were great natural problems to contend with – vast wadis which had to be spanned by twenty-arched bridges: sandstone hogsbacks which had to be cut and blasted through. The track was in need of constant maintenance: the ballast of the embankments would subside and leave holes under the rails; drifting sand would block the culverts; floodwaters would fill them with detritus and wash the banks away; Bedu raiders would damage the tracks. The labourers worked in troops of twenty to fifty together, always armed, always with sentries posted in high places to warn them of the approach of Bedu parties. No Bedui was permitted to come near a station without permission upon threat of being shot down, and in the Hejaz almost every station was protected by a stone fort, each with its underground water-cistern, equipped with loopholes and steel shutters, and entangled by barbed wire. If the sentries spotted raiders approaching, they would give a signal to the working parties, who would jump aboard their trolleys and rush to the station. Sometimes they were attacked by the marauders before they could reach safety and cut down man by man: frequently they were obliged to hold out for several days. The Bedu were uncontrollable. They trusted no one and were constantly in arms against the government and against each other, yet they were united in their hatred for the railway, which had reduced the carrying trade, and enabled the Turks to strengthen their control in the Hejaz.

In January 1914, with the new Governor and his eight battalions on the way, Hussain had played his Bedu card swiftly. He mustered the Sheikhs of the tribes and informed them of Vehib's arrival and his objectives. 'The railway will ruin you completely,' he told them. '. . . Once the Turks can rush troops from one part of the Hejaz to the other, they will no longer need to pay gold to the Bedu.'[12] The tribes saw where their interests lay, and gave the Emir their assurance of support. When Vehib arrived he found chaos: the telephone wires had been cut by Bedu tribesmen and the towns were starving; raiders were plundering shops in Jeddah and attacking caravans; his chief of police had disappeared, kidnapped by Bedu tribesmen on the Pilgrim road. The Governor dispatched a desperate message to Istanbul, and for a moment it looked as if the Turks might send a punitive expedition by ship from Smyrna. In the event, though, they backed down and offered 'Abdallah 250,000 gold sovereigns to persuade his father to end the insurrection, promising in addition half the revenues of the railway once extended to Mecca. 'Abdallah realized astutely that once the railway had been completed such promises would be as solid as the wind.

Whether he had come to Cairo that February specifically in order to sound out the British attitude to Turkey is uncertain. He had already had in mind the prospect of fomenting a rebellion among Arab units in the Ottoman army in Syria and Mesopotamia and, with British diplomatic help, of securing first the independence of the Hejaz and then, perhaps, of a wider Arab state. It may or may not have been fortuitous that, at an official reception, 'Abdallah bumped into Lord Kitchener, British Agent, but *de facto* ruler of Egypt, whose concern in the Hejaz was with the safety of Indian pilgrims performing the Haj – the annual pilgrimage to Mecca and Medina. At their first meeting it was this subject which they discussed. The following day, though, 'Abdallah visited Kitchener and inquired tentatively what the attitude of Britain would be if a conflict should develop between the Hashemites and the Turks. Kitchener was circumspect. He himself already considered Turkey a prospective enemy which would threaten the crucial

Suez Canal in the event of war: this was, in fact, why he, an Englishman, was the effective power in Egypt – a country still technically a part of the Ottoman Empire. Officially, however, his hands were tied. He explained to 'Abdallah that Turkey was a friendly country which Britain had fought a war in the Crimea to protect. Britain was thus unlikely to intervene in any conflict between the Hejaz and the Sublime Porte.

In Istanbul, 'Abdallah's protests to the Committee of Union and Progress fell on deaf ears, and he returned to Cairo in April 1914 fuming at his reception. By now, however, the Porte's spies had got wind of his manoeuvres with the British and had dissuaded Kitchener from meeting him. Instead, 'Abdallah spoke to Ronald Storrs, Oriental Secretary to the British Agency, from whom he requested a consignment of machine guns for 'defence' against the Turks. Storrs replied that 'in principle' the British Empire's only interest in the Hejaz was the welfare of its pilgrims and repeated that Britain could not intervene. Secretly, though, Storrs was sympathetic, and by carefully chosen words intimated that Britain's answer was not in fact so final as it seemed. The two men liked each other: Storrs, the traditional British Orientalist – suave, vain, sophisticated, perhaps bisexual, a lover of fine art and music: 'Abdallah, the Arabian prince – worldly-wise, cultivated, truculent, highly popular, an incessant quoter of Arabic verse and lover of young boys. It was perhaps as these two highly intelligent representatives of their nations faced each other in the Abdin Palace that, in scarcely perceptible signs, hints and attitudes, the Arab Revolt was born.

It was not until that autumn, when Turkey's entry to the war seemed inevitable, that Kitchener was able to come out into the open. On 24 September he sent a cable from London, instructing Storrs to dispatch a secret and highly trustworthy messenger to 'Abdallah in the Hejaz to find out whether the Hashemites would be with or against the British in the event of war. Storrs commissioned a veteran Persian agent named 'Ali Asghar – known to posterity as 'Messenger X' – to go to Mecca disguised as a pilgrim. 'Ali left Suez on 5 October, reached Jeddah three days later, hired a donkey for £2 and, having ridden all night, arrived in the Holy City the following morning. After several days' wait, he managed to contact 'Abdallah. He arrived back in Cairo before the end of the month, with a message conveying a response Kitchener had not anticipated. He would have been happy had the

Arabs merely agreed to stay out of the war. Instead, to his surprise, 'Abdallah promised to remain neutral for the time being, but, with sufficient diplomatic support, 'to lead his immediate followers into armed revolt'.[13] The text was cabled to London on 29 October: the Ottoman Empire declared war formally on Britain two days later. By early December, Lawrence, Woolley and Newcombe had been posted to Cairo's General Staff.

10. Cairo is Unutterable Things

Cairo and Mesopotamia
1914–16

When the black and white taxi deposited me in Ezbekiyya Square, Cairo, I had some difficulty at first in spotting the Grand Continental Hotel. I suddenly realized that it was the dismal, mouldering heap opposite the Ezbekiyya Gardens, half hidden by a row of very drab shops. In the Bodleian Library in Oxford, I had seen a picture of the place as it had been in 1914, embossed on the head of a letter written by T. E. Lawrence, and it was difficult to equate this mildewed tenement before me with that great colonial château whose guest-list – A. & C. Black's guidebook for 1916 had assured me – once read like a page out of the *Almanac de Gotha*. That grand world of Egypt's *belle époque*, when Cairo had been a fashionable winter resort rivalling Nice and Monte Carlo, was lost, hidden like the hotel itself beneath the seedy façade of a hectic modern city. In the dark lobby, a fly-blown man with a two-day stubble showed brown teeth when I pressed him for the price of a room: 'This place hasn't been a hotel in ten years,' he said. In what had been the Front Desk Manager's office – a place of peeling paint and faded velvet upholstery – a wizened man called Khalid groped in some filing cabinets and brought out a colour postcard of the hotel as it had looked ten years previously: precisely as neglected as it looked now, I thought. 'They said it was beyond repair,' he told me. 'They couldn't use it as a hotel any more, so they turned it into offices.' There was no chance of me seeing the rooms upstairs, he said, but he would show me the downstairs area, and, fetching a great ring of keys, he led me like a gaoler across the lobby and unlocked a steel flange nailed across the dining-room doors. The room was astonishingly vast, with a plush carpet, once wine-red, perhaps, but now faded and rotten and covered in rat-droppings and bits of plaster fallen from the ceiling. 'I was a bellboy here in the old days,' Khalid said. 'Kings and

Princes used to come from all over the world. It was the best hotel in Egypt.' He showed me the fine frescos of ancient Egyptian gods and Pharaohs which adorned the walls. 'Italian artist,' he said. 'Done more than a hundred years ago.' Lawrence must have known them well, I thought, for the Grand Continental had been his base for nine months from 1914 to 1915, and he had taken breakfast, lunch and dinner in this room almost every day. In the lobby, you could see the remains of a travel-agent's kiosk, a worn-out sign announcing Nile cruises, and a jeweller's shop, and Khalid showed me what had been the bar – though all that was left were the mirror-mosaic shelves where the bottles would have been on display. 'Here they had whisky,' he said, and I imagined the great and good of Cairo in 1914 – Ronald Storrs, Bertie Clayton, George Lloyd, Aubrey Herbert, Stewart Newcombe and others – nursing their drinks and turning over in their eminently civilized heads their dreams of Empire, their dreams of the Arab Revolt.

I walked out of the lobby into yellow sunlight and a swell of traffic, and trudged around the perimeter of the Ezbekiyya Gardens, which stood directly opposite the hotel. They had been closed to the public ever since a girl had been raped there in broad daylight, Khalid had informed me. Through the railings, the gardens looked faded and unkempt, but on 15 December 1914, when T. E. Lawrence took up his quarters in the Grand Continental, they were the showpiece of the city, bursting with exotic shrubs such as Australian beefwood, Madagascan flame and Cuban royal palm. Lawrence found Cairo very much alive. Though war with Turkey had been declared two months earlier, the news had done nothing to diminish the appeal of its winter season, and the frenzied circuit of receptions, masked balls, dinner parties, picnics, gymkhanas, race meetings and tennis parties went on unabated. The high points of the season were the glittering galas orchestrated at the Sultan Hussain Kamil's Abdin Palace, and at the British Residency at Qasr ad-Dubbara, where Sir Hugh Mc-Mahon had recently succeeded Lord Kitchener as British Agent. There were other gaieties and amusements aplenty for the gentleman with time on his hands. He might play a round of golf or even some polo at the Khedivial Sporting Club on Zamalek island, sip coffee at two piastres a cup at Groppi's or the Café Egyptien, quaff Bass ale at the Savoy Buffet, ogle the prohibited but no less *risqué* performance of

Ghawazi dancing-girls at the Eldorado, join a moonlit donkey-ride to the Pyramids at Giza, or enjoy a comfortable weekend's snipe-shooting in the Nile delta.

Imminent war had lent a certain dash to the figures of British officers residing in elegant hotels such as the Continental and Shepheard's, and eligible subalterns were much in demand among wintering débutantes. After dark, dozens of stiff-backed young men in tailored uniforms and highly polished Sam Browne belts and boots, with forage-caps worn at the regulation angle, would float like peacocks through Ezbekiyya. Second-Lieutenant Lawrence did not appear to belong among these magnificent editions of British manhood. Small, long-haired, dishevelled, he was so far from possessing a military bearing that he rarely looked at anyone directly in the eye. Indeed, he claimed that he would not even recognize his own mother if she arrived unexpectedly, and had perfected the art of talking for twenty minutes without revealing that he had no idea whom he was talking to. Certainly, he did not emulate the sartorial style of his military peers. His trousers were slack and unpressed, his buttons unpolished, his pockets usually undone, his Sam Browne belt, if worn at all, was worn loose and dangling. He often wore the insignia of different ranks on either shoulder-strap, so that it was impossible to tell at any given moment whether he was a humble Second-Lieutenant or an unlikely-looking Lieutenant-Colonel. His cap was worn askew, with his straw-coloured hair protruding from beneath, and was not even graced with a badge – the ultimate snub to military convention, and the visible expression of his conviction that he was a 'civilian in uniform'. In place of carefully bulled boots he wore patent-leather evening shoes, and a blood red tie instead of a khaki one. His future commanding officer in the Hejaz, Lieutenant-Colonel Pierce Joyce, would later write of his first encounter with Lawrence that he recalled only 'the intense desire on my part to tell him to get his hair cut and that his uniform and dirty buttons sadly needed the attention of his batman'.[1] His lack of cap-badge led him into difficulties for which he seemed to have a bizarre relish. Once, while attempting to cash a cheque at Messrs Cox and Co. in Cairo, for instance, the manager inquired as to his unit. 'Haven't got one,' Lawrence replied, without elaborating. The manager then had the Army List brought. 'Don't trouble yourself,' Lawrence told him, 'my name is not on it, but I *should* like to have my cheque cashed.' Finally, as Lawrence refused to produce any references, the manager regretted that he would have to cable to Britain before he could cash the cheque.[2]

Lawrence tended to saunter rather than march, and ignored all salutes given to him as assiduously as he ignored his superior officers, speaking to everyone, whether senior or junior in rank, in the same matter-of-fact, studious, eccentric, pedantic Oxford tones. He gave the impression, carefully cultivated, in fact, of being a misplaced and absent-minded Oxford don who had somehow drifted into military uniform, and actually referred to the Intelligence Department as 'the faculty'. He made no secret of his disdain for regular army officers, for red-tape military bureaucrats and for public-school hunting-shooting-and-fishing hearties, though he still took a certain snobbish pride in telling his mother that he was working alongside 'Lord Anglesey, Lord Hartington and Prince Alexander of Battenburg'.[3]

His eccentric appearance belied his incisive mind, however, and he vowed to end incompetence. Put in charge of all maps supplied to GHQ by the Survey of Egypt, he determined to go through map-production like a dose of salts. The topography of many theatres of the war was little known, and place-names were spelled in a wild variety of different ways, many of them bearing little relation to the way they were pronounced by natives. Although Lawrence knew that there was no foolproof system of transliterating Arabic, and would later take great pride in spelling Arabic names 'anyhow', he recognized that a consistent scheme must be developed which bore some resemblance to the actual pronunciation. He lost no time in criticizing the Survey's transliteration system to the Director of the Reproduction Office, W. H. Crosthwaite, who had himself invented it. He similarly affronted W. M. Logan, Director of the Map Compilation Office, who objected strongly to being bossed about by this impudent little upstart. Ernest Dowson, Director of the Survey, recalled, however, that 'it was not only the pompous, the inefficient and the pretentious whose cooperation Lawrence's ways tended to alienate. Many men of sense and ability were repelled by the impudence, freakishness and frivolity he trailed so provocatively.'[4] Cairo was very far in spirit from Carchemish, where Lawrence had been one of only two Europeans in a vast area, a sort of unofficial consul, a local employer and a man of great consequence. He was suddenly aware, perhaps, that the game he was playing here was a much bigger one, and with his instinctive feelings of inadequacy and low self-esteem, he was seeking desperately to establish himself in a position. He stood aloof from the social whirl, and was definitely not one of those to be found decorating the bar-stools in the Continental: he was not teetotal, he said, but merely lacked the sociability to enjoy a cosy drink. He had always felt ill at ease with the Egyptians, but his few forays into the streets now convinced him that they actually hated their British overlords. 'Cairo is unutterable things,' he wrote after settling in. 'I took a day off last month and went and looked at it: no more: – and to think that – this folly apart – one might have been living on that mound in the bend in the Euphrates, in a clean place, with decent people not far off. I wonder if one will ever settle down again and take an interest in proper things.'[5]

In February 1915 Lawrence's racing bicycle arrived from England, and he would cycle to work every morning from the Continental to GHQ in the Old Savoy Hotel, which stood in what is today Talaat Harb Square, on a site now occupied by a department store. The Intelligence Department to which he had been posted was directed by his friend Stewart Newcombe, and consisted to begin with of only three other officers: Leonard Woolley and two Unionist MPs recently drafted in, George Lloyd and Aubrey Herbert. Despite congenial stories which later emerged about 'The Five Musketeers', there were two factions in the office from the start, for Newcombe, Lawrence and Woolley knew each other well from the Negev survey, while Lloyd and Herbert were both Welshmen, both old Etonians, and had both served as Honorary Attachés to the British Embassy in Constantinople. They were Oriental dabblers of the Hogarth stamp, speaking a dozen languages between them, and Herbert already had a reputation as an adventurer, having fought alongside the Turks in the Balkans and in Yemen. A younger son of the Earl of Carnarvon, he was later immortalized as John Buchan's Sandy Arbuthnot in *Greenmantle*: 'You will hear of him at little forgotten fishing ports where the Albanian mountains dip to the Adriatic. If you struck a Meccan pilgrimage the odds are you would meet a dozen of Sandy's friends in it. In shepherd's huts in the Caucasus you will find bits of his cast off clothing, for he has a knack of shedding garments as he goes.'[6] Lawrence was both attracted and repelled by the self-assured, dilettantish aristocrat, and thought him 'quaint' and 'a joke, but a very nice one'.[7] Herbert reciprocated Lawrence's half-admiring, half-deprecating attitude, call-

ing him 'gnomish' and 'half-cad', but admitting that he had a touch
of genius. Lloyd, who divided his time between his constituents, the
East, and his work as director of a bank, was another upper-class
Welshman whom Lawrence found 'exceedingly noisy' but valued for
his knowledge of trade and politics, and his air of confidence. He
remained in touch with Lloyd after he and Herbert left for Gallipoli
and travelled with him later in the campaign. Both Lloyd and Herbert
were uncomfortable with Newcombe, however, and objected to taking
orders from this highly intelligent and able, but sadly 'underbred'
Sapper. Lawrence's view was different: 'Newcombe is . . . a most
heavenly person,' he wrote. 'He runs all the spies, & curses all the
subordinates who don't do their duty and takes the raw edges off
generals and things. Without that I should have gone mad, I think.'[8]
Newcombe's immediate superior was the *éminence grise* of Middle East
intelligence, Lieutenant-Colonel Gilbert 'Bertie' Clayton, a veteran of
the Egyptian army, who had fought the Dervishes at Omdurman
beside Lord Kitchener. Clayton was the archetypal grey man: quiet
and unassuming, he was, as Lawrence discovered, 'far bigger . . . than
[he] appeared at first sight'. Before the war he had served as Sudan
Agent in Cairo, and Intelligence Director to the Sirdar or C-in-C of
the Egyptian Army, Sir Reginald Wingate – who doubled as Governor-
General of the Sudan. In 1914, he had been brought back into the
army by General Sir John Maxwell, the General Officer Commanding
British Forces in Egypt, who had given him *carte blanche* to run intelligence operations. Clayton's position was all-powerful, and he took it
upon himself not only to gather intelligence but also to nudge policy
judiciously where he felt it was required. Even before war with Turkey
had been declared, Clayton had received Storrs's suggestion of raising
an Arab Revolt with enthusiasm, and was an early supporter of the
Hashemites. He had sent a letter to Kitchener early in 1914 urging an
immediate approach to Hussain. Lawrence later confessed admiration
for Clayton's far-sightedness and detachment and particularly for the
free hand he gave to his subordinates, yet his description of his influence,
'like water or permeating oil, creeping silently and insistently through
everything', is not entirely flattering.[9] Lawrence also got to know Storrs
well, and the two men found each other convivial company. They
shared literary tastes, and Storrs would often return to his flat to find
Lawrence already there, curled up in an armchair reading Latin or

Greek: 'I found him from the beginning an arresting and intentionally provocative talker,' Storrs recalled, 'liking nonsense to be treated as nonsense and not casually or dully accepted or dismissed. He could flare into sudden anger at a story of pettiness, particularly official pettiness or injustice.'[10] Lawrence later admitted that he thought Storrs the most brilliant Englishman in the Middle East, but commented that his influence would have been even greater had he been more single-minded. Storrs was sometimes irritated by Lawrence's lack of social etiquette, recalling that he had once arranged a special dinner party of four guests for Lawrence, who had failed to turn up without offering any excuse: 'He only told me long afterwards,' Storrs wrote, 'that I had more than "got back at him" by explaining that I shouldn't have minded if he had warned me in time to get someone else.'[11]

Lawrence referred to himself as 'bottle washer and office boy pencil sharpener and pen wiper' of the department, but in fact, though the most junior officer in rank, he shared fully in the work. The *raison d'être* for the British presence in Egypt was the defence of the Suez Canal, and opinion was divided as to how this should best be accomplished. There were those 'Westerners' who believed that the Western Front in Europe was the 'real' war, and an active campaign in any other theatre merely a 'sideshow'. They lobbied for a purely defensive policy in Egypt, a policy which Lawrence, like the rest of the Intelligence Department, actively contested. They were 'Easterners', who believed that attack was the best means of defence and pushed for a British invasion of the Ottoman Empire, specifically a landing at Alexandretta on the coast of Syria. Lawrence, who was later to claim falsely that the Alexandretta scheme was his idea, was certainly one of its most passionate advocates. He believed that the moment the British landed in Syria, the Syrians would revolt against the Turks, and Arab elements in the Ottoman armies would mutiny, establishing an Arab government there before the French, who had designs in Syria, could prevent them. Lawrence had scented revolution in the air while at Carchemish in 1913, and well knew that the ordinary Syrians were not prepared to get rid of one foreign master merely to make way for another and even more alien one. Though the Alexandretta landing proposal was well received by the cabinet, it was vetoed by the French, who recognized as well as Lawrence the dangers it entailed for their colonial policy. Soon it was eclipsed by plans for a mass landing at Gallipoli, and Lawrence turned his attention to the Assir, the mountainous and fertile region of Arabia which lay immediately south of the Hejaz. The Porte held little sway in this remote corner of Arabia, and the Assir's ruler, al-Idrisi, was a notorious opponent of the Turks. In February, the Anglo-Indian Government concluded a treaty with al-Idrisi, paying him a stipend of £7,000 per year, and for a while Lawrence nurtured high hopes that his followers would revolt against the Turks and carry the revolution north in the name of the Emir of Mecca: 'I think Newcombe & myself are going down to [Qunfidhdha – in the Assir] as his advisers,' he wrote. 'If Idrisi is anything like as good as we hope we can rush right up to Damascus, & biff the French out of all hope of Syria. It's a big game and at last one worth playing.'[12] Al-Idrisi proved a damp squib, however, and as for the Emir of Mecca himself, throughout the first part of 1915 he had maintained an ominous silence.

In late 1914, an Indian youth had been arrested by the British authorities while attempting to cross the North West Frontier from Afghanistan and India. Sewn into the seams of his clothing were pieces of linen which carried the details of a world-wide plot to raise an Islamic Jihad or Holy War against Britain, France and Russia, the powers of the Triple Entente. The youth was the emissary of an Indian renegade called Barakat Allah, an agent of the Turkish government in Kabul, and had been on his way to meet contacts in India, who were to encourage Indian troops in the British army to mutiny, assassinate their foreign leaders and attack their quarters. He was, it turned out, just one of thousands of agents, preachers, scholars, holy men, spies and agitators being dispatched by the Committee of Union and Progress to infiltrate India, Persia, Egypt, Afghanistan, Arabia, Mesopotamia, the Libyan desert and the Sudan. The Jihad plot was intended to set the Islamic world ablaze. On 7 November, only a week after the declaration of war, the Sheikh al-Islam – the highest religious official in the Ottoman Empire – had declared the *fatwa*, making it the personal duty of every Muslim to take up arms against the Allies. A central tenet of the Jihad, though, was the protection of the Holy Cities, Mecca and Medina, and without the blessing of their steward, Sharif Hussain, the *fatwa* was a worthless scrap of paper.

His blessing Hussain had refused staunchly to give. In November he had written to Enver Pasha, Ottoman Minister of War, that he would support the Jihad with all his heart and pray for its success, but he could not endorse it openly for fear that the British Red Sea fleet would immediately launch a blockade. The population of the Hejaz was dependent on grain imported from British India, and its people would eventually be faced with famine, and might even – he suggested – revolt against Ottoman rule. He paid lip service to the Porte to the extent of raising a force of *mujahidiyyin* – Islamic volunteers – but simultaneously contacted the great chiefs of the Arabian Peninsula: Ibn Sa'ud of the Nejd, Ibn Rashid of the Shammar, the Imam Yahya of Yemen, and al-Idrisi of the Assir, in great secrecy, explaining why he had failed to support the Jihad, and eliciting their attitude towards the Turks. Of these, Ibn Sa'ud, who was receiving a substantial stipend from the Anglo-Indian Government, resolved to stay neutral and watch the outcome. His rival Ibn Rashid – who feared him – decided consequently to throw in his lot with the Turks. The Imam Yahya, facing the British in Aden, did the same, and al-Idrisi, now receiving a cash incentive from Britain, had always been implacably anti-Turk. Jamal Pasha, Military Governor of Syria as well as Commander-in-Chief of Turkish forces there, was preparing the Ottoman 4th Army for an assault on the Suez Canal. The attack was scheduled for February 1915, and the CUP hoped it would spark off a revolt by the Egyptians against their infidel masters, the British. That Hussain refused to play his part in stirring up his co-religionists infuriated them, and although they were powerless but to accept his refusal officially, they decided to get rid of him secretly by assassination or arrest. Unfortunately, the principal of the plot, Vehib Pasha – Governor of the Hejaz – mysteriously lost a trunk containing compromising documents, which was handed to 'Ali, Hussain's eldest son. The Sharif now had first-hand proof of the Machiavellian duplicity which lay beneath the Porte's assurances that the Hejaz railway was the only bone of contention between them. He decided to send his third son, Feisal, to Istanbul to confront the CUP with the evidence of its own calumny. Meanwhile, he was able to take some comfort from the fact that the Hashemites were not entirely alone.

In January, an Arab officer who was to be attached to his personal bodyguard, Fawzi al-Bakri, a young member of a prominent merchant clan of Damascus which had long enjoyed cordial relations with the Hashemites, had brought a verbal message from al-Fatat, a secret

Arab nationalist society in Syria. The message, which Fawzi had whispered into the Sharif's ear as he sat gazing imperturbably out of the window of his palace in Mecca, was that nationalist leaders in Syria and Iraq, including certain Arab officers in the Turkish army, were in favour of a revolt against the Turks for Arab independence, and invited Hussain to be its leader. The cautious Sharif, secretly gratified, made no immediate reply, but, on Feisal's departure for Istanbul, charged him to halt in Damascus for the purpose of hearing the proposals of al-Fatat. Feisal arrived in Damascus later that month and courteously turned down an invitation from Jamal Pasha, staying instead at the al-Bakri clan's farmhouse outside the city. It was here, under the watchful eye of Nasib al-Bakri, Fawzi's elder brother, that Feisal was initiated into the secrets of the Syrian Nationalist Societies, al-Fatat and al-'Ahd. The result, which Feisal collected the following month on his way back to the Hejaz, was the famous 'Damascus Protocol', a document specifying the frontiers of a possible independent Arab state after the war, proposing the abolition of all privileges granted to foreigners, but advocating a defensive alliance with Great Britain and the future independent Arab state.[13] In mid-July, having discussed the Damascus Protocol with his sons and advisers, Hussain felt strong enough to act. His terms for Arab intervention in the war against Turkey reached the High Commissioner in Cairo, Sir Hugh McMahon, by secret emissary, on 18 August.

1915 had been a bad year for the British Empire and for Lawrence personally. In January, twelve British and four French capital ships led by HMS *Queen Elizabeth* – the biggest warship ever seen in Mediterranean waters – had attempted to force the straits of the Dardanelles. After only a day's battle, the entire fleet had been sent packing by 176 Turkish guns dug in on the peninsula, only four of which had been put out of action. It was the swansong of the myth of British naval supremacy: Britannia no longer ruled the waves. At the end of April, the British had launched a massive amphibious landing at Gallipoli, where Medforce – the first of almost 200,000 Allied troops to be landed on its beaches – was cut to ribbons by Turkish artillery and machine-gun fire. Medforce had been expected to reach its objectives by the third day, but three months later it was still fighting desperately just to remain where it was. The failure of the Gallipoli landings was an appalling indictment of the inefficiency of British Intelligence, for, as even Lawrence admitted, Medforce was 'beastly ill-prepared, with no knowledge of where it was going, or what it would meet, or what it was going to do'.[14] Indeed, its maps were archaic, inaccurate, and of considerably less value than a copy of Baedeker: Lawrence recorded that the expedition 'came out with two copies of some quarter-inch maps of European Turkey as their sole supply'.[15] The element of surprise was completely missing, since security was non-existent, and as for assessment of enemy forces, no one even knew how many Turkish troops opposed it. In the end, no one believed it really mattered. Lawrence himself expressed the general air of complacency when, just before the landings, he wrote, 'Poor old Turkey is hanging together . . . Everything about her is very sick.'[16] The largest amphibious operation ever mounted in the history of war thus took place on the basis of virtually zero intelligence, and a vain belief in the superiority of the 'white man': after all, as one Australian infantryman wrote before the landing, 'Who was going to stop us? Not the bloody Turks!'[17] But the 'bloody Turks' did stop them, and not even the repulse of Jamal Pasha's assault on the Suez Canal in February could easily redeem that fact.

On the Western Front there was stalemate, and in May Lawrence received the distressing news that Frank had been killed by shellfire while leading his platoon. He wrote soothing letters to his parents, and to his brother Will maintained the appropriate 'stiff upper lip': 'Frank's death was as you say a shock, because it was so unexpected,' he wrote. 'I don't think one can regret it overmuch, because it was a very good way to take after all. The hugeness of this war has made one change one's perspective, I think, for one can hardly see details at all.'[18] He told his mother to keep a brave face to the world: '. . . we cannot all go fighting,' he wrote, 'but we can do that, which is in the same kind.'[19] Secretly, though, his conscience was pricked. Not for the first time, perhaps, he asked himself if it was right to go on enjoying a comfortable desk job, far from the fighting, when his peers were risking their lives at the front. Newcombe and Woolley had already served on the Western Front, and now Lloyd and Herbert were at Gallipoli. He valued his contribution to the war effort, and knew that his specialized knowledge would be wasted if he became mere 'cannon fodder', but he also knew at a deeper level that it was his lifelong terror of being hurt which was really keeping him from the front. Lawrence was far from being a hero by nature, and though his self-imposed ordeals had given him a certain nodding acquaintance with physical suffering, he still feared it more than anything. His life had been spent in escaping from conformity rather than in seeking action, and he found danger almost physically crippling: 'one reason that taught me I wasn't a man of action,' he wrote later, 'was [the] routine melting of bowels before a crisis.'[20] After the war, his brother Arnie would write that he was not a 'natural hero or naturally brave . . . and knowing this . . . he put himself through severe tests and overcame his natural weaknesses'.[21] George Lloyd thought him 'not in the least fearless like some who do brave things'.[22] In the summer of 1915, there seemed little to justify his existence. His plans for the Alexandretta landing and for the al-Idrisi revolt had fallen though: 'Arabian affairs have gone all to pot,' he wrote. 'I've never seen a more despicable mess made of a show. It makes one howl with fury – for we had a ripping chance there.'[23] All efforts were bent towards success at Gallipoli, in which he could play little part, and he kept himself busy in writing geographical digests and reports for the High Command, tracking the movements of Turkish forces, and periodically interviewing Syrian prisoners of war. Though he prided himself on being able to pinpoint the districts they came from merely by their dialects, hard intelligence on Syria and Palestine remained poor. He rumbled periodically on a borrowed motorbike between the Savoy and Bulaq, where the Survey offices were situated. He wandered disconsolately in the bazaar, buying the occasional carpet for his family and the odd Hittite seal for Hogarth, who was still struggling to find a war job. He had dinner with Lady Evelyn Cobbold, who had lent him money at Petra. He enciphered and deciphered telegrams, supervised the printing, packing and dispatch of maps, and made more abortive and inappropriate plans for attacks on Syria. He read *The Greek Anthology*, Hérédia and William Morris. Woolley was sent to provide liaison with the French navy at Port Sa'id, and the Department was augmented by Philip Graves, a former correspondent of *The Times*: other personnel came and went like passing ghosts. Lawrence went on a brief excursion to improve liaison with the Intelligence office in Athens, but on his return he felt even more weighed down by what he called 'official inertia'. He began to toy with the idea of going up to Gallipoli: he wondered, even, if life would be better in a trench. Cairo was hot, dusty and squalid, and Lawrence summed up his feelings when he told Hogarth: 'Everything is going to sleep . . .'[24]

Into this atmosphere of almost palpable lethargy, Sharif Hussain's letter dropped like a bombshell. Storrs, who went over the missive line by line, was astonished to see that the Sharif was demanding virtually the whole of the Arab dominions of the Ottoman Empire in return for Arab help: he could hardly believe Hussain's effrontery, and found himself murmuring as he read it:

> In matters of commerce the fault of the Dutch
> Is offering too little and asking too much.[25]

For all Kitchener's flaunting of a Caliphate, Sharif Hussain was actually regarded by the British as a minor Arab chieftain, who represented no one but his own family, the Hashemites, and should, in their view, have been well pleased with independence and autonomy for the Hejaz. Storrs was highly amused by the message, whose pretensions, he felt, 'bordered on the tragic-comic' – he could only believe it was a preposterous opening gambit in a process of bargaining such as one might hear in the bazaar: '. . . it may be regarded as certain,' he wrote, 'that [the Sharif] has no sort of mandate from other potentates . . . and that he knows he is demanding, possibly as a basis for negotiation, far more than he has the right, the hope, or the power to expect.'[26] As a result, McMahon's reply – composed by Storrs and dispatched on 30 August – was non-committal. He merely confirmed Kitchener's original assurances, but refused to be drawn on the issue of frontiers, stating that it was a waste of time to discuss such things under the stress of war. Hussain answered almost immediately, expressing amazement at British hesitation: the negotiations, he wrote, depended solely and fundamentally on whether or not they accepted the proposed borders.

By the time this second note reached Cairo in September, however, the situation had changed. In that month a young Arab officer called Mohammad Sharif al-Faruqi had slipped through the Turkish lines at Gallipoli under the pretext of leading a burial party, and defected to the British. Sent to Cairo, he was interrogated by Lawrence among others, and what he had to say astonished them. Al-Faruqi was an Arab from Iraq, and claimed to be a descendant of the third 'Right Minded' Khalif of the Muslims, Omar, whose nickname had been al-Faruq – 'The Divider'. He was, he said, a member of al-'Ahd, the secret society of Arab officers in the Turkish army, which with its sister society, al-Fatat, had devised the Damascus Protocol on which Hussain's demands were based. Although al-Faruqi was not the official spokesman for al-'Ahd the British at first believed him to be, he revealed a great deal about the aims and organization of the nationalist secret societies in Syria that neither Lawrence nor his colleagues had been aware of. To the delight of Clayton and Lawrence, he confirmed that the Sharif did, indeed, speak for more than just the Hashemites.

Nevertheless, McMahon was unable to concede all that the Sharif asked, since the French, with whom his government were about to enter an agreement over the fate of Syria, already considered the western portion of the country to be rightfully theirs. In his next letter he agreed to Hussain's proposals with certain exceptions, including the districts west of Aleppo, Hama, Homs and Damascus which he claimed – almost certainly with Lawrence's prompting – were not 'purely Arab'. These areas – the Syrian littoral and its hinterland, which formed parts of the Ottoman Sanjaq of Lebanon and Vilayet of Beirut – were claimed by Britain's French allies and had been earmarked as regions of possible French interest in a report made by Lawrence himself earlier that year. Hussain replied that he could not accept that these districts were not wholly Arab, and once again the negotiations faltered over French demands. It was, Lawrence commented, not the Turks but the French who were the real enemy in Syria.

The nights grew cooler in Cairo, but there appeared no light at the end of the tunnel. At the same time, it was becoming horribly clear that the Gallipoli operation had failed: 'I don't like the look of things up there,' Lawrence wrote, 'and the worst is, it was such an easy business till we blundered.'[27] He was brightened temporarily when Hogarth arrived, still looking for a job, but after his friend went off to Athens he became feverish with malaria for the first time in a year. 'Official inertia' had set in once more, and Lawrence confessed that he had 'the nausea of it'.[28] Though his days were full, they were monotonously similar. Newcombe was posted to Gallipoli and replaced by Colonel A. C. Parker, a nephew of Kitchener's, who had once been Governor of Sinai. Parker was highly regarded by the Bedu, who knew him as *Barkal* – the absence of a title such as 'Bey' or 'Pasha' denoting their affection. He had a reputation for being a tireless camel-rider and an indefatigable walker, who would track sand-grouse through impossible country as nimbly as an ibex. Lawrence, who may have found himself slightly jealous of Parker's reputation, thought him knowledgeable about Sinai, and very little else, and threatened to 'murder' him one day. His despondency increased when, at the end of October, he received the news that Will, an observer in the Royal Flying Corps, had been shot down and lost on the Western Front: 'I'm rather low,' he wrote Edward Leeds, 'because first one, and now another of my brothers has been killed . . . they were both younger than I am and it doesn't seem right, somehow, that I should go on living peacefully in Cairo . . . I wish one might have an end sometime.'[29] All winter the negotiations with Hussain staggered on interminably, while the situation at Gallipoli went from bad to worse. Finally, in January 1916, the shattered remains of Medforce was evacuated from the Dardanelles. This was a dangerous moment for the British Empire. Not only had she been humiliated by 'the bloody Turks' before the eyes of the world, but thousands of Ottoman troops were now free to launch an invasion of Egypt with renewed brio. Already the Arabs were wavering, and the inconclusive bargaining between McMahon and Sharif Hussain had only exacerbated the situation. Both the Sharif and the Syrian Nationalists were suspicious of European encroachment in the East, and now it was beginning to look as if the Allies were less than a match – in military terms even – for the Ottoman Turks. In the Libyan Desert an Islamic Fundamentalist group, the Senussi brotherhood, were gathering silently, awaiting only the opportunity to strike at Egypt from the west. On the frontiers of the Sudan there was trouble from the pro-Turkish Sultan, 'Ali Dinar. If the Arabs in Syria and the Hejaz joined the Turks instead of rebelling against them, British ambitions in the Middle East might well be lost.

Then, on New Year's Day 1916, Sharif Hussain made a supreme gesture of his faith in British 'decency', and informed McMahon that he would waive a full discussion of the frontier until after the hostilities. It was a courageous but politically fatal act, which would later lead to accusations that he had 'sold out' to the Allies. Near the end of his life, he would tell historian George Antonius that his experience of British straightness in international affairs had impressed him deeply as a young man, and he had developed a 'solid belief in English standards of honourable dealing'. Having received McMahon's promise on the fundamental question of the area of Arab independence, he was willing to let secondary considerations ride for the time being, trusting implicitly that the British government's word was its bond.[30] His faith was sadly misplaced. A few weeks after McMahon had concluded his agreement with the Hashemites in February 1916, the British government signed the Sykes–Picot agreement with France and Russia, cynically carving up the Middle East between them in the event of a victory to the Triple Entente. By then, however, the General Staff in Cairo were already deeply distracted by another disaster in the making. In Mesopotamia, the 6th Indian Division under Major-General Sir Charles Townshend lay stranded and starving on a loop in the Tigris river at the village of Kut, where the British Empire faced the most humiliating surrender in the entire history of its arms.

It might almost have been a scene from the glorious annals of *Pax Britannica* – of redcoats, jammed Gatling guns and broken squares and the desert running with blood. Certainly, Townshend had been remembering the valiant days of his defence of Chitral, when he had told his men: 'It is our duty to our Empire, to our beloved King and Country to stand here and hold the Turkish advance . . . we will make this a defence to be remembered in history as a glorious one.' But Imperial glory was in short ration by that spring. Indeed, it was the ineptitude of Townshend himself and two other British commanders which had led to the impasse in the first place. His Division had originally been ordered only to protect the British oil refinery at Abadan and to prevent any threat to British shipping in the Gulf. In the event, goaded on by his superiors, Generals Beauchamp Duff in India and Sir John Nixon in Basra, Sir Charles had found himself euphorically chasing Turkish battalions up the Tigris. The enemy units had simply melted away, until, at Ctesiphon, he had met his nemesis in the form of 20,000 well-trained and determined Osmanli veterans. The Division had sustained 4,000 casualties before being forced to retire. If Townshend had then withdrawn tactically all the way back to the British HQ in Basra, the bulk of his men might still have been saved. Incredibly, he had chosen instead to make a 'heroic' stand at Kut, where he had immediately been surrounded by the Turks.

For five months they held out against the 20,000 troops who daily bombarded the town, sniping at any soldier unwise enough to show himself, and lobbing bombs from an old howitzer which the Tommies, with characteristic gallows-humour, christened 'Fanny'. Three times a relief column of the British Tigris Corps from Basra tried to smash its way through the Turkish blockade, and three times the Turks threw it back with appalling losses. Almost daily, aircraft of the Royal Flying Corps droned over the grid of streets in a vain attempt to drop supplies of flour and sugar, most of which either splashed into the Tigris or fell to the Turks. By April even the dogs and cats had been eaten, and the troops were being issued with opium pills to relieve the effects of hunger. The men, lethargic, dispirited and famished, had begun to give up hope.

By the time Lawrence arrived in Mesopotamia, more than 20,000 men had already been killed or injured in vain attempts to relieve the garrison. The British could not go on indefinitely feeding their soldiers into the furnace – they simply did not have the men. The question, then, was how to save Kut without wasting the lives of thousands more. To the British military hierarchy, any strategy other than the sledgehammer frontal attack seemed inconceivable. They had failed even to encircle the Turkish units investing the town, leaving open their lines of communication and supply. The solution to the problem of Kut required an obliqueness of thought of which the generals were incapable. It required a subtle and ingenious mind, unhampered by the conventions of the hereditary British warrior-class. It required such a mind as T. E. Lawrence possessed.

Despite his lack of war experience, Lawrence was confident of his ability to solve the problem. His superiors must have had confidence in him too. He had been sent to Basra with a letter of introduction from High Commissioner McMahon, stating that he was under orders from the War Office to lend his services in regard to Arab matters. 'He is one of the best of our very able intelligence staff here,' the letter ran, 'and has a thorough knowledge of the Arab question in all its bearings.'[31] If the Arab tribes of the Hai and the Euphrates could be raised in revolt, Lawrence believed, then the garrison at Kut could be saved without the wholesale butchery which had marked its progress so far. Should this fail, though, Lawrence and Aubrey Herbert – who had been brought back especially for the assignment – were authorized to offer a selected Turkish general a bribe of £1 million (later increased to £2 million) to let Townshend's division go.

Lawrence disembarked at Basra, where he ran into several old friends from his Carchemish days, including Gertrude Bell and Camp-bell-Thompson – who were both serving in the Basra Intelligence Department under Sir Percy Cox – and Hubert Young, the Arabic-speaking officer who had helped him mould gargoyles for the roof of the Expedition House in 1913. Young, who had liked Lawrence on their first meeting, was on this occasion utterly disappointed in him: 'He seemed to me thoroughly spoilt,' Young wrote, 'and posing in a way that was quite unlike what I remembered . . . It was then that I first noticed his anti-regular soldier complex and . . . resented it hotly.'[32] If Young's resentment is understandable, so is Lawrence's: on the Western Front, at Gallipoli and now in Mesopotamia, regular soldiers had already squandered thousands of innocent lives – those of his brothers among them. Lawrence began to scour Basra for Arab con-tacts. He had been hoping to meet Sayid Taleb of the Pan-Arab party, but found he was out of the country. On 7 April he met Sulayman Fayzi, a Basra notable and former associate of Sayid Taleb, who had been a member of the Ottoman Parliament. Fayzi recalled that Lawrence had begun by saying that he liked the Arabs and wished them success. Britain was intent on giving them independence, he continued, but could do so only if the Arabs revolted against the Turks. 'The British have authorised me to initiate this revolt,' Lawrence told him, 'and to offer what it may need in money and arms . . . I have selected you to perform the task of sparking the fire of the revolt.'[33] Fayzi replied that he could not raise a revolt since he was not a tribal chief. 'With money you could do wonders,' Lawrence told him. 'You could pitch a great many tents, employ many guards and attendants, offer hospitality to all who visit you and grant valuable gifts to sup-porters. With all this you could become a great leader and would soon find yourself at the head of a great army.'[34] Fayzi said that he would consult with his friends – remnants of the Pan-Arab party's committee – but came back later saying that they had rejected the proposal. Lawrence had been hoping to take some of them with him to the front before revealing the full details of his plan, but in the event he was forced to go off alone.

He left Basra on a paddle-steamer with an infantry detachment on 9 April and steamed up the Tigris, a viscous brown stream, stitched in a baroque pattern of switch-back channels and sandbreaks across a brooding, dead world of black and grey flint. On the first night the ship moored at Qurna – the confluence of the Tigris and the Euphrates, and the putative site of the Garden of Eden. Staring into the brown waters as they swirled and mingled, Lawrence thought with nostalgia of his friends at Carchemish, and wondered if he would ever see Dahoum again. Although he did not know it then, Dahoum was almost certainly dead – killed by the terrible famine and epidemics of 1916 which the war had exacerbated. Carchemish had been his own private Garden of Eden: 'till the war swallowed up everything,' he wrote later, 'I wanted nothing better than Carchemish, which was a perfect life.'[35] It might have been a requiem for an entire generation, for the holocaust in which he and his peers found themselves was a nodal point in world history – the point beyond which the traditions and assumptions which had governed European life for centuries would ultimately be swept away.

He arrived at Wadi – where Tigris Force had made its H Q – six days later, to be given short shrift from the senior members of staff. The relief campaign was faring badly, yet the generals intended to send in still more waves of troops. That his countrymen were being sacrificed like beasts on the altar of their leaders' ambition distressed Lawrence as abjectly as it was to distress the war's most celebrated poet, Wilfred Owen:

> What passing-bells for these who die as cattle?
> – Only the monstrous anger of the guns.
>   Only the stuttering rifles' rapid rattle
> Can patter out their hasty orisons.[36]

The Anglo-Indian generals did not wish to consider Lawrence's ideas. Such unorthodox strategy, they said, was incompatible with the ideal of 'military honour' – that same 'honour' which had already cost thousands of lives without gaining them a single inch of ground. For them, any kind of secret or subversive activity in war was tantamount to 'cheating'. It was precisely the same emotion which in earlier times had caused British officers to order their redcoats to fight in the open, since it was 'cowardly' to hide behind trees. But it was not only a matter of this misplaced conception of honour. The Anglo-Indian mandarins were horrified at the idea of an Arab Revolt. They felt that it would provide a dangerous example to India's millions of Muslim subjects, the possibility of whose insurrection gave them sleepless nights. The generals would have their frontal offensive. Lawrence was struck down by fever at the critical moment, and could do little but thrash helplessly on his bunk.

At first light on 22 April, he was woken up by a shocking barrage of shellfire from the British guns. For forty minutes the cannon boomed with slow, deliberate percussion, then suddenly the rhythm increased to a crescendo – the prelude to an attack. The Turks were holding five lines of trenches at a place called Sannaiyat, in a narrow bottle-neck between a treacherous salt-marsh and the riverbank. It was an almost impregnable position, but in order to reach Kut, Tigris Corps had no alternative but to punch a way through. At point of the spearhead – 19th Brigade – were the Highlanders: the bloodied remnants of the 2nd Black Watch and the 1st Seaforths, so decimated from previous assaults that they had been hastily cobbled together into a single battalion for this fight. At 7 a.m. precisely, 19th Brigade moved out. Turkish machine-guns and artillery blazed at them from positions concealed by the dappling heat-haze, and the Highlanders rushed straight into the rattling maw of the guns. It had been estimated that it would take them seven minutes to broach the Turkish line. It took them four. As the men came into the range of their own artillery they waved their red markers frantically for the bombardment to stop. Then they drove themselves on through the waterlogged ditches, only to find their rifles so clogged with mud that they could not be fired. Moments later, the Turks swept in from the flanks with a massive counter-attack, and 19th Brigade was swamped. The position looked hopeless. One by one the spearhead battalions withdrew, leaving only the Highlanders – who ignored the order to retreat. Incredibly, they tried to continue the advance, making three separate assaults on the third line defences. From these three attacks, not a single man returned.

By 8.20 a.m. it was all over. The assault had lasted one hour and twenty minutes, and in that time 19th Brigade had lost over 1,000 men. They had advanced and retreated a little more than half a mile. The Highland Battalion had suffered more than 600 casualties – the 2nd Black Watch, the 1st Seaforth Highlanders, and the 6th Jaht Rifles together now consisted of fewer than 160 men. General Young-husband, commanding the Division, knew that the relief mission to Kut had failed. He could not ask them to advance again. 'I cannot speak too highly of the splendid gallantry of the Highlanders, aided by a party of the Jahts, in storming the Turkish trenches,' he wrote. 'They showed qualities of endurance and courage under circumstances so adverse, as to be almost phenomenal.'[37]

Once again, their valour had been wasted. A week later, white flags fluttered over Kut, and the 13,000 surviving troops of the 6th Indian Division were marched off into a captivity in which more than half of them died. General Townshend, the principal architect of the disaster, abandoned his division and spent an 'honourable' captivity in a hotel on the Bosphorus accompanied by his beloved dogs – the only animals which had not been eaten by the starving garrison. Sir Charles had great affection for his dogs, but as to his men, he never once inquired about their welfare. The Turks not only laughed at the British plan to bribe them, but also made political capital from it. Lawrence and Herbert met the Turkish generals for a parley on 29 April, but found that nothing could be salvaged from their plans but the exchange of a few wounded prisoners. The tragedy of Kut had cost the British 38,000 casualties in all, yet not an iota of political advantage had been gained. The British Empire had scarcely been at such a low. There had been slaughter on the Western Front, defeat at Gallipoli, Turkish attacks on the Suez Canal, and now, the débâcle at Kut. Lawrence returned to Basra disillusioned, deeply disappointed by his failure to have his strategy adopted, and disgusted with the attitude of the Anglo-Indian generals, still convinced that an Arab movement could have saved the day. All his hopes had been dashed: 'I did nothing,' he wrote, 'of what was in my mind and power to do.'[38] On the ship back to Cairo he drafted a report criticizing them so scathingly that it had to be bowdlerized before being presented to Sir Archibald Murray, who had just replaced Sir John Maxwell as Commander-in-Chief.

Back in Cairo, Lawrence found that Medforce had now been amalgamated with the British Force in Egypt, and that Murray was already planning to use the extra troops in a pre-emptive strike into Sinai. This, at least, he thought, was a move for the better. His approval was not to last for long: Murray turned out to be another orthodox soldier of the old school, who mistrusted intelligence departments and Eastern veterans like Clayton. He divided the now expanded Department, moving many of the officers to his new operational GHQ at Ismailiyya, and leaving only seven – including Lawrence – to make up Cairo Intelligence at the Savoy. Lawrence was glad to see Hogarth, who had arrived in Cairo in March wearing the uniform of a Lieutenant-Commander in the RNVR. At last he had found himself a war job in the Geographical Section of Naval Intelligence, but had been seconded to Egypt where he would help set up the new 'Arab Bureau', which was to be knocked together from Clayton's remnant intelligence officers at the Savoy, but was to answer to the civil authority – High Commissioner McMahon. The Bureau was to be run under the aegis of the Foreign Office, and to be responsible for political developments in the Middle East. In effect, 'Intrusive' – as it was codenamed – had been created not only to foment and support insurrection among the Arabs, but also as a tool to spread the gospel of such insurrection into the most exalted circles of British power: 'We meant to break into the accepted halls of British foreign policy,' Lawrence wrote, 'and build a new people in the East.'[39] To begin with, though, Lawrence was not a member of the 'band of wild men', as he put it, but retained his old job in Cairo Intelligence. He was, nevertheless, given the task of editing the Bureau's intelligence summary, the *Arab Bulletin*. This was work after his own heart, for his excursion to Kut had confirmed him in the belief that he was no man of action. He had made his pilgrimage to the front line, and was now resigned to spending the rest of the war in the office: 'the most interesting place there is,' he wrote, 'until the Near East settles down.'[40] There were hopes in the Hejaz, of course, but despite the lengthy negotiations, no one really believed that, when the chips were down, the Sharif would fight. Then, the day before the first issue of the *Arab Bulletin* was published, a dramatic development took place. At dawn on 5 June 1916 – the day on which Lord Kitchener was drowned in the North Sea – Sharifs 'Ali and Feisal raised the scarlet banner of the Hashemites under the walls of Medina, and, in the name of all the Arabs, declared an end to the rule of the Ottoman Turks.

PART TWO

THE WARRIOR
October 1916–October 1918

11. *The Biggest Thing in the Near East Since 1550*

The Outbreak of the Arab Revolt
1916

It was a harsh land, a thirsty land, a land scorching under a sky of burnished cobalt blue, an inferno of blazing light. It was a place of naked peaks, scarred, cracked and hammered into fantastic forms, a place where dust-devils unreeled across the aching loneliness, a place of deep dry valleys, of saltbush, thornscrub and sedge, of waterless swathes of sand, of crunching black gravel and dark volcanic stones the Bedu called *harra*. Its name – al-Hejaz – signified 'The Barrier', yet for countless generations it had been a highway for pilgrimage and trade. Long before Islam, great caravans had tramped its wastes carrying frankincense from the spice kingdoms of South Arabia to the ports of the Levant. Bilqis, the legendary Queen of Sheba, had passed this way on her journey to King Solomon's court. No great civilizations had ever flourished here, but scattered through these skeletal, glittering hills and plains were oases of millions of palm-trees – Medina, Yanbu' an-Nakhl, Tayma, Khaybar, Daydan, Ta'if – like vast green islands in the wastes. At Mecca, a place set in a valley so arid that cultivation was impossible, lay a sacred enclave – a *haram* – where no beast might be hunted, no tree cut, nor human blood spilt. Since the Time of Ignorance, men had come there to worship before the great black stone of *al-Ka'aba* which had fallen from the stars.

Between such oases, the wilderness was trawled by the desert and hill folk – the Bedu – a people in endless movement, endlessly changing, endlessly adapting to the whims of the land: now staying in one place long enough to plant seeds, now furling their black tents and setting their camels' heads towards some distant pasture. The changes came slowly, generation by generation, and the Bedu, who had virtually no history, could not remember that things had ever been different, and believed their ways immutable and hallowed by time. Their records, enshrined in verse and handed down from mouth to mouth, were endless tales of war upon war, or clan against clan and tribe against tribe, of interminable raids and skirmishes. Such wars were fought with 'white weapons' – the swordblade and the spear. Fighting with these arms, a man could scarcely be slain without his killer being known to the entire world. Vengeance would be certain. It was the absolute law of *lex talionis* – an eye for an eye, a tooth for a tooth – that prevailed, and the Bedu had a saying which underlined the slow inevitability of the vendetta: 'Forty years on, the Bedui took his revenge.' By Bedu tradition, vengeance might fall on any adult male relative of the killer within five generations – which was as far back as anyone could recall his own true ancestry. Beyond one's great-great-great grandfather, genealogy passed into the nebula of myth. The tribe itself was something of an abstract entity, consisting of a number of five-generation families who simply felt they belonged together while not necessarily being related by blood. Yet this tribe was the refuge and sanctuary of every individual. Though the tribes were violently independent and quite often in a state of hostility with one another, within them there was a feeling of passionate unity and solidarity known as *'asabiyya*, and in it lay the true strength of Arabia. Individuals owed no personal allegiance to any other: they owed their loyalty eternally to the tribe.

In the Hejaz, the Bedu lived on the milk of their she-camels, on dates and grain from their own oasis gardens, for here there was no transition from the desert to the sown. The great tribes of western Arabia – the 'Utayba, the Harb, the Juhayna, the Billi, the Muttar and the Bani 'Atiya – consisted of families who lived in a continuum of lifestyles, from fully nomadic, to semi-nomadic, to villagers who scarcely moved at all. Yet while the more mobile tended to sneer at the more settled, they were kinsmen, and all were considered honourable, and derived honour from the reputation of the tribe. For though the individual members of a tribe were equals, and the Sheikhs simply *primes inter pares*, the tribes themselves were not. The tribes which were most powerful at any given moment were considered the most 'noble', and altered their genealogies accordingly. There were certain outcast tribes, such as the Shararat, the 'Awazim and the Hutaym, who were not accepted as warriors, and with whom no one would marry, and an anomalous folk called the Solayb, who were tinkers, hunters and medicine-men. Another group, the 'Agayl, fitted none of these categories. Mostly settled villagers from the Qasim oases of Najd, the 'Agayl were not a tribe but a brotherhood of camel-dealers and caravan guides known everywhere in Arabia as honest brokers and superb camel-handlers, and a force of mercenaries respected as brave fighters, who would remain loyal to those they had undertaken to protect. Though the 'Agayl were not Bedu, they were considered honourable in every part of the land. Bedu life was hard, but the idea that it was a 'death in life', as Lawrence later claimed, shows more about his own character than the nature of the Bedu. In fact, their culture was so perfectly adapted to the desert that they felt at home there. Their herds of camels, goats and sheep were their survival machines: much that they used could be garnered from their own materials – the rest they could trade for in the towns. They lived not by material wealth – a transient thing in such desolation – but by the cult of reputation. A man gained honour by displaying courage, endurance, hospitality, generosity and loyalty, and while no strange caravan, nor traveller, nor rival tent was free from his depredations, there was no more honourable travelling companion nor host once he had shared bread and salt. Raiding for camels was the spice of his life, and a means of acquiring reputation, and his hand was turned against every man, unless it suited him. His services could be bought with gold, but his soul could not.

The hardest facet of Bedu life for a stranger to grasp was not its physical aspect, but its spiritual one. The Bedu lived in a different space-time continuum from the European – a world which was flat, a world in which the sun crossed the sky, a world in which the stars were merely lights in the heavens, a world which could not be measured by kilometres or miles. They inhabited a world in which everything – every tree, stone or pool – had its individual spirit, but in which everything was related in God: in which a man must accept what befell him because it was the will of God. The Bedu had no lust to explain, no thought to solve, no notion to improve – the answer to every question lay not in reason but in faith. They lived in a world without physical security, where death – from raiders, thirst, hunger, accident or disease – might strike at any moment. Yet they possessed existential security – like the medieval European, they had an absolute knowledge of who they were, a sense of purpose, a sense of meaning, a sense that

God moved everything for the best, a sense of belonging to the earth and to the universe, which modern Europeans had lost.

Johan Lutwig Burckhardt and Richard Burton had penetrated Mecca and Medina disguised as Muslims in the first half of the nineteenth century, and Charles Doughty had travelled *in forma pauperis* in Arabia in the 1870s. Yet of the land itself, little was known to the outside world: 'Up to 1914,' David Hogarth would tell the Royal Geographical Society in 1920, 'our best knowledge of the Peninsula of Arabia was everywhere sketchy, and of more than half of its great area . . . it scarcely amounted to anything worth mention. The virtually unknown regions lay in the centre – especially on its western half . . . The greater part of this last region had been barred as a Holy Land to European explorers unless they would risk themselves in furtive disguise which hindered, if it did not absolutely preclude, them from observing and recording facts and features of geographical interest.'[1] The Tihama, or Red Sea coast of the Hejaz, was still as little mapped as the Antarctic. The British had no reliable map of the interior, could not say for certain how far the Hejaz railway lay from the coast, and could not even enumerate its stations south of al-'Ula. For the 200-mile stretch between there and Mecca, they could not fix the longitude of any given point, and indeed, did not know exactly where Medina lay nor what it looked like. The only plan they had of the town was a sketch made by Burton seventy years previously. When Lawrence stepped ashore at Jeddah on 19 October 1916, he was aware that he was entering *terra incognita*.

The revolt was then four months old, and dangerously near crisis. The initiative had been regained by the Turks. It seemed to the British that the Sharif had acted precipitately, though Hussain himself had seen no other choice. In January 1916 he had sent his son Feisal to Damascus, accompanied by a bodyguard of forty tribesmen, to foment mutiny among Arab Divisions of the Ottoman army in Syria and Mesopotamia. To his dismay, Feisal had found that there were no longer any Arab Divisions *in* Syria, for the resourceful Jamal Pasha – the Military Governor – had sent them off to other fronts and replaced them with Osmanli Divisions. Jamal's new policy was repressive. In April, he had ordered the public hanging of twenty-one Arab nationalists – including prominent magistrates, writers and intellectuals – in Damascus and

Beirut. He was also on the point of dispatching Khairy Bey with an additional 3,500 specially picked and trained soldiers to the Hejaz, ostensibly on their way to the Yemen, to escort a German field mission under Baron Othmar von Stotzingen, but actually to strengthen his hold on the Hejaz. Hussain recognized that the executions symbolized a new confidence on the part of the Turks, encouraged by their successes in Gallipoli and Kut, and suspected that the true purpose of the Khairy Bey mission was to depose him. He knew that he must act before the fresh troops reached Medina. He had already taken the Sheikhs of the Harb, the 'Utayba, the Juhayna and others into his confidence, and knew he could count on Bedu levies. He had his own trained and blooded camelry of 'Agayl mercenaries and his Bishah tribal police – highlanders from the hills of the fertile Assir – but virtually no regular troops and no modern equipment, particularly machine-guns or artillery. Nevertheless, Hussain felt confident of his Bedu troops, and only one factor stayed his hand: his son Feisal was still in Syria, and would be seized by Jamal as soon as word of hostilities leaked out. Feisal solved the problem cleverly by gulling Jamal into believing that he was returning to the Hejaz only to bring back a force of volunteers for the Turkish army. On 16 May he left Damascus, putting his forty men under the command of his friend Nasib al-Bakri of al-Fatat, with instructions to flee as soon as they received a coded password. By the third week in May he was back in Medina, and the Sharif was free to strike.

At first light on 10 June, the voice of a single muezzin rang out from the minaret of the Grand Mosque at Mecca. It was still cool at that hour, but already the sky was clear as a burning-glass and the eddyless air held the threat of furnace heat. There were dark figures in the streets, Bedu wrapped in cloaks and mantles, with their headcloths tightly knotted across their faces, mingling, hardly noticed, with towns-men hurrying to perform their prayers. At the Jirwal barracks on the Jeddah road, where the garrison commander had spent the night, the Turks slept on, confident in the belief that they were protected by the sentries and guns of the Jiyad fortress – a massive, many-towered redoubt squatting on a stump of shale above the town. The troops were few – less than 1,500 men – for during the sweltering summer season, the Governor moved to cooler quarters in Ta'if with the bulk of the garrison. In the Hamdiyya building, which housed the Ottoman

Government Offices, the Vice-Governor, who was already awake and making his ablutions, paused for an instant to take in the beauty of the muezzin's song. Not far away, in the Hashemite palace, Sharif Hussain was listening carefully to the same clear notes, gazing out of the window, and observing the slowly milling figures in the streets. The Call to Prayers finished abruptly, and for a second there was silence. Then the Sharif picked up his rifle, and, with slow deliberation, fired from the window the shot which officially opened the Arab Revolt.

It was the signal the tribesmen had been waiting for. Instantly, they threw off their cloaks, and let rip a hail of bullets at the three Turkish fortresses, the barracks, the guard-posts and the offices. The troops at the Jirwal awoke to find bullets buzzing through their windows like flies, and, rolling out of bed, the Commander looked about him in confusion. He was under attack, but he had no idea by whom. He listened attentively for the boom of artillery or the rattle of machine-guns which would have accompanied an Allied assault, but heard only the coarser crack and thump of musketry. Glancing out of the window, he saw a scarlet flag flying from the Hashemite palace, but did not distinguish it as the Hashemite emblem, for the Imperial Ottoman banner was also scarlet. Quickly, he cranked the telephone and spoke to the Commander of the battery in the Jiyad fort. Almost at once a terse order brought the gunners to their posts. Puffs of smoke appeared at the gun-ports of the fortress, followed by the crashing roar of shells bursting in the streets. To the Bedu attackers, the guns sounded like thunder-demons. They were armed only with muzzle-loading muskets, and had never heard artillery before. At the Jirwal barracks the Turks had recovered from their initial surprise, and, emboldened by the artillery barrage, were now firing back vigorously. The Commander next telephoned the Sharif: 'We are under attack by the Bedu,' he reported. 'Can you do something about it?' 'Certainly,' Hussain replied calmly, and gave the signal for a renewed attack.

At nine o'clock, when the lambent heat of the day could already be felt in the tight streets, the Commander asked for a parley. The local Arab civil officer marched up to the barracks under a white flag, and informed him: 'This country has declared its independence from the Ottoman Empire. Hostilities will only cease when your force evacuates the barracks and surrenders it entire armoury to the Arab commander.'[2]

Startled by the revelation, but determined to hold out now he knew whom he was fighting, the Commander at once ordered the Jiyad battery to open up. Firing continued sporadically all that day and all through the night, and the next morning a wedge of Bedu, screaming warcries and brandishing daggers and scimitars which flashed venomously in the sunlight, rushed the main guard-house near the Grand Mosque, stove in its doors, and captured its defenders. The following day they attacked the Hamidiyya Building, where the Vice-Vali had by now entrenched himself with his escort. All night he and his men had kept up a withering fire at anyone who came within range, and had shot dead a number of people who were merely plodding to prayer at the mosque. Worming their way from door to door, the Bedu suddenly launched a charge from close range, leaping out of the shadows screaming like banshees. The Turkish soldiers, cowed by their ferocity, dropped their rifles and raised their hands in fright. They were marched up to the Hashemite palace, from where the Vice-Governor sent letters ordering the troops at Jirwal and Jiyad to surrender. The Turkish units adamantly refused to budge, and kept up a continual, rhythmic barrage of shells, ranging them so indiscriminately into the town that they set fire to the *Kiswa* – the embroidery covering the sacred *Ka'aba* – the holiest shrine in Islam. They also managed to damage the shrine of Abraham, and to splinter a bas-relief commemorating the life of the Khalif Othman. All of these acts provided excellent propaganda against them, and the last was held up as an ominous sign of their disfavour, since the name Othman was linked with the eponymous ancestor of the Ottoman Turks. The situation was now stalemate, however. The Arabs could not attack the Jiyad with its deadly batteries, and the Turks were unable or unwilling to sally forth. The situation remained static until the beginning of July, when two batteries of mountain-guns arrived with a detachment of Egyptian artillerymen under the command of Sayyid 'Ali Pasha. Though the guns were archaic, sent hurriedly by Sir Reginald Wingate, Sirdar of the Egyptian Army, from Port Sudan, they were effective at close quarters. Almost at once the batteries knocked out some of the Turkish guns in the Jiyad, and breached the walls, so that the Bedu, who had scaled the surrounding heights, were able to hurl themselves into the fort, where they cut down or captured the entire garrison. They also took five artillery-pieces, 8,000 rifles, and hundreds of thousands of rounds of ammunition. The mountain-guns were then turned on the Jiwal barracks, and a shell-burst set the building ablaze, spreading poisonous smoke through it. The Turks, who had no water to put out the blaze, surrendered on 9 July. In a month's fighting the Arabs had killed and wounded almost 300 Turks, and had captured the rest. The opening gambit in the Arab Revolt had been an astounding success.

Jeddah, Mecca's port, had long since been taken. Here, Hussain had used gold to raise a section of the Harb – notorious freebooters and highway brigands – under Muhsin ibn Mansour, a brave and highly respected Sharif. The Harb were recalcitrant and unruly, and not entirely to be trusted, but they fought for gold. For days they had massed around Jeddah, and on the morning of 10 June, 3,000 tribesmen had mounted their camels and horses and raced recklessly towards the city gates. The Turks began to rake the plain with artillery, planting great mushrooms of smoke among the running camels, and spattering the vanguard with machine-gun fire. The Harb turned abruptly and withdrew out of range, and Muhsin sent a squadron of camel-riders around to the north-west side of the town to cut off the water supply to the Ottoman garrison, which stood outside the walls. The following day, the Indian Marine ship *Hardinge* and the light cruiser *Fox* of the British Red Sea Patrol Squadron beat into the harbour and scourged the garrison with concentrated fire, killing three Turkish gendarmes. The bombardment was repeated daily, until, on 16 June, the carrier *Ben-My-Chree* dropped anchor off the reef and disgorged a flight of seaplanes which soared over the town walls dropping anti-personnel bombs. The Turkish garrison was demoralized and thirsty. On receiving advice that no reinforcements were on their way, the Commander surrendered to Sharif Muhsin. There was similar success at other ports along the Red Sea Coast. Medina's port, Yanbu', and Rabegh – about 120 miles north of Jeddah – were taken by the end of July. Lith and Qunfidhdha, to the south, were captured about the same time, and at Umm Lujj the Turkish troops fled in the desert when *Fox* put a round up the mainstreet of the town and holed the fort. Ta'if, in the Hejaz highlands seventy-five miles south-east of Mecca, however, had proved a harder nut to crack.

Ta'if, lying on a sandy plain amid fruit orchards and olive groves, 5,000 feet above sea-level, was a walled town which served as a market for the 'Utayba – one of the most powerful Bedu tribes of central

Arabia – as well as a number of smaller semi-nomadic tribes. 'Abdallah had been sent there with seventy 'Agayl riders on 1 June, as soon as Hussain had heard the news of Khairy Bey's advance. He had made a camp near the town, and informed the local Commander, Ahmad Bey, that he was on a raid against the Baqqum, a nomadic tribe of 500 tents inhabiting the wadis of the Assir. Ahmad Bey had been suspicious, but had reckoned that whatever it was the young Sharif was up to, with only seventy poorly armed 'Agayl he offered very little threat to the Turks, who numbered 3,000, and possessed ten mountain-guns. 'Abdallah proceeded to send messengers to the camps of the 'Utayba and other tribes, inviting them to join him, offering money and arms. The Bedu arrived in their camels in small unobtrusive parties over the next few days, and with astonishing speed 'Abdallah built up his force from seventy to 5,000 men. Ahmad Bey, who visited his camp every evening, watched the foregathering of tribesmen and camels with disquiet. Within a week, the Sharif was ready to order the attack. Then, on the eve of his planned strike, his presence was suddenly requested by Ghalib Pasha, the Governor of the Hejaz. 'Abdallah's chiefs counselled caution, but the Sharif rode boldly to Ghalib's palace escorted by only two Bedu, whom he posted outside the office, instructing them quietly that if anyone tried to arrest him they were to hold off any threat from outside while he dealt with the Vali. 'Abdallah swept into the Governor's presence, and found that Ghalib simply wanted to advise him against carrying out his raid on the Baqqum: 'Rumours are about,' the Governor said, 'that a revolt may take place any day now. You see how the people of Ta'if are leaving their homes with their children.'³ 'Let me carry out the raid,' 'Abdallah protested, 'and the people will regain their confidence.' At that moment Ahmad Bey entered the room, looking grave, and 'Abdallah tensed himself for action. The Commander whispered to Ghalib, confessing his suspicions and suggesting that he should arrest 'Abdallah forthwith. The Sharif watched anxiously, fingering his revolver beneath his cloak. After a few minutes, though, the Governor waved his Commander aside, and 'Abdallah left freely. No sooner had he regained his camp than he sent his 'Agayl to cut the telegraph wires to Mecca, and ordered his scouts to stop any messengers leaving or entering Ta'if, by shooting them dead if necessary. On the night of 10 June, his forces surrounded the northern quarter of the city. They were easily repelled, however, for Ahmad Bey had strengthened the town walls with earthworks and trenches. 'Our attack was made with great violence,' 'Abdallah wrote. 'In the centre our riflemen made a raid and returned with some prisoners and loot. At sunrise the Turkish artillery began to shell us heavily. We were fortunate there was no infantry offensive as well.'[4] Over the next few days, the Arabs tried continually to raid individual positions, only to find themselves scattered by the noise of the Turkish guns. The Bani Sa'ad – a local cultivating tribe – were so unnerved that they abandoned the Sharif and decamped for their villages. 'Abdallah bided his time patiently, however, until, in mid-July, the Egyptian mountain-guns arrived, having been carried in pieces up the Wadi Fatima from Mecca, together with a howitzer the Arabs had captured there. Yet the stand-off continued. 'Abdallah said later that he had not made as much use of the artillery as he should have done, while the Egyptian gunners later told Hubert Young that the Bedu had been afraid to attack, and had never taken advantage of their bombardments. Eventually, the Sharif's patience paid off, however: the garrison at Ta'if surrendered on 22 September, and the Governor was taken prisoner.

With a little assistance from the Royal Navy, but with few trained troops and little modern equipment, the Hashemites had captured most of the vital towns of the Hejaz, taking some 6,000 prisoners and a vast amount of military hardware. More than this, they had scored a brilliant propaganda success: Turco-German dreams of a Jihad or Holy War were dead. Jamal Pasha admitted as much publicly in a speech, in which he called Hussain a 'traitor' and a 'vile individual'. For the Arabs, the problem was that Medina, not Mecca, was the key to the Hejaz, and they had not captured it. Medina was not only a self-supporting oasis, far beyond the range of British naval guns, but it was also linked directly to the outside world by the Hejaz railway. By June it had a large garrison of at least 12,000 men under a gifted, resolute and ruthless commander named Fakhri Pasha, the notorious 'Butcher of Urfa'. Hussain and his sons slowly realized that they had underestimated the power of the railway. While Medina remained in Turkish hands, the Turks could move any amount of men and material into the Hejaz at will, and launch a counter-attack at their leisure.

After raising the flag on 5 June, 'Ali and Feisal had divided their force of Bedu into three detachments, one of which had torn up the railway tracks north of Medina with their bare hands and flung the rails down the embankment. This achieved nothing, for without explosives they could do no permanent damage, and the Turks, who had repair teams in their fortress-stations, had no shortage of spare track. Muhit was the first station on the railway, thirteen miles north-west of Medina, a solid building of black basalt, guarded by a massive blockhouse, standing under a crust of low hills. On the morning of 8 June, 'Ali's snipers poured fire into the buildings from concealed places in the surrounding hills, while another detachment skirmished across the open plain towards the position. The Turks were well-entrenched and easily turned back the advance with a clatter of machine-gun fire. Worse, a large force of infantry under the personal leadership of Fakhri Pasha had sallied forth from Medina, and fell on them from the rear. The Arabs retreated into the hills and regrouped, making a massed sortie against Medina which was again met with a solid wall of fire from artillery and machine-guns. The noise of the cannon so terrified the Bedu that they turned and ran. The 'Utayba and the 'Agayl took shelter among the black stones of a lava scree and refused to budge. Feisal, riding a white mare and dressed conspicuously in his finest Sharifian robes, paced up and down steadily through a rain of Turkish bullets and bursting shells trying to rally them. It was to no avail; the Bedu had no experience of this kind of carnage. Feisal had been relying on the Bani 'Ali, a tribe of cultivators who inhabited the village of 'Awali outside the town walls, to hold the city's water supply. But the roar of the guns and the flight of the Bedu irregulars were too much for them. They asked the Turks for a truce, and while they were parleying, Fakhri's men encircled the village. Then, on a signal, they moved in with fixed bayonets and massacred every man, woman and child, burning the houses and setting machine-guns at the gates to cut down the fleeing victims as they ran out. Feisal and a handful of Bedu who came to the rescue too late were appalled. This wanton butchery of women and children was an atrocity which they would never forget. It was the final nerve-shattering blow to their morale, and the Hashemites were obliged to retreat, first to Bir Mashi, south of the city, and then to Wadi Aqiq. The Turks pursued them as doggedly as bloodhounds, driving them from place to place, until they split up, Feisal taking his troops to Yanbu 'an-Nakhl – a palm oasis in the hills on the Medina–Yanbu' road – and 'Ali to Wadi Ithm, about thirty miles to the south-west of Medina, where, almost out of food, he barely managed to hang on. The Turks now began to push forward relentlessly, collecting camels from the surrounding tribes for transport, capturing and fortifying wells and strong-points. The Arab forces were almost out of supplies and ammunition, and what little they had was reaching them from Mecca, rather than from the beach-head at Rabegh. In mid-July 'Ali's force was increased by a detachment of regular Arab soldiers – former members of Ottoman Divisions seized by the British as prisoners-of-war, and released from prison-camps in Egypt as volunteers for the Arab cause. They were under the command of a highly capable young Iraqi artillery officer called Nuri as-Sa'id, who, on reaching 'Ali's position, saw that his situation was hopeless. 'Ali had no information about the enemy's movements, and Nuri had to locate the three Turkish battalions tracking him by sending out his men as decoys to draw fire. Ammunition was low, and the Turks were in possession of the nearest water sources. Nuri felt that the Bedu troops were incapable of holding a Turkish advance, and advised 'Ali to withdraw to the coast, where, in the comforting shelter of British naval guns, the nucleus of a regular Arab army might be formed under the command of Aziz 'Ali al-Masri – another distinguished and brilliant Arab defector from the Turks, who had fought with the Senussi in the Libyan desert, and had now devised a detailed strategy for the Arab Revolt. Al-Masri proposed to form a 'flying column' of trained Arab volunteers 8,000 strong, which, with eight mountain-guns, would move north from the Hejaz into Syria, wrecking the railway but never fighting pitched battles with the Turks. The scheme, later to be adapted by Lawrence, was scotched by Hussain, who was suspicious of his Syrian officers and felt that such a 'flying column' would be beyond his control. Indeed, the guerrilla strategist al-Masri was later sacked by the Sharif – an irreplaceable loss to the revolt. For now, however, Nuri advised 'Ali to withdraw to Rabegh. In doing so, the Sharif could also find out why none of the thousands of rifles and tons of supplies the British had landed there had reached them in the field.

In Rabegh, 'Ali quickly discovered the answer to this last question: the supplies had been stolen by Sheikh Hussain ibn Mubeiriq of the Zebayd Harb, who had been put in charge of the port. Ibn Mubeiriq, who had an old blood-feud with the Hashemites, was secretly a Turkish sympathizer. 'Ali sent word to his youngest brother, Zayd, who arrived with Ahmad bin Mansur and a troop of his Bani Salem, took possession of ibn Mubeiriq's villages by force and seized the stores, driving the 'traitor' and his men out into the hills where they lingered like malevolent spirits. Instead of returning to the field, however, 'Ali and Zayd settled down to wait for al-Masri and Nuri as-Sa'id to build up their forces, leaving Feisal to face the Turks alone. The situation was fast becoming critical. Feisal, who had taken up a position on the *Darb Sultani* – the main road to the coast – had under his command 4,000 irregulars with rifles and the Egyptian artillery, whose ancient field-pieces were far outranged by the Turks' Krupp mountain-guns. In Medina, Fakhri's forces now amounted to twelve battalions with sixteen mountain-guns and two heavy field-pieces – thanks to the railway, fresh troops were arriving all the time. Feisal's forces were unable to meet the Turks head-on, and the Sharif sent camel-mounted raiding-parties, under the ferocious young Sharif 'Ali ibn Hussain of the Harith, to harass them by night, hitting guard-posts and convoys and fading back into the hills. These pinpricks were hardly felt by the enemy, but they were costly in Arab lives, and Feisal's Bedu were melting rapidly back to their tents and villages. Feisal could not prevent them: they were hired on a daily rate, and he had no money to pay them with. He was obliged at one point to have a chest filled with heavy stones and put a guard on it at night to convince his troops that he was still solvent. Feisal felt that at the very most he could hold out for three weeks, but to push the Turks back to Medina was now impossible. At the end of August he rode down to the coast, where at Yanbu' he met Lieutenant-Colonel Cyril Wilson, who had been posted to Jeddah as British representative. Wilson, who was actually Governor of the Red Sea Province of the Sudan, was spokesman for Sir Reginald Wingate, the officer responsible for supplying the Hashemites from neighbouring Port Sudan. This had been Feisal's first meeting with a British officer, and he had complained volubly about the lack of ammunition and supplies, which were supposed to be reaching him from the beach-head at Rabegh. He wanted machine-guns, modern artillery and aircraft, as well as a contingent of British troops at Rabegh. The Turks were clearly building up for an advance on Mecca, for which Rabegh, as the major source of water on the *Darb Sultani*, would be a vital stepping-stone. The Arab regulars at Rabegh were not yet ready to hold it, and the Bedu could not hold it either. Feisal felt that the only solution was to land a seasoned British brigade. Hussain agreed that such a landing was necessary, but thought it should be limited to 300 men. He feared to allow Christian soldiers – or even Muslim soldiers in Christian pay – to land *en masse* on sacred soil, for the Turks, who had now appointed a rival Sharif, 'Ali Haydar, as Emir of Mecca in his place, were already declaring that Hussain had 'sold out' to the British infidels. On recapturing Mecca, their first act would be to hang Hussain publicly as a traitor and install 'Ali Haydar as Emir. Feisal met Wilson for a second time in early September, together with Lieutenant-Colonel A. C. Parker – now posted to the Hejaz as intelligence officer – and repeated his urgent request for British troops at Rabegh. Wilson and Parker were convinced that the Arab Revolt was about to collapse, and had rushed to Cairo on the *Dufferin* to persuade Murray to send a British force. As September faded into October, though, no such force arrived. The weather grew cooler and a Turkish advance on Mecca looked increasingly imminent. All that stood in the way of the juggernaut was the thin, ragged band of Feisal's Bedu, hidden in the hills.

12. Fallen Like a Sword into Their Midst

First Mission to the Hejaz
October 1916

In 1916 Jeddah was a tiny walled port, only half a mile square. Today it is a thriving metropolis, covering an area several hundred times larger, served by two international airports, and almost drowned under a continually roiling stream of motor cars. I flew there in high summer and when I arrived the wetness in the air clung to me like a sweater. I was pleased, though, to find that odd bits of the old port survived. The lagoon, still stinking of sulphur, was no longer used as a harbour, but along the wharfs there were the fractured hulls of *sambuks*, and the old sea-gate, by which Lawrence had entered the town, had been restored as a monument to the past. Among the air-conditioned shopping malls and the marble walkways, I came across examples of the baroque coral-and-limestone skyscraper houses Lawrence had described in *Seven Pillars*. Some were on a modest scale, listing dangerously from exhaustion into the narrow alleys of the suq, while others were vast and palatial, with heavy doors of carved teak, rambling façades of timbered bow windows, tiers of ornate latticework, mock balconies and balustrades, *mashrubat* slats like huge light-filters, great edifices of shutters and crosspoles, curving around the entire front of the building. In the pedestrian precinct of the Old Town, I drifted along in the sauna-heat, blessedly far from the noise of cars, amid the smells of cinnamon, coffee and sherbet, among men in scarlet Mosul headcloths, and women flitting like faceless shadows in black, and tried to imagine for an instant that I had stepped back in time. In 1916, of course, these alleys would have been dark, earth-floored conduits, shaded with sacking through which the light strobed in golden shafts, obstructed by donkeys and laden camels, and – during the Pilgrim season – crowded with shaven-pated men of almost every conceivable race – Turks, Baluch, Indians, Pharsees, Malays, Javanese, Africans from Zanzibar and the Sudan. That October, though, Lawrence had found Jeddah almost deserted: 'hushed, strained, furtive' he wrote – a ghost town, where doors shut silently as he approached. Dodging traffic, I followed his route from the stinking wharfs, and came upon the house that had once been the British Agency – a squarish block with well-carved lattice-windows, shining brilliantly with white paint, but sadly devoid of the rambling asymmetry which had made some of the old houses in the suq attractive. It had been restored over-zealously as the Municipal Museum, and stood on a triangular island in the harbour ring-road, opposite a vast glass-fronted shopping mall and dwarfed by the towering concrete-and-glass blade of the National Commercial Bank.

Lawrence and Storrs had arrived at this building at 9.30 on the morning of 16 October 1916, to find Cyril Wilson seated in a darkened room behind an open lattice. He had welcomed them politely but without much enthusiasm. He was essentially an honest, honourable and forthright man, who thought Storrs effete and devious, and Lawrence, whom he had once met in Cairo, a know-it-all and 'a bumptious young ass'. He knew that they did not share his opinion that a British force should be landed at Rabegh, and was embarrassed that his promises to Feisal had not been fulfilled. He had arranged a meeting with 'Abdallah, who, fresh from his victory at Ta'if, had pitched his tents near Eve's Tomb, four miles outside the town. That morning, Wilson and Storrs rode out to meet the Sharif, and in the afternoon 'Abdallah returned the compliment, riding through the Mecca gate on a white mare with an escort of slaves. Stylishly turned out in a yellow silk headcloth, a camel's-hair cloak, a white silk shirt and knee-length boots of patent leather, he dismounted at the Agency and was shown into a meeting consisting of Storrs, Wilson, Lawrence, and two Arab officers – Aziz 'Ali al-Misri, the Hashemite Chief of Staff, who had travelled down in the *Lama* with Storrs and Lawrence, and Sayyid 'Ali Pasha, the Egyptian general commanding the artillery with Feisal in the hills. After describing conditions in the Hejaz, 'Abdallah revealed his concern about the danger to Rabegh. A Turkish advance now might take away all the Arabs' hard-won victories: the urban population was not undivided in its support for the Hashemites, and even among the Bedu there were elements of the Harb, the Billi – and some of the Juhayna

– who were not entirely to be trusted, and who might easily go over to the enemy. He asked anxiously about the possibility of landing the British force, which had more than once been promised. This was the moment Storrs had secretly been dreading. In a conference at Ismaeliyya on 12 September, which both he and Wilson had attended, Sir Archibald Murray, the GOC, had savaged the idea of sending British soldiers. Murray needed his troops for the serious business of protecting the Suez Canal, and was wary of 'sideshows' which, like the Gallipoli campaign, could quickly escalate out of all proportion and swallow men and arms needed elsewhere. Murray was also of the opinion that the Hashemites had botched the revolt: 'The Sharif, as might have been expected, has muddled the business,' he wired to the Chief of the Imperial General Staff, General Robertson, in London; 'it is not unlikely that, in spite of the numbers against them, the Turks will suppress the rising . . . I do not think we should send British troops . . . if we begin by sending a Brigade of infantry the demands will never cease – we shall begin with infantry, then artillery, then engineers . . . followed by . . . the whole impedimenta of a campaign in the desert . . .'[1] Wilson and Parker were pushing hard for a British landing, and Murray had an orthodox soldier's instinctive dislike for such 'experts': 'I have little faith in the judgement on a military question of any officer who has spent the best part of his life in this country [i.e. Egypt],' he wrote. 'Men like Wilson and Parker, now with the Sharif, are good Arabic scholars and know the habits and customs of the country, but their recommendations as to the military action are often futile and impossible of solution.'[2] Murray had firmly rejected their recommendations, and in London Robertson had supported his decision. It was Storrs's embarrassing task to explain to 'Abdallah that not only would the promised troops not be sent after all, but that the £10,000 granted was to be withheld, and the flight of aircraft which had already been dispatched to Rabegh to be withdrawn. 'Abdallah, Storrs knew, would view this as tantamount to treachery. Though Storrs was relieved that he 'took it like a fine gentleman', he wrote in his diary: 'The moment when we had to explain that the withdrawal of our promise of the Brigade included the aeroplanes was not pleasant and I do not wish to have to show HM Government to an Arab a second time in that light.'[3] In fact, 'Abdallah was astonished and angry, and after the meeting went straight to the French Agency to talk to

Lieutenant-Colonel Bremond, who had just arrived to take charge of a tiny French military mission. 'Abdallah hinted to Bremond that because the British had refused to help, the Hashemites might be forced to sue for peace with the Turks. Bremond felt that if the Arabs withdrew from the conflict, then, in the event of victory, the British alone would claim the lands of the Near East. The French could not spare large numbers of troops from the Western Front, and only his small contingent in Jeddah would ensure a place at the Peace Conference afterwards. If that mission had to retire, then all French hopes in Syria might be dashed. Bremond later hurried round to Wilson with the news, and after a flurry of cables, the British agreed to reconsider the question.

This was to come later. For the moment 'Abdallah sat out the meeting stoically. Lawrence, who had spoken little, had taken an immediate dislike to him. The Sharif, he admitted later, was 'too clever'. He knew that 'Abdallah was his father's right-hand man, and highly popular among the Arabs. He had been the prime mover in the revolt from the beginning – indeed, in many ways it might be said that 'Abdallah had *created* the Arab Revolt. Cheerful, extrovert, highly cultured and sophisticated, he did not fit Lawrence's concept of the 'noble savage', and bore no relation to his 'innocent' Dahoum. He was of strong character – highly intelligent, worldly-wise, experienced, blooded in battle, and a superb chess-player – more than a match for Lawrence's manipulation. If the British were to influence the situation to their advantage, Lawrence realized, they must find and set up as a figurehead a leader who was more malleable and susceptible to their design. He had been monitoring affairs in the Hejaz closely since June, and knew that the situation was critical. The revolt, he said, was 'standing still, which, with an irregular war, was a prelude to disaster'.[4] Secretly, though, he was against sending British troops, but for other reasons than those argued by Murray. First, as an arch-propagandist, he was aware that guerrilla wars were fought partly on an ideological level, and to have infidel soldiers in the Hejaz would make Hussain look like a Muslim renegade ready to hand over the Holy Cities to unbelievers. Secondly – and to Lawrence even more important – if the British were to fight Arab battles for them, the Arabs would have little claim, at the end of the war, to an independent state. They must, at least, be *seen* to be conducting their own revolt. Lawrence had a

16. Tent in the Wadi Rum, Jordan. A unique geological formation, created by the irruption of sandstone strata elsewhere confined under limestone, the Wadi Rum was considered by Lawrence to be the most spectacular sight in the whole of Arabia. Many of Rum's Howaytat Bedu still live in traditional black tents as they did in Lawrence's day.

17. Howaytat woman, Wadi Rum. Proudly displaying the facial tattoos she received as a girl on the eve of her wedding, this matriarch of the Howaytat, one of the celebrated bards of her tribe, still chants poems recalling the days of Lawrence and Auda Abu Tayyi.

18. The author with Sabah ibn 'Iid at Mudowwara well, Jordan. Lawrence's patrol watered at the pool here on 17 September 1917, on their way to attack Mudowwara station, which lies about three miles away. The Turks had deliberately polluted the water with dead camels, ensuring that Lawrence's British gunners came down with diarrhoea. Today, due to local irrigation projects, the well is completely dry.

19. Loading a camel at Mudowwara well. A Bedui of the Howaytat loads his camel at the same point from which Lawrence's patrol moved south to hit the railway near Hallat Ammar. They watered again at Mudowwara well on the exfiltration to Wadi Rum.

20. Wrecked railway wagon, Mudowwara. This wagon of 1914–18 vintage stands near the site where, on 19 September 1917, Lawrence and his patrol successfully mined a train drawn by two locomotives, and killed seventy Turks by machine-gun and mortar fire within ten minutes – one of the most perfectly executed guerrilla operations of the war.

21. A Bedui filling a waterskin. Lawrence wrote that the ways of the Bedu were hard even for those brought up in them, and for a stranger terrible – a death in life. The Bedu saw things differently, however: the desert offered them what to their eyes was a relatively comfortable way of life.

22. Azraq castle, exterior. Lawrence used the castle as a base for his later campaign in Syria, notably in November 1918 after the failed raid on Tel ash-Shehab bridge, when his men took down part of this wall to allow them to bring in their camels at night. Though the breach has been refilled, the place can be seen clearly in this picture.

23. Inside the gate-tower, Azraq castle. Lawrence himself occupied this room above the castle gate, where, on cold winter nights, his men would huddle around the fire in their cloaks, telling stories from Bedu folklore – including the tale of the ghost-hounds of the Bani Hillal, which were supposed to haunt the castle.

24. Bedu women of the Rwalla, Syria. Under their powerful Sheikh, Nuri ash-Sha'alan, the Rwalla – the largest camel-breeding tribe in Syria – joined the Hashemite forces for the final operations around Dara'a, and the push on Damascus in 1918.

25. The author at the postern gate, Azraq castle. Azraq's two gates consisted of slabs of rock weighing several tons, which were ingeniously pivoted so that one man could close them. Lawrence had the front gate permanently blocked, and used only this one – the postern gate – which was closed by a sentry at sunset, its slamming reverberating round the walls of the castle.

26. Sayl al-Haysa, Jordan. Marking the natural border between the hills of Edom to the south, and Moab to the north, it was in the Sayl al-Haysa that Hashemite scouts engaged Turkish cavalry pickets on 25 January 1918 – an engagement leading to the pitched battle in defence of Tafilah, when the Turkish forces were routed by the Arabs.

27. Shobek (Monreale) castle, Jordan. Lawrence stayed at this castle several times during the Dead Sea campaign in 1918, once, notably, on his winter ride from Guweira having secured a fresh supply of gold for the projected but abortive invasion of Moab.

(*top*) 28. The battlefield at Tafilah, Jordan. Set on a rolling, rocky panhandle dividing the Tafilah gorge from the Sayl al-Haysa, Lawrence described the battlefield as roughly triangular. On 25 January 1918, Turkish troops occupied ridges to the right and left, but were driven back when Arab forces out-flanked them and attacked suddenly from the rear.

(*bottom left*) 29. View from Shobek (Monreale) castle. Lawrence thought the castle an inspiring sight: 'We went over the ridge,' he wrote, '. . . and down to the base of a shapely cone, whose mural crown was the ring-wall of the old castle of Monreale, very noble against the night sky.'

(*bottom right*) 30. View of the Belqa uplands from Kerak, Jordan. Much of Lawrence's later campaign was fought not in the desert, as often imagined, but in these hills, bordering the eastern shore of the Dead Sea. A wheat-growing area inhabited by cultivating peasants, the plateau was snow-covered in winter 1918, and its muddy tracts often proved hard going for Lawrence's camels.

31. A Bedui of the Haywat, Jordan. One of the small Bedu tribes inhabiting southern Jordan and the Sinai peninsula, the Haywat joined the Hashemite forces on Lawrence's final push on Aqaba in July 1917.

passionate belief in the cause of Arab freedom, but though he wished to see the Arabs free of the Ottoman Turks, it is unlikely that he ever believed they could be entirely independent. From the beginning he envisaged not a single Arab state but a congeries of petty states, nominally independent but actually under the benevolent aegis of the British Empire, which would naturally fill the vacuum in the Near East left by the collapse of the Ottoman Empire. The war had to be won, and British and Arab interests dovetailed at this point: both wanted victory against the Turks. Lawrence could therefore happily serve both the cause of British victory and Arab independence, satisfied that, for now, there was no conflict between them. If such a conflict arose, though, he had no doubt where his true loyalties lay: 'I'm strongly pro-British and also pro-Arab,' he would tell Clayton later, 'France takes third place with me: but I quite recognize that we might have to sell our small friends to pay our big friends, or sell our future security in the Near East to pay for our present victory in Flanders.'[5] Though he may secretly have divined that the Hashemite problem lay in poor leadership, and privately decided that he could provide the guidance they needed, he was a committed intelligence officer, and never saw himself 'leading from the front'. Indeed, he had not expected, nor wished, to be sent into the field. He firmly believed that his place was behind a desk, and in the past months had done an excellent job in designing and having printed a set of Hejaz postage stamps whose object was to establish before the eyes of the world that the Hejaz was, in fact, already independent.

Lawrence's first mission to the Hejaz had come about in an indirect way. In May, General Murray had made more changes to his intelligence organization, stripping Clayton of his *carte blanche* and assigning him solely to the work of the Arab Bureau, which was now under the direction of Major Kinahan Cornwallis. The Intelligence Department in Cairo, of which Lawrence remained a member, was to be reunited with its Ismaeliyya counterpart under the command of Major G. V. W. Holdich. The Bureau and the Intelligence Department were to remain quite distinct entities. Lawrence did not wish to be separated from Clayton, and had sounded out the possibility of a transfer to the Bureau. When Holdich had barred any such transfer, Lawrence had resorted to guerrilla tactics, plaguing senior officers by correcting the grammar in their reports, and mocking their poor knowledge of geography and customs in the Near East. One morning a staff officer had phoned him, demanding to know where certain divisions of the Turkish army were currently located. Lawrence had given him a thoroughly competent description of the composition and location of the divisions, to the extent of pinpointing the actual villages in which they were quartered.

'Have you noted them in the Dislocation files?' the officer asked.

'No,' Lawrence replied, 'they are better in my head until I can check the information.'

'Yes,' said the officer. 'But you can't send your head along to Ismaeliyya every time.'

'I wish to goodness I could,' Lawrence concluded, ringing off.

Such ploys amounted to insubordination, and had not endeared Lawrence to his superiors. Finally, he had taken his case to Clayton, who had agreed to request his transfer through London, in order to circumvent Holdich. Meanwhile he managed to get Lawrence out of the way by asking to 'borrow' him from GHQ. Clayton's major problem with the Hejaz was that, bereft of any intelligence officers in the front line, he had little idea of what was really happening, or how many troops were involved. Parker – the Hejaz IO – was largely confined to Rabegh, and while both he and Wilson had met Feisal, they felt that the Sharif tended to exaggerate, claiming, for instance, that the Turks massed against him numbered 25,000 strong. This was clearly nonsense, but Clayton wondered what other exaggerations were being passed off in the name of truth. Frankly, he did not trust Wilson's judgement either, and suspected him of doctoring intelligence reports to agree with his own assessments, and indeed, he sometimes wondered if Wilson was entirely *compos mentis*. What were the actual dimensions of the threat from Medina? Parker, in Rabegh, had been pressing Clayton for some time to send an officer inland to obtain desperately needed intelligence, and had clearly hoped to go up country himself. On 9 October, though, Clayton wrote to Wingate that Storrs was being sent back there to see 'Abdallah and possibly Hussain. 'I propose to send Lawrence with him, if GHQ will let him go,' he wrote. 'They ought to be of use, and between them bring back a good appreciation of the situation.'[6] They had left Suez on the *Lama* on 14 October. Lawrence would later claim to have gone down to the Hejaz on his own initiative, to find 'the master spirit' of the revolt, and wrote that he had asked for two weeks' leave. Storrs, on the other hand, claimed that he had requested Lawrence for the expedition, simply because he enjoyed his company, and had thus created 'Lawrence of Arabia' as well as the Arab Revolt. The leave was a fact – a technicality designed to undermine any protests Holdich might have produced – but Storrs's claim to have applied for him, like his own claim to have gone there of his own choosing, was spurious. He had been sent to the Hejaz by the Arab Bureau, and he had been sent with a particular – and vital – mission in mind.

Lawrence knew that in order to make a proper appreciation he would have to visit Feisal on the *Darb Sultani*, and the thought did not attract him. He was well aware that the Hejaz was crawling with informers and Turkish sympathizers, and if captured he might be shot as a spy. Moreover, no Christian officers – not even Wilson or Parker – had ever been allowed to visit the front. However, he used all his charm with 'Abdallah, pretending to support the Sharif's view that a British landing was necessary, and suggesting obliquely that the decision not to send troops was by no means final. He argued that if he were allowed to speak to Feisal, and see the situation for himself, he might be able to give his backing more convincingly to 'Abdallah's case. 'Abdallah was doubtful. He telephoned Hussain in Mecca to ask his opinion, and the Sharif greeted the proposal with mistrust. This was perhaps the most crucial moment in Lawrence's entire life. If 'Abdallah had put the phone down, the story might have ended there and then. Lawrence might have gone back – not unhappily – to his desk in Cairo, and Colonel Lawrence, 'Lawrence of Arabia', might never have been born. But for some reason, 'Abdallah did not put the receiver down. He pushed his father on the point, then handed the phone to Storrs, who supported the idea with all the rhetoric at his command. Reluctantly, against all his principles, the Sharif agreed that Lawrence might ride up the Wadi Safra to visit Feisal. There was to be no turning back: the die had been cast, and the legend-in-the-making had found its path.

In AD 624, the army of the Prophet Mohammad engaged a rival Meccan force at Badr, where the Wadi Safra meets the coastal plain. The Muslims were then but a small sect, and had they lost the battle of Badr, they might well have disappeared. More than 1,000 years later, the Prophet's direct descendants found themselves in a similar plight. In 1916, Sharif Feisal and his Bedu army were retreating slowly down the Wadi Safra with a Turkish brigade behind them. If the Turks had launched a massive counter-attack at that moment, they would probably have broken through into the coastal plain and taken Rabegh, then Mecca, and the Arab Revolt would have been at an end.

In the Prophet's day, Badr was an important watering-station on the route to Mecca. Today, though, it is little more than a truck-stop on the motorway, without even a place to stay. I arrived there on a bus from Jeddah, late on a steamy night, and stood by the side of the road for an hour desperately trying to flag down a lift. Finally I gave up, bought two small bottles of mineral water, and walked along the soft asphalt for a mile until I found a sandy drywash, where, after carefully avoiding snake and scorpion tracks, I laid out my sleeping-bag. It was too hot to sleep, so I lay watching the stars until morning, and when dawn came, I saw that I was in a wadi forested with patches of thorn-trees and tamarisk, from which granite foothills rose steeply, their sharply carved facets turned at angles to the sun like cut jewels, flashing in the early light. The lower slopes were covered in a down of mustard-yellow goatgrass, which from this distance looked almost like a growth of lichen staining the rock. This yellowish growth solved the riddle of the valley's name, for Wadi Safra means 'The Yellow Wadi' in Arabic. I hiked back to the truck-stop and after half an hour a young Bedui of the Bani Salem Harb agreed to take me to Hamra and Medina in his pick-up for 100 riyals. The *Darb Sultani* – the road which crawled up the Wadi Safra – opened like a long twisting corridor, climbing up steadily until a vast panorama of mountains lay before us, silver and grey, like successive waves of cloud extending into the distance until they appeared to merge into the sky itself. We passed village after village of ancient baked-mud houses, now standing roofless on the rocky sides of the valley, in forests of date-palms: Jedida, Hussainiyya, Wasta, Kharma. In Lawrence's day these villages were the heartland of the Bani Salem, and produced almost all the tribe's grain and dates. The Bedu remained in the villages for five months of the year, spending the rest of the time wandering with their herds and flocks and leaving the villages and palm-groves to their slaves. These slaves, who were mostly of African origin, had no legal status, and numbered about 10,000 at the time of Lawrence's visit.

My Bedui driver asked what I was about, and when I mentioned 'Lawrence of Arabia' he asked, 'Who?'

'An Englishman who helped lead the Arab armies in the Great Arab Revolt.'

'What?'

'When the Hashemites were here.'

'Oh, the Hashemites! That was long ago. This is the country of the Saudis now!'

Was he being deliberately obtuse, I wondered, or could tribal memories really have become so short? His people, the Bani Salem, were one of the main clans of the Harb – a major Bedu tribe in the Hejaz. This youth's grandfathers and grand-uncles had actually fought with Feisal, while many of the Masruh Harb – their rivals – had sided with the Turks, under the 'traitor' Sheikh ibn Mubeiriq. It was only after a while that I remembered that it had been the Bani Salem who had run from the Turks at the crucial moment. Perhaps, after all, it was a memory the tribe would rather forget.

Hamra took me by surprise. I had imagined some tiny hamlet in a cleft in the wadi side, but the scale of the place was enormous, with thousands of palms whose heads moved slowly like sea-grass to the tune of the wind. The wadi was about half a mile wide here, lying between two steep, stony walls, and the ruined houses stood on a long ridge at the foot of the northern spur, and on high earth mounds rising steeply from the wadi bed. Lawrence had numbered the houses at about 150, but there were obviously many hundreds more, and there was also the remains of a Turkish fort, a shapeless mud stump on an island in the sea of palms. This village had for generations been a station on the Pilgrim Road from Yanbu' al-Bahr to Medina, and when Richard Burton had halted here, disguised as a Persian doctor, in 1852, the fort had been manned by a platoon of Albanian soldiers. I climbed the ridge and scrambled among the warren of ruptured and leaning mud walls, eroded into surreal sculptures by the rain, and tried to picture what this village must have been like in late October 1916, when the wadi was full of Feisal's defeated troops, and three camel-riders, one of them an Englishman, had suddenly appeared on the outskirts of the village.

*

Lawrence and his two *rafiqs* had left Rabegh on 21 October, under the cover of darkness. From a distance, all three might have been mistaken for Bedu, since Lawrence wore an Arab headcloth and had thrown a cloak over his uniform. Close up, though, he would easily have been recognized as a foreigner. Not only was he cleanshaven and pink-faced, he obviously knew nothing about camel-riding. When he had travelled with camels in the Negev two years previously, he had preferred to walk. Sharif 'Ali, the eldest of the Hashemite sons, had reluctantly provided him with his best camel and an escort of two Bani Salem – Sheikh Obeyd and his son 'Abdallah – to take him to Feisal's camp. Though Lawrence was to masquerade as a Syrian, 'Ali had ordered Obeyd not to let him talk to anyone: the desert and the hills were full of Turkish spies, and the 'traitor' ibn Mubeiriq, whose tribal district they were passing through, would happily have killed Lawrence or sold him to the Turks. The riders cleared Rabegh's palm-groves and stalked out into the endless coastal plain of the Tihama. There was no moon, and the night yawned infinitely before them, its silence broken only by the soft percussion of the camels' feet on the flat sand. As the darkness closed in, Lawrence felt suddenly apprehensive. He had entered a hostile and unknown dimension, into which few Europeans had been before him, and from which even fewer had returned alive. He was unsure, even, that he could trust his companions. He knew, of course, that the role of companion or *rafiq* was a solemn office to the Bedu: every traveller who wanted to cross a tribal district must have a *rafiq* from the local tribe or one allied to it to frank him through. For a *rafiq* to turn on his charge once accepted was a heinous affront to the Bedu code of honour, and a Bedui found guilty by his fellow-tribesmen of the crime of *bowqa* – treachery – would be ostracized for life, and never allowed to marry from his own folk. To be tribeless in a tribal society amounted virtually to a death sentence, for any marauder might kill the outcast without the risk of starting a blood-feud – the one social institution in Arabia which prevented bloodshed on a large scale. Nevertheless, Lawrence reminded himself, like the English code of the 'gentleman', the rules the Bedu lived by were only an ideal. The German explorer Charles Huber, for instance, who had come this way in 1884, had been murdered by his Harb *rafiqs* near Rabegh, when the Arabs had discovered that he was a Christian.

They slept for a few hours that night, wrapped in their cloaks, and were up in the chill of dawn, reaching the well at Masturah in the mellow flush of early light. Some Bedu of the Masruh Harb were crouching under an awning of palm-fronds, and their eyes followed Lawrence's party suspiciously as they passed. They dismounted by a ruined wall, and Lawrence sat down in the shade. Obeyd and his son took the camels off to water them at a stone shaft, twenty feet deep, with footholds built into its side. While Obeyd held the camels, 'Abdallah tucked up his *dishdasha* into his cartridge-belt and slung a goatskin over his shoulder, then descended into the well, feeling for the footholds deftly with his bare feet. He filled the goatskin, shinned up again as surely as a lizard and poured the water into a stone basin. When the animals had drunk their fill, Obeyd carried over a bowl of water for Lawrence to drink. Finally, the two Bani Salem drank themselves. Then they sat down with Lawrence in the shade, to watch the Masruh watering a herd of thin she-camels. 'Abdallah rolled himself a cigarette.

It was at this moment that Lawrence had a vision. As they watched, he wrote, two young riders came trotting in on richly caparisoned thoroughbred camels, and couched them by the well. One of them, dressed in a fine cashmere robe, tossed his headrope carelessly to the other and ordered him to water them. The young lord strutted arrogantly over to where Lawrence and his *rafiqs* were sitting, and sank down on his haunches next to them. He was a slim man, little more than a boy, with a slightly pugnacious, inquisitive face, his long hair dressed in plaits, Bedu style. He was powerful-looking and appeared supremely confident. He offered Lawrence a cigarette, freshly rolled and licked, and then inquired if he was from Syria. Lawrence left the question hanging in the air, and asked if the youth was from Mecca. His companion, meanwhile, was making little progress in watering his camels. The Masruh herd was pressing lustily around the stone basin, and the herdsmen had not given the youth a chance to water his beasts as the customary etiquette to travellers demanded. 'What is it, Mustafa?' the lord shouted. 'Water them at once!' 'Mustafa' approached him shamefacedly, and began to explain that the herdsmen would not let him, whereupon the other jumped up with an oath and beat him savagely three or four times about the shoulders with his camel-stick. 'Mustafa' looked resentful, but stayed silent. The Masruh, watching from the well, were embarrassed that their own lack of hospitality had caused the boy's humiliation, and not only gave the young man a place at the water immediately, but offered his camels some fresh shoots to eat. After the animals had eaten and drunk, the young lord climbed upon his camel without couching her, simply pulling her head down gently and stepping on her neck. 'God requite you!' he told the Masruh, and rode off with his companion to the south.

No sooner had they gone than Obeyd started to chuckle. Later, after Lawrence and his *rafiqs* had mounted their camels and were riding north, he explained that the young 'lord' was Sharif 'Ali ibn Hussain of the Harith, and 'Mustafa' actually his cousin, Sharif Muhsin. Sharif 'Ali was a trusted lieutenant of Feisal's, and despite his age had an outstanding reputation for courage. He had been one of Feisal's picked bodyguard in Damascus, and had fought next to him on the bloody plains outside Medina at the beginning of June. Later, he had led the raids against the Turkish advance at Bir Darwish. The Harith and the Masruh were blood-enemies, and if the herdsmen at the well had suspected their identities, they might have been driven away. They had invented the charade of master and servant, Obeyd said, to deceive them. Lawrence was entranced by Sharif 'Ali. For the rest of his time in Arabia, he would be captivated by the image of the 'noble' boy-warrior he had glimpsed at Masturah, on his first journey into the desert.

Like several of the questionable incidents in Lawrence's story, the meeting with Sharif 'Ali makes no appearance in any official report – though Lawrence often gives details of a far more minor nature. In *Seven Pillars*,[7] this vision sets the scene for the world of deception, conflict and cruelty in which he now found himself: a world of handsome young men who resort frequently to the stick, a world in which the tribes are ancient blood-enemies that only an idea of great influence can unite. Since Obeyd knew the identities of the two Harith Sharifs, though, it seems unlikely that the Masruh at the well would not have recognized them. The Bedu were extremely observant, not missing a single detail – tribesmen who could remember the track of every camel they had ever seen, who could distinguish families and clans simply by the difference in the way they tied their headcloths, are unlikely to have been deceived by the rather amateurish performance, and it would have been obvious from 'Mustafa's' appearance, bearing, clothing, saddlery, and a thousand other tiny details, that he was no servant or slave. Secondly, the story has a ring of familiarity common to many tales in *Seven Pillars*: the boyish pranks of the young Sharifs are a preview of the 'naughtiness' later practised by Lawrence's servants 'Farraj and Da'ud', and the masochistic element – the 'submission', 'humiliation' and beating of one of the boys – is clear. Such flagellation and public humiliation also play a large role in the 'Farraj and Da'ud' story. Sharif 'Ali emerges from *Seven Pillars* as Lawrence's beau ideal of the desert Arab – the aristocratic Bedui, counterpart of his pre-war love, Dahoum. It seems at least possible, though, that this vision of male beauty Lawrence claimed to have experienced at Masturah was no more than an interior one, since Sharif 'Ali makes his first appearance in Lawrence's field diary on 8 March 1917 – five months later – and in this hand-written entry Lawrence describes the Sharif as if seeing him for the first time.

From Masturah, they passed out of the territory of the Masruh and into that of the Bani Salem, to which Lawrence's *rafiqs* belonged. Obeyd showed Lawrence the stone which marked the frontier of his own tribal district. What struck Lawrence most forcibly was the thought that, though Europeans saw the desert as a barren wilderness, to the Bedu it was home. Every tree, rock, hill, well and spring had its owner, and while it was Bedu custom to allow a traveller to cut firewood and to draw water enough for their own use, woe betide any foreign spirit who tried to exploit it. By noon, Lawrence was beginning to feel the strain of the journey. His legs and back were raw and aching from the constant jolting of the camel, his skin blistered from the sun and his eyes painful from peering all morning into the glare of the burning flint. He had been two years in the city, commuting from hotel to office, he realized, and now had suddenly been dumped in the desert without the slightest preparation. As the sun dipped and melted into the west, they arrived at a village of grass huts called Bir ash-Sheikh, belonging to the Bani Salem. The Bedu couched their camels by one of the huts, and were greeted by a woman who showed them a place to sit, and kindled a fire for them outside. Obeyd went off and begged some flour, which he mixed with a little water in a bowl, and kneaded into a flat oval patty. He buried it carefully in the sand under the embers of the fire, waiting twenty minutes, then brushed them away, delved in the sand, and brought out a piping hot, hard-baked loaf. He clapped it with his hand to remove the last grains of sand and broke it into pieces, which the three of them shared. Although Lawrence later claimed that the Arabs thought it 'effeminate' to take provisions for a journey of less than 100 miles, this was untrue. The fact was that no Bedui would bother to take food while travelling in his own tribal district, since he could always be certain of obtaining nourishment from his fellow tribesmen on the way. The *libbeh* – unleavened bread baked in the sand – was the Bedu's standard fare, and would soon become nauseatingly familiar to Lawrence. For now, though, he ate a little with the best grace he could muster. Afterwards, Obeyd invited him to look at some nearby wells, but he was so stiff after the ride that he declined.

There was a further stretch that night, and at dawn they reached Bir ibn Hassani, the village of Ahmad al-Mansur, one of the great sheikhs of the Harb. As they passed, a camel-rider came loping out of the village and tagged along with them, asking a string of questions, to which Obeyd and his son made short, unwilling, answers. The Arab, whose name was Khallaf, insisted on them eating with him, and forced them to couch their camels. He brought an iron pot out of his saddle-bag, full of baked bread, crumbled and sprinkled with sugar and butter, and offered it to them. Once they had eaten, he told Lawrence that Feisal had been pushed back the previous day from Bir Abbas to Hamra, a little way ahead of them, and he listed the names and injuries of each tribesman who had been hurt. He tried to engage Lawrence in conversation, inquiring if he knew any of the English in Egypt. Lawrence replied in the Aleppo dialect, and Khallaf began asking him about Syrians he knew, then shifted to politics and asked what he thought Feisal's plans were. Obeyd cut in abruptly and changed the subject, and shortly the man left them. They discovered subsequently that he had been a spy in Turkish pay.

By noon they had come to Wasta, a large village of the Bani Salem, consisting of 1,000 mud houses set on earth mounds and long rocky ridges across the wadi-bed, and above the thick palm groves. Lawrence learned that many of the houses were empty. This year a flood like a tidal wave had broken through the embankment, destroyed many of the palmeries and leached away the carefully preserved topsoil. To cap it all, there had been a terrible plague of locusts which had reduced the harvest still further, driving many of the inhabitants away. They rested in Wasta until early afternoon, then rode up the wadi. Almost at once they began to pass squadrons of Bedu crouching around cooking fires or sitting, smoking in the shade of the trees, and there were caravans laden with provisions on the move. These were Feisal's men – many of them Bani Salem – who called out greetings to Obeyd as Lawrence's party passed. Shortly, they saw the village of Hamra before them. They crossed a small stream, and were led up a walled pathway, couching their camels in front of one of the houses. A slave with a scimitar led Lawrence inside, to a smoky room where Feisal was holding court with his military *aide*, an Iraqi cavalry officer named Maulud al-Mukhlis, and Sheikhs of several Bedu tribes, including the Faqir, the Billi, and the Rwalla – a tribe based in Syria. According to Lawrence, Feisal was already standing at the door when he approached, 'waiting for him nervously' – but this is not the Arab way. It is far more likely that when Lawrence entered, the Sharif and his company merely rose to their feet in customary fashion – this was the manner in which they greeted kings and tribesmen alike – while Lawrence shook hands with each of them in turn. He was impressed by the Sharif's stately appearance, which, he said, reminded him of the monument to Richard the Lionheart – the hero of his youth – at Fontevraud in France. He found Feisal more regal and imposing than his brothers, and this was important: Lawrence's first reaction to the Arabs had always been aesthetic and the propagandist in him knew that, to appeal to the British, the Arab Revolt should have a leader who at least *looked* like the European idea of the 'noble Arab'. While 'Abdallah was too round and jolly, and 'Ali too sickly and effete, Feisal fitted the bill admirably. For all his noble appearance, though, Lawrence also thought the Sharif looked dog-tired, much older than his thirty-one years, with bloodshot eyes and hollow cheeks, his skin shrivelled with lines of pain. He smoked incessantly. Lawrence claimed in *Seven Pillars* that he had known instinctively that this was 'the man who would bring the Arab revolt to full glory',[8] yet he told Liddell Hart that in reality he had simply thought that Feisal could be 'made into a hero of revolt' more easily than his elder brothers. According to Lawrence, they sat down together among the Bedu, and Feisal asked him: 'How do you like our place here in the Wadi Safra?'

Lawrence answered: 'Well; but it is far from Damascus.'

'The word had fallen like a sword in their midst,' he wrote. 'There was a quiver. Then everybody present stiffened where they sat, and held his breath for a silent minute . . .' It was Feisal, he said, who eased the tension. The Sharif lifted his eyes, smiling, at Lawrence, and said, 'Praise be to Allah. There are Turks nearer to us than that!'[9]

On the first night, Lawrence and Feisal sat in the smoky room and argued for hours, while the fire crackled and burned down, the dring-drang of the coffee mortar rang out, the coffee and tea went its rounds again and again, and Feisal stubbed out butt after butt. Lawrence found the Sharif most unreasonable. Feisal was indignant that few of the arms he had requested from Wilson had turned up, especially the artillery, and Lawrence became the target of his indignation. Lack of artillery, Feisal maintained, was the Arabs' main problem: with two field-guns he could have captured Medina. The Bedu were terrified of the very sound of shells, and the merest hint of a barrage sent them scampering for cover like rats. This was not because they were cowards, the Sharif explained – for the Bedu would face bullets and swords steadfastly – but because they could not endure the thought of being blown to bits. Feisal talked about artillery endlessly, and Lawrence perceived that the power of the guns, and the carnage at Medina, had made an ineradicable impression on him. He saw that Feisal's nerve had been shattered by what he had seen on that day: 'At [the] original attack on Medina,' he told Liddell Hart, 'he had nerved himself to put on a bold front, and the effort had shaken him so that he never courted danger in battle again.'[10] His spirit had been restored by the arrival of the Egyptian battery, but broken again when he saw that the mountain-guns were helpless against the Turkish heavy field-pieces – a shell from the Turkish guns had actually struck his own tent. Privately, Lawrence viewed his regard for artillery as 'silly', and felt that, guns or no guns, he had never been near capturing Medina. He also felt that the Sharif had not grasped how to use the Egyptian mountain-guns, whose main advantage was their mobility. He tried to persuade Feisal that irregular soldiers should never try to fight pitched battles, anyway, but should attack in small, self-contained mobile groups. The Turks were dogged defensive fighters, as the British defeat at Gallipoli had demonstrated to their bitter cost, and Lawrence reckoned that a single company of Turks, well-entrenched, could defeat the entire Hashemite army. But the Turks' strength lay in concentration of numbers, while the strength of the Arabs lay in diffusion: the Bedu, in their tribal wars and forays, had always fought in this way. Feisal disagreed. For weeks now small parties of Bedu had been making lightning strikes on Turkish positions, trying to slow down their advance, and these flea-bites had failed to hold the Turks back: what the Arabs needed was artillery. The Sharif planned to make a massive assault on two of the stations of the Hejaz railway, Buwat and Hafira, just north of Medina, with a 3,000-strong force of Juhayna now stationed at Khayf Hussain. The Turks had concentrated at Bir Darwish, with no less than five battalions of infantry, two Mule Mounted companies, a camel-mounted mountain-gun battery, field-gun batteries, three aircraft and a regiment of 'Agayl camel-corps. A diversion to the north, Feisal thought, might cause them to retire. Lawrence disliked the plan. He thought that, even with the support of 'Abdallah to the east, and with Zayd's force replacing him in the wadi, the Turkish force would only be drawn off by a third, and the remainder might seize the opportunity to push through the Wadi Safra to Rabegh.

Lawrence had been quartered with the Egyptian artillerymen, whose commander, Zaki Bey, had a tent pitched for him. He retired unsatisfied, however. At first light, Feisal and Maulud al-Mukhlis came to see him again, and they argued solidly for five and a half hours. Lawrence had slept well, and, rested after his journey, he made full use of his powers of persuasion. Today, he gradually began to feel that his arguments were telling. Privately, he perceived that Feisal, though highly intelligent, was by nature cautious, and a weaker character than his brother 'Abdallah, of whom he was notoriously jealous. The Sharif told Lawrence later that when he had advised his father to delay his declaration of the revolt, 'Abdallah had called him a coward: he referred to his elder brother as *mufsid*: 'the malicious one'. Feisal was susceptible to advice, whereas 'Abdallah was not; in fact, Lawrence told Liddell Hart, 'his defect was that he always listened to his momentary adviser, despite his own better judgement.'[11] This was a very different picture, of course, from the one Lawrence presented in his official dispatches, where he emphasized the fact that Feisal was regarded as a hero by his men, and had risked his life at Medina to hearten his troops. He represented him as impatient and impetuous, hot-tempered and proud, 'full of dreams and the capacity to realise them'.[12] It was not, Lawrence said, the fact that Feisal had been unnerved by a shell through his tent which had caused him to order his troops back from Bir Abbas, but because he was 'bored with his obvious impotence' – a languid emotion which smacks more of the Oxford common room than the heat of battle. In reality, he thought Feisal timid and terrified of danger, and this private view was echoed by others who knew Feisal well, such as Pierce Joyce, who wrote that Feisal was 'not a very strong character and much swayed by his surroundings'.[13] Lawrence felt that Feisal's passion for Arab freedom had forced him to face risks he hated, and since his own masochistic nature obliged him to do the same, he had great empathy with the Sharif. For the British establishment, though, the leader of the Arab Revolt must appear heroic, and Lawrence resolved to 'make the best of him', even if this meant portraying his character falsely in his dispatches.[14] He was no novice in manipulating the facts and the media to get his way, and he was as passionate about the Arab Revolt as Feisal was: 'I had been a mover in its beginning,' he wrote, 'my hopes lay in it.'[15] This was not pure altruism. Lawrence had been romantically attached to the Arabs since his experiences at Carchemish. He saw Feisal and the revolt as an expression of his own rebellion – the same emotions which had led him to bring Dahoum and Hammoudi to Oxford – the competitive spirit, the 'beast' within, which craved others' notice, yearned for recognition that he was 'different' and 'distinct'. His attitude to the Hashemites was an extension of his attitude to Dahoum, for just as he had written that he wished to help the boy help himself, so he would tell Graves that his object with the Arabs was 'to make them stand on their own feet'.[16] Lawrence felt he knew what was best for Dahoum, and now he knew what was best for the Hashemites. The problem of the Arab Revolt was lack of leadership, he concluded, and he, Lawrence, would provide that leadership through his proxy, the malleable Feisal. For his part, Feisal was moved by Lawrence's masterly rhetoric, and encouraged that British GHQ were taking a closer interest in his affairs. He had the impression that Lawrence was empowered to make definite promises. Above all, Lawrence's mysteriousness and whimsicality began to win the Sharif over. At the end of their second discussion, they parted amicably for lunch.

In the afternoon, Lawrence made it his business to stroll around the wadi, chatting with Feisal's troops. He felt that they were in fine fettle for a defeated army. The Bedu, who had made camp in the palm-groves, mostly belonged to the Juhayna, a large tribe based in the Wadi Yanbu' to the north, and to the Harb, their deadly enemies. Lawrence saw that Feisal had done a remarkable job in reconciling the traditional foes to fight side by side for the Hashemite cause. He was under no illusion though: it was Hashemite money – ultimately from British coffers – which had bought the Bedu's allegiance, and if things went badly, they might easily desert to the enemy. The British conception of the tribal levies as a feudal army under the noble Sharifs was quite wrong. In feudal Europe serfs had been the chattels of their lords and bound to military service when required. Not so the Bedu. They were not bound to anyone or anything but their own tribe, and for this reason would not consider it *bowqa* – treachery – to change sides, as long as such a defection were agreed by the tribe or the family as a whole. The people they served – Hashemites or Turks – were aliens. The Turks already had Bedu irregulars working for them. The Billi, a powerful and xenophobic tribe to the north, were still wavering, and one of their Sheikhs, Suleyman Rifada, had already declared for the Turks. If the Billi went over to the Turks *en bloc*, then the Juhayna might follow. Nevertheless, Lawrence reckoned that the Turks were spending £70,000 a month on attempts to buy the tribes, and were receiving mostly empty promises in return. He believed that ultimately the Hashemites had a sentimental appeal to the Bedu which the Turks could not equal.

This was the first time Lawrence had been close to the Bedu, and he was thrilled by their appearance, and awed by their toughness. Not all were nomads – most, indeed, were cultivators and semi-nomads, and many were armed slaves and retainers of the desert folk. Their ages ranged from twelve to sixty – small, dark, spare, bird-like, elegant men, clad only in loose *dishdashas*, baggy *sirwals* and headcloths, bristling with cartridge-belts and rifles which they would fire off at any excuse. They were superbly fit, and could run and walk in the sun for hours barefoot over rock and burning sand. They moved with a quick nervousness which gave the impression of the need to burn off boundless energy. Lawrence thought they would make superb guerrilla fighters and, when trained properly, excellent snipers. They would run and climb long distances in order to find themselves the right niche for a shot, though they were as yet more used to their slow old muskets than modern rifles with sights, and were accustomed to engage their enemies at short range. They had an intimate knowledge of the terrain and their tracking skills appeared almost supernatural. As conventional troops, though, Lawrence felt that they would be useless. For one thing, the actual personnel were constantly shifting as tribesmen returned home to visit their wives, handing their rifle to a brother or a cousin to take their place. Sometimes an entire clan would get bored and quit. They would not take orders from anyone but their own tribal Sheikhs, and would not serve beside an enemy tribe unless they were under the command of a Sharif, who was thought to be above tribal politics. As individuals they were brave and reckless, but the cult of reputation by which they lived made them poor team-players. Every man was his own master, and he would not readily obey commands, fight in line, or help strangers merely because they happened to be in the same army. The Bedu were obsessively clannish: 'Me and my cousin against a stranger, me and my brother against my cousin,' was their *modus vivendi*. Their traditional raid or *ghazwa* was fought to specific rules – an attack was never made by night; women, children and unarmed shepherds were inviolate; at least one camel was always left so that the victims could survive. It was also fought for property – usually camels – rather than life. Their way of fighting did not allow of high casualties, which the ancient rule of *lex talionis* – blood-feud – had for generations proscribed. Their way was the way of the individual warrior – this new-fangled method of warfare, of faceless armies and weapons that killed indiscriminately from afar, was beyond their ken. To the Bedu, each fellow-tribesman was a valued individual rather than just another soldier, which was why they had traditionally turned tail when faced with resolute opposition or greater numbers. As early as 1830, Burckhardt described Arab warfare as that of partisans whose main object was to surprise the enemy by sudden attack and plunder his camp:[17] 'I could adduce,' he wrote, 'numerous instances of caravan-travellers and peasants putting to flight three times their number of Arabs [Bedu] who attacked them: hence . . . they are reckoned miserable cowards and their contests with the peasants always prove them such.'[18] C. S. Jarvis called them 'very good ten minute fighters' – and added, 'there is nothing to savage and terrifying as Arab horsemen dealing with a demoralised enemy; and nothing quite so easy as the same Arabs with the "wind up" '.[19] Pierce Joyce would write that the Bedu were 'more of a bluff than a real menace', and felt that the notion of working to a set programme was an impossibility for them.[20] Alec Kirkbride would say later: 'You could get a terrific charge out of them.

If it came off, splendid, but if it didn't, well, they ran away. That seemed the only sensible thing to do.'[21] Lawrence thought that they would be good for dynamiting the railway, plundering Turkish caravans or stealing camels, and noted in his report later that while one might sneer at their mercenary nature, despite considerable bribes from the Turks the tribes were not helping them, and the Hashemite supply caravans were still plying through the hills unmolested.

Later that afternoon Lawrence saw Feisal again, and this time they got on much better. If Feisal's plan to distract them failed, Lawrence thought, the Turks' next move would probably be to advance on Mecca through Rabegh. In this case the Bedu irregulars could best be used to hold the Subh hills around the Wadi Safra, which formed a natural defensive line. The Turkish army would have no choice but to advance through the wadis, and their twists and turns would be a godsend for guerrilla troops. Even the Turkish artillery would not benefit them much in the hills. He thought that the Arabs should be strengthened with Lewis machine-guns, and some modern field artillery for the sake of their morale, and that they needed technical advisers, better liaison with the British GHQ and even wireless sets. Though the tribal force would never be capable of an offensive, he thought, it would make a strong defensive screen behind which a regular field-force recruited from slaves, townsfolk and peasants could be built up. Lawrence felt that if Feisal could just hold out in these hills for two months, then al-Masri could train up his column of Arab regulars in Rabegh. As for landing British troops there, Lawrence thought that nothing would be more certain to destroy the Hashemite cause. He noted in his report that Feisal and his aides had no sympathy with the Arab Nationalists hanged in Damascus and Beirut, because they had been in league with the French, hinting strongly to his superiors that the Arabs had no intention of handing their country over to another foreign master, and would thus be highly suspicious of any massed landing of British troops. The intuition was correct, but the facts were almost certainly a fabrication – in Feisal's case at least, for there are eye-witness reports that he was outraged by the Nationalist hangings when he heard about them in Damascus. In his reports, Lawrence also misrepresented the tribesmen as being intensely nationalistic: in fact they were chauvinistic, xenophobic and fanatically anti-Christian. A British landing would be certain to shatter Hashemite prestige, and drive the tribes into the arms of the Turks. He left at four o'clock in the afternoon of 24 October, with an escort of fourteen tribesmen of the Juhayna, heading for Yanbu', not expecting to see the Sharif again. He was satisfied that in Feisal the British had a hero they could influence and manipulate, or as he put it, with characteristic ambiguity, a leader 'with reason to give effect to our science'. He was also confident that he had solved the conundrum of Rabegh: 'I told my chiefs,' he wrote, 'that Mecca was defended not by the obstacle of Rabegh, but by the flank threat of Feisal in [the Subh hills].'[22]

13. Not an Army But a World is Moving upon Wejh

Yanbu' and Wejh
December 1916–January 1917

It was wishful thinking, of course. The Bedu had never been defensive fighters, and when Fakhri Pasha finally emerged from Medina that December with three full brigades, he outflanked the Bani Salem holding the Wadi Safra and sent them scattering to their villages without a fight. Despite Lawrence's assurances, they had never received either machine-guns or artillery, and the Turks broke through into the coastal plain within twenty-four hours, proving what Lawrence later dignified as 'The Second Theorem of Irregular War' – 'that irregular troops are as unable to defend a point or line as they are to attack it'.[1] Professional soldiers such as Sir Reginald Wingate had been saying this from the beginning without any elaborate 'theorem', which was why British troops had been thought necessary to defend Rabegh in the first place. By then, though, it was too late. Lawrence had returned from the mountains like Moses, with the solution to the problem of Rabegh graven in stone. If a British force had landed in the Hejaz, he said later, not a single Arab would have remained with the Sharif. This, as he well knew, was exactly what General Murray wanted to hear, and the provision of machine-guns, artillery and military advisers Lawrence requested seemed to the GOC a small price to pay for the conservation of one or two brigades. Lawrence's star was suddenly in the ascendant at GHQ, and he realized that he was in a uniquely powerful position. No one had been to the front before him, and none followed him: he was the only British officer who had seen the conditions there for himself. By presenting the evidence, carefully pruned to suit his own objectives, he had now become a major player in the Arab Revolt. His information had also given him a private channel to the other players. On his way back to Cairo, he had not only met Admiral Wemyss, commanding the Red

Sea Fleet, who was, like Murray, an opponent of intervention, but had also called at Khartoum to be debriefed by Wingate, who was a staunch supporter of it. That he had managed to convince both parties that each was right was a tribute to his shape-shifting power. After the debriefing, Wingate – who was shortly to move to Cairo as High Commissioner in place of McMahon – wrote: 'I understood him to agree that in an emergency the Arabs would welcome [a British Brigade] . . . and cling to this hope of success rather than acquiesce in the certain defeat that failure to hold Rabegh would mean.'[2] Lawrence had not – as far as he was concerned – agreed to any such thing, and Wingate was enraged when later he read Lawrence's memorandum on the subject. But by then the die was cast, and Clayton managed to convince the Sirdar that Murray had obliged Lawrence to write the document, anyway.

Lawrence continued to see himself working from his office in Cairo, helping to direct the Revolt from a safe distance. His expedition up the Wadi Safra had done nothing to convince him that he was a field officer. He was now formally transferred to the Arab Bureau under Clayton, who assigned him the post of Propaganda Officer – a role for which he was well suited. Wingate, however, had other ideas. The Sirdar felt that his exceptional knowledge of the Arabs would be wasted in Cairo, and told Clayton to send him back to the Hejaz as liaison officer with Feisal. Clayton was loath to let him go. Lawrence, who learned of the posting on 19 November, also objected strongly, arguing that he was not cut out to be a man of action, and had no experience in leadership. This argument was not entirely true, for he had emerged from his four years at Carchemish with formidable management skills. He also maintained that Feisal was headstrong and almost impossible to advise – a claim which he himself later revealed as spurious. He was desperate to stay away from the fighting, and was prepared to use all his rhetorical skills to do so. Yet it was to no avail. The Sirdar had ordered it, and the Sirdar would have his way. Wingate conceded only that Stewart Newcombe, now promoted Lieutenant-Colonel, should take over his posting at Yanbu' – Feisal's current base – as soon as he was available, releasing Lawrence once again for the Arab Bureau. Lawrence realized that the time for action had come. Fate had decreed that he should go into the field, and there was no avoiding it. Once he had accepted it, he summoned all the willpower he had built up in his youth, and galvanized himself for action. He feared that his nerve would not hold out in the face of danger, yet he drew on those long years of self-punishment, the close acquaintance with pain and deprivation he had forced upon himself, and hoped desperately that it would be enough. On 25 November, he sailed once more for the Hejaz.

He arrived in the eye of the gravest crisis the Revolt had suffered so far. On 1 December, Fakhri Pasha's outriders had found an unguarded road into the Wadi Safra, and pushed quickly up behind the Bani Salem units guarding the wadi. Finding Turks behind them, the tribesmen had simply fled, anxious for their villages, and Feisal's youngest brother, Zayd, who had been in command of the regular force of Egyptian soldiers lent by Wingate, had pushed forward to Hamra and had been stopped by a hail of machine-gun fire. Zayd himself had only narrowly escaped capture. He was retreating towards Yanbu' on the coast, and the Turks, now occupying the Wadi Safra, were in a position to threaten both Yanbu' and Rabegh. When the Turkish breakthrough had occurred, Feisal had been up-country recruiting a force of Juhayna to march north along the coast and attack the port of Wejh, which remained in Turkish hands. The capture of the Wadi Safra had not only cut him off from Mecca and Rabegh, but had also robbed him of his support among the Bani Salem. He was left with only the Juhayna, whose loyalty, he thought, would certainly not survive the capture of Yanbu' and Rabegh. His spy-system had broken down, and wildly contradictory reports were coming into his camp. On 2 December he dashed to Nakhl Mubarak – a large palm oasis in the Wadi Yanbu' – with 4,000 tribesmen, ready to repel any Turkish threat to Yanbu' port, which was now his last refuge.

Lawrence arrived at Nakhl Mubarak with 'Abd al-Karim al-Baydawi, a Sharif of the Juhayna, just before midnight, to find a scene of utter confusion. The wadi was full of woodsmoke, and echoing with the bleating and roaring of thousands of camels. Half-naked tribesmen were running about barefoot, babbling, cursing and firing off rifles. Lawrence's party warily hid their camels in a disused yard, and 'Abd al-Karim went to investigate. He returned with the news that Feisal had just arrived, and shortly they found the Sharif sitting calmly amongst the madness, on a rug in the wadi, dictating letters by

lamplight. With him were his *aide* Maulud al-Mukhlis, and Sharif
Sharraf, the Hashemite Governor of Ta'if – his second in command.
Feisal was relieved to see Lawrence. The whole camp was on the verge
of panic, and messengers were coming and going constantly, couching
and rousing their camels around the Sharif's tiny island on the rug.
Bedu patrols loped into camp or scattered into the night noisily.
Baggage trains were being unloaded, mules and horses bucked and
shied, and as they talked, a recalcitrant baggage-camel bolted and
dropped its load, showering them with hay. Feisal listened to every
messenger, petitioner and plaintiff patiently, and spoke to his men
with dignity and composure. He was fighting a desperate internal
battle, Lawrence realized. He had been shocked by the suddenness of
his brother's retreat, and was privately 'most horribly cut up' about
it. Publicly, though, he was magnificent. Lawrence watched him
address the Sheikhs of a troop of Bedu he was sending out to picket
the Turks: 'He did not say much,' Lawrence wrote. 'No noise about
it, but it was exactly right, and the people rushed over one another to
kiss his headrope when he finished.'[3] Once again, Feisal blamed lack
of artillery for the Turkish success, and feared that the defection of
the Bani Salem would have a domino effect on the other tribes:
'Henceforward, much of the Harb will have to be ruled out,' Lawrence
wrote to Clayton. 'The Hawazim [the section of the tribe which had
run from the Turks] are most openly wrong, and all the other Bani
Salem will tend to hedge, and try to make peace with the people
occupying their palm groves.'[4] Lawrence and Feisal snatched some
sleep and were up only an hour later, in the chill of dawn, to the
ringing of the coffee-mortar. Lawrence made a reconnaissance of the
camp and talked to the Bedu, particularly the Juhayna, whom he
thought unsettled and uneasy. Later that day Feisal's force moved out
of the wadi, which they suspected might soon flood, and made camp
to the north. The whole army mounted together, making a swath for
Feisal to ride through on his mare, followed by his lieutenants and
Sharifs, his standard-bearer, and a bodyguard of 800 armed 'Agayl
and Bishah on camels. Despite the desperate situation, Lawrence was
thrilled by the pageant of an Arab tribal army on the move.

It was at this point, Lawrence claimed, that Feisal invited him to
wear Arab dress, and presented him with a gold-laced *dishdasha* his
aunt had recently sent him from Mecca. Feisal's reason for this move,

Lawrence said, was because the Bedu did not feel at ease with khaki uniforms which hitherto they had only seen being worn by the Turks. It is doubtful if Feisal ever used this argument, because the Egyptian artillerymen and the Arab regular officers such as Maulud al-Mukhlis, Nuri as-Sa'id and Aziz 'Ali al-Masri all wore khaki. It is more likely that the idea was Lawrence's own. He had become accustomed to wearing native dress in Syria, and his natural sense of empathy, now applied to Feisal in particular, demanded that he wear the same clothes. Not only was it a compliment to the Arabs, it also gave him a psychological advantage, for by wearing the rich robes of a Sharif of Mecca, his status would be more obvious to the rank and file. In Syria he had escaped notice in local dress among the plethora of races, but not even Lawrence believed that anyone would mistake his rosy, clean-shaven English face for that of an Arab. There was also a practical element: Arab clothes were far more comfortable for camel-riding and living in the desert than anything Europeans had designed. The long, loose shirt enabled a layer of cool air to circulate around the body, and the thick headcloth, which could be knotted around the head, or across the face in a sandstorm, used as a towel, a blanket, a rope, a water-strainer, or a bandage, was eminently versatile. The long skirts also provided a screen when answering the call of nature, often necessary in the open desert. In sum, the adoption of Arab clothes was in both practical and ideological senses an excellent idea.

Lawrence remained with Feisal long enough to lay out a crude runway near his camp for the RFC flight which would shortly be operating out of Yanbu'. The Turks were on their way, and he was convinced that Feisal's shaken army would not stand and fight. They would have no alternative but to flee to Yanbu' port, where Major Herbert Garland of the Royal Engineers was busy training the Bedu for attacks on the railway. The port was poorly defended, and if it was to be held at all, Lawrence knew, it could only be with the aid of the Royal Navy. On 4 December he mounted his camel and rode back to Yanbu', arriving at half past three in the morning, exhausted after three almost sleepless nights. At once, he cabled to Captain Boyle of the Red Sea Patrol Squadron, and finally he wired Clayton in Cairo, blaming his pessimistic tone on his tiredness, but adding, 'All the same, things are bad.'[5]

Garland, whom he had hoped to find in Yanbu', was sleeping aboard a ship in the harbour, but Lawrence found his house anyway, and fell asleep on a hard bench. He was up in time to see Zayd's defeated column of 500 troops from Wadi Safra marching in, and thought it remarkable that they displayed no obvious shame at having endangered the future of the revolt. Zayd himself seemed 'finely indifferent', he thought. Within twenty-four hours, five ships of the Red Sea Patrol steamed into harbour, including the battleship *Dufferin*, and *M.31* – an amphibious assault vessel with a shallow draught, specially designed for offshore bombardment. They arrived none too soon, for on the 9th Feisal's 'Agayl, Bishah and Hudheil – his household troops – came streaming into the town having withdrawn from Nakhl Mubarak. Lawrence went to take a photograph of the defeated Sharif riding in, and noticed that the Juhayna irregulars were not with him. Wondering if they had finally gone over to the Turks, he hurried to meet Feisal, who told him that the enemy had arrived suddenly the previous day, with three battalions of infantry, some Mule Mounted companies, a host of Bedu camelry, and a guide from the Juhayna's ruling family, Dakhilallah ibn Baydawi. They had shelled Nakhl Mubarak with seven field-guns, he said, against which Feisal's tiny battery of two archaic German fifteen-pounders without sights or range-finders had been powerless, except to encourage the tribesmen by their noise. His Syrian chief of artillery, Rasim Sardast, had blasted off salvo after useless salvo with profligate abandon, and the din alone had sent the Bedu forward. Things had been looking well, Feisal claimed, when the Juhayna on his left flank had turned tail and retreated until they were behind his household forces, for no obvious reason. Scenting treachery, Feisal had ordered Rasim to save the guns, and had pulled back with his own troops – the 'Agayl, Bishah, and others – all the way to the sea. Lawrence wrote that a Sheikh arrived at Feisal's house in Yanbu' the following day, though, to report that his Juhayna had only retired to 'make themselves a cup of coffee', and had fought on for another twenty-four hours after Feisal had left. Feisal and Lawrence had rolled with laughter when they heard the story, though whether it was the irony of the defeat or the lameness of the excuse which amused them, Lawrence does not say. Certainly, it was the kind of aristocratic tale that he loved: the Bedu had not fled the Turks, but had been so unruffled in the face of the enemy that they had merely taken a coffee-break when it suited them. It was a very English tale – Aubrey Herbert fighting at Mons with an alpenstock, and taking charge of a Turkish company that had lost its way – but was it the truth?

The Egyptian artillery officers who had been eye-witnesses to the battle at Nakhl Mubarak told a different story. They said that the Turks had not come in force, and had opened fire with only three mountain-guns and a machine-gun battery. The Bedu, they reported, had put up no fight at all, and many of the Juhayna had simply fled back to their villages in the Wadi Yanbu' without firing a shot. Having taken Feisal's shilling, they had evaporated at the first sign of trouble, just as the Bani Salem had done before them in the Wadi Safra. This story must have been generally known at the time, for when Ronald Storrs met Feisal a few days later, he countered his complaint about the lack of artillery by suggesting that 'the courage of his Arab tribesmen stood in some need of vindication in the eyes of the world; even if they were for the moment unable to face their foes in the open field, their intimate knowledge of their own mountainous country would surely render them more redoubtable enemies in guerrilla warfare'.[6] Storrs was looking at the situation, however, as if the Juhayna and Harb were British regiments under a rigid chain of command. As Feisal well knew, the Bedu were far from being cowards. In fact, when they felt their tribal honour to be at stake, they were capable of the most heroic valour. In the Arab Revolt, though, they were fighting as mercenaries: their aim was simply to be on the winning side. To Englishmen like Storrs this might not seem quite honourable, but to the Bedui, whose whole world was his tribe, it was eminently so. What mattered to the Juhayna was the survival of the Juhayna, not the survival of the Hashemites, who were – in the end – just another tribe. Feisal knew that Storrs credited his family with more control over the tribes than they actually had – the Bedu would always suit themselves. In fact, he was now virtually bereft of tribal support, and despaired for the future of the revolt, which he thought would peter out within three weeks. He wrote a bitter note to General Murray, stating that many of the Turkish units that had come against him had been withdrawn from the Sinai front, in the British zone of operations: 'The relief to you should be great,' the message ran, 'but the strain upon us too great to endure. I hope your situation will permit you to press sharply towards Beersheba, or feign landing in Syria, as seems best, for I think the Turks hope to crush us soon, and then return against you.'[7] In forwarding the message, Lawrence added as a postscript, 'I infer Sharif had been offended.'[8]

There was no time for recriminations, however. The situation in Yanbu' was grave and the Turks were expected at any minute. The total number of Arab troops in the town did not exceed 1,500. Feisal sent the remnants of the Juhayna back up into the hills to harry the Turkish lines, and when he returned Garland took charge of the physical defences, refurbishing old entrenchments, strengthening the 300-year-old coral town walls, unreeling barbed wire and posting machine-gun crews. Boyle signalled to the carrier *Raven*, riding at anchor in Sharm Yanbu' – a creek eight miles north of the port – to dispatch its brace of seaplanes against Turkish positions, and then came ashore to survey the ground. Yanbu' was built on a peninsula with the sea on three sides, a flat, dusty plain on the other, which was entirely devoid of cover. If the Turks attacked they would have to attack at night, he thought, and then the Navy would be waiting for them. At sunset on 11 December, a hush fell upon the port. No one slept. At about ten o'clock, the Turkish advance-guard, which had crept silently down from the hills with a Juhayna guide, engaged Arab pickets only six miles from the town walls. Town criers alerted the garrison. British naval spotters on the minaret of the mosque signalled to the ships in the harbour, whose crews immediately began to traverse the plain with powerful searchlights and to train their guns. The troops stood to arms in utter silence, and waited tensely for the Turkish assault. But the attack never came. The Turks lost their nerve at the sight of the eerie spotlights playing across the open plain like the fiery eyes of monsters hidden in the darkness. They turned south towards Rabegh, leaving Yanbu' unmolested – a decision, Lawrence wrote, which ultimately cost them the war.[9]

Now all eyes were turned towards Rabegh, the key chess-piece in the game. Soon, Fakhri Pasha's advance-guard was within thirty miles of the port, which was defended only by al-Masri's anaemic army of half-trained Arab regulars, and a flight of aircraft under Major Ross. Sharif 'Ali, in command of the Rabegh garrison, decided to march out boldly with his forces to engage the Turks, to take the pressure off Feisal in Yanbu' and to make a final stand. When the Turks had evacuated Nakhl Mubarak, Feisal returned there and by a tremendous effort of rhetoric convinced the Juhayna to join him again. The following day his entire force went in pursuit of the Turks, hoping to trap them in the hills between his army and 'Ali's. It was not to be, however. 'Ali's bold spirit deserted him as soon as he was out of sight of British naval guns, and he retreated when he heard a false rumour that the local Harb had gone over to the Turks – much to the disgust of his War Minister, al-Masri. Feisal pulled his Juhayna back to Nakhl Mubarak with equal disgust. Zayd and 'Ali had both sat in Rabegh while he had faced the Turks alone on the *Darb Sultani*, and now both had proved ineffectual. Meanwhile, in Mecca, Hussain panicked, and against all previous misgivings demanded a British brigade to defend Rabegh. In November he had scored another diplomatic home-goal by declaring himself 'king' of the Hejaz. It was a title alien to Arab tradition, for while the Arabic counterparts of the words 'Sultan' and 'Emir' have connotations of authority, the Arabic word for king, *malik*, implies ownership. Hussain had announced his change of status without previous warning and without consulting his allies: the move was of no real advantage politically, and could only serve to infuriate other Arab potentates such as ibn Sa'ud in the Najd. At a meeting with Wilson in Jeddah on 12 December, he accused the British of defaulting on their promise to cut the Hejaz railway, a promise which had never, in fact, been made. It was bluster designed to excuse the Hashemites' blunders. If Rabegh fell, then Mecca would fall and Hussain and his sons would be executed. The only way to save Mecca seemed to be a landing of British troops at Rabegh, but if this happened, then Hussain might lose all Muslim support anyway. After much deliberation, Wingate informed the Sharif that the two brigades on standby at Suez would be dispatched to Rabegh only on receipt of his own written request. Hussain prevaricated. The British troops never came. Zayd had lost the Wadi Safra. Feisal had withdrawn to the Wadi Yanbu'. 'Abdallah was inactive in Hanakiyya, near Medina, short of food, water and ammunition. 'Ali had marched out of Rabegh and promptly marched back. The Arab cause seemed lost.

It was obvious to the Hashemites and to their British advisers that a decisive move was necessary. Wilson pushed Feisal to reactivate his plan to march on Wejh, 200 miles up the coast – the last Turkish-held port in the Hejaz. Once Wejh had fallen, Feisal would be in a position to menace the Hejaz railway north of Medina, and Fakhri Pasha would inevitably be distracted from Rabegh. Feisal now justified Lawrence's trust in his diplomatic powers, and by a combination of superb oratory and British gold he managed to regroup the Juhayna, and to assemble a force of thousands of camelry – including 'Utayba, Harb and Billi – in the Wadi Yanbu'. Though the irregulars had proved ineffective in the field, Lawrence continued to see their worth. He realized that it had been the potential threat to the railway which had caused Fakhri Pasha to hesitate for so long, and if the Arabs threatened the railway, then the Turkish flank would be extended up to Damascus, 800 miles away, and the Turks would be obliged to spread their troops thinly across that entire distance. Lawrence and Feisal between them came up with a two-pronged plan. First, to move Sharif 'Abdallah and his 5,000 Bedu from Hanakiyya to the Wadi 'Ais, where he could strike at the Hejaz railway more easily, and yet remain within reach of Yanbu'. Second, to march on Wejh with Feisal's entire force of tribes-men, leaving only a skeleton unit to defend the port. These two moves would certainly put the Turks on the defensive, Lawrence thought. Feisal hung back, however, fearing for Rabegh. He would sooner die in defence of his family than be cut off helplessly from them when the axe fell. On 27 December, Wilson arrived in Yanbu' and gave Feisal his personal assurance that the navy could hold Rabegh until his troops reached Wejh. A week later, Feisal's Bedu army rode out of Nakhl Mubarak with banners flying. It was a magnificent, barbaric sight, the like of which had not been seen in the Hejaz in living memory. This was no tribal *ghazwa*, but massed tribes on the march. The army was divided into nine sections, and Sharif Feisal rode at the head of his 'Agayl bodyguard, with Lawrence slightly to the rear, and behind him three standard-bearers carrying banners of purple silk, and three kettle-drummers pounding their great drums to the rhythm of the camels' feet. The 'Agayl, 1,200 of them, fanned out to the right and left, with their camels pressed together almost flank to flank in a wildly snorting mass, taking up the refrain of an improvised camel song, led by the tribal bard. Their greased, shoulder-length plaits, bleached with camels' urine, swung from beneath their headcloths, their brilliantly coloured shirts billowed, and the tassels on their saddle-bags swung majestically, as every man sang for all he was worth 'the deep-throated roaring of the tribes', so that the camels pricked up their ears, lowered

their heads, stretched out their necks, and lengthened their pace. Day
by day, their numbers increased as Bedu contingents from almost
every tribe in the Hejaz flocked to the Hashemite banner, until the
force was 8,000 strong. Suddenly, the dismal image of defeat began
to recede: suddenly, even the capture of Damascus looked possible.
Feisal and Lawrence knew that this was the real beginning of the
revolt, for after this historic massing of the tribes, the Hejaz would never
be the same again. Lawrence called it the 'biggest moral achievement of
the new Hejaz government': for the first time in memory, he said, an
entire tribe had marched into another tribe's district without thought
of plunder or blood-feud, complete with transport and supplies, united
in a military goal against a common enemy. It was, as Auda ibn
Hamad, Sheikh of the Rifa'a, told Feisal, 'not an army, but a world
which is moving on Wejh'.[10]

At dawn on 23 January, a small flotilla of British ships, including *Fox*,
Espiegle and *Hardinge*, nosed through a blanket of seafog off the Red
Sea coast near Wejh. Admiral Wemyss, scanning the shore with his
binoculars, could make out the shape of a stone Martello tower standing
on a high cliff, but there was no sign of Feisal, Lawrence, or the Bedu
column. Wemyss concluded that Feisal had not made the rendezvous,
and he was perplexed. On board *Hardinge* were 600 Arab volunteers,
mostly ex-slaves of the Juhayna, and Feisal's Bishah tribal police, who
had been picked up from Umm Lujj. They were to fight under their
own Sheikhs, 'Amr and Salih, with the nominal direction of Major
Charles Vickery and Captain N. N. E. Bray, both experienced Arabic-
speaking officers who had been assigned by Wingate to his Military
Mission team. Wemyss was faced with the choice of waiting for Feisal
to appear or making the assault without him. The Arabs on *Hardinge*
could not be kept aboard much longer, for they lacked food and
sanitary arrangements. But could they take the town? Wejh was mostly
inhabited by anti-Hashemite Egyptian immigrants from Qusair, which
stood directly opposite across the Red Sea, and its Turkish garrison
consisted of 800 men, with about 500 irregular camel-corps of the
'Agayl. Wemyss decided that, with his fifty naval guns, and a landing
party of 200 naval ratings to support them, the Arabs could take it,
even without the backing of Feisal's much larger force. *Hardinge* slipped
through the mist and dropped anchor two miles beyond the town.

The Arabs, dressed in camel-hair cloaks against the chill, smelling of sheep, scrambled barefooted into lighters, and put ashore in a sheltered bay, protected by a rocky coral cliff. The mist was clearing, and two miles south the naval guns began their thunder, a deep, bass booming which seemed to the Arabs to shake the earth itself. On the beach, though, there was terrible confusion. Half the tribesmen sat down and refused to budge. The rest of them, game for plunder, split up into three sections, one of which went straight over the bluff and charged, bellowing ferociously, towards the town. The Turks had been expecting a massive assault from the south, and were poorly organized. The sentries in the houses on the northern perimeter looked out of the windows to see a mob of shrieking tribesmen rushing straight towards them. A ruckle of shots rang out, hitting two or three Arabs, who slumped down like dark bundles among the rocks. This was the only defence the Turks managed, for by then the Arabs had reached the first house, and, tearing open the door, they shot down three Egyptian civilians and started tearing up mattresses and smashing furniture in a frenzied hunt for loot. Afterwards they skirmished from house to house, killing and looting. Meanwhile a second and third group of Arabs had engaged the Turkish trenches, one section covering with rifle fire, while the other, under Sheikh Salih, advanced slowly towards them. The tribesmen walked unhurriedly over the cool stones, feeling their way easily, with their *dishdashas* tucked into their cartridge-belts, and their rifles carried on the shoulder muzzle-forward in Bedu style. They were 1,000 yards from the Turkish position when the enemy opened fire, and at once they broke into a slow trot, making for a ridge, behind which they rolled and bobbed up shooting, hitting ten or eleven Turks. Vickery, who had advanced with them, signalled to *Hardinge* with a mirror, and at once the battleship began lobbing shells into the Turkish entrenchments. The Turks fled, and the bombardment stopped long enough for the Arabs to advance. They came forward steadily, and almost collided with the landing-party of 200 bluejackets. They slept in their positions that night, and on the morning of the 24th moved into the quarters of the town not yet captured, to find that most of the Turkish garrison, including the commander, had fled in the night. The few troops left were hiding out in the mosque, and staggered out weaponless as soon as *Fox* knocked a gaping hole through its wall. Wejh had been taken, at a cost of twenty Arabs killed, one

RFC officer mortally wounded, and a bluejacket shot in the foot.

Feisal's tribal levies, with Lawrence, and Stewart Newcombe – whom they had picked up at Umm Lujj – arrived the following day to find the town already in Arab hands: 'It was a fine sight to see his contingents scattered over the undulating plain to the south east,' wrote Captain Bray. '. . . Feisal himself led the van, his presence denoted by his standard-bearer, carrying a huge red banner, the only splash of colour in his army.' The Bedu trotted into the town on their horses and camels, singing, capering and executing mock charges. Bray noted that they appeared very light-hearted, 'which was rather to be wondered at,' he added, 'since they had failed us – quite inexcusably, I think, in spite of the explanations which were later given by Lawrence and Feisal . . . no attempt whatsoever was made to keep faith, and it was a reflection, both on Feisal's leadership and still more on his British advisers . . .'[11] It was, indeed, a sad end to Lawrence's 'spectacular march' of 200 miles, and privately he was mortified by the failure. Publicly, though, he blamed the delay on lack of water, the weakness of Feisal's camels – many of which had died – and on the ineptitude of his Juhayna guides. He defended himself by attacking Vickery's impatience, implying that the assault had been made prematurely, and that the number of casualties had been unacceptable for an irregular army. He pointed out, correctly, that to the Arabs casualties were not statistics but personal tragedies, called the attack a 'blunder' militarily, and decried the looting and smashing of the town, which was, after all, required as an Arab base. Lawrence had met Vickery at Umm Lujj during the march, and they had taken a mutual dislike to one another. Vickery had thought Lawrence a braggart for boasting that the Arabs would be in Damascus by the end of the year. For his part, Lawrence, always critical of professional soldiers, condemned this gunner of ten years' experience in the Sudan as insensitive because he had drunk whisky in the presence of Feisal, a devout Muslim. He regarded Vickery as one of those colonial officers who, though perfectly fluent in Arabic, was accustomed to patronize the natives, and could not distinguish between ordinary tribesmen and 'noble' Arabs such as the Hashemites. Lawrence's style was very different. He tried to get 'under the skin' of the Arabs and emulate their ways: to see the best in them, even when their behaviour seemed unacceptable to European culture. His irritation with Vickery, though, arose from his unconscious shadow – the submerged feeling that despite his mask, he and Vickery were in essence the same, differing only in approach. Drinking whisky before Feisal might have been insensitive, he reflected, but it was at least honest (and Feisal, being broadminded, had laughingly accepted it), while his own assumption of an Arab persona was a charade. His criticism of Vickery was largely unjust, however. First, it had been Admiral Wemyss rather than Vickery who had decided not to wait for Feisal's force: second, the Arabs had been largely beyond Vickery's control, and third, the looting and smashing of the town had been no less appalling to Vickery and Bray than it had been to himself. Lawrence took no personal responsibility for Feisal's failure to make the rendez-vous, and his excuses were lame. Elsewhere he boasted of the Bedu's ability to march long distances on minimal food and water, and, as Bray pointed out, he could quite easily have sent a small advance-guard of the 8,000 men ahead to Wejh to join in the attack. On the other hand, the propagandist in Lawrence appreciated that the march had been a success by its very occurrence: Feisal's ability to assemble such a formidable force of tribesmen, to move them 200 miles through the desert, and now to threaten the Hejaz railway, would, he knew, have a devastating effect on Turkish morale.

Another great blow to Turkish morale, though, had been delivered by Sharif 'Abdallah, who, on 13 January, while on the march to Wadi 'Ais with 5,000 Bedu, had run into a Turkish column under the former assassin Ashraf Bey, near the oasis of Khaybar. 'Abdallah, who even Feisal admitted could act with lightning decision when necessary, had sent in his horsemen so swiftly that the Turkish machine-gunners had only managed to get off sixty rounds before being swamped. He had captured the entire column, including Ashraf himself, together with £20,000 in gold, carpets, clothes, a machine-gun, howitzers, and boxes of pistols. 'Abdallah had then crossed the railway in the Wadi Hamdh and had left a letter for Fakhri Pasha between the rails, informing him that the Arabs had Ashraf Bey, and making all manner of dire threats. 'Abdallah had sent a messenger to Feisal with Ashraf Bey's own jewelled dagger as a present, while he and Lawrence were encamped at Harrat Ghalib on the coast. There had been great feasting and rejoicing: the tribal bard, Lawrence wrote, had composed an ode to the victory 'within sixteen minutes'. The Arabs had lingered an extra day at Abu Zeraybat in the Wadi Hamdh to celebrate, and it was this delay, rather than lack of water, which had cost them the rendezvous at Wejh.

The capture of Ashraf on 13 January, together with news of the march on Wejh, ended Fakhri Pasha's designs on Rabegh. In the Wadi Safra, the Harb were harassing his caravans, not for the sake of the Hashemites, but simply for their own benefit: his supply-lines were dangerously over-extended, and lay through hostile country. The British had air superiority in Rabegh, since the Turkish flight in Medina was grounded, and Ross's aircraft had several times buzzed Medina itself. The Turks were also weakened by a new and even more subversive enemy – the cholera bacillus – which was claiming twenty soldiers a day. News that the Arabs were operating north of Medina was the final straw. On 18 January, five days after the loss of Ashraf, and six days before the fall of Wejh, Fakhri ordered his battalions back to Medina and the railway. The threat to Rabegh had evaporated, and the Turks never stirred again from Medina for the duration of the war.

14. I Do Not Suppose Any Englishman
Before Ever Had Such a Place

Wadi 'Ais and Wadi Hamdh
March–April 1917

We sighted Aba an-Na'am station an hour before sunset, when the saltbush and tamarisk were throwing elastic shadows like exclamation marks across the hard grey shingle on the valley floor. From afar, glimpsed through the folios of thorn-trees, the station buildings were a nest of dark geometrical symmetry amid the fractal patterns of nature, tiny against the gleaming granite walls of Jabal Unsayl, which towered behind it. This was the Wadi Hamdh – the frontier of Juhayna and Billi country – but my driver, Mifleh, was Bani Salem and considered it a foreign district. I had tried to find a camel, to make the pilgrimage to the places where Lawrence had first attacked the Hejaz railway in the slow and leisurely manner they deserved, but in Saudi Arabia today there are no riding-camels. Sadly, I had been obliged to hire a Land-Cruiser at Medina. All afternoon we had been following the line of the railway. The rails and sleepers had long ago been removed, and in places it was scarcely identifiable but for its embankment, a low shelf cutting through sand and shale. The stations had been placed roughly at thirteen-mile intervals, and in 1917 it had been the custom of the Turks to patrol the line every day, using a clockwork system, which had made their movements predictable to Lawrence's demolition parties. A patrol from each station would clear exactly half the distance to the next station, then, having encountered their neighbours, and exchanged talk and cigarettes, would retreat back down the line. There were six stations between Medina and Abu an-Na'am, and almost all of them brought an image from the Lawrence story – Muhit, where in June 1916 'Ali and Feisal had been forced back and attacked in the rear by Fakhri Pasha; Hafira and Buwat, which Feisal had planned to attack in force with his Juhayna; al-Buwayr, where a complete locomotive still stood, rusted to its rails and covered in painted graffiti, in the station yard; Istabl 'Antar, where 'Abdallah had crossed the line on his way to Wadi 'Ais, standing under a mountain with distinct double-fanged peaks, supposed in Bedu folklore to be the place where the hero 'Antar ibn Shaddad tethered his gigantic horse. It was Abu an-Na'am which claimed my interest most, though, for it was here that Lawrence had fought his first engagement with the Turks, and 'fingered the thrilling rails' of the Hejaz railway for the first time. The mouth of Wadi 'Ais was visible to the west, and the low ridges of the Dhula – before which Sharif Shakir had laid his artillery, to bombard the station from 2,000 yards. Hamdh, 'The Sour Wadi', had a wooded feel, almost African – in Lawrence's day there were leopard, hyena and ibex here, and at some time in the past there must have been ostrich also, for the name Aba an-Na'am means 'Place of the Ostrich'.[1] Mifleh thought there were still hyena and ibex, and perhaps even the odd leopard, though he didn't know anyone who had seen a leopard in recent years. No one he had spoken to, not even the old men, had ever seen an ostrich in Hamdh. We passed a patch of wild colocynth melons, small yellow-green globes, with a camouflage pattern, joined by succulent runners. Mifleh stopped to collect some, saying that you could make a medicine from them which was good for diabetes. The melons were poisonous to humans, but donkeys would eat them boiled, and the Bedu had once made tar from their seeds which they used for proofing water-skins. Like the Bedu, they were superbly adapted to aridity: when the sun dried them into husks, the wind would bowl them through the desert scattering the seeds as they went.

Aba an-Na'am was built on a similar pattern to the other stations we had seen and consisted of three main buildings – a substantial fort, the station itself, and an oval water tower – not circular as Lawrence had described it. To the west stood a tiny mosque and a well-house. The buildings were made of black basalt blocks, and the upper storey of the fort and part of the water-tower had clearly been rebuilt after the Arabs' bombardment. Mifleh and I explored the fort, which was solidly constructed – rooms opening off a central yard buried under generations of guano, a steel ladder leading down into an underground water-cistern, a staircase taking you to the upper floors, with walkways and battlements. With binoculars, I swept the wadi towards the line of broken outcrops which guarded the entrance to Wadi 'Ais. The valley was full of *rimth* sedge set in low, golden clusters like islands, and there was a knot of camels grazing peacefully on the saltbush. I wondered what the Turkish commander of the fort had seen and felt as he stood here on the morning of 30 March 1917, hearing the first, terrifying report of Sharif Shakir's guns, just before the building began to fall in on him. There had been no fewer than 400 troops defending the station then, sleeping in tents pitched around it, and the place had been encircled with barbed wire. The Turks had been aware that there were Arab patrols in the area, and had been anticipating an attack, because on the evening of the 28th Lawrence's men had fired a few rounds at the fort, to make sure the troops stayed inside. Later, opposite the door, Mifleh showed me the twisted iron chassis of a railway-wagon, with its bogeys a little way off, half buried in sand. The metal was hot to the touch. This was probably another relic of Lawrence's attack – for one of Shakir's shells had hit the first of six wagons attached to a locomotive standing in the siding, detonating its highly flammable cargo which had erupted in flames. The engine had steamed off south directly towards the place where Lawrence had laid his first mine.

Wejh had been taken as a base from which the Arabs could cut the Hejaz railway, and Feisal's ultimate objective remained the slow strangling and final capture of Medina. In one sense, his march on Wejh had been an overwhelming success – it had mobilized the Bedu tribes of the northern Hejaz and beyond, and brought them flocking to the Hashemite colours. In February alone, Feisal received visitors from the Shararat, the Howaytat, the Bani 'Atiya and the Rwalla – tribes from Syria or the Syrian marches – and from the Wuld 'Ali and Billi tribes of the Hejaz. His aim was to mould the tribes into an 'Arab Nation', and his first task was to try to end the blood-feuds which had riven them for generations. He listened carefully and patiently to every petitioner, investigating the history of every claimed wrong, balancing the rival claims with *diyya* or 'blood-money' where this was acceptable, or invoking the cause of Arab solidarity in the name of his father Hussain, the King of the Hejaz, where it was not. Adherents to the cause were made to swear to Feisal personally on the Holy Quran that they would 'wait while he waited, march when he marched, yield obedience to no Turk, deal kindly with all who spoke Arabic . . . and put independence above life, family and goods . . .'² The Bedu swore, but whether they believed themselves to be an 'Arab nation' is doubtful. They hated the Turks, wanted them out of their tribal districts, and were willing to go along with the Hashemites towards this end, but they valued their independence more highly than gold, and if their thoughts strayed beyond their own territory, it was generally in terms of gain or plunder: their nation would always be the tribe, the tribe and the tribe.

Already, Lawrence noticed, the Juhayna were drifting back to their homes in the Wadi Yanbu', feeling themselves foreigners in Billi country. Ironically, it was only the 'Agayl, who were neither a tribe nor even nomads, who were willing to travel far beyond their own frontiers, and the 'Agayl had troubles of their own. On 12 February they mutinied against their leader 'Abdallah ibn Dakhil, ransacked his tent, and thrashed his guards, then rushed the camp of the 'Utayba, with whom they had a blood-feud. They were dissuaded only by Feisal himself, who strode among them barefoot, laying about with the flat of his sword, but by the time peace had been restored two men had been killed and thirty wounded. As for Lawrence, his temporary assignment with Feisal was now officially completed, for Newcombe was in the field to replace him. However, Feisal and Lawrence had grown attached to each other, and neither wished to part from the other *in medias res*. Lawrence saw that his place was to be official adviser and unofficial spur of the Arab Revolt. On the day they had ridden into Wejh, a cable had reached Clayton from Jeddah containing Feisal's personal request that Lawrence should stay with him, since he had been 'of very great assistance'.³ Clayton had no choice but to accept. On 1 March he wrote to Major Hugh Pearson – who had temporarily replaced Wilson in Jeddah – that 'Lawrence with Feisal is of inestimable value and an Englishman to take a corresponding place with 'Ali could immensely increase the probability of cooperation among the armies'.⁴ It was inevitable, given Lawrence's faculty for empathy, that he should identify with the Arabs and the Arab Revolt, and he now felt his hand on the reins of power. His earlier reservations about being in the field were forgotten, and he became engrossed in his work to the exclusion of almost everything else. Now, dressing habitually in Arab robes, speaking Arabic constantly, he had stepped into his Arab persona and had half forgotten that he was a captain in

the British army, regarding himself of being 'of Sharif Feisal's household'. He had 'chosen' Feisal as the revolt's figurehead, and he alone
would guide him to victory. He knew that Feisal was easily influenced,
and since this was so, he intended to be the Sharif's adviser for as long
as he could: 'The position I have is a queer one,' he wrote home, 'I
do not suppose any Englishman before ever had such a place.'⁵ Feisal
had come to rely on Lawrence because he recognized that the Englishman had a quality indispensable to a true leader – he inspired confidence. Lawrence could not only generate great charm, but was one
of those individuals who always seemed to be able to supply the right
answer, who always appeared to know the right course, and was always
capable of reassuring others that things would turn out for the best.
As Sir Herbert Baker later said, 'he appeared to radiate a magnetic
influence'.⁶ Although Lawrence's self-assured demeanour actually disguised an inner lack of confidence, and a turmoil of doubt, like his
mother Sarah he showed a different face to the world. His influence
was subtle, however. He did not try to dictate strategy to Feisal, neither
did he harangue Arab councils with his opinions. He did not command,
but suggested a course: '. . . he would make brilliant suggestions,'
Leonard Woolley commented, 'but would seldom argue in support of
them: they were based on sound enough arguments, but he would
expect you to see these for yourself, and if you did not agree he would
relapse into silence and smile.'⁷ In his *Twenty-Seven Articles*, intended as
advice for other officers dealing with the Hashemites, Lawrence
revealed his *modus operandi* with Feisal: he would try to ensure that the
Sharif first put his plans before him privately, and would always accept
them and praise them, and then modify them imperceptibly by drawing
suggestions from Feisal himself, until they accorded with Lawrence's
own opinion. Once they were in agreement, he would hold him to it
firmly and push him, so subtly that the Sharif was hardly aware of it,
towards its execution. In front of others, though, he would always
appear to defer to the Sharif, and would strengthen Feisal's prestige
at the expense of his own. While in the Sharif's camp, he would not
visit him formally, but would remain in his company constantly, eating
with him and being present at all audiences, continually dropping
ideas into the casual talk. When tribal Sheikhs came to declare for the
Hashemites, though, Lawrence would vanish, realizing that a first
impression of foreigners in Feisal's confidence would do harm to the

cause. Lawrence brought his immense powers of concentration to bear on the Sharif's affairs and immersed himself totally in Arab culture: he watched and listened and chewed over every detail, delved into motives and machinations beneath the surface, analysed the characters he had to deal with. He was always on his guard, tried never to speak unnecessarily, constantly watched himself and his actions. Pierce Joyce, who saw him at dozens of conferences with the Arabs, recalled that he rarely spoke: 'He merely studied the men around him,' Joyce said; 'he knew beforehand that his plan would be accepted, while the task of kindling enthusiasm among the tribesmen was best left to the Arab leaders.' 'It was not as is often supposed by his individual leadership of hordes of Bedu that he achieved success . . . but by the wise selection of leaders and providing the essential grist to the mill in the shape of golden rewards for work well done.'[8]

Lawrence was aware that the march on Wejh had been a great moral triumph for the Hashemite cause, but to professional British officers, who were less aware of the nature of a propaganda war, the Arabs had been found wanting – their major successes had been made possible only by the Royal Navy. Lawrence realized that a more independent victory was needed to vindicate the movement in the eyes of his British commanders, and to vindicate himself personally, for he was well aware of what officers such as Bray and Vickery thought of Feisal's failure to make the rendezvous at Wejh, and of his part in that failure. A startling coup by the Arabs was needed to make the British stand up. That chance seemed to be offering itself when, on 10 March, the patrol ship *Nur al-Bahr* put into Wejh with the electrifying news that Fakhri Pasha had been ordered to evacuate Medina with all his force.

A Turkish retreat from Medina at that moment would have been a great victory for the Arabs, but for the British a disaster. In December 1916 Murray's Egyptian Expeditionary Force had crossed Sinai, and Murray was now preparing for a massive push against the Turkish defences in Palestine, which ran from Gaza on the coast to Beersheba inland. To have the entire Medina garrison – 12,000 Ottoman troops with full artillery – arrive suddenly on his right flank would have been most unwelcome. In a letter to Lawrence, Clayton stressed that Fakhri Pasha's force must be attacked and destroyed before it could reach Palestine. Under no circumstances should it be allowed to get through. Newcombe and Garland were still up-country on demolition-raids, and since Lawrence was the senior British officer in Wejh, he had no choice but to take charge of the situation. His first task required all his diplomacy, and called on the relationship of trust he had built up with Feisal. He had to explain to the Sharif that Arab priorities must be sacrificed in this case for British ones. Feisal, to whom Lawrence had recently revealed the terms of the Sykes–Picot agreement, had been anxious to push north into Syria to consolidate the Arab position there before the French could claim it. It was a great tribute to Lawrence's persuasive power that he brought Feisal round within the space of a few hours to accept the priority of British requirements. Once done, he and Feisal sat down to decide on the distribution of their forces. Messengers were rushed off to 'Ali and 'Abdallah to alert them to the new situation. 'Ali was to move north-east with the Juhayna and Bani Salem, 'Abdallah was to be sent dynamite and instructed to hit the railway at any point and at any cost. Maulud al-Mukhlis and Rasim Sardast were to go to Faqir with the Mule Mounted Infantry and a mountain-gun, Sharif 'Ali ibn Hussain of the Harith – the 'young lord' Lawrence had encountered on his first ride to Hamra the previous October – was to go to Jayala to harass the line. Sections of the Billi and Wuld Mohammad were to take machine-guns and menace the station at al-'Ula. The plan, made on the spur of the moment, was to contain the Turks south of that line. If they managed to pass al-'Ula then they would be in the protection of the large Ottoman garrison at Tebuk. A key point in their retreat would be the station at Hediyya, the only permanent water supply for 200 miles, and Lawrence ear-marked this as his own target. Even before arriving in Wejh he had talked about the possibility of visiting 'Abdallah in Wadi 'Ais. Now, he decided, he would travel to 'Abdallah's camp, explain the new strategy, have a look at the railway, mine a train, and if possible capture a station. He set off for Wadi 'Ais with an escort the same night.

This was Lawrence's first major operation in the field. He was not a trained field-officer, as he had always insisted, but a political officer, and his proper place was by Feisal's side. Garland and Newcombe, both Sappers, had preceded him in action against the railway. However, this was an emergency, and Lawrence felt that 'Abdallah's force, sitting in Wadi 'Ais, had done little to justify its existence over the previous months. He would now act as a spur to 'Abdallah, as he had done so effectively with Feisal, and in the process would strike at the key point on the railway himself. As he rode out of Wejh with his escort, it must almost have seemed to Lawrence that the entire future of the Near East campaign rested on his shoulders. As soon as he was on the road, however, the old terror of being injured reasserted itself with a vengeance. Almost every moment of profound stress in Lawrence's life is marked with illness: his journeys in Syria had ended in malaria and dysentery: at the crucial point on his mission to Kut in 1916 an attack of fever had laid him out. The malaria was genuine, but it returned at intervals when his fear brought his psychological defences down. His ride to Wadi 'Ais, the terrible responsibility of his position, the necessity of doing right both by the Arabs and by his British masters, and the prospect of standing between the Turkish wolf and its home ground, took their psychical toll. By the second evening, when his party camped at the pool of Abu Zeraybat, where Feisal had lingered on his march to Wejh, Lawrence was suffering from fever, boils and dysentery. The following day – 12 March – the party set out early. Lawrence's companions – a Moroccan named Hamed, a Syrian cook, some 'Agayl, Rifa'a, a Merawi and an 'Utaybi – spent the day arguing continuously. The going was difficult, and for Lawrence agonizing. After a short break at mid-morning they rode up a narrow water-course towards the Sukhur – vast striated masses of cracked and faulted volcanic rock – where they were obliged to dismount and drag their camels up over rocky shelves and a knife-blade ridge. They descended into a valley, which opened into another, and another, until they strayed into an area of black basalt boulders known as a *harra*, where the camels tripped and stumbled. The sun came out with a vengeance, and twice during the day Lawrence fainted. It was all he could do to stay in the saddle. In the afternoon they were obliged to make two difficult and steep descents which only added to his fatigue. Finally, at 4.15 they halted for the night in a stony water-course called Wadi Khitan, where Lawrence unhitched his saddle-bags and threw himself into the shade of some rocks, exhausted, with a headache and raging fever. What happened next forms one of those mysterious hiatuses which feature so commonly in Lawrence's life, when we seem to be passing from the realms of solid fact – times, distances, numbers and dates, with which he crammed his diaries and letters – into a subterranean world of nightmares and shadows.

According to Lawrence's description in *Seven Pillars*, his feverish reveries were suddenly disturbed by a crisp gunshot at close quarters. This did not bother him, as he imagined one of his Bedu was shooting a hare for supper. Not so. He was shortly roused by Sulayman, the 'Utaybi, who led him over to another gully to show him the dead body of an 'Agayli called Salem, with a gaping bullet wound in the temple. Lawrence clearly saw that the skin was burned at the edges, suggesting a shot from close quarters. At once he suspected Sulayman himself, remembering the feud between the 'Utayba and the 'Agayl, but 'Ali – the senior 'Agayli – assured him that the murderer had been none other than Lawrence's own servant, Hamed the Moor. Lawrence sent the men to search for Hamed, and had just crawled back under his cloak when he heard a rustle. Opening his eyes wide, he saw the Moor lifting some saddle-bags nearby, evidently intending to load his camel and make off. Lawrence drew his pistol and stopped him in his tracks. The other Arabs came rushing back, and at once held court. Hamed confessed that he and Salem had argued, and he had lost his temper and shot the 'Agayli at point-blank range. 'Ali and the other 'Agayl demanded an eye for an eye. Lawrence knew that this was the ancient desert law, and was anyway too shattered to argue the case for clemency – he agreed that the murder of Salem had been an unforgivable crime. It was clear that Hamed had to die, but who would perform the execution? If he died at the hands of an 'Agayli, this would start another blood-feud between the 'Agayl and the Moroccans, of whom there were many in Feisal's army. Only Lawrence, who stood in the role of a Sharif, and above tribal feuds, could safely execute the condemned man. He made the Moor enter a sandy gully which shrank to a crack a few inches wide, and allowed him a brief pause to come to terms with himself. Hamed crouched sobbing on the ground. Then Lawrence ordered him to stand up, and shot him in the chest with a trembling hand. The Moor collapsed, coughing blood, and Lawrence shot him once more but only fractured his wrist. Hamed lay in the sand, screaming, and Lawrence stepped close to him, laid the muzzle of his pistol under his jaw, and shot him for the third time. The body shivered slightly. Lawrence called the 'Agayl to bury him, staggered over to his baggage and collapsed in his sleeping space. His diary entry for 12 March consists of a rough sketch-map of the Wadi Khitan with an arrow pointing to a place labelled 'deathcrack', and – in very spidery writing – the words: 'Slept here. Terrible night. Shot.'[9]

Now, to kill in the red heat of battle is one thing, but to deliberately shoot a helpless man dead at close quarters must be an ordeal which few could stomach easily, especially while shaking with fever. Lawrence was not a hardened soldier: indeed, he had never fought in a battle. Even at the very end of the war, two years later and after all the killing he had seen subsequently, Alec Kirkbride wrote that he 'appeared to be genuinely shocked by the free use which I made of my revolver . . .' 'Occasionally someone turned nasty . . . and I shot them at once . . . Lawrence got quite cross and said "For God's sake stop being so bloody minded!" '[10] This does not sound like the kind of person who would find it easy to place the barrel of a gun under a man's chin and shoot him in cold blood. The contemporary entry in his diary suggests that something or someone was 'shot' that night, but it is characteristically cryptic. The fact is that there is no hint of the incident in Lawrence's reports, and neither does he ever refer to it subsequently, though one would have imagined that such an experience would have a lasting residue. In his dispatch, written afterwards, he claims to have left Wejh with 'four 'Agayl and four Rifa'a': given that he may have neglected to mention his servants, the Syrian and the Moroccan, there still remains the mysterious 'Utaybi, Sulayman, who is not mentioned in any diary or dispatch, but only appears in *Seven Pillars*. Lawrence's field-diary entry for 13 March reads: 'with us 12 camels and men, Syrian, Zilfi, Rass, Anyza, Merawi, Rifaa'. There was a seventh name, but this has been heavily crossed out. Though this obviously does not add up to twelve, Lawrence is more specific in his later, typewritten dispatch. The '12 men' is missing, and the entry for 13 March – the day after the alleged shooting – now reads: 'I have with me a Syrian, a *Moroccan*, a Merawi, four Rifaa, and three men from Aneizah, Rass and Zilfi [i.e. 'Agayl] respectively.' The only discrepancy, then, is that of the Moroccan – presumably Hamed – whose name has apparently been scrubbed off the list in the earlier, handwritten diary, but appears in the later, official typewritten document. Is it plausible that one scrubs out a name violently – presumably from remorse – in one's diary, and then includes the name in one's official report? The obvious implication is that the name was scrubbed out *after* the official dispatch was published – suggesting that Hamed the Moor was alive and kicking on 13 March – the day after he was supposed to have been shot by Lawrence. On close reading, too, the description in *Seven Pillars* does not ring true. Lawrence describes the 'Agayl as 'running frantically about' when he arrived to see the corpse, and says that he later sent them 'to search for Hamed'. Yet the 'Agayl and the Rifa'a were men who had spent their lives in the desert, tracking enemy raiders and stray camels: their first reaction to such a problem would certainly have been a methodical examination of the murderer's tracks. In the *Seven Pillars* account, Lawrence says that they halted in Wadi Khitan after sunset, which would indicate that the entire adventure took place in darkness. He does not explain how, if this was so, he was able to see the dead man's wound clearly enough in the dark to distinguish the powder-burns. In his official report, though, he states specifically that the party halted at 4.15 p.m. – a good two hours before sunset, which would indicate that the murder occurred while it was still light, when any tracks would have been clearly discernible. It is true that Khitan was a rocky wadi in which tracks might not appear, yet there were also evidently sandy patches where they had made camp, for no self-respecting Bedui would ever halt his camels on rocks, simply for fear of injuring the animals' knees, and besides, Lawrence mentions the 'sandy gully' in which he shot his man. Finally, there is a familiarity about the pattern of the story – it is curiously similar in context to the tale of his near-murder at Tel Bashar in Syria in 1909. In both cases, Lawrence's dreams of Herculean achievement failed due to illness and physical weakness, and in both cases he appears to present a trauma in order to expiate that failure. Is it significant that Lawrence's apparent first reaction to the murder was 'the feeling that it need not have happened today of all days, when I was in pain'? Did Lawrence shoot Hamed the Moor? Did someone else shoot him? Or was Hamed still alive on the 13th? Perhaps someone was killed on the night of the 12th, but given Lawrence's character, and given the fact that he never referred to the alleged incident subsequently, it seems unlikely that he personally ever shot a man dead in cold blood.

They were off at three in the morning, and Lawrence was now so sick that his men had to lift him on to his camel. After two more days of slogging through the maze of washes and *harras* that surrounded the Wadi 'Ais, Lawrence and his escort – which may or may not have included Hamed the Moor – couched their camels at the water pool of Abu Markha, where 'Abdallah was about to pitch camp amid a great confusion of tribesmen and roaring and whinnying pack animals.

Lawrence had preserved just enough strength to greet 'Abdallah, hand him the instructions from Feisal, and retire. He waited for a tent to be pitched for him, then threw himself down on his bed. He did not leave the tent for eight days.

It was now 15 March. Feisal and Lawrence had hoped to have the Arab forces in position within ten days, and only five of those days remained. Lawrence was virtually paralysed by malaria, riddled with dysentery, and whether this was from nature, fear, or the added burden of conscience over a man's death, he was *hors de combat*. If Fakhri Pasha's forces got through to Tebuk, and subsequently managed to reach the Palestine front, the whole balance of the war would be upset. A major part of the Arab failure, he felt, would be down to himself. As he lay there, hour after hour, staring at the roof of the tent, a confused mass of visions began to swirl about in his mind. He thought of his childhood longing for the East, the feeling he had had at school about 'freeing' the Arabs, the series of synchronicities which had brought him to Syria, to the Negev, and finally here to Arabia. All the events of his life had been leading to this point. He had never been a man of action. Yet one thought dropped into his mind with the cool clarity of a water-droplet striking the surface of a pool: he, Lawrence, was now as much in command of the campaign as he chose.[11] The British looked at the revolt through his eyes, and his close liaison with Feisal meant that the Arabs saw the British largely from his perspective. He, Lawrence, was the pivot: he, Lawrence, was the uncrowned king of Arabia. He bestraddled the flow of information between the Arabs and the British and could manipulate events any way he pleased. His delirium stove through the barriers of his consciousness in a way that he had never experienced before: the fortifications broke down, and the barbarian tribes came rushing in. He experienced a powerful sense of connection, a profound sense of meaning. The liberation of the Arab nation and the winning of the war for the British: these two objectives it had been given to him to achieve. His first reaction to the revolt had been driven by the needs of the moment, but so much had been overlooked. Until now, everyone, including himself, had been obsessed with the capture of Medina, but what on earth was the good of Medina? A string of thoughts snicked into place like ratchets, and made him smile with sudden, thrilling insight. The war in the Hejaz was already won! It had been won the day Feisal's army had marched into Wejh. From the moment the Arabs had threatened the railway the Turks had had no choice but to waste their strength in defending it. The Turkish garrison was stuck in Medina eating its own transport animals, steadily reducing its own power of movement. The Arabs did not need to take Medina, and to cut the railway entirely would merely give the enemy an excuse to march out. In Medina, they were no threat to the Arabs, nor to the British flank. Soon, his mind began instinctively to calculate. How big was Arabia? Perhaps 140,000 square miles. How could the Turks defend that vast region against its own people? To do so effectively, he reckoned, they would need a fortified post every four square miles, manned by at least twenty troops. That made 600,000 men for the whole of the Arabian theatre! Clearly, to defend Arabia was beyond the capacity of the Turks. Yes, they could defend it with an entrenched and fortified line as they had against the British in Palestine, but only if the enemy marched in formation, with banners flying. But suppose the Arabs were simply an influence, an idea, a thing intangible, invulnerable, without front or back, drifting about like a gas?[12] They were not obliged to engage the Turks head-on. The prevailing military philosophy of Clausewitz, that the aim of war was to concentrate the largest force at the enemy's strongest point, and destroy him by sledgehammer blows, need not apply to the desert. Killing Turks was a luxury. In small, mobile parties, the Arabs could strike the enemy at his weakest point, and run away back into the wilderness, their sanctuary – a place where the Turks could not follow. Their advantages were speed, range and time, not firepower. They had no need to fight a pitched battle, nor present a target to the enemy. They could not sustain large numbers of casualties like a regular army, but a war of fading ghosts, waged against objects – machines, technical equipment, rails, stations and bridges – would achieve their purpose without exposing them to great risk. The desert was an ocean in which the Arabs cruised unseen, ubiquitous, independent of bases, communications or fixed points. Using the desert they could harass the enemy, evade decisive battles, sever lines of communication, hit hard and withdraw hastily. Lawrence saw with visionary clearness that the desert was his great ally: he had discovered 'desert power'.

After eight days of fever, the mists began to clear, and he remembered that he had been sent to prevent the Medina garrison from marching back to Syria. It was now almost two weeks since he had left Wejh, but there had been no move from Fakhri Pasha. In fact, although Lawrence did not know it, Fakhri had adamantly refused to abandon Medina, which was not to be evacuated until after the war. Lawrence wanted to resume his plan to hit the railway, not to cut it completely, but to dissuade the Turks from leaving Medina at all. On 20 March, he dragged himself out of bed long enough to talk to 'Abdallah, whom he found indolent and complacent – his instinctive dislike of the Sharif came to the fore. He reported to Wilson later that the conditions in the camp were 'unsatisfactory'. 'Abdallah's force of 3,000 'Utayba seemed to him inferior as fighting men to the Harb and Juhayna, and he found their Sheikhs ignorant and lacking in enthusiasm for the war. Just as he had used his rhetoric to boost 'his' Feisal, so he left no stone unturned in discrediting 'Abdallah. He represented him as an obese playboy, 'lazy and luxurious', who ate well, read the newspapers, talked about the royal families of Europe, played cruel jokes on his 'court jester', and remained largely confined to his tent. He exercised no supervision over his men, rarely visited tribal Sheikhs, and allowed only intimates into his presence. 'Abdallah was little interested in Syria – Lawrence's obsession – but was making plans to annex the Assir, and subordinate the Yemen. Lawrence thought enough of his political acumen, at least, to take the possibility seriously, yet in general his observations are so scathing as to suggest that he felt a sense of rivalry with 'Abdallah, who would not bend to his will. Indeed, his need to convince Wilson that 'there was nothing between them' was clearly an *excusatio non petita* – the unrequested denial which proves the fact. 'Abdallah himself was not happy about Lawrence's arrival. He had not wanted any foreign officers in Wadi 'Ais, for the disconcerting effect a Christian presence might have on the tribes. In his memoirs he wrote that one of his Sheikhs asked him, 'Who is this red newcomer, and what does he want?' while another, a fanatic Wahhabi, castigated him for befriending Christians. He wrote that Lawrence had 'an adverse influence on the fanatical tribes' and that the general dislike of his presence among the Bedu was clear. The Sharif was concerned with taking Medina, and believed that a pincer movement by the three Arab armies – 'Ali's force in Rabegh, Feisal's in Wejh, and his own in Wadi 'Ais – would capture the city. He disagreed with the idea of dissipating Arab strength by attacking too many points on the line.

His view had something to be said for it: *if* the Arabs could have captured Medina, it would have been a tremendous moral victory, and would have freed all three Arab armies to move into Syria. Lawrence was now convinced, however, that the Arabs could not capture Medina, and a defeat there, with its multiple casualties, would have ruined the Hashemite cause. 'Abdallah treated Lawrence kindly, but ultimately his attitude was that Hashemite strategy was no business of an Englishman, and that he should not interfere.[13]

Lawrence was, however, more successful with 'Abdallah's second in command, Sharif Shakir, a slim, boyish-looking fellow of twenty-seven who had been a childhood companion of the Hashemite princes. With Shakir, Lawrence's aesthetic sense was brought into play, for while he thought 'Abdallah undignified, Shakir seemed to him 'the born aristocrat', who nevertheless identified with the Bedu, calling himself an 'Utaybi, wearing his hair in plaits in Bedu style, deliberately cultivating head-lice, and even wearing the *brim* – a girdle of thorns supposed to confine the belly. Here was another 'noble Arab' to add to the list which included Feisal and 'Ali ibn Hussain al-Harithi, but which definitely excluded the 'vulgar' – but intellectually gifted and fiercely independent – 'Abdallah. Lawrence said that the 'Utayba 'worshipped' Shakir, and would take orders from him rather than his chief, but he clearly appreciated Shakir most for the simple reason that he was amenable to the 'congenial guidance' which Lawrence could give him – guidance to which the headstrong 'Abdallah was immune. Lawrence's position with the Arabs – great and small – had always been paternalist: he knew what was best. Specifically, Lawrence liked Shakir because he agreed to his plan of striking at the railway immediately. Lawrence also appreciated the help of Dakhilallah al-Qadi, the hereditary lawgiver of the Juhayna, a man of forty-five – short, tough, weatherbeaten, with the 'manner and appearance of a toad'. Dakhilallah had been with the Turks in Wadi Yanbu', and indeed, it was he who had guided them down to the town on the night of 11 December 1916, when they had been scared off by the ethereal patterns of the naval searchlights. It was he who, by way of compensation for that act, had blown the bridge near Aba an-Na'am station about three weeks previously – the only action, Lawrence reminded his superiors, that 'Abdallah's forces had executed since moving to Wadi 'Ais. Dakhilallah had his own reason for being attentive to Lawrence: he wished to make peace with

Feisal after having helped the Turks. This was useful, for without Dakhilallah's influence Lawrence would have been unable to organize anything at all.

Though his spirit was willing to start at once, his body was still weak. Fever, boils and swellings returned and confined him to bed for the next two days. On the 22nd he managed to send a message to Pierce Joyce, who had taken command in Wejh, saying that he hoped to organize a force of his own shortly, and intended to get down to the railway the following day for a reconnaissance. He said that he would stay in Wadi 'Ais for a time, to make sure something was done, and asked Joyce to beg Feisal not to stay in Wejh, as the mere knowledge that he was moving against the railway would both inspire the Arabs and frighten the Turks. Lawrence's insistent tone in the message, in fact, is indicative of the ascendancy he had already gained over the Arab leader: he told Joyce to say that 'he hoped most strongly to find [Feisal] at Jayadah or 'Ain Shefa soon'.[14] He had decided to leave on Sunday the 25th, but the following day he wrote in his pocket diary, 'am still beastly ill really.'[15] He finally started the day after, intent on attacking the station at Aba an-Na'am, which lay, conveniently, almost opposite the mouth of the Wadi 'Ais, shielded from its view by an outcrop of ridges – the Dhula. Lawrence collected about thirty 'Utayba, and a handful of Sharifs, which would be the scouting party of a much larger force commanded by Sharif Shakir, equipped with howitzers and machine-guns. They left the camp just after first light, their camels' feet crunching on the hard flints of the wadi floor, and by a tremendous effort of will Lawrence put his fear behind him. After riding for two days the party reached the Dhula, where they made camp in the lee of the rocky outcrops, amid some great tamarisk trees. Leaving camp, Lawrence climbed a 600-foot ridge to spy on the station, and found himself shattered after his fever, panting and halting to get his breath frequently. At the top, though, he was rewarded with a clear view of the station, which lay about 6,000 yards away: three large buildings, and the twenty-arched bridge which Dakhilallah had blown previously – now repaired. The original plan had been to send a force of tribesmen to occupy the hill behind the station – Jabal Unsayl – and attack it from the rear. When Sharif Shakir arrived with the main body the following afternoon, though, Lawrence discovered that he had brought with him only 300 men – a third of the number promised. He judged this force inadequate for an infantry assault, and instead he and the Sharif decided to bombard the station with their artillery, while mining the railway on both sides. One party was dispatched to the north to dynamite the rails and cut the telegraph line at dawn, while Lawrence led another – a group of 'Utayba – to mine the track between Aba an-Na'am and Istabl 'Antar – the next station to the south. There was no talking, and the camels loped along in silence, until, at about 11.15, they arrived at a deserted stretch of line. This was the first time Lawrence had seen the railway close up, and he found the touch of the rails thrilling. He placed the mine – a twenty-pound Garland-Martini, designed by Herbert Garland himself – under the rails, and set up a pressure switch which would detonate when the metals were depressed by the weight of a train. Then he sited a machine-gun and its crew in a water-course about 500 yards away, behind some thick bushes. Leaving the gun crew, Lawrence and the rest of the 'Utayba mounted up and rode a little farther south, to cut the telegraph wires. As none of the Arabs could climb a telegraph pole, Lawrence had to shin up himself, and, having severed the wires, lost his grip and plummeted sixteen feet to the ground, only to be saved by his guide, Mohammad al-Qadi. At last, though, everything was in place: the plan was for Shakir's artillery to open up on the station at first light next morning. The Turks would immediately try to telegraph for reinforcements, but, finding the lines cut, would be forced to send off a train towards Medina, which would run straight into Lawrence's mine and be derailed or destroyed. When the crew jumped out to salvage it, the machine-gun would cut them down.

Lawrence's party reached their camp just before dawn, to find that Shakir was already in position with his guns. At 6.30 precisely the battery belched fire and smoke across the valley, the crack and boom ricocheting around the rock walls. The first few salvoes crumpled the upper storeys of both the fort and the station building, and three or four shells punched into the water-tank, knocking it out of shape and sending water cascading down the tower walls. The next few salvoes set the Turkish camp ablaze, destroyed the woodpile kept to refuel locomotives, and hit the wagons of the train. The locomotive uncoupled and rumbled off towards Medina, and Lawrence watched with bated breath as it approached his mine. Suddenly, there was a loud explosion and a cloud of dust, and the train came to a halt. The mine had detonated late, Lawrence realized, and only the front wheels had been derailed. A crew of seven men sprang out at once and began to jack up the wheels, and he waited keenly for the sound of the machine-gun. It never came. The gunners had grown tired of waiting and had packed up, and moved back to camp. Lawrence was furious, but was obliged to watch impotently as the train crew got the locomotive back on the line within half an hour, and moved off slowly to the south. Meanwhile, though, the battle for the station was becoming hotter. The 'Utayba were skirmishing towards the buildings under the cover of billowing smoke, leaping barefoot from bush to bush and firing as they went. They assaulted two of the Turkish outposts, cutting down every man in one, and capturing the other, then closed in on the northern part of the station, taking twenty-four prisoners – all of them Syrians, whom Lawrence later interrogated. He also had a chance to examine the brake-van of the train, which had been left behind, and discovered that it was lined with cement. However, the Turks in the fort were too near to linger, and the smoke was too dense for shooting. The Arabs broke off the action and withdrew, having killed and wounded seventy-two Turks. Within two days they were back at 'Abdallah's camp.

Lawrence considered his first attempt at railway-mining only a limited success: after all, the train had escaped. He also criticized the 'Utayba, who, he wrote in his report, had not been asked to do much, and probably would not have done it if they had been. He was determined to have another try with the pressure-switch mine, and decided to hit the railway again between Hediyya and Mudahrij – second and third stations north of Abu an-Na'am respectively. He set off on 2 April, with a party which included the Juhayna law-giver Dakhilallah al-Qadi, his son Mohammad, and twenty of their Juhayna tribesmen, a couple of Sharifs, a machine-gun crew and a section of Syrian infantrymen. Once again, they marched up Wadi 'Ais and turned into Wadi Hamdh, where they slept on a sandy flat and were disturbed in the night by a heavy shower of rain. The following day the temperature soared, and the sun burnished the soil to such a heat that Lawrence could no longer walk barefoot as the Bedu did, but had to put on his sandals. Thunder rolled across the hills all morning and the peaks around them were shrouded in ragged clouds of sulphurous yellow and blue. Suddenly, Lawrence realized that the clouds were columns of dust, over 1,000 feet high, spinning in a double vortex steadily towards them. The storm hit them like a slap only three minutes later, ripping at their cloaks, filling their eyes with stinging grains of sand, spinning round the camels and clashing them together. The whirlwind lasted only eighteen minutes, but it was followed by sleeting rain, which moulded the Arabs' cloaks to their backs and had them shivering in the saddle. In the afternoon they climbed a steep crag to observe the railway, but found their view obscured by swirling mist: on the way down, an 'Utaybi slipped on the wet rock and plummeted forty feet, smashing his skull on the stones beneath. This was, wrote Lawrence, the only casualty they sustained during the mission.

After dark, Lawrence, with the al-Qadis and an 'Utaybi Sheikh called Sultan, crossed the plain to the railway. Mudahrij – a small station without a water-tower – lay behind a steep escarpment where the line curved sharply to the east. Soon after they moved out, they heard the bugle-call from the station that signified supper, and resented it, for tonight they would be too near to the Turkish sentries to light a fire. They came upon the track at about ten o'clock and rode along it, searching for a suitable machine-gun position. Visibility was too poor to identify one, however, so Lawrence chose a place at random – Kilometre 1121 – in which to lay the mine, and the party couched their camels silently. Lawrence's mine was this time a slightly more complicated affair, and laying the hair-trigger igniter was, he admitted, 'shaky work'. He placed two rail-cutting charges about thirty yards apart, and connected them to the pressure-switch, which he laid half-way between. This meant that, whichever way the train was heading, at least one charge would be certain to explode beneath its body. It took two hours to complete the mine-laying, and while he worked a light rain began to fall, caking the sandy surface around the railway embankment, which became plastered with footprints. Whenever a train was due, Lawrence knew, a Turkish patrol would search the line thoroughly inch by inch, looking for suspicious signs, and the elephant-like tracks they had left would be a certain giveaway. They were too deep to be concealed, so instead Lawrence and his party brought their camels and trampled the ground for 100 yards on either side of the charge, and out into the desert beyond, to make it look as though a large force had merely crossed the railway in the night. Then they rode off to a safe distance and concealed themselves behind a ridge to wait for sunrise, shivering fitfully and gasping in the intense cold through grinding and chattering teeth. Dawn spread crimson veins across the jagged hills like a benediction, and the heat melted the clouds and spread fire through Lawrence's body. He prayed that there would be no action until he was thoroughly warm. At first light the machine-gun crew arrived, and Dakhilallah al-Qadi crawled up to the top of the ridge to find out what was happening. At 7.30, an armed patrol of eleven Turks worked its way along the line, and halted at Kilometre 1121. They began an exhaustive search of the sand and the ballast, and although the mines had been well hidden, Lawrence watched with his heart in his mouth. To his relief, however, they continued to the south and met up with the patrol from Hediyya, the next station. An hour later, Lawrence heard the rumble of a train, and saw a locomotive and nine wagons approaching from the south. Astonishingly, it passed over the mine safely – much to Lawrence's secret relief, for it was full of women and children – though, as a demolitions artist, he was chagrined that the pressure-switch laid so painstakingly had proved a dud. It would need replacing, he decided, but at that moment the Turkish sentries posted in guard-sangars in the hills above Mudahrij spotted the Bedu who had crowded into his position to see the train, and opened fire at a range of 5,000 yards. Though this was too far to do any damage, Lawrence and his party knew that the Turks had well over 1,000 men at Mudahrij and Hediyya, and mounted patrols would soon be out hunting for them. They beat a dignified retreat, keeping their camels at a walk so as not to exhaust the mule carrying the heavy machine-gun, which they towed behind them. They laid up in another wadi for most of the day, and in the later afternoon walked their camels coolly back, under a renewed flurry of fire, towards the railway to replace the faulty trigger. The Turks were in the habit of shooting at any troop of Bedu who came near the railway, and from a distance they had no way of knowing that Lawrence's party was actually a guerrilla unit. Dakhilallah thought of a brilliant ploy to alleviate their suspicions by having everyone couch their camels by the railway, and perform the evening prayer, standing in line, with himself as Imam in front. The Juhayna were not assiduous in their religious practice, and Lawrence thought they had probably not prayed for a year, while he himself was a complete novice. Nevertheless, he followed their movements – bowing, kneeling, and touching the ground with the forehead – and felt that the watching Turks had been convinced: 'This was,' he wrote later, 'the first and last time I ever prayed in Arabia as a Muslim.'[16]

Sunset came, and it was time for Lawrence to face the unpleasant task of searching for the buried trigger mechanism in pitch darkness. If ignited by accident, he reckoned, the two charges would lacerate the line for seventy yards, and anyone within that distance would almost certainly be blown to bits. To make matters worse, the whole force of Juhayna insisted on accompanying him for moral support, and as he groped for the firing mechanism with tremulous fingers, he had dreadful visions of blowing up not only himself but the entire patrol. It took him an hour to locate it, and at once he understood why it had failed to ignite: it had subsided a fraction of an inch, due to the soft ground or his own faulty laying. He quickly reset the mechanism, and then he and his party ran for their camels and rode north towards the bluffs behind which Mudahrij was hidden, laying charges as they went. The Juhayna in Lawrence's party were all Garland-trained dynamiters, and they scurried about like ants in the darkness, setting charges on a four-arched culvert and on the rails. Lawrence shinned up a telegraph pole and cut the wires. Within a few moments, the silence of the night was torn apart violently as the charges went off almost in unison, cutting dozens of rails and shearing the head off the bridge. As soon as it was done, the Arabs dashed for their camels and rode back to their base-camp at a canter, so wildly, in fact, that they were mistaken for the enemy by their own machine-gunners, who let fly half a belt at them in the darkness. Fortunately no one was hit, and Lawrence slept contentedly, to be woken at 7.30 by the distant thud of his mine going off. Two scouts he had left behind to watch the track reported that a train carrying 300 troops from the Repair Battalions, and stacks of replacement rails, had set off the mine, the charges going off fore and aft of its wheels. Though the damage was not as great as he would have liked, Lawrence was satisfied that the mine had worked, and that his party had done enough damage to close down the railway. He had learned that Garland mines were almost impossible to detect, and that the Turkish garrisons on the railway were nervous and trigger-happy. His keen mind, ever questing for principles, had absorbed profound lessons about the Bedu, too. They were, he concluded, 'odd people': 'Travelling with them is unsatisfactory for an Englishman,' he wrote in his report, 'unless he had patience as deep and wide as the sea.'[17] He called them slaves of their appetites with no stamina of mind – addicted to coffee, milk and water, gluttonous consumers of mutton and smokers of tobacco. They would dream constantly about sex, he said, and titillated each other continually with bawdy tales. It was, he concluded, only the hardship of their lives which made them continent: given lush circumstances they would be pure sensualists. If they suspected one of driving them, they would resist or run away, but if one had the patience to present things from their own point of view, they would 'do one's pleasure'. 'Their processes are clear,' he wrote, 'their minds moving as [ours] move, with nothing incomprehensible or radically different, and they will follow us, if we can endure with them, and play their game.'[18] He had survived his first major action under enemy fire, had risked his life in groping for a hair-trigger igniter, and had not been found wanting. Now, the thrill of war, the intensity of balancing on the edge of the abyss almost every moment of the day, gave him a sense of connection and purpose which he had never experienced before. This, Lawrence suddenly understood, was what he had been destined for: the years of wandering had all been preparation for this.

The party rode back through the Wadi Hamdh, singing, and two days later they arrived back in 'Abdallah's camp at Abu Markha, where Lawrence found a letter from Feisal which demonstrated once and for all the esteem in which he was held in the Sharif's camp: 'My Dear Affectionate Friend,' the letter ran, '. . . I want to see you very much because I have many things to tell you. The destruction of the railway is easy. Major Garland has arrived and we can send him for this purpose. You are much needed here more than the destruction of the line because I am in a very great complication which I never expected . . .'[19] In fact, as Lawrence later reported, the Sharif was annoyed that he had stayed away so long, and was in a nervous and exhausted state. After receiving 'Abdallah's assurance that he would launch attacks on the railway on a nightly basis, he set out with Mohammad al-Qadi and three 'Agayl and arrived in Wejh on 14 April, to encounter a man with whom his fate was inextricably linked: the near-legendary warrior-chief of the Howaytat, Auda Abu Tayyi.

15. It is Not Known What are the Present Whereabouts of Captain Lawrence

Auda Abu Tayyi was the most feared fighting-man in Arabia. Tall, lean, predatory, with a nose like the hooked beak of an eagle, and eyes that had grown into slits from peering at the sun, his very presence carried with it the aura of danger. Auda seemed to be possessed by a demon which might today be described as psychopathy – a tendency to fall into a blind rage which could only be assuaged by violence. He had no control over his mouth, and would openly insult people by telling scandalous lies about them in public, daring them to challenge him. He claimed to have killed seventy-five men in battle, many at close quarters, and was reputed to have torn out and eaten the hearts of several of his enemies.[1] In 1909 he had opened fire on a party of Turkish gendarmes who had descended on his camp to demand taxes, killing two and sending the others packing. Ever since, he had been on the run from the Ottoman government, which had declared him an outlaw and issued a warrant for his arrest.

Auda had not been born to the sheikhdom of his tribe, which traditionally belonged to the ibn Jazi section of the Howaytat. In Bedu custom the authority of a hereditary Sheikh simply ceased when it was no longer acknowledged by the tribe – so the Howaytat Sheikh 'Ar'ar ibn Jazi had been deserted by his people, first for Harb Abu Tayyi and later for Auda, who retained authority by dint of his reputation for courage, energy, cruelty and generosity. He was not rich, no well-respected Bedui ever could be, for the Bedu revered open-handedness rather than wealth, and stood in awe of the man who acquired much and gave most of it away. Even in a land where people prided themselves on their munificence, Auda's hospitality was legendary. Under his leadership, and the guidance of his cousin Mohammad adh-Dhaylan, the Towayha section of the Howaytat had been transformed within one generation from a clan of nomad-farmers to the most efficient force of raiders in the entire peninsula, known to strike as far north as Aleppo and as far south as Wadi Dawaasir on the borders of the Empty Quarter. Inspired by Auda's truculence, they had acquired an *élan*, a ruthlessness and a persistence which had led them into so many encounters that their numbers had been reduced in a few decades from over 1,000 fighting men to only 500. Unruly, anarchistic, uncompromising, the Howaytat had eccentricities which displayed the shortness of their history as nomadic camel-breeders and raiders: they were disorganized on the march and would argue incessantly over where to camp, they owned land, they carried parasols and bottles of mineral water on raids, and they had a reputation for treachery, for ignoring blood-ties, and for flouting the Bedu code. Lawrence later characterized the Howaytat as 'true' Bedu – in fact they were despised as *parvenus* by the great Bedu tribes of the desert such as the Rwalla and the Shammar, yet none of these could ignore their ferocity, and even Sheikhs such as the powerful Nuri ibn ash-Sha'alan, Emir of the Rwalla, pretended friendship to Auda Abu Tayyi.

Indeed, Auda's bitterest enemy was Hammayd ibn Jazi, a descendant of 'Ar'ar, with whom he had disputed a point of honour. A scion of ibn Jazi had taken a camel from a certain Sharari tribesman who happened to be under the protection of Auda's family. Auda and some kinsmen had arrived at ibn Jazi's tent demanding restitution, whereupon they had been fired on: Auda had shot dead the son of one of his opponents and seized the camel. From that moment, the ibn Jazi and the Abu Tayyi had been at each other's throats, and the feud had resulted in the murder of Annad, Auda's son, who had been cut down by five riders of the Motalga ibn Jazi at Bair in the Ard as-Suwwan. Auda's only remaining son, Mohammad, from whom he was rarely parted, was a little boy of eleven. In 1914 the various branches of the Howaytat had made an uneasy truce, and moved east of the railway to the desolate Jefer plain near the Wadi Sirhan, from where they had plundered Turkish caravans and raided the Bani Sakhr – a powerful Bedu tribe to the north. They were also at war with the Shararat – the despised clan of camel-herders – to the south. Finally, around the beginning of April 1917, Auda had turned up in the camp of Feisal near Wejh, with eleven-year-old Mohammad as his only protector, and declared in favour of the Hashemites. This was a great victory for Feisal, for to have such a man as Auda with him not only added to his prestige, but gave him the key to the crucial region of Ma'an and the hinterland of Aqaba – now the only major Red Sea port still held by the Turks. Moreover, the Howaytat were accustomed to menacing the railway – in 1909 they had threatened to destroy all the bridges in the Ma'an district unless the Governor paid protection-money. Although the blackmail had been paid, Howaytat raiders continued sporadically to attack and loot stations. When Lawrence returned to Wejh in mid-April 1917, bursting with his new guerrilla doctrine, and convinced that Medina should hereafter be ignored, he found in Auda the very ally he required.

The idea of capturing Aqaba was not Lawrence's: it had been discussed from the very beginning of the war. In August 1916, before Lawrence had even arrived in Arabia, General Murray had broached the idea with the Chief of the Imperial General Staff, General Robertson, in London: 'As for Aqaba,' Robertson cabled him, 'the thing to do is to work out your scheme and let us know what it means – and then we will decide whether it should be undertaken or not.'[2] However, all the schemes mooted for the occupation of the port envisaged an assault from the sea – an approach which Lawrence had realized as ineffective, probably as early as 1914: he had certainly argued against it in a report he wrote in 1915. On 1 March 1917, Charles Vickery sent a telegram to Clayton to sound out his attitude to the question of taking Aqaba with troops from Feisal's army. 'Sharif Feisal is very anxious to occupy the town,' Vickery wrote, 'as he thinks ... that its capture and occupation by him would have an excellent political effect on the Syrians.'[3] However, Feisal clearly had in mind a seaborne landing with the support of British troops and naval artillery. Clayton's reply, which came a week later, stressed political rather than military objections: '... it is questionable,' he wrote, 'whether, in the present circumstances, the presence of an Arab force at Aqaba would be desirable, as it would unsettle tribes which are better left quiet until the time is more ripe.'[4] In May, though, he revealed the true nature of his reservations in a report to McMahon: 'the occupation of [Aqaba] by Arabic troops might well result in the Arabs claiming that place thereafter and it is by no means improbable that after the war [Aqaba] may be of considerable importance to the future defence scheme of Egypt. It is thus essential that [Aqaba] should remain in British hands after the war.'[5] On his return to Wejh, Lawrence found Feisal depressed and disheartened. The Sharif had originally been intent on Medina, but now planned to press on into Syria as soon as possible, for in late March he had heard the disturbing rumour that 60,000 French troops had already landed or were about to land in Syria. Since he believed that the arid Hejaz could not exist as an independent country without the support of fertile Syria, the prospect of the country falling into French hands at this eleventh hour was tragic. Lawrence agreed. He went to see the British OC Wejh, Pierce Joyce, in his tent by the beach, to persuade him to drop the strike against al-'Ula which he was planning, with the object of cutting off the Medina garrison. Lawrence now saw this plan – originally devised by Newcombe – as folly: to hold a middle point on the railway would mean exposing it to a pincer attack from the Medina force and the strong garrison in Tebuk. He explained the epiphany he had had in Wadi 'Ais – his sudden insight that it was to the advantage of the Arabs if the Turks stayed in Medina. He expressed again his fears that if there were large casualty lists, the Bedu would lose heart. To keep the railway just crawling along and to induce the Turks into passive resistance, he felt, would be the most rewarding strategy. Joyce refused to listen. Plans for the assault at al-'Ula were already in progress: Garland and Newcombe were both poised to strike, and if Medina were captured Feisal could then move north very quickly.

Seeing that he would make no convert of Joyce, Lawrence turned to Auda. A seaborne landing at Aqaba was out of the question, and he had long been meditating on an alternative course. Aqaba's defences and the fortifications at the mouth of the Wadi Ithm faced the sea – that was the direction from which the enemy was expected. A deep infiltration raid by a small force of picked men, who would appear suddenly out of the desert in the Turkish rear, would certainly take them by surprise. It was an original and audacious plan – the model for all the deep penetration raids later undertaken by Special Forces units throughout the century. It was also incredibly hazardous. To reach Aqaba by way of Wadi Ithm required a circuitous route of 600 miles across some of the worst desert in Arabia, including a stretch called al-Houl – literally 'The Terror' – where not even a fly or a blade of grass could survive. There would be no sophisticated equipment – no artillery, no machine-guns, no wireless – and no supply caravan or trained regulars.[6] Such a raid required hardened desert men who could live off the land. Ironically, the Bedu were ruled out because they would not fight beyond their tribal districts. This left only Feisal's 'Agayl, the tough professional mercenaries recruited from the oases of the Najd. Only a small party – no more than squadron strength – would be viable in these waterless wastes if the supply problem were to be solved, but with such limited firepower the long-range patrol would have to avoid contact with the enemy, for once behind hostile lines they would be at the mercy of any larger force and without a clear escape route. Within striking distance of their target, they would be obliged to recruit local volunteers, for such a small patrol could not, on its own, capture Aqaba. Thus the mission would entail some persuasive preaching as well as great hardship and danger. They decided to adopt a circuitous turning movement through the Wadi Sirhan, a major corridor of communication between Arabia and Syria, where the Howaytat grazed their camels. Even if the patrol were spotted by Turkish spies in Sirhan, its objective could not be accurately guessed – the direction of march would suggest an attack on Ma'an, Dara'a or even Damascus rather than Aqaba, and Lawrence would launch lightning raids on the railway as far north as the Yarmuk valley in order to confirm this suspicion. At the very last moment, his force would turn sharply to the south-west and dash across empty desert to the gates of Wadi Ithm. This, Lawrence guessed, was where the key battle would be fought.

Without Auda Abu Tayyi, though, the plan would be doomed. Auda's Howaytat controlled the Aqaba region, and not only their good will, but also volunteers from the tribe would be needed if the assault were to come off. Fortunately, Lawrence found Auda receptive, and together they formulated the details of the raid. With his British colleagues, he remained vague as to the actual nature of the operation, for he had read Clayton's reply to Vickery and was perfectly aware that the British intended to keep Aqaba in their sphere of influence. However, he reasoned, the capture of Aqaba by the Arabs, once a *fait accompli*, would satisfy everyone. For the British it would place the last Ottoman Red Sea port in Allied hands, thus securing Murray's right flank as he pushed into Palestine; for the Arabs, it would provide a supply-base for operations in Syria, and for Lawrence it would provide the master-stroke which vindicated the Arabs and his work amongst them in the eyes of his masters. He could not risk a direct order to desist, and did not specify his plans in any report to GHQ. Wilson clearly believed that Ma'an was the objective, for on 1 May he telegraphed Cairo: 'in about 10 days time . . . Sheikh Auda Abu [Tayyi] of the eastern [Howaytat] will proceed to his country east of [Ma'an], probably accompanied by Captain Lawrence, he is at once to commence demolition work against the railway . . . his first objective will be the capture of [Ma'an] and consequent clearing of the posts from there to [Aqaba].'[7]

Lawrence was now on his own: his operation had not been authorized, and its true aim was not even known. The risk was huge, but Lawrence satisfied his conscience by reflecting that he was not subtracting anything from the railway operation at al-'Ula apart from himself and a small group of men. He spent his last few days in the Wejh area travelling in aircraft and armoured cars, locating a plane which had crashed in the desert. On 8 May, he and Sharif Nasir took charge of the £25,000 in gold they would need to raise the Bedu levies on the other side. Nasir, whom Lawrence thought the most able guerrilla fighter of all the Hashemites, would command the mission, and he would be accompanied by two Syrians, Nasib al-Bakri and Zaki Drubi, who would help recruit the Syrian peasants to the Hashemite cause. The Howaytat included Auda, his cousin the highly capable strategist Mohammad adh-Dhaylan, and his nephew the notorious raider Za'al Abu Tayyi. With them were only seventeen 'Agayl fighters under their chief, ibn Dgaythir. Lawrence presented revolvers to Nasir, Auda and Mohammad adh-Dhaylan and the following day each of them drew half a sack of flour, filled their waterskins, crammed spare cartridges into their belts, and roused their camels, groaning and spitting, to begin one of the most daring raids ever attempted in the annals of war.

It was now high summer and the days suffocatingly hot. On the second morning they were so dazzled by the blazing reflection of the sun on the rocks that they halted at eleven o'clock, despite Auda's wish to press on, and lay at the foot of some acacia bushes, slinging blankets over the thorns to provide a few square feet of shade. By the third day, Lawrence's fever, boils and swellings had returned. As at almost every crucial juncture in his life, the great enterprise was to be marred by physical weakness. The going soon became execrable, and in the narrow valleys Lawrence and his men were forced to dismount and pull their camels by the headropes, then to work in tandem, one man dragging, the other driving from behind. The sun rained down hammer-blows like bitter steel, and Lawrence staggered along, almost fainting from the heat, the fever and the effort. Finally, the way followed a ledge by overhanging rocks, so perilous that two camels, already weakened by mange, slipped and fell, smashing their legs in the pass. The Howaytat slithered down to them and slaughtered them with their razor-sharp daggers, butchering the meat expertly and doling it out among the men. To avoid any further casualties, though, they were obliged to dump the camels' loads and repack them. After a few days of slow progress they reached the pool at Abu Ragha, and by now Lawrence's terrible fear of the risks ahead, dormant while safely in Wejh, came out to haunt him: 'The weight is bearing down on me now,' he wrote in his pocket diary on 13 May, '. . . pain and agony today.'[8] He became frustrated by the slow ponderousness of the march: accustomed to running about on lightly laden camels, this slow desert trekking was irksome to him. The camels were feeble with mange, and Auda knew that they must be spared if they were to reach journey's end. To the Bedu, the camels must come first, for to lose them meant certain death. Lawrence, faced with the most fearsome experience of his life, though, was pushed instinctively to flee forward to the fear, and the constant delays sickened him: '[if we could] only get on . . .' he wrote on 14 May.[9]

His mood was temporarily alleviated, however, when, camping at the water pool, he met two young 'Agayl boys named 'Ali and Othman, who were due to be punished for having set fire to the camp. Although Lawrence later wrote in *Seven Pillars* that the pair had implored him to take them with him, evoking the reply that he, Lawrence, was a simple man who had no desire for servants, he wrote in his field diary that he had actually 'begged them' from Sa'ad al-Gharm – chief of Sharif Sharraf's 'Agayl escort – which they met at the pool. 'Othman soft-looking,' he wrote, ''Ali fine fellow. Both apparently plucky.'[10] Lawrence insisted in *Seven Pillars* that he had never been 'lofty' and had never had cooks or body-servants, only his guards, who were fighting men. This was untrue: in the Hejaz he had travelled with a Syrian cook called Arslan; Hamad the Moor – whether or not Lawrence had executed him – was clearly a servant of some kind. When Lawrence met 'Ali and Othman, he had already had a substantial entourage of his own: three 'Agayl named Mukhaymar, Marjan and 'Ali: Mohammad, a fat peasant from the Hauran in Syria, and Gasim, a bad-tempered, yellow-toothed fellow from Ma'an, who had lived among the Howaytat. Lawrence noted on his equipment list for the Wejh–Aqaba trek that he had provided four revolvers for his 'servants'. He wanted the 'Agayl boys simply because they were attractive, or 'clean', as he put it, but he justified himself by maintaining that Gasim and Mohammad were useless, and declared that he must have extra men.

'Ali and Othman were to become immortalized in *Seven Pillars* as 'Farraj and Da'ud' – the puckish figures whose mischief seems to counterpoint the grimmer side of the action in the text with remarkably opportune timing. So opportune, indeed, Lawrence's friend Vyvyan Richards observed wryly, that 'had all the Arab campaign been planned by some Shakespearian dramatic genius he could not have imagined a more delightful human relief for the great story than this astonishing pair'.[11] Lawrence represented them as homosexual lovers with a deep devotion to one another – an example of the Eastern 'boy and boy affection' which, he said, the segregation of women made inevitable. He suggested that such coupling was commonplace, and on the second page of *Seven Pillars* launched into a lengthy description of homosexuality among the Arabs, illustrated by passages of an overtly sensual character: 'friends quivering together in the yielding sand with intimate hot limbs in supreme embrace'.[12] The story of 'Farraj and Da'ud' owes much more to Lawrence's Uranian connections than to Arab culture: even the 'fleshiness' of the prose is evocative of Uranian novels, such as Rolfe's *Don Tarquinio*, which Richards listed as one of Lawrence's favourite books while an undergraduate. The homoerotic theme in *Seven Pillars*, while purporting to be ethnographical, is actually an expression of Lawrence's own suppressed desires: it is possible that the idea of 'friends quivering together' is what he imagined was happening, but it is unlikely to have been the truth. Homosexuality, accepted only tacitly among Arab townsmen and villagers, was taboo among the Bedu, for whom merest suggestion of it would be likely to bring out daggers. The explorer Wilfred Thesiger, who travelled among them for five years in the 1940s, living closely with his companions day after day, far from their womenfolk, recorded that he had never encountered among them a single instance of homosexuality. No doubt it existed, but it was so much frowned upon as to be carefully hidden – certainly it was never flaunted in public as Lawrence claims was the case with 'Farraj and Da'ud'.

'Ali and Othman were only two of a new contingent of 'Agayl Lawrence's column borrowed from Sharif Sharraf at Abu Ragha, bringing their numbers up to thirty-five. On 16 May, the day Lawrence acquired his new servants, he reported himself 'still waiting and still savage'.[13] The following day, though, much to his relief, the enlarged patrol finally mounted their camels and drew off across volcanic *harra* – a maze of basalt clinkers so thick and angular that the camels were obliged to travel in single file. Lawrence's internal desolation was now matched by the surreal strangeness of the landscape: it was as if they had passed into another dimension. Nothing here was reassuring or ordinary – everything seemed other-worldly, odd, hostile, inimical to life. At last they crossed a fifty-foot ridge of vast, twisted columns, and came into the sandy bed of the Wadi 'Aish, where there were scattered thorn-bushes and waterholes. They couched their camels, unloaded and piled up their baggage, then sent the beasts out into the scrub to fill their bellies on the green stuff. No sooner were they out than someone screamed 'Raiders!' and Lawrence glanced up to see riders racing towards them, hanging together in the heat-haze like a swarm of flies. There was the chilling crack of rifles and the sound of bullets buzzing through the air, and whanging off the stones around him. Some of the 'Agayl fell flat and fired back at once, while others rushed hazardously towards the enemy, whooping out challenges. The raiders had not been expecting so large a party or so aggressive a defence. Almost at once they reined in their camels, and pulled away. Auda identified them from the cut of their clothes as a party of Shammar, whose Emir, ibn Rashid, had taken the side of the Turks.

On 19 May, ten days after setting out from Wejh, they filled their water-skins at the pools at Dira'a, and in the evening crossed the railway at ad-Dizad. There was a Turkish fort nearby which seemed to have been abandoned, and the trained dynamiters among the 'Agayl quickly got to work on the rails, setting up a relay of gun-cotton and gelatine charges which they detonated in sequence, filling the valley with deafening explosions and billows of smoke. Auda, who had never seen explosives before, burst into delighted laughter and made up a

1. T. E. Lawrence (Ned) aged about ten or eleven. A detail from a studio photograph in Oxford, c. 1900.

2. Sarah Lawrence with her children, in the porch of their home at Fawley on the shores of Southampton Water. Ned is sitting with his brothers Will, baby Frank and Bob. The photograph may have been taken by their father, Thomas Lawrence, shortly after their arrival in England, c. 1894.

3. In 1896 the family moved to Oxford, and Ned and his elder brother Bob went to school at the City of Oxford High School for Boys. Ned is sitting on the ground in the centre, surrounded by his form mates and their teacher, c. 1900.

4. *Portrait of Gray*, by Henry Scott Tuke. This painting, apparently showing Lawrence as a young soldier, was found among his possessions after his death and claimed as evidence of his disputed service in the artillery whilst still a schoolboy, perhaps in 1906. Though Lawrence may have met Tuke as a boy, the artist listed this portrait as having been painted in 1922. How it came into Lawrence's possession is unknown.

5. In 1909 Lawrence spent three months travelling through Syria, visiting crusader castles. In August he spent three days at Kala'at al-Husn (Crak des Chevaliers), inspecting and photographing it. He wrote later that it was 'the best preserved and most wholly admirable castle in the world'.

6. The castle of Sahyun, with its slender needle of rock supporting the centre of a drawbridge, was one of the highlights of Lawrence's 1909 tour.

7 . Lawrence visited many other castles, including *left*, the Norman keep at Safita (this view from inside) and *right*, Harran, photographed on a subsequent visit in 1911.

8. Lawrence's years at Carchemish were the happiest of his life. Here he worked with Leonard Woolley (*right*) over five seasons from 1912 until 1914. In this photograph they are standing on either side of a large Hittite slab.

9. Carchemish, a Hittite capital as early as 2500 BC, had been built on the intersection of two waterways and centred on a 130-foot acropolis which dominated the flat landscape.

10. Lawrence had two close friends among the local workforce at Carchemish: *left*, Dahoum, Salim Ahmad – the water-boy – and *right*, Sheikh Hammoudi, a former bandit, who was the foreman. Lawrence took these photographs in 1911.

11. (*above*) Workmen dragging up a large block of masonry at Carchemish. Photographed by Lawrence in 1911.

12. By the outbreak of war in 1914 Lawrence had already mastered Arabic and had managed to pass himself off occasionally as a native in northern Syria, where many non-Arab races intermingled. However, though he wore Arab dress throughout the Revolt he never imagined that he could masquerade as a true Arab, and though his Arabic was fluent witnesses say he spoke with a noticeably foreign accent.

13. Lt.-Col. Stewart Newcombe, Royal Engineers, who first met Lawrence during the Negev survey in 1914. He subsequently became his chief at the Intelligence Department in Cairo, and played a major role in the Revolt. Much admired by Lawrence, he was to remain a lifelong friend.

14. Lawrence travelled with camels in Syria before the war, but did not learn to ride until his first visit to the Hejaz in 1916. He quickly became an expert, though accounts of his fabulous rides which circulated after the war were often exaggerated.

Aziz el Masri

15. The two principal instigators of the Arab Revolt: Sharif 'Abdallah (seated) and Ronald Storrs (in white suit) at Jeddah in October 1916.

16. Sharif Feisal's army falling back on Yanbu' on the coast of the Red Sea, December 1916. Feisal was at the apex, surrounded by his bodyguard.

17. Feisal's camp at dawn, December 1916. Four thousand tribesmen were gathered at Nakhl Mubarak, a large palm oasis in the Wadi Yanbuʻ. Lawrence arrived there at night on 2 December to find a scene of utter confusion; the wadi was full of woodsmoke and echoing with the noise of thousands of camels.

18 and 19. Feisal and his army captured Wejh in January 1917 and made it their headquarters for the next six months. From here Lawrence would attempt to cut the Hejaz railway.

20. Auda Abu Tayyi (*left*) of the Howaytat – one of the most feared raiders in the whole of Arabia. This photograph was taken by Lawrence in Wejh in May 1917, just before the expedition to take Aqaba – the turning point in the Arab Revolt and the crucial success of Lawrence's life.

21. Auda (*centre*), with Sharif Nasir on his left, in a Howaytat tent in the Wadi Sirhan, June 1917. Auda, guide and strategist of the Aqaba mission, and Nasir, its commander, were in their different ways the most feared and able guerrilla leaders among the Hashemite forces.

22. Mohammad adh-Dhaylan (*centre*) with other Howaytat tribesmen.

23. The Turkish forces on the Hejaz railway had fully equipped repair battalions whose sole job was to maintain the line and repair it after an attack by Arab forces. Here a patrol repairs a stretch of track near Ma'an.

24. The bridge at Tel ash-Shehab, which Lawrence attempted to dynamite on the night of 7 November 1917. The daring assault was foiled when an Arab tribesman dropped his rifle, alerting the Turkish guard. For Lawrence, this failure was one of the most bitter personal defeats of the war.

25. Nasib al-Bakri, scion of a famous merchant clan of Damascus, was one of the founders of the Arab Revolt and a major contributor to the 'Damascus Protocol' which defined Arab policy in the event of victory against the Turks. He accompanied the Aqaba mission, but was isolated by Lawrence, who felt that his plan for a general rising in Syria was premature.

26. Dakhilallah al-Qadi, hereditary law-giver of the Juhayna. He initially fought with the Turks, then threw in his lot with the Hashemites, and dynamited the bridge at Aba an-Na'am. He and his son joined Lawrence on his first raids against the Hejaz railway, at Aba an-Na'am station and Kilometre 1121, in 1917.

verse about it spontaneously. The 'Agayl lunged for their camels, and while they were mounting up, Lawrence cut three telegraph wires and dragged the poles down by attaching them to half a dozen mounts. They trotted on for five miles until the going became too difficult, then made camp on a ridge. Lawrence lay in the darkness listening to the shouts of Turkish soldiers in the stations and outposts down the line, and the occasional salvo of shots they fired at imaginary raiders in the shadows. He dared not light a fire or send up a signal-flare to contact the baggage-party, which had become separated from his riders in the darkness. Later, two scouts returned and led Lawrence and his men on to where the main body were encamped, safe behind a sand-dune. They managed to snatch a few hours' sleep, but it was still dark when they mounted again, and Auda guided them across hills and dunes until, at dawn, they found themselves on the edge of a vast, shimmering plain which stretched endlessly to the east, falling steadily until it merged with the haze of the eastern sky. This was al-Houl, 'The Terror' – a vast anvil of sand and stone without a tree, a bush or a single blade of grass.

For five days they rode across the wilderness in the teeth of a smouldering sand-storm which leached their bodies dry of moisture. Yet they could not drink more than a few mouthfuls a day, for their water was limited and there would be no major water-sources till they reached the Wadi Sirhan. As the day drew on, Lawrence would see strange will-o'-the-wisp luminosities which licked suddenly out of the nothingness, and dust-devils that fumed across the hot flints like pillars of fire. Not only was there no life here, there was no sign of life. As his party rode forward reluctantly into the emptiness, weighed down by the awesome vastness of the sky, Lawrence looked in vain for the tracks of lizards, rats, insects or birds. The hugeness of this plain, so ancient, so still, so silent, reduced them to black specks on its redness, and it seemed to Lawrence that they made no progress, for the horizon remained always the same distance before them, the same distance behind: 'we ourselves felt tiny in it,' he wrote, 'our progress across its stillness an immobility of futile effort.'[14] The only sound was the splash of water in the goatskins, the mesmeric creak of the saddles, and the clink of the camels' feet on the dry stones. By noon on the first day, a hot wind was boiling off the horizon, bringing with it the spice-taste of the great Nafud desert which lay beyond. The 'Agayl drew their headcloths tightly across their mouths, but Lawrence decided to 'face out' the storm simply from masochistic perversity, and as a result developed badly chapped lips and a throat so hoarse with dust that he could not eat properly for the next three days. They rode from dawn till sunset, for even Auda felt too ill-at-ease in such a void to travel at night, with the risk of losing the way and thrashing about in unknown desert until they died of thirst. Soon the flint country merged into *gi'an* or salt-flats, which gleamed blindingly white in the sun, a sensation so painful that several times Lawrence almost fainted. At last, on 24 May, he sighted the first significant animal life he had seen since entering al-Houl – two ostrich, strutting rapidly across the horizon – and when one of the 'Agayl ran up with ostrich eggs, he, Auda, Nasir, and Nasib al-Bakri halted to breakfast on them. Lawrence caught up with the main party hours later to find that his servant Gasim – the ill-favoured peasant from Ma'an – was missing. His camel was there, complete with his saddle-bags and rifle, but of the man himself there was no trace.

The 'Agayl suggested that he had fallen asleep in the saddle during the night and tumbled off, hitting his head on a rock, or even that he had been the victim of a grudge-killing. It was clear that Gasim was lost, and that the 'Agayl – to whom he was merely a bad-tempered stranger – were not prepared to go back and look for him. Lawrence realized that the onus fell on him. He considered ordering one of his servants to go back on his camel, but realized that such a shirking of his duty would always be remembered. He begged half a skin of water from the 'Agayl – the last water they had – and turned his camel silently, forcing her back along the line of camel-riders and into the desert beyond, cursing his need to live up to Bedu ideals. Within twenty minutes the caravan was out of sight, and the terrible loneliness of the desert descended on him. The only sign that humans had ever survived in this void was a pattern of threshing-pits across the flints of the desert floor, where in the past the Fajr Bedu had worked grain from the wild grass *samh*. The pits were tiny pools of sand like eyes in the stony waste, and Lawrence urged his camel across them deliberately so as to leave some trace of his outward journey. He rode on for an hour and a half through a series of mirages which cast ghostly sparklers of light and haze, and sighted at last a tiny dark blemish on the desert's surface. This was Gasim. When Lawrence approached, he saw that the man was blundering about in confusion, half blinded by the sun, his arms held out and his mouth gaping. Lawrence couched his camel and Gasim snatched the water-skin from him, spilling the precious liquid down his shirt in his eagerness to drink. Lawrence sat him on the camel's rump, then mounted himself and set off on a compass-bearing, hoping desperately that he could now find the caravan. He traced the tracks he had left on the threshing-floors, and Gasim clung on behind the saddle, blubbering. Within an hour, though, he spotted a black bubble in the distance, which gradually split and swelled, resolving into the forms of three camel-riders. For an anxious moment, Lawrence wondered if it was the enemy. Then, suddenly, he recognized Auda and two of Sharif Nasir's 'Agayl, who had come back to search for him. Lawrence yelled sneers at them for abandoning a man in the desert. Auda replied that Gasim was not worth the price of a camel: Lawrence interrupted him. 'Not worth half a crown, Auda!' he said. Gasim claimed to have dismounted to urinate and lost the caravan in the darkness, but Lawrence suspected that he had actually halted and gone to sleep. Soon they caught up with Sharif Nasir and Nasib al-Bakri. While the Sharif appreciated Lawrence's act of courage, Nasib was angry that he had endangered his own life and Auda's – and consequently the entire mission – for the sake of a single worthless man.

The rescue of Gasim was Lawrence's most courageous single deed, and did much to enhance his reputation after the war. Though he apparently tried to play down the heroism of the act in *Seven Pillars*, by portraying his irritation that the duty of rescuing the man fell on him, the fact that it occupies an entire chapter is significant. There is no mention of Gasim in any official reports, but in an article in *The Times* written in 1918, Lawrence claimed that 'many of his party' were lost in crossing al-Houl – a claim less indicative of success than of failure. According to the *Seven Pillars* account, at least one man *was* lost in al-Houl, a slave of Nuri ash-Sha'alan's whom nobody went back for, since he was believed to know the country well. His mummified corpse was discovered weeks later. Although the rescue of Gasim has the characteristics of one of Lawrence's departures into fantasy, in this case we have solid evidence, from his diary entry for 24 May 1917, that he actually *did* go back to look for him, for that evening Sharif

Nasir apparently beat 'Ali and Othman – Lawrence's newly acquired servants – for allowing him to return alone. He also wrote in his diary that he 'wasted two hours and a half' looking for Gasim, which has been taken by some to suggest that the rescue attempt actually failed. Lawrence was precise in his choice of words, and a master of linguistic nuances: is it likely that he would have chosen to write 'wasted' if he had really returned with the lost man? If Gasim was indeed rescued, why does his name not appear again in the text of *Seven Pillars* when he was Lawrence's servant, and the party a relatively small one? The absence of his name following the incident is considered the most convincing evidence that Lawrence's heroic rescue attempt was a failure.

Now, it is the case that 'Gasim' is not referred to by this single name after Lawrence had supposedly brought him out of the desert, but three weeks after the incident, he does refer to a man called 'Gasim ash-Shimit' in a tale he tells in an attempt to parody Auda's epic style of rhetoric. This tale, it is true, is set at Wejh before the Aqaba expedition, but the important question is whether 'Gasim ash-Shimt' and the Gasim of the rescue story are the same man. First of all, the name: 'ash-Shimt' means 'he who rejoices in another's misfortune'; it is not a family name, nor is it *kunya* – a name defining the named person in relation to someone else, such as 'the father of so-and-so'. It is clearly a nickname, and as such it certainly seems to evoke the character of Gasim as Lawrence described him. It so happens that in *Seven Pillars* there are two references to an Arab Lawrence simply calls 'The Shimt' following the incident in al-Houl – the first at the battle of Aba l-Lissan, about a month later, when Lawrence, searching for Auda on the battlefield, asks 'The Shimt' where his horsemen have gone. The second reference is indirect: in his description of the Mudowwara raid which took place the following September, Lawrence notes that 'The Shimt's boy – a very dashing fellow'[15] had been killed in the attack. If 'The Shimt' and Lawrence's Gasim are the same man, then it seems probable that Lawrence did indeed bring Gasim out of the desert and save his life. Moreover, the phrase 'wasted two and a half hours looking for Gasim' does not, in the English idiom, necessarily mean that the rescue attempt was abortive – it could indicate only that Lawrence was annoyed because Gasim had needlessly wasted time and energy by his incompetence: throughout the trek to Aqaba his diary entries frequently express his impatience to get on. Finally, Lawrence also wrote in his diary the phrase 'not worth a camel's price' – which he said later was spoken by Auda, and to which he is supposed to have replied, 'Not worth half a crown, Auda!' Such comments smack of deliberate admonishment to someone who has done a stupid thing – such as going to sleep in the desert when the rest of the caravan is moving on: they are scarcely the kind of remarks likely to be made about a comrade – no matter how disagreeable – who has just been lost. The balance of evidence seems to me to suggest that Lawrence did return alone into al-Houl and save the life of Gasim – a remarkable act of bravery for a man who was terrified of being hurt.

That night was a terrible one: the party had no water, and could neither drink nor bake bread. Instead, they lay tossing and turning sleeplessly on the desert floor with thirst and hunger pangs tearing at them: 'Tonight worst yet in my experience,' Lawrence wrote in his diary.[16] When the day dawned, however, they found themselves in the great Wadi Sirhan, and knew that they had crossed al-Houl: the terror of thirst lay behind them, the ordeal was over. They struck camp at first light and by eight o'clock they had arrived at the well of Arfaja, an eighteen-foot shaft containing cream-coloured muddy water which both stank and tasted horrible. Nevertheless, it was all there was, and a blessing after the waterless waste behind them, and they drank until their stomachs swelled. They dumped their baggage, watered the camels, drove them out into the grazing and sat down to enjoy a well-deserved respite after the strain of crossing the 'Devil's Anvil'. They had not been resting more than a few minutes, though, when they were startled by the cry of 'Raiders! Raiders!' and Lawrence saw a wedge of Bedu cantering towards the wells on fast camels with rifles in their hands. At once he and Nasir mustered the 'Agayl, who fell on their bellies with cocked rifles behind their baggage, ready to defend the camp. Za'al Abu Tayyi rushed for his camel and rode bravely towards the interlopers, who, seeing organized resistance, turned and retreated into the desert. They had not gone far, however. That evening, Lawrence and his men were sitting around the fire being served with coffee in turn by an 'Agayli called Assaf. Suddenly a fusillade of shots rapped out of the darkness, hitting the coffee-server – the only man standing – who was mortally wounded and died only minutes later. Lawrence's men doused the flames at once and rolled into the dunes, located the position of the enemy from the flashes of their rifles, and shot back with such concentrated fire that the raiders gave up and disappeared into the night: 'Tonight we were shot into,' Lawrence wrote in his diary; 'an [Agayli] killed just after giving men coffee.'[17]

No other incident marred their welcome into Sirhan, and within two days they had located the camp of 'Ali Abu Fitna, a Howaytat chief, where they were to remain for several days, feasting royally on Howaytat sheep. Auda left them here and rode off north to meet Nuri ash-Sha'alan, the paramount chief of the powerful Rwalla, whose help, tacit or explicit, they would require if the operation were to be a success. Lawrence, Nasir and their patrol made slow progress along the wadi, which to Lawrence began to appear sinister – even actively evil – with its snakes, brackish wells, salt-marsh, stunted palms and barren bush. This view was a reflection of his inner state, for the further he moved into enemy territory the more the fear gripped him. He was also troubled by the job of recruiting levies, for as groups of Bedu appeared in his camp each night to swear allegiance to Feisal, he was obliged to reassure them that the Arabs were fighting for independence, not to further Allied objectives in the Near East. This had been easy in the Hejaz, which would almost certainly receive independence if the Allies were victorious, but Lawrence was less able to convince himself of the honesty of his preaching here in Syria: he was quite aware of the Sykes–Picot agreement, and that Britain and France intended to carve the region up between them afterwards. He despised Arab Nationalists like Nasib al-Bakri who believed in development and modernization: he had fallen in love with the 'Old Syria' and hated the thought of change: he wanted the East to remain the mystical, romantic land he had encountered in 1909, but without the oppressive government of the Ottoman Turks. He admired the Bedu and the semi-nomadic or tribal peasants such as Dahoum and Hammoudi – these were the 'real' Arabs. The 'fat, greasy' townsmen of Syria and Palestine were, he considered, of a different race, despite the fact that they were linguistically, culturally and racially homogenous. He perceived the East through a set of highly romanticized – and therefore ethnocentric – ideas. His idea of 'self-determination' was in reality determination by certain traditional and reactionary elements – the Bedu, the Hashemites, the conservative Sheikhs and Islamic elders – who represented his own romantic idea of what the East *should* be like: not the 'will of the people', but the superimposition of a romantic structure of his own. That Lawrence believed in these ideas passionately, and believed that they were right for the Arabs, is beyond question: from early childhood he had seen himself always as the clever 'elder brother'. It is similarly likely that his views changed as he moved into Syria: the wily intelligence officer who had at first accepted the *realpolitik* of sacrificing Arab priorities to those of the Allies became increasingly plagued by doubt. Though the guilt niggled at him more and more strongly, his chameleon-like quality never allowed him to abandon the pose of the tough, practical politician with his own side. War correspondent Lowell Thomas, who actually spoke to him only a few months later, reported his opinion that the British could never keep the 'promises they had made to the Arabs, and that, in wartime, promises were made to be broken'.[18] Lawrence made a great deal of his anguish in having to deceive the Arabs in *Seven Pillars*: no doubt this is part genuine, part 'elaboration'. Beneath this role of martyrdom lies the stratum of Lawrence's masochism – the constant need to be punished for mankind's transgressions, and to be seen to be punished: 'In the contradictory and paradoxical phenomenon of [masochistic] exhibitionism,' Lyn Cowan has written, 'the roles of masochist and martyr interchange in the same actor, their distinction almost obliterated in the spotlight's glare.'[19] The fear and the hypocrisy, the divided loyalties, the divided soul, the sheer inertia of the heavy days in Sirhan, wandering from tent to tent, stuffing himself against his will with vast quantities of mutton and rice in order to placate his hosts, receiving delegations, exchanging pleasantries, telling lies: all this began to inflate his emotions to bursting point.

At Agayla, many black tents were pitched in the wadi, and Lawrence was rejoined by Auda with Durzi ibn Dughmi of the Rwalla and a troop of his horsemen. This suggested a favourable response from Nuri ash-Sha'alan, and the prospective assistance of the powerful Rwalla changed the situation dramatically. Now, even Damascus seemed open to them, and Nasib al-Bakri, eager to raise the revolt in Syria, began to argue for an attack to the north instead of the planned move on Aqaba. Sharif Nasir and Auda were swayed by his argument, but Lawrence was outraged. If the Hashemites attempted to raise the tribes of northern Syria at this juncture, and captured Damascus, he thought, then they would be totally isolated. The British Expeditionary Force still lay behind the Gaza–Beersheba line and would be physically incapable of supporting them. The insurrection in Damascus would easily be crushed and the Hashemite cause would fizzle out. Timing was crucial, because the tribes would not rise a second time. Meanwhile, Aqaba lay on the British flank in Palestine, and Lawrence was convinced that, in order to be fully acknowledged, the revolt must move in concert with the British advance. He feared al-Bakri, as he feared all sophisticated Arab townsmen, and in *Seven Pillars* branded him spitefully as a 'fool', a 'rat' and 'petty'. Nasib, who had been one of the founders of the Revolt, was certainly neither a fool nor a traitor to the cause of Arab Nationalism, but, like the Sharif 'Abdallah whom Lawrence despised equally, he was capable of independent thought, and had no truck with Allied aspirations in his country. He was not gulled by Lawrence's double-talk. Nasib was exactly the kind of supposedly 'volatile and short-sighted' Arab Lawrence and the British disliked: they felt more empathy for the conservative elements in Arab society, and in *Seven Pillars* Lawrence tapped this traditional orientalist view of the essential congruency between the 'honourable' English 'gentleman' and the Bedui – a category into which he pressed those members of the Hashemite family of whom he approved, despite the fact that they had been raised in Istanbul. Thus, he indicated that while Nasib frowned on his heroic rescue of Gasim, Auda and Sharif Nasir – two of 'nature's gentlemen' – fully understood. When the feasting in the Wadi Sirhan grew too much to bear, Nasib and his aide, Zaki Drubi, had retired, while Lawrence and Nasir had had the grace to honour their hosts by sticking the meal out to the end. In Lawrence's writing a man's 'nobility' is frequently defined by his table-manners and eating habits. By such rhetorical devices, he sought to demonstrate how the English and the 'real Arabs' – that is the Bedu – had more in common than either had with the 'ignoble', 'petty' and 'treacherous' town Arabs, even though these townsmen were the vast majority in the Arab world, and therefore, by another definition, might be considered 'the real Arabs'. The 'real Arabs' did not, of course, exist – the idea was simply an ideological concept which was of great use to the colonialists, but was in reality nebulous: referring to the Bedu as 'the real Arabs' was in fact no more satisfactory than calling the British royal family 'the real British' and trying to forget the remaining millions of the population. In any case, it was not by honourable means that Lawrence got his way with al-Bakri. First, he went to see Auda and explained that, if they were to strike north through Rwalla territory, then it would be the Rwalla and not the Howaytat who received the credit and the bulk of the British gold. He spoke privately with Nasir, too, fanning the instinctive jealousy between the Hashemites – direct descendants of the Prophet – and the al-Bakris, who claimed descent – spuriously, Lawrence hinted – from the Prophet's first Khalif, Abu Bakr as-Sadiq. Eventually he won them both over, and it was agreed that, after the recruitment was completed, Nasib should ride off to the Druse mountains to prepare the way for an eventual march on Damascus. Lawrence tried to make sure that he had insufficient funds to raise a proper revolt by persuading Auda and Nasir to ask for the £7,000 Feisal had given him to spend in Syria. The strain of this double-dealing, with holding to the course he had set himself at Wejh, with lying day after day to the Bedu recruits, play-acting the Bedui, now became too much to bear. Ever since they had started from Wejh, three weeks previously, Lawrence's overwhelming fear had nagged at him, telling him constantly to move on towards the thing he feared most. The inertia of the movement in Wadi Sirhan had been agonizing for someone of his masochistic temperament, and at last, something inside him snapped: 'Can't stand it another day,' he wrote in his pocket diary on 5 June. 'Will ride N[orth] and chuck it.'[20]

'Chuck it' clearly suggests that he had in mind a suicide-mission, and such a reaction would be in keeping with the 'flight-forward' tendency he had displayed so markedly even as a youth. Riding alone – or with a small escort – deep into Turkish-held lands was the psychological equivalent for Lawrence of diving through the ice into the frozen Cherwell: 'a bodily wound would have been a grateful vent for my internal complexities,' he wrote, 'a mouth through which my troubles might have found relief.'[21] Before leaving, though, he scribbled a melodramatic note to Clayton in a journal he was to leave behind, suggesting that his motive was simply frustration at being expected to raise the Bedu on a fraud: 'Clayton,' he wrote, 'I've decided to go off alone to Damascus, hoping to get killed on the way: for all sakes try and clear this show up before it goes further. We are calling them to fight for us on a lie, and I can't stand it.'[22] No doubt Lawrence thought the note would make a suitably noble epitaph, but his true motivation for this flight-forward is much more likely to have its origin in his unusual psychological make-up – his 'internal complexities' were less the martyrdom of 'lying for the cause' than the perennial pressure of overwhelming fear which had blighted all his days.

There was certainly method in Lawrence's recklessness too. He guessed that Nasib al-Bakri would soon be visiting the principal Arab leaders around Damascus, and was terrified that he would goad them into rising too soon. As Feisal's emissary, he believed he might be able to persuade them to hang fire until the time was ripe. He left Nabk some time on 5 June with two tribesmen, and rode at furious pace across the Syrian Desert to Burga, Seba Biar and 'Ain al-Barida, near Palmyra, averaging more than forty miles a day. The going was too hard for Lawrence's camel, which had foundered by 9 June, when he arrived at the tents of the Kawakiba 'Anaza, pitched beneath the crags of the Tadmor hills. Lawrence's objective here had been to compose the blood-feud between the Bishr – another section of the 'Anaza – and the Howaytat, but he realized now that time was against him. Instead, he turned to the Kawakiba Sheikh, Dhami, whom he found 'a good man', and an ardent pro-Hashemite. Lawrence thought that Dhami would make a suitable middle-man between the Howaytat and the powerful 'Anaza, and could provide men to destroy the railway bridges on the Orontes river when the time was right. Dhami not only gave Lawrence a replacement for his exhausted camel, but also helped him enrol thirty-five Bedu for an immediate attack on the railway at Raas Baalbek. Though Lawrence had no intention of cutting the line at this northern latitude, he reasoned that a small demolition would have untold propaganda value, not only suggesting to the Turks that an attack was imminent, but also exciting the local Arabs of the Metawila sect, whom Lawrence had first encountered years before at Nabatiyyeh. The Bedu brought up their camels and left almost at once, heading due west towards the Anti-Lebanon range, whose white peaks seemed to float insubstantially above the desert as they padded on. They skirted the mountains, and drove straight in to the railway, coming up on a plate-girder bridge which Lawrence blew with a four-pound charge. The effect on traffic, he wrote, was slight, but the alarm was tremendous. A report obtained by British Intelligence a month later made clear that the Turks believed the Metawila respon-sible for the assault, and claimed that they had 'burned the station' at

Raas Baalbek. While this was an exaggeration, the threat of a Metawila insurrection was considered serious enough to divert no less than six battalions of Ottoman troops from the front line at Gaza – an incredibly profitable return on only four pounds of explosive.

Lawrence parted with the Kawakiba after the raid, and, having received Dhami's promise to meet him at Bair with a force of tribesmen in a few days, he rode south with a small escort towards Damascus. At the village of al-Qabban, three miles outside the city, he met with 'Ali Ridha Pasha ar-Rikabi, a covert Arab nationalist who was then mayor of Damascus, and whom Lawrence had once met at Carchemish. He warned ar-Rikabi not to take any action prematurely, though the Pasha replied that as he had only 500 Turkish gendarmes and three unarmed labour battalions in the city, he was in no position to do anything even though he might have wished to. Lawrence then rode south again, meeting Sa'ad ad-Din, Sheikh of the Leja, and Hussain al-'Atrash, leader of the Druses, who informed him of the terms on which his people were prepared to rise against the Turks. Finally he rode to Azraq, an oasis standing on a lake where the Wadi Sirhan debouched into the Syrian desert, and where he hoped to meet Nuri ash-Sha'alan of the Rwalla, and his son, Nawwaf. In 1927, the Arabist Carl Raswan, who lived among the Rwalla, heard a story that Nuri's scouts had found Lawrence asleep in a wadi near Azraq, and had identified him as an Englishman. Nuri had by this time got wind of the Sykes–Picot agreement, revealed to the world by the Bolsheviks, who had just seized power in Russia. He was inclined to regard Lawrence as a dangerous spy, and debated whether to kill him or not. Though the Bedu considered it cowardly to kill a sleeping man, Nuri posted guards with instructions to shoot or capture him as soon as he made a move, to prevent him claiming *daakhil* – the Bedu right of protection, which could be gained by touching a tent-rope, spitting on a slave, or various other ploys. The guards watched him for three hours, and in that time Nuri decided to spare him. When he awoke the Emir called him into his tent, and slapped a fat file of documents in front of him, demanding to know which of the contradictory British promises was to be believed. Nuri was the most powerful Bedu chief in Syria, and Lawrence realized the success or failure of the Hashemites might depend on his answer. It was with some agony of mind, he said, that he told Nuri to trust the most recent of the contradictions. Lawrence said later that Nuri was inclined to sit on the fence: he did not wish to commit himself to the Hashemite cause, but was circumspect enough to countenance the possibility that they might defeat the Turks, in which case he ought to be on the winning side. For now, his support would remain tacit: 'he is willing now to compromise himself to any extent short of open hostilities,' Lawrence wrote in his journal, 'pending the collection of his year's food supply.'[23]

Lawrence arrived back in Nabk on 17 June, having made a trek of 560 miles through enemy-held territory. He had blown a bridge and caused the Turks to move six battalions from the front, had met many of the principal leaders in the region, and had surveyed the prospective battlefields. It was a magnificent achievement – certainly one of the great intelligence-gathering missions of the war – and deserved the highest accolade. Yet if the northern ride is shrouded in uncertainty, Lawrence himself bears much of the blame for his incorrigible habit of self-mystification. In *Seven Pillars* he alluded only fleetingly to the expedition: 'the results,' he said, 'were incommensurate with the risks, and the act artistically unjustifiable, like the motive.'[24] Vyvyan Richards suggested that there was a purely literary motive in Lawrence's skating over the ride: to have described it in detail would have detracted from the action in the Aqaba mission, and produced an anticlimax. Several biographers have concluded that the story was a fabrication, and Nasib al-Bakri, speaking forty years after the event, told Suleiman Mousa that he was certain Lawrence had never left Wadi Sirhan even for a day, and accused him of 'double-dealing, slander and dissemination of discord'. The tone of the denial, though, suggests strongly that Nasib's memory was coloured with anger at Lawrence's remarks about him in *Seven Pillars*.[25] Nasib also reported that while Auda and Nasir had asked for the return of the £7,000 given to him by Feisal, on the grounds that their own funds had run out, he had refused to give it back. Nasir, he said, had revealed confidentially that Lawrence lay behind the demand, and they had pretended that Nasib had surrendered the money, whereas in fact he never returned a single pound. Against Nasib's insistence that he never left camp, though, there is Lawrence's diary, which, while the writing is often illegible and the entries sometimes incomprehensible, makes it clear beyond reasonable doubt that he did visit Raas Baalbek and the other places mentioned in his later report. Why, then, did he later tell Robert Graves: 'in my report to Clayton . . . I gave a short account of my excursions from Nabk northward. It was part of the truth. During it some things happened, and I do not want the whole story to be made traceable . . .'[26] Why, if the story was true, did Lawrence not wish it to be traceable, and what did he mean by his earlier statement that the motive was 'unjustifiable'? There are two possible answers – or rather two complementary answers representing two levels of Lawrence's psyche. First, on the rational level the purpose of the ride was to prime the Syrian tribes for a general revolt which would coincide with any British invasion of Palestine. The information Lawrence gathered at so much risk to his life provided a detailed report for GHQ showing the various groups of Syrian Arabs ready to strike. It was partly on the basis of this report that vast funds and resources were eventually assigned to the Arabs. However, the Syrian revolt was never to come off completely, and not even partially until the last days of the campaign. The masterplan which Lawrence conceived on this northern ride went askew because, when the time was ripe, he lost his nerve and failed to call a general uprising in Syria. His feelings of guilt over this failure are clearly expressed in the Oxford version of *Seven Pillars*, and may have prompted him to cut the details of his northern ride. The second reason probably lurked on the shadow side of his mind. That the ride had actually been initiated by his masochism – his need to ease tension by fleeing forwards – is clear from the note in his diary stating that he was going north to 'chuck it'. Afterwards, he could not forget the fact that he had been moved by fear rather than the more chauvinistic brand of courage others expected. He was later awarded the Companionship of the Bath on the strength of his own report, and might have had the Victoria Cross had another officer been present. The idea that he should be rewarded for what, in his own eyes, amounted to 'cowardice' amused him acidly: 'A bit of a handicap, is funk,' he wrote, 'to people of the VC class, in which reputation would put me! Of course, I know in myself I'm not a brave person: and am not sorry. Most brave people aren't attractive.'[27] The idea that cowardice and bravery were two aspects of the same quality occurred to him later, when he declared that a man who could run away was a potential VC. His attitude to bravery is summed up in a letter to Charlotte Shaw: 'When a VC . . . passes an army guard-room the guard turn out and salute,' he wrote; 'the poor shy soldier wearing it isn't thereby puffed up to believe himself brave. He convicts himself of fraudulence . . .'[28] Lawrence's low self-esteem; the feeling that he was 'not a brave person', that he was 'fraudulent'; the notion that he had been driven forward by fear rather than some idealistic notion of 'higher courage' caused him to coil his bravest act within a labyrinth of conundrums which would make it almost impossible for posterity to discover its exact nature.

All was now ready for the assault on Aqaba. Nasir, Nasib and Auda had recruited 535 men of the Towayha Howaytat, and 150 Rwalla and Shararat. Dhami was also there, with thirty-five of his Kawakiba from Tadmor. Nasir and Lawrence detached 200 of these Bedu to guard the tents in the Wadi Sirhan, and on 20 June the remainder loaded their camels and horses and turned south-west, riding to the ancient wells at Bair, set in a depression in the stony wasteland known as the Ard as-Suwwan. Here, they found that the three principal wells had been blown with gelignite, probably by Auda's blood-enemies, the ibn Jazi Howaytat, under the supervision of the Turks. There were traces of perhaps 100 cavalry in the ruined *khan*. The work had been done badly, however, and though one of the wells had been filled in, the other two were only slightly damaged. The charges had been poorly laid, Lawrence concluded: 'I took out two sets on the end of a rope,' he wrote in his journal. 'Nasty job, for all well-lining was very loose.'[29] There was a fourth well, some distance from the others, however, which had not been blown at all, and since this well belonged to the ibn Jazi, Auda's suspicions were confirmed. The party settled down to occupy Bair, while a scout was sent to the next group of wells, al-Jefer, to find out whether the Turks had destroyed these, too, and a small caravan of camels with local brands was dispatched to Tafilah in the hills of Edom, to buy flour. Nasir opened negotiations with the ibn Jazi Howaytat, hoping to bring them under the Hashemite umbrella and settle the feud with the Abu Tayyi, and put out feelers to the small sections of Howaytat whose tents were pitched in the Wadi Ithm. Meanwhile, Lawrence rode off with Za'al Abu Tayyi to visit several other Arab leaders and to dynamite a bridge near Minifir in the Yarmuk valley, as a further diversionary measure to convince the Turks that their objective lay farther north. The plan was unsuccessful, but on their return they attacked the lonely station of Atwi, killing three Turks and plundering a flock of sheep. They returned to Bair on 28 June to find that their food supply caravan had come in from Tafilah with a week's ration of flour for the whole party. This meant that they must take Aqaba within a week or starve. Their funds had already run short, and Nasir had been obliged to pay the Bedu in promissory notes to be drawn ultimately on the British government. They pulled out of Bair the same day, and as they rode there arrived a messenger from Nuri ash-Sha'alan, informing them that a regiment of 400 Turkish horse with four machine-guns was now scouring the Wadi Sirhan for them. Nuri had lent the Turks his nephew Trad as a guide, to be certain they lost the way and made slow progress. This was a further incentive to hasten the attack on Aqaba, for until the cavalry returned from Sirhan, the Turks would assume that Lawrence's party were still there, and would not be on their guard in the Aqaba district.

By 30 June they were at Jefer – Auda's headquarters – a tiny oasis of thorn-trees in a plain of mud cracked into filigree patterns by the sun, and dazzling white with salt-licks, from which the railway station at Ma'an was just visible on the horizon. Here, too, the wells had been blown by the Turks, but by carefully sounding them with a mallet, the 'Agayl discovered that one – the 'King's Well': Auda's own property – had not been damaged, but was merely plugged with earth. They spent hours digging it out in the sun, while Nasir dispatched a messenger to the Dumaniyyah Howaytat – the signal for them to attack the Turkish fort at Fuweilah, dominating Aba l-Lissan, a watering-place at the mouth of the great pass at Nagb ash-Shtar, through which they must descend to reach Aqaba. This was the opening gambit in the carefully-laid plan for the advance, and the direction of the campaign depended on the success of this first attack. All day they waited tensely for news, crouching in the shadow of sparse bushes near the wells, with their camels and horses ready-saddled. In the evening an exhausted rider stalked into camp: Fuweilah had been taken, and the Ottoman garrison massacred to a man. The Howaytat, under their Sheikh, Gasim Abu Dumayk, had, in fact, opened fire as soon as word had reached them that morning, but at first the Turks had driven them off. Believing that this was merely a tribal outburst, the Turkish garrison had sent out a mounted pursuit-party which had come across an undefended Howaytat camp and had slit the throats of six women and seven children and stabbed to death an old man. Outraged, the Howaytat had rushed down from their hill-top, cut off the Turks' retreat and slaughtered them all. They had then turned on the fort with renewed fury, taken it in a ferocious charge, and shot dead every Turk they could find, though a few had escaped and retreated back to Ma'an. This was the news Lawrence's party had been waiting for, and within ten minutes they had mounted and were riding across the Jefer plain towards the station of Ghadir al-Haj on the Hejaz railway, en route for the head of the pass at Aba l-Lissan.

The guerrilla column rode on through the miasma of dust, until the railway line with its telegraph poles like strange totems in the emptiness appeared suddenly before them. The Turkish patrols, seeing a horde of raiders coming silently and suddenly out of the mirage, were petrified, and retreated quickly to the blockhouses. Lawrence's 'Agayl jogged from bridge to bridge laying charges, knowing that the thuds of their explosions would reach Ma'an and bring a Turkish relief force down upon them. But by that time, they would have vanished back into the desert like a cloud. The 'Agayl blew ten bridges and ruined scores of rails, and in the spreading dusk they moved five miles into the plateau of Shirah, west of the line, intending to spend the night there. No sooner had they lit their cooking-fires, though, than three horsemen cantered into camp with the news that a Turkish battalion of the 178th Regiment had marched from Ma'an and recaptured Fuweilah from the Howaytat. This was bad news, for unless the Arabs could clear the pass down into Wadi Ithm, the road to Aqaba would be denied them.

Instantly, Nasir gave the order to march, and the Arabs threw their saddle-bags across the camels' backs and rode off at once with their fresh-baked bread still in their hands. All night they rode across the basalt, wormwood-strewn plateau of Shirah, and when dawn came Lawrence dismounted to take in the entrancing view of the Guweira plain, thousands of feet below them, soft golden-red in the new sun, traced with a map of drainage channels, and bounded by the great weathered massifs of the Wadi Ithm and the Wadi Rum. Gasim Abu Dumayk and his Howaytat, still bloody from their fight with the Turks, were waiting for them near Aba l-Lissan, with the news that the Turkish battalion, encamped in the natural depression around the spring, was still asleep. Cautiously, making use of the curves and contours of the ground, the Arab snipers encircled them. Once in position, they opened fire suddenly, bringing the Turkish sentries to full alert. Za'al Abu Tayyi and a cavalry detachment galloped away to cut the telegraph line to Ma'an. The Turks rallied, wiping sleep from their eyes, and blazed back salvoes of musketry into the hills. Soon their mountain-gun was puffing whoffs of smoke and shells were ripping out of the hollow, exploding far beyond the Arab lines. The Arab snipers ran, rolled and fired, moving too quickly for the Turks, who were blinded by the sun and confused by the shadows, and were unable to judge their range. The Turkish artillerymen had only twenty rounds, which were soon exhausted. That day the sun was demonic. On the plateau the Arab snipers baked slowly among the rocks, whose hot surface sheared off their skin in strips, and there was no water to ease their raging thirst. It was so hot by late afternoon that Lawrence crept into a cleft where he had located a dirty trickle of water and sucked some from the sleeve of his shirt. He was quickly joined by Nasir, panting through cracked lips. Auda, who came upon them lying there, sneered at the two of them, saying: 'Well, how is it with the Howaytat? All talk and no work!' Lawrence rounded on him, declaring that the Howaytat shot a great deal but hit nothing. Auda turned pale with rage and stalked off. Lawrence and Nasir called for their camels and rushed after him, just in time to see Auda, at the head of fifty Howaytat horsemen, charging straight downhill towards the Turkish lines with their carbines cracking and their sabres flashing. The enemy were braced together under a cliff, and let off an uncertain tattoo of bullets. A few horsemen fell and Auda's horse went down under him – but the momentum of the downhill charge could not be halted. Many of the Arabs had no stirrups, and could not check their mounts at full gallop even if they wanted to. The tiny wedge of horsemen smashed through the Turkish ranks like a battering-ram. The enemy broke up in confusion. Lawrence and Nasir, watching from the crest of a hill to the east, at the head of 400 camelry, saw a chance to cut off the enemy retreat. Lawrence felt the blood rushing to his head. This was the moment he had feared all his life: close contact with an enemy intent on killing him. But it was too late for doubt. Nasir screamed '*Yallah!*' and the entire troop, with Lawrence in the van, plunged over the hilltop and raced downwards like a whirlwind into the retreating Turks. Four hundred camels, fully caparisoned, with their great swan-necks arched out and their huge limbs working, ridden by long-haired Bedu with savage, snarling faces, were too much for the Turks. They let fly a few unaimed shots, screeched in terror and rushed off. In an instant the whirlwind shivered into their flank, and Lawrence, still cantering, fired wildly about him with his revolver. There was a dreadful mix of bodies, heaving, screaming and swaying. Then, suddenly, Lawrence's camel went down like a dead weight, hurling him from the saddle. He hit the ground with such force that the breath was knocked out of his body, and his world went black. When he recovered a few moments later, the battle was already over: the Arabs were advancing shoulder to shoulder cutting down the last knot of Turks. The entire Turkish relief battalion had been wiped out or had surrendered, the OC had been taken prisoner and the mountain-gun captured. Hundreds of corpses were strewn across the ground in low heaps. Lawrence later discovered that he had shot his own camel in the back of the head.

It had not been the war of ghosts which he had envisaged, but it had been an astonishingly successful action. The Arab irregulars had engaged a trained enemy of slightly superior numbers, and had killed 300 and taken 160 prisoner at a cost of only two men dead. Auda was delighted: two bullets had smashed his binoculars, one had pierced his revolver-holster, three had struck the blade of his scimitar, his horse had been shot from under him, and still he had survived. Aba l-Lissan was the crucial battle in the capture of Aqaba, for the pass of Nagb ash-Shtar was now open to them. Standing on that crest, where Lawrence and Nasir had stood at that crucial moment in the Revolt, eighty years on, though, I saw plainly how the Arabs had won. The hollow of Aba l-Lissan, now occupied by a village, is a natural amphitheatre, which would have been impossible to defend. Once the Turks had occupied the spring and failed to send out pickets to cover the heights around, the battle was as good as lost. They could not see the enemy hidden behind the hills, could not attack effectively uphill, and could only, perhaps, have retreated back to Ma'an. The topographer in Lawrence must have known that the ground had favoured them intensely, and that not all battles would be won so easily. However, for now the bulk of the fighting was over, and that night Lawrence did a curious thing: he walked round the battlefield alone by moonlight, inspecting the corpses, moving them and arranging them in regular rows. His masochism pushed him forwards to look death, his ultimate fear, literally in the face. He later made an oddly surreal and strangely emotionless sketch of himself arranging the matchstick bodies: 'I put them in order, one by one,' he wrote, 'very wearied myself, and longing to be one of these quiet ones.'[30]

Three more Turkish posts lay between them and Aqaba, but the garrison at Guweira – 120 strong – had already surrendered to the local Howaytat Sheikh, ibn Jad, who had waited to see which side would win at Aba l-Lissan before declaring for the Hashemites. Leaving the next post, Kathira, for ibn Jad's men to assault in the darkness of the lunar eclipse due that night, Lawrence's party pushed on down the Wadi Ithm, and found post after post abandoned. The Turks had fled to Khadra at the mouth of the wadi – the last bastion standing between the Arabs and the sea. The following night hundreds of Howaytat and Haywat tribesmen joined the Hashemite force, swelling their numbers to over 1,000 men. In the morning, Khadra surrendered without a fight. A British gunboat – later identified as *Slieve Foy* – had lain off the Gulf at dawn and had put a couple of shells into the hills. Lawrence and Nasir rode fast out of Ithm and across the great Wadi 'Araba, where they glimpsed the blue of the sea through a powerful haze, but *Slieve Foy* had weighed anchor and was gone. They would have to take the news of the victory to Cairo themselves, by camel.[31] They found Aqaba town ruined and deserted – smashed to bits by the shellfire of British gunships weeks before. The Hashemite patrol which had marched 600 miles through smouldering deserts to get here took possession of its prize without a single shot being fired.

16. An Amateurish Buffalo-Billy Sort of Performance

Crossing Sinai: The Mudowwara Raid
July–September 1917

Of all Lawrence's camel-treks, the one I most wanted to reconstruct was his classic traverse of Sinai in forty-nine hours, to take the news of the capture of Aqaba to the British at Suez. The Howaytat I met in Wadi Rum insisted that it was impossible, so I brought one of them, Sabah ibn 'Iid, to Sinai to make the crossing with me, and prove to them that it was not. Sabah's grandfather had ridden with Lawrence on several of his raids, but the Bedu of Jordan had grown used to four-wheel drive vehicles, I thought, and no longer knew what camels and men were capable of. Unlike them, the tribes of Sinai still rode their camels, and I bought four of the best mounts I could find from the Nuwayba' Tarabin. Though I had Lawrence's own map, copied from the Royal Geographical Society archives, reconstructing the route proved far more difficult than I had anticipated. For a start, Aqaba and Sinai were now separated by the narrow strip of Israel, and the border at Ras an-Naqab (called Nagb Akaba in Lawrence's day) – between Israel and Egypt – was closed. I had to find an alternative route up the escarpment which approximated to the one Lawrence had taken, and which would take us to Ras an-Naqab. An old camel-man of the Tarabin named Furrayj showed me Wadi Tuwayba – a tortuous way running parallel with Lawrence's pilgrim route, but starting at Taba on the Egyptian side of the border. Furrayj would accompany us as guide and *rafiq* for the first part of the journey: another *rafiq* of the Haywat would be waiting for us at Themed. My wife, Mariantonietta – an experienced camel-rider and fluent Arabic speaker – made up the party of four.

As the day loomed nearer, I began to grasp more clearly the magnitude of the task we had undertaken. At first sight, a ride of forty-nine hours was a flea-bite compared with the 271 days it had taken Mariantonietta and me to cross the Sahara's 4,500 miles. But to stay in the saddle for two full days and two full nights virtually without rest suddenly seemed an effort of a shorter duration but an equally demanding order. Lawrence had had great incentive, of course: not only had he won a startling victory, he had also left a Hashemite force at Aqaba so short of food that it was eating its own transport. According to the Oxford version of *Seven Pillars*, he had left Aqaba on the afternoon of 7 July, the day after capturing the town, and arrived at Suez on the afternoon of the 9th, '49 hours out of Aqaba'. He felt that this was 'a fair time', considering that both men and camels had been exhausted before they started: 'Unfortunately the camels by now had done 1,000 miles in five weeks, and were all jaded,' he wrote in a report for *The Times* soon after the war, 'so that it took the men two days to get to Suez.'[1] This was not modesty but litotes, and it was mischievous, for Lawrence well knew that his non-stop trek was a record – it was celebrated in his own life as one of the great camel-dashes of all time: 'The great sagas sung throughout the desert, of phenomenal rides dating back to the time of Harun ar-Rashid,' wrote Frank Stirling, 'have all been eclipsed by Lawrence's achievements . . . Such endurance . . . is almost incredible.'[2]

Our start was marked with a violent argument with the Taba Bedu who surrounded our tiny nest of camels as we saddled up. We had with us a *rafiq* from the Tarabin, they argued, but Tuwayba was Haywat territory and we must take another from the Haywat. We finally managed to placate them, and trudged up the steep track, dragging the camels after us by the headstalls. As we climbed the Gulf of Aqaba came into view beneath us, a translucent, shimmering blue, with the jagged edges of the Midian hills in the Hejaz beyond. Sunset came on us as we cleared the top of the escarpment, a zig-zag of gold etched into a scroll of dark cloud. It had taken us roughly four hours to make the ascent, which cannot have been far off Lawrence's time: however, we were still fresh, and Mariantonietta pointed out the anomaly that Lawrence's men and camels had been 'trembling with fatigue'. I put this down to the fact that his animals had been weak before they had started, and that the men had just fought a battle at Aba l-Lissan.

It was a moonless night, and the darkness closed in around us, locking us in an endlessly long tunnel from which there was no escape but morning. A bitter wind, bone-chilling as only a desert wind can be, was blasting in our faces. We were on the plateau of Sinai, the 'great and terrible wilderness', a vast shelterless plain of stone, whose great winds could freeze a man to death, and whose dust-storms could suck the body dry. The breathtaking force of the wind, the weight of the darkness, numbed our senses as if we were travelling in a dream. The camels pressed together haunch to haunch for comfort in the dark, and paced out bravely, their pads clicking on the rubble of rocks. We talked less and less, spinning away in our private universes, and between smatters of talk there was nothing but the sound of our saddles creaking and the familiar rhythmic slap of water in our jerry-cans. Furrayj smoked cigarettes furiously. Sabah began to sing a camel-song, a verse repeated again and again and again, but I was glad, for the sound of it kept us awake and anchored in reality. I knew from long experience that hallucination could be a far more dangerous enemy in the desert than bodily fatigue. We rode on for hour after hour, and slowly sleep began to stalk us. Sabah said that he could make out mountain peaks in the shadows where there were none, and at one point I looked over my shoulder to see another camel-rider following us, and only realized after minutes that no one was there. Even Lawrence had written of the 'silence of the night so intense that we turned round in the saddles at fancied noises away there by the cloak of stars'.[3] The world was so dim and silent, indeed, that it would not have surprised me to have come upon Lawrence's party. We came, instead, upon a rich vein of thornscrub – presumably the one in which Lawrence and his eight Howaytat had halted for an hour to let their camels browse. Sabah kindled a fire quickly and efficiently and Mariantonietta made coffee. It was now ten o'clock, and we had been travelling for a solid seven hours without a break. Themed, the only watering place on the route, lay at least thirty-five miles away. Yet Lawrence claimed to have reached Themed by midnight on the first day. I acknowledged that he might have had better camels than ours – though his insistence that they were tired out before the start of the journey tended to neutralize that fact – but, even so, was it possible that he could have been so far ahead? Sunset had come upon him at the top of the escarpment – as it had for us. How, then, had he jumped forward to Themed in five or six hours? The only explanation I could think of was that his party had been running their camels. At a fast canter, they could just about have covered the distance in the time. But Lawrence had specifically stated that they had walked them: 'If we rode hard,' he wrote, 'they might break down with exhaustion . . . we agreed to keep them at a walk, however tempting the surface.'[4]

The night seemed endless. The wind gusted stronger and more chilling, and Furrayj, who was seventy years old, became almost frozen to the saddle. Unlike us younger ones, he did not have the luxury of dropping down to the desert floor and stamping off the cold at a walk. In the saddle we would be overcome by that terrifying feeling of losing touch with the real world and drifting into the dimension of nightmare – or of falling asleep entirely and dropping from the camels' backs on to the sharp stones. On foot, though, I was haunted by another fear which by day I had shrugged off, but which, as the night drew on, grew stronger and stronger: the fear of blundering into a minefield. There were live mines in Sinai – plenty of them – left over from the Six Day War in 1967, and though the Bedu declared that they knew where the mines lay, no one could be absolutely certain. In the saddle, high above the desert, I felt more confident, but as we tramped on on foot, I had unnerving visions of an unexpected crack and puff of smoke, and one of us lying in the cold desert with his or her leg blown off. The hours passed by with agonizing slowness as we rode and tramped. Themed, which Lawrence claimed to have reached at midnight, was still far ahead – in my mind as far away as the north pole. Somewhere, in the early hours of the morning, there arose in my frozen and exhausted head the first faint possibility that Lawrence might not have been telling the truth.

An hour before dawn we stopped and made a fire to warm Furrayj, who looked deathly pale by the light of my torch, and who was now quaking so visibly with cold that I was afraid he would die of exposure. With great gallantry, Sabah threw his own sheepskin-lined cloak around the old man's bony shoulders. But he continued to shake, and we had to lift him on to his camel. He was saved only by the sun, which came up in a blaze behind us, sending pulses of golden light and unshrouding suddenly the stark immensity of the wilderness. We had reached the end of the tunnel. The night had closed us in a space a few yards square; now we were suddenly ants in an infinity of apricot-coloured rock, broken only by sharp crests like lone fangs, falling away into the depression of Wadi Themed. The sun warmed

257

us gently as we followed dry water-courses where there were scattered sedges for the camels to graze. Furrayj lost his paleness and began to breathe steadily again. Presently we came to the road, which wound down into a deep dustbowl, out of sight.

Themed well, where Lawrence had watered his camels, was still there, standing by a single building in the shade of a thorn-tree. On the shoulder of the wadi side I saw the ruin of the Sinai Police barracks which had been deserted on that day in 1917 when Lawrence had arrived. We couched our camels and slid heavily off. Old Furrayj wrapped himself in a blanket and fell asleep under a bush. We sat down in the shade to make tea. Sabah's leg was badly bruised from the saddle, and the soles of Mariantonietta's shoes were worn right through. It was already ten o'clock in the morning, which meant that Lawrence had arrived here ten hours earlier. That added ten hours to our journey at least: instead of staying awake for forty-nine hours – already a difficult task – we were now faced with the prospect of staying awake for fifty-nine hours – probably much more, since our pace would slow down as we tired. I judged this almost impossible, and decided, to my bitter disappointment, that we must give up the expedition at that point.

I flew back to London, troubled: this was, I felt, a serious defeat. I had been travelling in the desert for almost twenty years, and had covered almost 16,000 miles by camel. In fact, I was far more experienced than Lawrence had been when he had crossed Sinai in 1917. He had then been twenty-nine years old and had made his first real journey by camel only nine months earlier. I was able to conceive that Lawrence might have been minutes ahead, but after two decades of riding camels I refused to accept that the discrepancy could amount to ten hours. Even if Lawrence and his men were hardier than we were – a point I was perfectly willing to concede – how was it possible for debilitated camels to have travelled so much faster than ours, yet still kept to a walk? It was the magnitude of the difference which affected me. I knew we had done our best. We had not delayed but slogged on solidly for an afternoon, an entire night and most of the next morning, covering sixty miles at a walk, averaging three to four miles an hour – a pretty good time by most standards. Our failure to keep up with Lawrence – or within a reasonable margin – threw my whole life's experience into doubt.

A few days later I was working in the Manuscripts Room of the British Museum when an attendant put a small blue box on my desk. I almost got up to protest a mistake. I thought I had ordered Lawrence's wartime journals – written in a military signals-pad: but this box, no wider than the hand, obviously did not contain them. I examined the contents out of curiosity, and found two tiny pre-printed Letts' pocket-diaries, which I had never seen before. In fact, they were Lawrence's 'Skeleton Diaries', which he carried with him, and in which he entered the place he had slept every night of the campaign. They were, I suddenly realized, the most genuinely contemporary of all sources. Idly, I turned to 6 July, the day Lawrence had ridden into Aqaba. What I read astonished me:

> *Friday 6th July*
> *Entered Akaba 10 am. Read letter from Newcombe.*
> *Left in afternoon. Slept at the head of Negb Akaba*
>
> *Saturday 7th July*
> *Watered at Themed. [Bir] Mohammad sunset.*
>
> *Sunday 8th July*
> *Passed Nekhl [illeg] Medifeh (Sudr Heitan)*
>
> *Monday 9th July*
> *Slept in Suez, very well.*[5]

Lawrence had not made the journey in forty-nine hours! In fact he had slept at the head of the pass, 'Nagb Akaba', and far from reaching Themed at midnight as he had claimed, he had made it to the well just before sunset on the *following day* – for Bir Mohammad, traceable on the map, lay only a few miles farther on. This meant that we had actually arrived at Themed a good six hours *before* Lawrence: those hours he had spent sleeping at the top of the pass, we had been trekking stupidly into the night, trying to catch up with him. The diary entry made it clear that he had arrived in Suez not on the second but on the third day out of Aqaba – the forty-nine hour saga of *Seven Pillars* had been a lie. Why Lawrence had lied in *Seven Pillars* I could not fathom, for I realized that he had not lied to his superiors. When I re-read the report he had made to Clayton on 10 July – the day he arrived back in Cairo – I noticed that it ran: 'We entered Akaba on

July 6th . . . I rode the same day for Suez with 8 men and arrived at El Shatt on July 9th.'[6] This report, published in Garnett's letters in 1938, had been staring me and almost every other biographer in the face all the time.[7] It had taken an agonizing night ride across part of Sinai – and very nearly the death of one old man – to bring it out. Lawrence must have realized that some day someone would notice the discrepancy, and this led me to suspect it had been deliberate – part of the great game of 'whimsicality' he had been playing since he had been a child, intriguing others by a cloak of mystery, 'hoping [they] would wish to know whom that odd creature was'.[8] How effective his ploy had been, I thought: here we were, eighty years on, still trying desperately to find out.

Lawrence's perverse games do not, of course, lessen the fact that the capture of Aqaba was a brilliant achievement. It was the single great coup of his life. Though he was never to enjoy such an astounding success again, the Aqaba operation established him. It was imperative that Lawrence should have brought the news himself, for a messenger might not have been believed, but more than this, Lawrence was now able to convince his superiors that he was the indispensable conduit through which arms and money must flow to the Arabs. This, in turn, made his position among the Hashemites indispensable. Through Aqaba he became, as he himself put it, the 'principal' of the Arab Revolt. In Cairo he was fêted by his superiors. Clayton sent a special message to the CIGS, General Robertson: 'Captain Lawrence has arrived after a journey through enemy country which is little short of marvellous . . . He started at Wejh on 9th May with 36 Arabs and marched via Jauf and Nebk, crossing and dynamiting the railway en route.'[9] Robertson returned his personal commendation, and shortly Lawrence, the 'Temporary Second-Lieutenant Interpreter', found himself a full-blown major. Fortunately, his arrival in Cairo also happened to coincide with the appointment of General Sir Edmund Allenby as GOC. In early 1917, Murray's forces had twice attacked Gaza in Palestine, and had been thrown back with almost 6,000 casualties. Allenby, it was hoped, was made of sterner stuff. Lawrence, who was given an audience with the great man, wandered into his office barefoot, dressed in his soiled Arab clothes, and played his customary game of mystification. He had produced a detailed report based on his secret journey to the north, claiming that he could deploy no less than seven forces of Arab levies in various key positions, which could, by the end of August, threaten the lines of communication of the Turkish army in Jerusalem. This amounted to a general Arab rising in Syria, including the capture of Damascus – though Lawrence stressed that it could only take place if the main Turkish force was held down by Allenby's Egyptian Expeditionary Force on the Gaza–Beersheba line, and thus prevented from drafting new battalions to the Hauran. It was an ambitious – almost fantastic – proposal, and Allenby watched Lawrence curiously, unsure 'how much was genuine performer and how much charlatan'.[10] For Lawrence, the General was imposingly paternal, and would join the roster of father-figures which he spent his life compiling – a list which included Hogarth, and would one day include Thomas Hardy and Lord Trenchard. He would later complain that while service – 'voluntary slavery' – was his deepest desire, he had never found a chief capable of using him – it was Allenby, though, who came nearest to his 'longings for a master': 'What an idol the man was to us,' he wrote, 'prismatic with the unmixed self-standing quality of greatness, instinct and compact with it.'[11] Allenby's reaction to Lawrence is less easy to gauge. He later wrote that he thought Lawrence a brilliant war leader, and noted that his work was invaluable throughout the campaign. Yet he is also on record as saying that in reality the Arabs were no more than a distraction for the Turks, and that there were other officers who might have done an even better job than Lawrence. This was *post factum* speculation, of course. For now, Lawrence had just captured Aqaba, and even if his Arabs were simply a distraction, such a distraction was a million times better than having them join the enemy. Allenby was a realist, and knew that anything Lawrence did in Syria – even if it failed – would tie up Turkish forces. The General's massive inscrutability made it hard for Lawrence to judge how much he had 'caught' him, but as usual the performance worked, and Allenby promised to do what he could for his Arab allies.

Within days of the victory, *Euryalus*, the flagship of the Red Sea fleet, had anchored off Aqaba as a token of British support, and by 13 July *Dufferin* was disgorging arms and supplies. Feisal's forces were to be moved from the Hejaz to Aqaba – the camelry on the hoof, the Arab Regular battalions, now under the command of Ja'afar Pasha, by sea from Wejh. Feisal was to be put under Allenby's command, and from now on his forces would operate as the British right flank. Lawrence travelled to the Hejaz at the end of July, where he saw Feisal, and met Hussain for the first time. It was while in Jeddah that he received an intercept from Cairo apprising him that Auda Abu Tayyi was about to defect to the Turks: 'It is reported by Agent "Y",' the message read, 'that Auda [Abu Tayyi] who was Captain Lawrence's right hand man during the recent operations in the [Ma'an–Aqaba] area has written to the Turks giving as his reason for rebelling that presents had been given to Nuri [ash-Sha'alan – chief of the Rwalla] not to him but that he was now willing to come in under certain conditions and had twice written to the GOC 8th Army Corps asking for a present.'[12] Lawrence was alarmed, and by 4 August he was back in Aqaba, where he bought a famous camel called Ghazala and rode fast up the Wadi Ithm to Auda's camp at Guweira. The loyalty of the Howaytat remained crucial to the defence of Aqaba, for the Turks had already recaptured Aba l-Lissan and were bombing along the Wadi Ithm. A counter-attack on Aqaba was expected within two months, and Sharif Nasir had established four defensive outposts to protect the crucial pass of Shtar. One of these was Wadi Musa, at the gate of Petra, another at Dalagha in the Balga hills, a third at Batra, the highest point on the Shirah plateau, and the fourth at Guweira on the plain beneath, where, in the shadow of a single weathered crag of rock, there lay an ancient water-cistern. Until the Arab regulars arrived in Aqaba, these outposts were vital, and their continued viability depended on the Howaytat and Auda Abu Tayyi. Lawrence was received as a friend in Auda's camp, and when he touched on his correspondence with the Turks, Auda told him a cock-and-bull story about having pretended to go over to them in order to obtain money. Lawrence divined, though, that Auda was angry with the British. He had received no reward for taking Aqaba, and they had not yet sent troops or guns. Lawrence guessed that Auda's approach to the enemy had been more serious than he maintained. Though he wrote with romantic lyricism in *Seven Pillars* that Auda's heart somehow 'yearned for the defeated enemy', the prosaic fact was that the Howaytat, like the Hejaz tribes, were working for money rather than 'independence' and saw little farther than the solidarity of the tribe. Lawrence solved the problem by describing to Auda the vast amounts of arms which

would soon be pouring into Aqaba, and by explaining that Feisal –
who would soon be there too – would be 'extremely grateful' for his
services. Finally, he offered Auda an advance on the large sum he
could certainly count on receiving when Feisal arrived. Lawrence rode
back to Aqaba the same night, hoping his gambit had secured the
Howaytat at least until the regulars occupied the port. He resolved to
keep the secret of Auda's betrayal to himself: the British, with their
feudal values, would not understand the nature of Arab loyalty: they
wanted 'story book heroes', he believed. He would present Auda as
the brave Bedui raider, just as he had presented Feisal as the noble
Arab leader, manipulating the British image of the Arabs to the
advantage of the Arabs, the British, and Lawrence himself. He maintained that it irked him to have to serve two masters. He was, he wrote,
one of Allenby's officers, and Allenby expected him to do his best for
the British. But he was also Feisal's adviser, and Feisal expected honesty
and competence from him. He played one role off against the other:
'I could not explain to Allenby the whole Arab situation,' he wrote,
'nor disclose the full British plan to Feisal.'[13]

Lawrence had told Clayton frankly that Aqaba had been captured
on his initiative, and asked for command of 'Operation Hedgehog' –
the British Mission to the Arabs. This Clayton could not grant, because
although Lawrence was now promoted major, he was still a relatively
junior officer and could not be put over men like Newcombe and
Joyce. Officially, Joyce would be in command, but since Lawrence
would remain liaison officer with Feisal he would in practice have as
much power as he wished. On 18 August Ja'afar Pasha arrived at
Aqaba with two battalions of Arab regulars, consisting mainly of
Meccan townsmen or former Syrian soldiers in the Turkish army. Six
days later *Hardinge* landed Feisal with more supplies and troops. The
regulars, now about 2,000 strong, were supported by the French
Mission from Wejh under Captain Pisani, with a battery of mountain-
guns manned by Algerian artillerymen. Nasir had occupied his time
in recruiting the local Bedu, who had flocked to Aqaba in droves to
declare for the Hashemites. In late August a flight of aircraft was sent
to a temporary airfield at Quntilla in Sinai, from where a continuous
series of bombing raids was launched against Ma'an. To initiate the
campaign in Syria, the Hashemites were granted £200,000 in gold,
20,000 rifles, twenty Lewis machine-guns, eight Stokes mortars, 50

tons of gun-cotton for demolitions, and a squadron of armoured cars.

The arrival of Ja'afar Pasha and his regulars at Aqaba, together with the comforting guns of HMS *Humber*, meant that the town was now defended, and freed the Howaytat for raids against the railway. No one expected Ja'afar's troops to be able to stop a determined onslaught from the Turks, but they were an unknown quantity to the enemy and therefore a deterrent. By the end of August a Turkish offensive against Aqaba had, anyway, begun to look increasingly unlikely, for the Turks had a transport problem: their camels were few and weak and the pasture poor. Intercepted orders from the Ottoman HQ in Damascus revealed that the Ma'an garrison, 6,000 strong, had been instructed only to cut Feisal's units off from the fertile highlands of Balqa, whose grain supplies were needed by the Turkish army in Palestine, and whose timber was required as fuel for locomotives on the railway. A 'sitrep' from Clayton advised Joyce – now OC Aqaba – that the only offensive action the Turks envisaged was the occupation of Wadi Musa, near Petra, with two infantry battalions, a cavalry unit and some Mule Mounted riflemen. Clayton suggested that Feisal's irregular forces should 'raid the railway south of [Ma'an] and demolish it as far as possible in order to keep the [Turkish garrisons at Tebuk and Medina] cut off from their base'.[14] Demolitions on the line would also deter the Turks from a major offensive by diluting their forces. Many railway-cutting operations were planned for September, and for his own target Lawrence chose Mudowwara – a station south of Ma'an which possessed the only water in a long arid stretch: 'There are seven waterless stations here,' he wrote in a dispatch to Clayton from Aqaba, on 27 August, 'and I have hope that with the Stokes and Lewis guns we may be able to do something fairly serious to the line. If we can make a big break I will do my best to maintain it, since the need for shutting down [Wejh] altogether is becoming urgent.'[15] On 7 September, he rode out of Aqaba with two British gun-instructors, Sergeant Yells and Corporal Brook, and two Sheikhs of the Bani 'Atiya – a Bedu tribe inhabiting the Mudowwara area. His plan was to recruit 300 Bedu of the Howaytat at Guweira, ride to Mudowwara and take the station. At Guweira, however, he encountered opposition. The Howaytat were owed two months' pay, and were querulous. Auda, who was now trying to assert his authority over the entire tribe, did little to ease the situation. Instead, Lawrence rode five miles south-east across the Guweira plain to Wadi Rum, where, he reported, there were good springs, some pasturage and some beautiful sandstone-cliff scenery.

The Wadi Rum was, in fact, one of the most spectacular sights in the whole of Arabia: a maze of sandstone whose continual process of evolution was so clearly visible that the vast boulevards and buttresses of red rock appeared to be part of a living organism. No matter how many times Lawrence visited Rum, he never ceased to be transported by these great bastions of rock, skewered and scrolled and fissured and wrinkled by salt and sand and wind into shapes that no delirious mind could invent – *delirium tremens* embodied in rock and stone: the landscape of the unconscious mind. For Lawrence, Rum was a gateway to the cosmos – a road down which he might ride to that far-off, alluring sunlit space of eternal sleep: 'often . . .' he wrote, 'my mind used to turn me from the direct road, to clear my senses by a night in [Rum] and by the ride down its dawn-lit valley towards the shining plains, or up its valley in the sunset to that glowing square which my anticipation would never let me reach. I would say, shall I ride on this time, beyond the Khazail, and know it all?'[16]

For now, though, a war had to be won, and a railway had to be wrecked, and Lawrence rode between the grand walls of the wadi only as far as the great natural amphitheatre in the rock beneath Jabal Rum. This was the ideal hideout and base for guerrilla operations. Protected by sheer cliffs on three sides, it was invisible to anyone coming up the wadi until they literally rode into it, and here, fifteen minutes' climb up the hillside, lay the natural spring called Shallala, known to modern visitors as 'Lawrence's Spring'. The tents of the Howaytat were pitched in the lee of the sheer rock walls, hidden among thick *rattam* bush near the ruins of an ancient Nabataean temple. Lawrence's party camped there after dark and received visitors from various Howaytat clans, all of whom were disgruntled by what they saw as a Hashemite attempt to promote the Abu Tayyi. Of all the Bedu, none were so jealous of their personal integrity as the Howaytat – Lawrence wrote that every fourth or fifth man considered himself a Sheikh. The Dumaniyya clan under Sheikh Gasim Abu Dumayk – the valiant warrior who had led the fighting at Fuweilah – were openly rebellious. Lawrence realized that he could not win Gasim over, and declared furiously that he would enrol members of any other clan but the Dumaniyya for his raid on Mudowwara. Gasim stormed off, bellowing that he would join the Turks.

Feeling that he lacked authority to handle this mutiny himself, Lawrence returned to Aqaba, consulted Feisal, and rode back to Rum with a Sharif – 'Abdallah ibn Hamza – to smooth over the troubles. 'Abdallah managed to bring some of the Dumaniyya round, but Gasim himself remained defiant, not least because Za'al Abu Tayyi – whom Lawrence considered 'the finest raider alive' – was to accompany the raiding party, together with twenty-five tribesmen of the Towayha. None of the other clans of the Howaytat would accept Za'al's authority, neither would the separate clans even talk to one another. As 'Abdallah had returned to Aqaba, and the other Sharif with the party, Nasir al-Harithi, went blind on the first day out, Lawrence was the only individual sufficiently impartial to assume the direction of the raid, and, for the first time, he had to abandon his habit of working through a Sharif, and take on direct leadership himself.

Lawrence left Rum at dawn on 16 September, with 116 Bedu and his two British NCOs, each protected by a pair of Feisal's personal body-slaves, who were prepared to die in their defence. He guarded these British soldiers with solicitous care, first because their skills were crucial to the coming battle, secondly because their loss would have reflected badly on the Arabs, and thirdly because it was in his nature to care for others: 'He was ever thoughtful of us,' Brook remembered, 'and careful to see that the intense heat was not proving too much for us.'[17] They travelled along al-Ga'a – a vast swath of salt *sebkha* dividing Rum from the plateau of Shirah, whose bed of hard, flat clay made it a natural highway. Within a few hours, the gnarled sandstone blocks whose theme reached its crescendo in Rum mountain were playing out smaller and less distinct by degrees until the last outlying blocks stood no higher than a man. Sandstone gave way to cut-glass limestone slopes, and they rode towards a hogsback where the ridge drooped to a saddle between two bookends, marking the entrance to another clay *sebkha* on which they spent the night. The following day they crossed wilder country – intersecting limestone ridges relieved by knots of tamarisk and *rattam* trees. In the evening they came upon Mudowwara well, set in a valley between huge limestone plinths, no more than three miles from the station. Today, a few stunted palm-trees grow in that spot, indicating the presence of water, but the well itself is a sandy pit, completely dry. In 1917 there was abundant water, but it had been deliberately fouled by the Turks, who had hurled into it the carcasses of dead camels. Their bloated flesh was nauseatingly apparent to Lawrence and his party, but they filled their waterskins anyway – for it was the only water available to them – and both Yells and Brook later went down with severe diarrhoea.

At sunset, Lawrence, with Za'al and the two NCOs, stole forward on foot to the last ridge overlooking the station, where the Turks had built guard-sangars from the flaky grey rock. The sangars are still there, and one warm night, having arrived at Mudowwara riding a camel called 'Alyan, I crawled up the same crest to see the same station buildings, standing by the ghost of the line, from which the tracks and sleepers had been torn and piled up. On 17 September 1917, though, the line remained very much intact, and Lawrence looked down from the crest on the series of blockhouses along the station platform and saw their windows lit by cooking fires, and a host of tents in the foreground inhabited by about 200 milling Turks. Lawrence wrote later that the station was about 300 yards from the ridge, and thus out of range of the Stokes mortar. He decided that they must creep even nearer to find a better site. They crawled so close to the enemy, in fact, that they could hear them talking, and clearly saw the face of a young officer who left the camp to relieve himself, and lit a cigarette with a match. They withdrew to the shelter of the hill and discussed the prospect of an assault in whispers: the garrison was 200 compared with their 116 men, and Lawrence felt that the station buildings were too solid for the mortar shells. He decided not to chance storming the station, but to mine the railway down the line instead.

Looked at after an interval of eighty years, Lawrence's stated motives for aborting the attack seem less than justified. On the morning after my arrival, I paced out the distance between the hill crest and the station buildings, and found that it was less than the 300 yards he claimed – and in any case, the Stokes probably would have been effective from such a range. As for the station buildings being 'too solid' – I examined them closely and found that they were built of precisely the same basalt blocks from which all the other stations were constructed – a fact of which Lawrence must have been perfectly aware. The main obstacle was the disunity of the Arabs, and though Lawrence only hinted that this was a major consideration in the 1935 text of *Seven*

Pillars, saying 'we were not a happy family', he was more explicit in the earlier Oxford text, explaining that the Howaytat were so rancorous and feud-ridden that every Bedui feared lest another deserted him or even shot him in the back. It was his unsureness about the Howaytat which finally dissuaded him from the attack. Mining a train was not only easier to control, it was also much more to the Arabs' taste, since it involved easy looting. Lawrence later noted that the Bedu put more enthusiasm into blowing up a train than almost anything else.

They slept near Mudowwara well, and the following morning moved south across a plain then barren, but today greened by an agricultural project, to a belt of low hills, where the railway curved eastwards to avoid the instep of a fifty-foot terraced ridge. This, Lawrence thought, would be an ideal place for mining. The train would slow down to take the bend, and the terraces provided an admirable position for the Stokes mortar. It was a little high for the Lewis machine-guns, but since it faced due north it looked directly down the track and would make a superb base for enfilade fire. They hid their camels among some rocks farther up the valley and carried their weapons and tools back to the ridge. About 300 yards away, the metals crossed a two-arched culvert, which Lawrence chose as the site for his mine. Previously, he had used pressure-switches, but this time he was trying out an electrically donated charge which would be attached to a cable and a plunger, and set off by hand. Instead of burying it beneath the arches, though, he laid his fifty pounds of blasting gelatine in the sand on top, so that the downward blast would smash the bridge and derail the coaches, whatever happened to the train. It took almost two hours to lay the charge and another three to bury the 200-yard cable which stretched to some hollows near the foot of the ridge, where the exploder would be concealed. The cable proved troublesome: no sooner had one part been buried than another would spring out of the sand. Finally, Lawrence had to weigh it down with heavy boulders, then sweep over the sand with his cloak to disguise the tell-tale marks. Unfortunately, the culvert could not be seen from the firing position, so Lawrence decided that he would have to stand half-way between the track and the exploder in order to give the signal to Salem – one of Feisal's slaves – who had volunteered for the task of pressing the plunger. This, of course, meant that Lawrence would be in full view of the soldiers on the train.

All was set for the ambush, when things suddenly began to go wrong. The Bedu who had been left to guard the camels had climbed to the top of the ridge, merely to 'sniff the breeze', and could be seen clearly both from Mudowwara station, about nine miles to the north, and from Hallat Ammar station – four miles to the south. Lawrence shouted to them to come down, but the Turks had already spotted them, and an outpost opened fire from two and a half miles away. The Arabs were saved by the sunset, however, and Lawrence's party slept confident that the Turks would not come looking for them in the dark. Not long after dawn the next day, though, a detachment of forty Turks was observed advancing up the line from Hallat Ammar. Lawrence sent thirty Howaytat to engage them and draw them off, but at noon a much larger force – about 100 strong – left Mudowwara station and moved menacingly down the line to the south. Lawrence decided to pull out and leave the mine for another occasion. At that moment, however, the sentry on top of the ridge shouted out that there was a train standing in the station at Hallat Ammar. Lawrence rushed up to see, and as he did so the locomotive began to steam slowly towards them. He and Za'al screamed to the Bedu to get in position, and the tribesmen and the British NCOs jogged from their camping-place to the terrace on the ridge. Yells and Brook took their positions on the shelf, while the Bedu riflemen fanned out in niches and crannies along the track. As the train came up, Lawrence saw that it consisted of not one but two coupled locomotives and about twelve box-wagons crammed with Turkish troops, who, anticipating an attack, were shooting blindly into the desert from loopholes and sangars on the roofs. Lawrence was amazed to see the two engines and decided on the spur of the moment to fire the mine under the second, so that it would not be able to draw the carriages away if the first was derailed. At precisely the instant when the cab of the second engine crossed the culvert, Lawrence raised his hand. Down went the plunger, there was a thunderclap and a plume of smoke and dust 100 feet high through which lumps of mangled iron whanged towards them, including one complete locomotive wheel which whizzed past Lawrence's head and clanged into the desert. The culvert had been blown, the first engine derailed and the second smashed to smithereens. At once Sergeant Yells and the Arab crew opened up with the two Lewis guns, raking with deadly plunging fire along the roofs of the box-wagons, bowling the Turks over like ninepins, and cutting away the planking in showers of chips. According to Corporal Brook, Lawrence strolled calmly back to the gun-position on the ridge, 'with a complete disregard of flying bullets'. 'His bearing,' wrote Brook, 'made us feel that the whole thing was a picnic.'[18] From the terrace, Lawrence and the NCOs saw the Bedu, stripped down to their baggy trousers, leaping out of their holes and rushing towards the train. This was an unscheduled move, but it was too late to prevent them. The Turks were falling out of the doors on the eastern side of the wagons and taking shelter behind the embankment, firing point-blank at the leaping brown figures of the Bedu. They were huddled together, making a perfect target for the mortar, and Corporal Brook lobbed two shells at them, the second of which found its mark, killing a dozen men instantly. The terrified survivors began to run away across the desert, exposing themselves once again to the Lewis guns. Drum after drum of bullets throbbed into the retreating horde, until the sand was streaked with blood and littered with scores of bodies. The smoke and dust drifted away, the Turkish rifles fell silent. The battle was over, and, glancing at his watch, Lawrence was shocked to see that the whole engagement had lasted only ten minutes.

He ran down to the line to inspect the damage, and found the Bedu in a feeding-frenzy, ripping off the doors of the box-wagons, smashing cargo, tearing about yelling, shooting dementedly, plunging into the train and reappearing with bales and carpets. They had gone so wild that they pretended not to know Lawrence and three times Bedu snatched at his headcloth and his dagger, obliging him to fight them off. He found the first engine lying half on its side, and detonated a gun-cotton charge on its cylinder so that it should never be used again: 'I fear, however,' he wrote in his dispatch, 'that it is still capable of repair. The conditions were not helpful to good work, for there were many prisoners and women hanging on to me.'[19] Lawrence joined the looters, and chose for himself a fine Baluch prayer-carpet. The Bedu were beyond all control, grabbing at the nearest camel, whoever it belonged to, loading their booty on to it and making off. The Turkish patrols from the two stations were now closing in, shooting, and the Bedu began to streak off into the desert. Lawrence, Yells and Brook, who had returned to the ridge to retrieve the guns and the cable, suddenly found themselves alone. They were on the verge of abandoning the guns when Za'al Abu Tayyi and his cousin Howaymil rushed back on their camels, and helped to load them. Yells and Za'al made a fire of the spare drums and ammunition, laid twenty loose mortar-shells on it, then ran. The Turks, advancing on the train, were met by a barrage of fire from the detonating shells and cartridges.

The Bedu regrouped in safer ground, and were about to withdraw when, Lawrence wrote, he discovered that the slave, Salem, who had fired the charge, was missing. He asked for volunteers to go back for him, and the rest of the lost kit. Za'al, and twelve of his Towayha, agreed. They cantered back to the line on their camels to find the wreck crawling with Turks, and, realizing that Salem must be dead – for the Turks took no wounded Arab prisoners – made for their former camping ground, but were obliged to abandon the kit under heavy fire, and retired ridge by ridge covered by a Lewis gun manned by Sergeant Yells. They pulled back to the well at Mudowwara, where they watered, and then rode directly to Rum, arriving there the following evening. They had lost one Arab killed and two wounded, and had killed seventy Turks, wounded thirty, and taken ninety prisoner.[20]

The Mudowwara raid was one of Lawrence's most spectacular and most successful attacks on the railway: 'I beg to call attention once again to the gallantry displayed by Major Lawrence,' Clayton wrote in a message to Allenby, 'and the successful manner in which he managed his small force. I would also bring notice to the good work and steadiness of Sgt. Yells AIF and Cpl. Brooks RWF both of whom were relatively new to the work . . . the success of this small operation should have effects . . . beyond the importance of the action. It will raise the spirit of the Arabs . . . and will without doubt be reported and its magnitude will not lose as the news travels.'[21] Today, the ridge on which Lawrence sited his Lewis and Stokes guns stands on the border of Sa'udi-Arabia and Jordan, but, if you are willing to risk the hostility of the border-guards, you may climb it, lie on the rocky shelf in a stone sangar which may itself be a relic of that battle, and gain the same view of the track which Sergeant Yells saw through his sights on 19 September 1917. You will see, too, 500 yards away, the wreck of a railway wagon on its side. Sadly, this is probably not part of the train Lawrence mined, for it is an open wagon, whereas Lawrence specified in all his reports that the train drew ten box-wagons. At the foot of the ridge you may search in vain for the remains of the bridge

on which he laid his charge. It is no longer there: but if you are patient
enough to pace out the distance from the ridge to the embankment,
you will find, buried in the sand, the broken masonry of a two-arched
culvert, which may or may not be the one which Lawrence demolished on that day in September, eighty years ago, when, within the
space of ten minutes, he and his men cut down seventy Turks. Lawrence's reaction to this killing is difficult to judge. On 25 September
he wrote a letter to Major Frank Stirling, a colleague in Cairo who
was about to be posted to the Arab front, describing the attack in the
kind of gung-ho, boy scout language which he must have believed
appropriate to the professional soldier: 'I hope this sounds the fun it
is,' he commented. 'It's the most amateurish Buffalo-Billy sort of
performance, and the only people who do it well are the [Bedu]. Only
you will think it's heaven, because there aren't any returns, or orders,
or superiors; no doctors, no accounts, no meals and no drinks.'[22]
Lawrence was always adept at bluster and bravado, but beneath the
surface lay a sensitive soul. A very different picture of his feelings
emerges in a letter he wrote only a day earlier to Edward Leeds: 'I
hope when this nightmare ends that I will wake up and come alive
again . . . I'm not going to last out this game much longer: nerves
going and temper wearing thin . . . This killing and killing of Turks is
horrible. When you charge in at the finish and find them all over the
place in bits, and still alive many of them . . . and know that you have
done hundreds in the same way before and must do hundreds more
if you can.'[23] Whether one or both of these letters displays the 'real'
Lawrence, or whether both are simply reflections of the contrasting
characters of their recipients, is a question which cannot satisfactorily
be answered.

17. Ahmad ibn Baqr, a Circassian from Qunaytra

The Yarmuk operation and the Dara'a incident
October 1917–January 1918

On a morning in April I rode a bull-camel called Shaylan – a famous racer of the Howaytat – under the serried pagodas of Umm Salab, the 'guardian of Rum', and across the *sebkha* called al-Ga'a, towards the gash of Wadi Hafira. I carried *Seven Pillars* in my saddle-bag, and if Lawrence was correct, I should find, at the end of the wadi, a steep pass which would take me up 2,000 feet to the head of the Shirah plateau. I had felt the heat in the air long before the sun was up, and just after dawn long tongues of lemon and fire-orange shades had licked across the brownness of the hills, picking them out like sugared cakes, and gleaming on the mirror salt-licks of the Ga'a. Wadi Hafira itself lay in a haze which had steamed out from its thick green pastures of *rimth* and *rattam*. I reached the foot of the pass by noon, and climbed through the bed of a wadi which curved gently towards a snow-white pimple thousands of feet above. The wadi grew narrower and the walls steeper until I was hauling the camel by his headstall through a crack in the rocks which was only just wide enough to let us through. On and on I staggered, and suddenly the walls were so tight that when Shaylan passed, one of my jerrycans was scraped and punctured so that the water began to trickle out maddeningly. Since entering the wadi, doubts had nagged at me. Surely, this could not be the way Lawrence had come, I thought, with an entire army of Arabs, a squadron of Indian machine-gunners and hundreds of camels? They simply would not have got through. I was afraid that the wadi would become so narrow that I would not be able to turn the camel, yet for some reason I continued, stalking on through basting heat that bounced between the walls of the chasm, until I found that it ended abruptly beneath a towering cliff. This, certainly, had not been Lawrence's path. Cursing myself, I turned Shaylan about and headed back, but no sooner had I done so than there was a sudden savage peal of thunder. For a moment I stood stock still: there was a surge of cold air, and rain came slinging down, gouging up the sand in the wadi bed. I was gripped with terror. If the rain was heavy on the plateau, a wave of water might roll down the wadi and catch me here, imprisoned between its sheer walls. I looked about me, thinking that I should have to abandon the camel and climb as high as I could. Seconds later, though, the rain stopped, and, thanking providence, I almost ran the rest of the way back to the foot of the pass, pulling the recalcitrant Shaylan after me.

I realized now that Lawrence's route must have followed the shoulder of the wadi, but here the going was no easier. There was no clearly marked path, and often I stumbled over boulders, fell sprawling, cut my feet. I shimmied, half skating, down loose screes, balanced on ledges no more than eighteen inches wide, worked my way down into a weird broken water-course of purple stones and white felspar. Once I came so near to the edge of the precipice that Shaylan, bucking and shying, almost pulled me over. Again, I wondered that Lawrence's army could have come this way. True, he had reported that, on one of his ascents, two of the camels had been lost when they had slipped and fallen down the hillside, but on the other hand he had also described how, on another occasion, he had ridden down the pass without descending from his camel except in one or two difficult places. I shuddered at the thought of riding a camel over these sharp boulders and precipitous paths today. Yet it clearly was the same 'zig-zag broken pass', for gazing back down hundreds of feet, I could see the grassy street of Hafira terminating in a cone-hill which appeared to stand in the centre of the wadi, with the diaphanous mass of Rum brooding over it, exactly as Lawrence had described. Getting up that hill with a camel in tow was one of the most exhausting experiences I have ever had, and by the time I reached the top it was almost sunset. The ascent had taken me six hours. I could not believe that Lawrence had ever managed to ride up or down the steep, stony hillside virtually without getting out of the saddle – but perhaps, I thought, despite my years of experience, he had simply been a better camel-man than me.

Lawrence thought of Hafira as a passageway between Arabia and Syria, between heat and cold, between tamarisk and wormwood.

Indeed, the plateau was a very different world from the sandy swaths of Rum – a stony yellow moorland undulating almost featurelessly into the distance. In a cleft beyond the first undulation, I came upon a batch of Bedu tents. Dogs barked at me as I walked by, and a Bedui in a pitch-black *dishdasha* came out and invited me to stay the night. He showed me where to couch my camel, and five or six Bedu in ragged shirts helped me unload. They welcomed me into the tent where a fire of *rimth* was flickering in the square hearth and made a place for me. After dark they slaughtered a sheep, and we squatted by the fire, drinking tea and coffee, talking for hours, until the meat was carried in on a tin tray a yard in diameter – haunches and ribs of mutton, with the sheep's head set on top as centrepiece with its gaping maw frozen in a diabolic grin. This reminded me of the great food-tray Lawrence had described as a shallow bath, five feet across and set on a single foot, which had belonged to Auda Abu Tayyi. My Bedu hosts were Howaytat, and I asked after Auda's great tray. They told me that when the Jordanian army had occupied Jefer in the 1930s, they had looted much of Auda's property. Perhaps the tray had gone with them. My host, Mohammad ibn Salem, who had once served in the Desert Police camel-corps, told me that he remembered seeing an engraved tray at Jefer as a boy, 'but it wasn't five feet across,' he said, 'it was just the usual size.' I wondered if this was another of Lawrence's elaborations. In his original diary entry, he had written that the vessel was '3 feet wide', then crossed it out and written '5 feet wide'. Later, I read a report by Alois Musil, who had dined with Auda in 1910, and who described the dish – presumably the same one – as being of the standard size – about three feet across. If Lawrence had exaggerated about such a trivial thing, what of the Hafira pass, I wondered? I asked the Howaytat their opinion. The older men laughed, and Mohammad told me: 'In Lawrence's time Hafira was different. There were no roads and no cars then, and the pass was on the main caravan route from the Hejaz to Ma'an: it was used by hundreds of camels every day. The local Howaytat used to keep it in good trim – clearing away the stones that were washed down by the rains. But now, everyone has motor cars. There are roads which take you around to Naqab ash-Shtar. Only shepherds use the path now, and nobody bothers to clear it up. That's why you found it difficult. In the old times it was just like a motorway – you could easily ride up and down!'

I went to sleep in the tent that night, satisfied that these Howaytat had vindicated both Lawrence and myself.

My hosts were from the Dumaniyya section of the Howaytat – the people of Sheikh Gasim Abu Dumayk, who before the Mudowwara raid had raged that he would join the Turks. He had not carried out the threat, and when Lawrence had returned to Rum he placated Gasim by recruiting only the Dumaniyya for his next railway raid at Kilometre 589 south of Ma'an. It was during the march-in to this strike, on 1 October 1917, that he had climbed the Hafira pass for the first time. The raid lasted six days, and at last, after several days of waiting, Lawrence had mined and destroyed a train at Imshash al-Hesma, and claimed to have been injured in the hip when a Turkish officer had fired at him. In the following months his trained dynamiters destroyed seventeen locomotives and seriously hampered the working of the railway, precisely as he had planned. In mid-October, though, he was flown back to Ismaeliyya to meet Allenby for the second time.

Allenby was planning his major offensive against the Gaza–Beersheba line for November. In July, Lawrence had promised him a general revolt in Syria to secure the entire British flank, but now, three months later, he was loath to take such an irreversible step: the detailed report made to Clayton after the taking of Aqaba was, he said, 'ancient history'. It had achieved its immediate object – massive British support for the Arab Revolt – but now Lawrence realized he could not deliver, for if Allenby's offensive failed, or failed to reach Jaffa and Jerusalem, the rebel Arabs would be cut off and massacred by the Turks. The Arabs of Syria were not nomads but cultivating peasants, who lived in populous villages and would not be able to fade back into the desert like Lawrence's cameleers – they were a one-time weapon, and if fired off prematurely would be entirely wasted. To Allenby, perhaps, the Arabs were expendable, but not to Lawrence, whose passionate desire was that the Revolt should succeed. Instead, he decided to put his efforts into a proposal which had originally been but a small part of his master-plan – an attack on the westernmost bridge in the Yarmuk valley, at Jisr al-Hemmi – a complex steel structure spanning a plunging ravine, protected by only half a dozen sentries. The destruction of this bridge would, he calculated, stop railway traffic for two weeks. If the Arabs could blow the Jisr at precisely the moment when Allenby was driving the Turks before him, then their main line of retreat from Jerusalem to Damascus would be entirely cut off. They would be forced to withdraw on foot, and this would, perhaps, be the correct moment for the Syrian peasantry to rise and harass their retreat. Allenby approved the plan and asked Lawrence to cut the railway on 5 November, or one of the three succeeding days.

Lawrence planned to approach Yarmuk by the same gradual turning movement he had used to such great success at Aqaba. As on that operation, he would march in with fifty men, hopefully from Auda's Howaytat – the only Bedu he thought aggressive enough to capture the bridge in frontal attack. The route would hug the desert, from Rum to Azraq – the oasis in the Syrian desert where he had met Nuri ash-Sha'alan – and from there, having recruited a ladder of local Bedu tribes, the Bani Sakhr, the Bani Hassan, the Serahiyyin and the Sirhan, he would push quickly into the sown land of Syria and strike at the bridge. It was to be as close a facsimile of the Aqaba operation as conditions would allow, though this time the Bedu would be strength-ened by a squadron of Indian machine-gunners, under their Jemadar Hassan Shah, who were already hardened to camel-riding, having spent some months mining the railway in the Hejaz. Lawrence would be accompanied by Lieutenant Wood of the Royal Engineers, who would lay the mine if he was hit, and part of the way by George Lloyd, the former Welsh banker to whose conversation Lawrence had become addicted. In place of the charismatic Nasir, who was away on another job, OC Mission was to be Sharif 'Ali ibn Hussain al-Harithi, the brave, handsome 'young lord'.

There can be little doubt that Lawrence was attracted to Sharif 'Ali: 'No-one could see him without the desire to see him again,' he wrote, 'especially when he smiled, as he did rarely, with both mouth and eyes at once. His beauty was a conscious weapon.'[1] It has even been suggested that the 'SA' to whom Lawrence dedicated his book was not 'Salim Ahmad' at all, but 'Sharif 'Ali'. Like Dahoum, he was 'physically splendid', and while Lawrence's Syrian boy had been a 'wonderful wrestler', 'Ali was also as strong as an ox, capable, according to Lawrence, of kneeling down and rising to his feet with a man on each hand. Lawrence claimed that 'Ali could not only overtake a running camel over half a mile and 'leap into the saddle', but would have no one on his operations who could not do the same 'holding a rifle in one hand'.² The Sharif, wrote Lawrence, was 'impertinent, headstrong, conceited; as reckless in word as in deed; impressive (if he pleased) on public occasions, and fairly educated for a person whose native ambition was to excel the nomads of the desert in war and sport.'³ He was, in short, a younger and more desirable version of the heroic Auda Abu Tayyi. Lawrence referred to the Sharif affectionately as 'Little 'Ali' and represented him as having had at least one homosexual lover – a seventeen-year-old Bedui of the Bani Sakhr called Turki: '. . . the animal in each called to the other,' he wrote, 'and they wandered about inseparably, taking pleasure in touch and in silence.'⁴

Lawrence left Aqaba on 24 October with Lloyd, Wood, a yeomanry trooper called Thorne, and the Indian machine-gun company. They spent the night at Rum, where they were joined by Sharif 'Ali and an Algerian Emir named 'Abd al-Qadir, who was known to Feisal, and who owned several villages of Algerian exiles on the bank of the Yarmuk river. Lawrence thought that 'Abd al-Qadir's peasants might be of great use, and, since they were foreigners and hated by the local Arabs, might be able to strike at the Turks without causing a general rising, which he was keen to avoid. Lawrence had already received a telegram from Colonel Bremond of the French Mission, however, warning him that 'Abd al-Qadir was a Turkish spy. Lawrence saw no reason to suspect this. He put it down to mutual distrust, for 'Abd al-Qadir's grandfather had led Algerian resistance against the French – a qualification which did not diminish him in Lawrence's eyes at all. On the morning of 26 October, the raiding force climbed the Hafira pass. They crossed the railway with little incident on the 27th and arrived at Jefer the following day.

From here on, the good fortune which had so marked Lawrence's progress to Aqaba became conspicuous by its absence. First, the Towayha Howaytat, whom he encountered at Jefer, could not be persuaded to join the raid: even the notorious raider Za'al Abu Tayyi had become complacent since Mudowwara. Lawrence was obliged to recruit fifteen Bani Sakhr at Bair and thirty Serahiyyin at Azraq, none of whom expressed genuine enthusiasm for the attack. The Serahiyyin, indeed, told him that his target, the bridge at al-Hemmi, was out of the question because the nearby Ibrid hills were swarming with woodcutters in Turkish pay. He was now forced to change his plans, and agreed reluctantly to 'bump' Tel ash-Shehab – the nearest bridge geographically to Azraq, yet a dangerous objective since it would take them through inhabited country and cultivated land whose dampness would be hard going for camels and might prevent a hasty retreat. Then, on 4 November, 'Abd al-Qadir and his men suddenly disappeared from Azraq. Lawrence was astonished and troubled, but though he later wrote that he suspected the Algerian had gone to Dara'a to warn the Turks of their imminent attack, at the time he put his desertion down to simple cowardice: '. . . much talk and little doing,' he wrote to Joyce later; 'neither 'Ali nor myself gave him any offence.'[5]

The starting-point of the raid was the water-pool at Abu Sawana, where the patrol arrived on 5 November, just missing a scouting party of Circassian cavalry which had been sent by the Turks to reconnoitre the area. They left on the morning of the 7th, lay up until sunset on the plain two hours east of the railway, and crossed the line after dark, riding west until they dropped into a shallow depression at Ghadir al-Abyad, where they snatched some sleep among their still laden camels until first light. They could not move before dusk in case they were spotted, and then they must infiltrate forty miles to the bridge, 'bump' it, and exfiltrate across the railway by dawn the following day. They had thirteen hours of darkness in which to complete the operation, and Lawrence felt that the Indian machine-gunners were generally incapable of making the eighty miles required within that time. He selected six of their best riders to accompany him, under Jemadar Hassan Shah, with one Vickers machine-gun. He believed that the bridge could be taken with only twenty good men: the Indians could have done it, but they were too few in number. He mistrusted the Serahiyyin, and placed his faith in the Bani Sakhr under their Sheikh Fahad, whom he designated as storm-troops for the assault. To make the demolition easier, Wood repacked the blasting gelatine into thirty-pound loads which would facilitate its handling on the steep hillside in the darkness.

At sunset, they mounted their camels and padded silently out of their lying-up place towards Tel ash-Shehab, following the ancient Pilgrim Road. The mood was sombre. Lawrence himself had a bad feeling about this raid, and was miserable, disconsolate about 'Abd al-Qadir's desertion, and despairing of the success of the Arab Revolt. The going was sticky for camels: up and down gravelly ridges, and across ploughed fields or meadows riddled with rabbit warrens. The men were on edge. They came across a merchant and his family travelling with their donkeys, whom they were obliged to put under guard till dawn. Then a peasant fired a rifle at them again and again, taking them for raiders, and screaming out in the darkness. No sooner had they escaped him than they were startled by a stray camel and a barking dog. Suddenly, it began to drizzle and the ground became dangerously slippery, so that the camels slithered: two or three crashed down. The rain stopped and they passed under the telegraph line, to a place where they could hear the sound of water falling down the hillside at Tel ash-Shehab. They barracked the camels silently and Wood helped assemble the machine-gun, while Lawrence and his party carried the gelatine down a muddy slope towards the bridge. A train suddenly clanked past them, and Lawrence, flat on his stomach, had a momentary glimpse of uniformed soldiers, before continuing his crawl towards the bridge with Fahad. They snaked through the mud until they were almost within touching distance of the metals, and observed a single sentry on the opposite side, sixty yards away, clearly illuminated by a blazing fire. Lawrence and Fahad sneaked back to guide the men carrying the explosives, but before they could get to them one of the Serahiyyin dropped his rifle and fell noisily down the bank with a clang and a scuffle which shattered the silence as completely as a shot. Lawrence froze. The Turkish sentry shouted a challenge and snapped off a round in the direction of the noise, bawling for the rest of the guard, who rushed out of their tent and fired into the darkness. The Bani Sakhr blazed back out of the shadows, but the machine-gunners, who had been caught in the act of transferring the Vickers, could not get it into action. The Serahiyyin porters, terrified that the gelatine would go off if struck by a bullet, simply dumped it into the ravine. There was now general panic among the raiding party. The Serahiyyin rushed for their camels, quickly followed by Lawrence, Wood, the Indians and the Bani Sakhr. The shooting had alarmed the nearby villages, and lights began to go up, illuminating the dark countryside. The Serahiyyin came across a group of peasants and robbed them, only adding to the alarm. The villagers for miles around took to their roofs and began shooting volleys at Lawrence's party, while a troop of Arab horsemen charged them from the flank. The ground was still sticky, bowling the camels over as their flat feet tried to get a purchase. Lawrence and 'Ali took up the rear and goaded them on. They moved fast, driven by the demon of fear, and before long the shooting fell behind them. By first light they had reached the railway, hungry and exhausted. Lawrence heard the boom of Allenby's heavy artillery drifting across the landscape from the direction of Palestine, and took the sound as a reproach for his failure. If Allenby's attack succeeded, the Turks would now have a clear line of retreat along the railway: if it had been cut, not a man, a gun or a wagon need have escaped. The way would have been open for a general Arab revolt in Syria. Though he successfully mined Jamal Pasha the Lesser's train near Minifir the following day, Lawrence knew that all the great opportunities he had hoped for had now been lost. Dejectedly he returned to the castle at Azraq, arriving there on 12 November.

Azraq castle had stood since Roman times on the shore of a vast, shallow lake, where the waters of the great Wadi Sirhan collected after the rains. Until the 1960s at least it lay in an oasis unique in the Syrian desert – a region of woods and marshes inhabited by every species of water-bird, by leopard, hyena, wild boar and even buffalo. Once, it attracted hunters from all over the Arab world. In Lawrence's day the black basalt fortress must have stood out for miles across the sand-sheets and lava-fields. Today it is almost lost among ragged streets of breeze-block buildings, petrol-stations and barbed wire. The magic which Lawrence describes has gone, together with the waters of the lake, which have been siphoned off to Amman. I arrived in Azraq in a yellow taxi with my ex-Jordanian Special Forces friend, Mohammad al-Hababeh, and together we walked to the castle, and found it surprisingly well-kept inside. The guardian – an old Druse who seemed half crazy, and who was fond of interjecting English four-letter words into his conversation – showed us a photograph of his father, a Druse officer whom he claimed had served with Lawrence (though the Druses had not generally joined the Revolt until after the fall of Damascus). He shuffled around with us as we paced from wall to wall, following Lawrence's description in my coverless old copy of *Seven Pillars*. The most remarkable features of the castle were its two stone doors – giant slabs of basalt a foot thick, weighing tons, which had been ingeniously poised on greased pivots so that they could be opened and closed easily by the effort of a single man. Lawrence wrote that the main door was blocked during his sojourn, and a sentry posted at the postern gate whose job was to slam the great door to at sunset, so that the walls of the castle reverberated. We saw the mosque which had been used as a sheep-fold, until Hassan Shah, the Jemadar of the Indian machine-gunners, had had it cleaned out and sanctified once more, inspected the corner tower which Sharif 'Ali had chosen as his quarters, and even identified the breach in the wall – now restored – which Lawrence had had made so that the camels could be brought inside at night. Above the gate-house was the room Lawrence himself had occupied, a spacious garret with low windows through which shafts of light pierced the dust. I found Lawrence's description of how his men would light a fire on the stone floor on cold nights and gather around in their cloaks to recite poems and tell stories, as the coffee-cups went their rounds. On such nights, with the wind ravaging the castle walls, they had heard a ghostly wailing and sighing along the battlements, which the Bedu had attributed to the dogs of the Bani Hillal – the mythical builders of the fort – endlessly questing the six towers for a trace of their lost masters.

When Lawrence arrived back at Azraq castle on 12 November, he claimed to be nursing no fewer than five bullet wounds sustained in the railway attack at Minifir, and a broken toe sustained by a boiler-plate falling from the exploding train. This was the first movement in the concerto of his public chastisement for the failure at Yarmuk. The period between 14 November and his apparent 'return' to Azraq on 22 November marks another of those mysterious Lawrentian descents into the underworld about which nothing is certain. According to Lawrence himself, it was during this week that he suffered the most devastating and humiliating experience of his life: his capture, torture, and homosexual rape by the Turks of Dara'a. In the 1935 text of *Seven Pillars*, this sudden transfer from the conscious to the unconscious, from the specific to the general, is marked by the interruption of the dating-sequence. Up to 14 November, Lawrence specifies the date of events recalled on each page: for the next four pages he simply tells the reader that he is in 'November 1917'. The hiatus extends until 20 November, when he reappears at Dara'a, having jumped six days in the process. Where was Lawrence during those six days? His story is that he remained in Azraq for some time – long enough to oversee the refurbishment of the castle, to rest, and to receive hordes of guests and supporters. One of these guests was Talal al-Haraydhin of Tafas in the Hauran, a powerful figure amongst the Fellahin, and an outlaw with a Turkish price on his head. Lawrence told Talal that he would like to see the Hauran to reconnoitre for a future rising, and they rode off together, with two specially enrolled guards, an old man called Faris and a boy named Halim. They travelled by horse, and called at Umm al-Jamal, Umtaiye, Ghazala, Sheikh Miskin, Sheikh Sa'ad, Tafas, Tel Arar, Mezerib, 'Uthman, Dara'a, Nisib and back to Azraq, a distance of roughly 170 miles.

Now, Dara'a, the capital of the Hauran, was a key point on the railway, for it was here that the lines from the Hejaz to Damascus and from Haifa in Palestine to Damascus intersected. Any advance by the Arabs on Damascus, then, must necessarily take Dara'a into account. Lawrence decided to slip into the town in disguise to assess its strengths and weaknesses for a future assault. Talal could not accompany him, since his face was well known to the Turks, so Lawrence left the ponies with Halim, donned the boy's peasant garb, and walked into the town with Faris, 'an insignificant peasant'. Near the aerodrome, they were called by a Turkish sergeant, who grabbed Lawrence by the arm and told him roughly: 'The Bey wants you.' He ignored Faris and marched Lawrence in front of an officer to whom he gave 'a long report'. The officer asked his name, and Lawrence gave it as Ahmad ibn Baqr, a Circassian from Qunaytra. The Turk accused Lawrence of being a deserter, and he replied that Circassians were not subject to military service. This was a mistake, and the officer called him a liar, instructing the Sergeant to enrol him in his section 'until the Bey sent for him'. Lawrence was taken to the barracks and after dark was marched by three guards across the railway lines to the Governor's two-storeyed house. The Bey – Nahi – a bulky, spiny-haired man, was sitting on his bed when Lawrence was brought in. He inspected Lawrence's body, then flung his arms around him, trying to drag him down on to the bed. When Lawrence resisted he called in the sentry to pinion him, and stripped off his clothes, staring in surprise at his recent bullet-wounds. The Turk tried to touch his genitals, and Lawrence kicked him in the groin, making him stagger back, groaning with pain. He yelled for the guards to pinion Lawrence, then slapped him repeatedly in the face with a slipper, bit his neck until the blood flowed, kissed him, and drew a bayonet from one of the guards, pulling a fold of flesh over one of his ribs and working the blade through and twisting it, dabbling his fingers in the blood which poured over Lawrence's stomach. Lawrence said something in his despair, and Nahi answered, mysteriously: 'You must understand that I know: and it will be easier if you do as I wish.'[6] Lawrence raised his chin in a gesture of refusal, and the Bey instructed the guard corporal to take him out 'and teach him everything'.[7]

The guards stretched him over a wooden bench, and one of them brought a Circassian whip: 'a thong of supple black hide, rounded, and tapering from the thickness of a thumb at the grip (which was wrapped in silver) down to a hard point finer than a pencil'.[8] The corporal lashed him brutally. Lawrence was shocked by the pain, and though he had resolved to number the blows, lost count after twenty. He writhed and twisted, but the Turks were holding him tightly, kneeling on his legs and grasping his wrists. When the corporal was tired, the others took turns to beat him, and in the intervals between new series, raped him repeatedly. Often, they would pull his head round to see the wounds: 'a hard white ridge like a railway, darkening slowly to crimson leaped over my skin at the instant of each stroke'.[9] At last, Lawrence began to scream in Arabic, and when he was completely broken, they ceased, and he found himself lying on his back on the floor. The corporal kicked him with a hobnailed boot to get him up, damaging one of his ribs, but Lawrence grinned at him idly, 'for a delicious warmth, probably sexual, was swelling through me'.[10] The corporal slashed him twice in the testicles with the whip, and when he gained consciousness again, he was being raped by one guard while the others spread his legs. At this point, the Bey called, but when Lawrence was carried to him, sobbing and begging for mercy, the Turk rejected him as being too torn and bloody for his attentions. The guards carried him to a lean-to behind the Government House, where his wounds were washed and bandaged. One of the guards, who spoke with a Druse accent, whispered that the door of the next room was not locked. In the morning, he discovered that the next room was a dispensary, and found a suit of shoddy clothes hanging on the door. He put these on, climbed out of a window, and staggered out into the street, eventually making the rendezvous with Halim at Nisib, from where they rode slowly back to Azraq by horse. The only unexpected occurrence on the return journey was that a party of Wuld 'Ali raiders, who were not yet converted to the Hashemite cause, allowed them to go unmolested. The consideration of these raiders, given as if he deserved homage, Lawrence wrote, momentarily allowed him to carry the burden which the passing days confirmed: 'how in [Dara'a] that night the *citadel of my integrity* had been irrevocably lost'[11] (italics mine). Lawrence arrived back in Azraq on 22 November, two days after his ordeal, and the following day made an affectionate farewell with Sharif 'Ali, kissing and exchanging clothes just as he had done with Dahoum. He then rode for Aqaba, making the town by the 25th, having covered almost 300 miles by camel in only three and a half days.

This is the version of events Lawrence recorded in the final text of *Seven Pillars*. Certainly, if he had been captured, tortured and allowed to escape, such knowledge should have been reported to Military Intelligence, especially if, as he later maintained, he had been recognized. Yet, like the other mysterious incidents of his career – such as the shooting of Hamed the Moor – this one does not rear its head in any official report. There are no witnesses, no relevant diary entries, and no corroborating accounts whatsoever. Even the soldiers stationed in Dara'a, who were known to be mostly Arabs in Ottoman service, heard no rumour of the event. If Lawrence had not mentioned it himself, then it would have remained completely unknown to history. It was only in 1919, well after the end of the war, when he was already writing *Seven Pillars*, that the Dara'a drama emerged. In a letter to Frank Stirling, a former colleague from the 'Hedgehog' operation, who was by then serving as Chief Political Officer in Cairo, Lawrence used it to discredit the Algerian Emir Mohammad Sa'id by casting aspersions on his brother 'Abd al-Qadir, whom he claimed had defected to the Turks, ruined the Yarmuk bridge mission, and brought about Lawrence's capture at Dara'a by describing him to the Bey, whose real name was Hajim rather than the 'Nahi' used in *Seven Pillars*. Hajim, who was an 'ardent pederast', had taken a fancy to him, he told Stirling, and when he refused the Bey's advances he had been 'put in hospital' by his guards. He had escaped before dawn, he said, being not as badly hurt as Hajim thought. Lawrence maintained that the Bey had 'hushed up' the capture, having made such a muddle of it – and Lawrence had arrived back at Azraq 'very annoyed' with 'Abd al-Qadir, whose treachery, he said, he had learned all about from the Bey and his guards. In the original letter, this last line is interposed as an afterthought in the middle of another sentence, as if it had suddenly occurred to Lawrence that Stirling might wonder how he knew for certain that it was 'Abd al-Qadir's description which had led to his being identified. He does not, however, indicate how he knew that Hajim had 'hushed up' the incident. Moreover, this account differs from the *Seven Pillars* version, in which Lawrence was clearly not recognized: although some ambiguity is suggested by the sentence, 'You must understand that I know.' Lawrence concludes that 'It was evidently a chance shot' – thus severing any connection with a description which 'Abd al-Qadir might or might not have given – and this is confirmed when Lawrence notes that his companion, Halim, who entered Dara'a that night, probably in search of him, knew by the lack of rumour that the truth of Lawrence's identity had not been discovered. We have only Lawrence's word for it that it was 'Abd al-Qadir who 'shopped' him to the Turks, and the story of treachery was very much *post factum*. On 13 November, he had written Joyce that the Algerian had deserted 'out of fear' rather than defected to the Turks, and was then still sitting at Salkhad among the Druses – a friendly force. If this was so, then it is unlikely that 'Abd al-Qadir could have ruined the Yarmuk raid, which had already taken place. There is no independent evidence that 'Abd al-Qadir ever joined the Turks – he was anti-French and anti-Christian, certainly, but a fanatic Arab nationalist: the Turks may have wooed him, but Lawrence's assertion that he actually went over to them is unconfirmed. At the end of the campaign 'Abd al-Qadir and his brother Mohammad Sa'id had declared a government in the name of the Hashemites, and had tried to murder Lawrence personally in Damascus town hall when he objected. Lawrence had ordered them arrested and intended to have them shot, but Feisal arrived and spared them. 'Abd al-Qadir himself was killed by Feisal's guards in November 1917, but his brother, Mohammad Sa'id, a pan-Islamist, continued to cause problems for the Hashemites. Lawrence's letter to Stirling was written to provide evidence for the arrest of Mohammad Sa'id, which Feisal had demanded: 'I very much regret that Mohammad Sa'id has been given so much rope,' Lawrence wrote; 'Feisal has asked several times for his internment. He is the only real pan-Islamist in Damascus, and in his insanity is capable of any crime against us.'[12] Lawrence's first revelation of his torture at Dara'a thus has a clear political motive.

I travelled to Dara'a from Amman in a nondescript saloon with two Syrians and my friend Stephen White. Dara'a station, we discovered, was still standing, a large two-storey building of grey flint, jutting out like an iceberg from a market-place aboil with crowds. The whole railway yard, indeed, was a relic from the First World War. A rusting locomotive stood, disintegrating almost visibly, on a track by the engine-shed. I climbed up to the cab and found an engraved plate which read: *A. Borsig. Berlin-Tegel 1914*. This was evidently one of the German engines shipped by sea from Europe at the beginning of the war. There were other engines, of different patterns, in a similar state of trauma, sidings full of rolling stock of the same vintage – box-wagons, water-tanks, guards' vans – even beautifully built passenger-wagons which were obviously now used as toilets. We introduced ourselves to the station-master, who was assiduously playing cards with a group of employees. He knew of Lawrence of Arabia, he said, but he had no idea where it was that Lawrence was supposed to have been tortured, or even if the story was true. The railway here still functioned, he told us – there were two trains a week between Damascus and Amman.

We had *Seven Pillars* with us, and tried to reconstruct Lawrence's movements in Dara'a on 20 November 1917 – eighty years before. In 1917 the *serail* or Government House had stood south of the railway line, in the centre of Dara'a town, where Lawrence was arrested. At first sight it would seem logical that this was where his ordeal took place. Although he does not say so specifically, Lawrence does mention that after the beating he was taken to a lean-to building *behind* the Government House to have his wounds washed and dressed. He also says, though, that he was marched *across* the railway to reach the Bey's house, which must mean that it lay on the northern side of the railway, and thus could not have been the official *serail*. We crossed the tracks by the engine-shop, evidently a popular crossing-point for local people, and counted six lines, precisely as Lawrence had described. We turned left at a convenient hole in the fence, down a street of weary-looking palms, then right and into a square, where there stood a two-storey stone building. The building, which was large and detached, looked as if it belonged to the right era, and I noticed that some of the ground floor area was occupied by houses or shops with private doors. This would be consistent with Lawrence's description in the Oxford version, which mentions that the Bey's house comprised two storeys with a shop beneath. Had we discovered the place in which Lawrence had suffered the most devastating experience of his life? The details seemed remarkably accurate, even after eighty years. Yet it is perfectly possible that Lawrence picked up the geographical layout of the town not in November 1917, but in September 1918 when he stayed there for two days after it had fallen to British and Arab forces. An examination of his actual description raises some disturbing questions.

First, in the 1935 version, Lawrence writes that he entered Dara'a with a man called Faris who had been specially engaged for the Hauran reconnaissance. Yet in the Oxford text he gives his companion's name as Mijbil – a Biashr, whom he had recruited months earlier. Why was it necessary for him to change the man's name and conceal this fact, and why, for that matter, does he change the name of the Bey from Hajim to Nahi? Lawrence gives various reasons for changing names in *Seven Pillars*, but the most convincing is the one he gave Hubert Young, whose name he changes at one point in the text to 'Sabin'. When Young objected that 'it may perhaps be said that you put me under a false name . . . because you knew you were telling lies about me', Lawrence answered, 'But that *is* why I have put you under a false name.'[13] Secondly, many details of the flogging are not credible. The whip could not conceivably have had a point finer than that of a pencil. If Lawrence was not recognized, how could the soldier who arrested him possibly know that the Bey wanted him? What was the content of 'the long report' the soldier gave to his superior in Turkish, about a man he had merely picked up on the street whose name and origin he did not yet know? Lawrence might possibly have been mistaken for a Circassian from a distance when dressed in local costume, but how likely is it that he would consistently be taken for one when stripped naked?

These quibbles may be pedantic, and they do not prove that Lawrence invented the Dara'a incident, but put together they suggest, at least, a certain current of dishonesty in his account.

In the British Museum's Manuscripts Department, I turned to the pocket diaries which had shed some light on the Sinai trip, hoping that they would solve the enigma of Dara'a. Searching for the entry of 20 November, I discovered to my surprise that the page had been torn out. This was remarkable, for it was the only missing page in either of the two diaries for 1917 and 1918. At the bottom of the previous page, for 14 November, Lawrence's entry read 'Kasr [Azraq]' and then, added in another pencil, 'To the Hauran'. This suggested that he had been in Azraq on the night of the 14th and had left for the Hauran subsequently – it was impossible to say when, because of the missing page. I noticed that the pages had been numbered in Lawrence's handwriting, but this must have been *after* the removal of this page, since the numbers ran on as if no page was missing. This and the addition of 'To the Hauran' at the base of the previous page suggested strongly that it was Lawrence himself who had torn it out. What possible motive could he have had for ripping a page out of his diary, I wondered? Two answers immediately sprang to mind. First, that Lawrence had been so disgusted and ashamed of what had happened at Dara'a that he could not bear to re-read his diary entries. Second, that he had been covering up for something. In the first case, I thought, if Lawrence had been so disgusted by his treatment at the hands of the Turks he need not have made an entry in the diary at all: customarily, anyway, he entered little more than the place in which he spent the night. Consistently, then, the missing sheet would have included the names of the places he visited with Talal, and would have read simply 'Dara'a' for the night of 20 November. If this was so, there would seem to be little that could have disgusted him later. I also asked myself why, if Lawrence had truly wished to forget the incident, he should have brought it to light in the first place. If he had kept quiet, no one else need ever have known. A more logical conclusion was that he was *not* at the places he claimed to have visited between 14 and 22 November, and that he had removed the page to conceal that fact. The missing page covered six days: the next entry is 22 November, when Lawrence was 'back' in Azraq. The question was, did he leave Azraq at all?

The journey to Dara'a and back, allowing time for hospitality with Talal's family and an entire day at Dara'a, would have amounted to at least five days – perhaps five and a half. This would give a departure date from Azraq of 17 November at the very latest. Since it is certain that Lawrence returned to Azraq from the Yarmuk–Minifir mission on the 12th, his stay would have amounted to just five nights. Yet, turning to his *Seven Pillars* description of his time at Azraq, I found strong hints that he was there for a far longer period. He 'established himself' in the southern gate-tower, he wrote, and settled down to have a 'few days' repose' until the guests started coming in. When those few days were over, the guests began arriving 'all day and every day': 'we sat down to enjoy these dregs of Autumn – the alternate days of rain and shine' after which 'at last the world turned solidly to rain'. Visitors were converted 'very slowly' to the Hashemite cause; 'in these slow nights we were secure against the world.'[14] Taken together, these references indicated that Lawrence remained at Azraq for at least a week – probably longer. A letter sent to his parents on 14 December reads: 'I wrote to you last from [Azraq], about the time we blew up Jamal Pasha [actually the 14th November] and let him slip away from us. *After that I stayed for ten days or so there and then rode down to [Aqaba]* in three days: good going: tell Arnie: none of his old horses would do so much as my old camel.'[15] If, indeed, he had stayed at Azraq from 12 to 22 November, it would have added up to exactly eleven days.

Lawrence's reconnaissance in the Hauran would have been of great significance, I thought, for this was the area in which the last action of the campaign would be fought. Yet strangely, none of his superiors seem to have been aware of it. Moreover, a geographical report written by Lawrence himself on 15 December, for the benefit of future armoured-car operations, lists all the sites he had seen on his Yarmuk–Minifir operation, but none of those he supposedly visited with Talal, except a brief reference to Wadi Meddan, which might well have been supplied by an informant. It is the last act of the drama – the 300-mile ride to Aqaba – though, which casts the most profound shadows of doubt over the alleged incident at Dara'a. According to his testimony, Lawrence had arrived in Azraq on the 12th with five bullet wounds and a broken toe. At Dara'a a week later he had been thrashed severely. The annals of penal institutions hold numerous records of men who collapsed with heart-failure after thirty or forty strokes of the lash. Lawrence, who lost count after the first twenty, must have suffered at least this many. He had also been beaten in the face with a slipper, bitten, pierced with a bayonet, kicked hard enough to injure a rib, raped repeatedly, and received two vicious slashes directly to the groin which alone would have caused his testicles to swell so badly that he would have been unable to ride. How was it possible, then, for a man so badly battered to have made, within three days, the most distinguished camel-ride of his carer, covering eighty-six miles a day? Clearly, it is not possible. Either Lawrence was exaggerating about the ride, exaggerating about the extent of the treatment he received from the Turks, or the Dara'a incident did not happen at all.

Captain L. H. Gilman, who served on the Hedgehog Mission, told Lawrence's biographer John Mack that Lawrence had not mentioned a word about the Dara'a incident either to himself or any other officer who served in Arabia: yet he had no doubt that it happened: 'Lawrence was far too gallant and honourable a man to invent this experience,' he wrote; 'there would have been no point in it.'[16] Lawrence's official biographer, Jeremy Wilson, has echoed Gilman's words, writing that 'those who doubt that the event took place at this time are accusing Lawrence of an elaborate and pointless lie'.[17] Unfortunately, it is a proven fact that Lawrence *did* tell elaborate and, in some cases, pointless lies. His pre-war substitution of 'camel-bells' for 'mule-bells', for example, was demonstrably pointless (and it is inconceivable that someone with Lawrence's photographic memory should have forgotten or got muddled up). His claim to have crossed Sinai in forty-nine hours was certainly a lie – whether it was pointless or not is open to speculation. His ability to make up and sustain an intricately constructed untruth is evident from the story he was later to tell John Bruce, explaining his need to be flogged – a story which he kept up for a staggering thirteen years. Neither Wilson nor Mack disputed that Lawrence lied to Bruce, yet, paradoxically, both state that they found no evidence that Lawrence was a liar: as if lies told to a poorly educated working-class youth somehow did not count. Certainly, Lawrence could be gallant and honourable – he tried desperately all his life to live up to Sarah's image of him as the immaculate white knight – but some emotions are stronger than honourable desires. Bernard Shaw called him 'an actor' and noted that he was 'no monster of veracity', while Ronald Storrs, who knew him fairly intimately, said that his shortcomings were well known to his colleagues (presumably not Gilman) but were discounted because they were balanced by his brilliance. This seems to me perfectly normal: in the end none of us is an 'immaculate white knight', none of us is absolutely honourable or perfectly truthful. To expect this of Lawrence is to make him into a superman – an idea which he himself ridiculed. Even Achilles had a vulnerable heel: why should we expect Lawrence to be any better than Achilles? It may be that his compulsion to 'elaborate' was the shadow side of an otherwise 'honourable' man. Even Liddell Hart, who considered him a military genius, admitted that he had been too gullible with Lawrence's testimony, and Lawrence actually criticized Hart for accepting everything he said without question, just as he mocked others whose praise for his good qualities was not tempered by a little 'salt'. Moreover, his propensity for 'elaboration' is confirmed by his own admission: he confessed in his introduction to *Seven Pillars* that he often concealed the truth even in his official reports, and acknowledged elsewhere that he had a talent for deceit. Those who deny that he lied, therefore, are contradicting his own words and postulating a character which Lawrence himself refuted. He was a gifted intelligence officer – a member of a profession which almost by definition deals in lies, propaganda, and half-truths. Many have expressed incredulity that Lawrence's colleagues – among them men of the highest intellect and ability – could possibly have been misled by his 'elaborations', yet Lawrence himself, as a new recruit to the Map Department, boasted gleefully that such men were only too easily to be deceived by esoteric knowledge confidently declared. Just like others, the great and mighty believed only what suited them, neither were they themselves always paragons of truth: Richard Meinertzhagen, a highly respected senior intelligence officer at GHQ, for instance, who was credited with devising the ruse which led the Turks to believe that Allenby was going for Gaza instead of Beersheba, was later discovered to have deliberately forged entries in his own diaries. Lying brilliantly to the Turks was one thing, but lying to his own was not allowed. It is clear that Lawrence was so confident that he would be believed that he was prepared to 'elaborate' even when there were witnesses who could testify to the contrary. When Hubert Young asked him to alter what he had written about him on the grounds that the correct account might appear some day, Lawrence simply replied: 'Oh no it won't.'[18]

If the Dara'a incident was invented, then the 'point' lies not in the rational but in the unconscious mind. Lawrence was a masochist with a homosexual nature, who had from a very early age fantasized about being dominated by other men, especially in the ranks of the army. As he wrote repeatedly, the degradation of such a life appealed to him, for in the ranks one became a 'beast' – fed, clothed and watered and constantly available to be used by others. It is, perhaps, significant that in the 1935 version of *Seven Pillars*, Lawrence's page titles to the Daraʿa incident parody recruit-training in the army. The page on which he describes his arrest by the Turks, for instance, is entitled 'A Turkish Conscript' and the subsequent pages describing his ordeal, are entitled 'Recruit's Training', 'Further Lessons' and finally 'Passing Out'. At the age of seventeen Lawrence had tried to realize this fantasy by joining the Royal Garrison Artillery, and in 1912 the fantasy was extended when he was arrested as a deserter at Khalfati and possibly beaten by the Turks.[19] It is significant that Lawrence mentions the Khalfati incident in relation to his alleged torture and rape at Daraʿa, for the key to Daraʿa may lie here. Daraʿa may have been an elaboration of what happened at Khalfati, relived and magnified by Lawrence in his imagination over many years. The positioning of the Daraʿa incident immediately after the failure at Yarmuk is also significant. Lawrence had been terrified of failure all his life and was mortified to have let down Allenby, whom he saw as a father-figure. It is not insignificant that in his description of his meeting with Allenby a few weeks later, he evokes the fantasy of standing before the Bey: 'It was strange to stand before the tower with [Allenby],' he wrote, 'listening to his proclamation, and to think how a few days before I had stood before Hajim listening to his words. *How seldom we paid so sharply and so soon for our fears*. We would have been by now, not in Jerusalem but in Haifa or Damascus or Aleppo, had I not shrunk in October from the danger of a general rising . . . By my failure I had fettered the unknowing English and dishonoured the unknowing Arabs.'[20] The humiliation he brought on himself by inventing the Daraʿa trauma may have been an expiation of his self-adopted failure – not only his failure to blow the bridge, but to raise the revolt in Syria as he had originally promised Allenby. The same pattern may be traced in at least two of the mysterious incidents of his life: the attack by a tribesman in Syria during his 1909 walk, and the shooting of Hamed the Moor. Both followed a sequence of private failure and public expiation by apparent violence, a pattern which had its origin in Lawrence's early childhood, when his mother's beatings became a means of expiating his 'improper' thoughts. It is perhaps no coincidence that in revealing the apparent trauma at Daraʿa he should use precisely the same terminology – 'the circle of my integrity' – which he employed when talking of his mother's psychical threat.

Lawrence's *Seven Pillars* was never intended purely as a historical document: it was, he would tell Charlotte Shaw later, 'a survey of myself to Feb 1920 . . . people who read it will know me better than I know myself.'[21] His true self was, he said, 'a beast' and the book was 'its mangy skin, dried, stuffed and set up squarely for men to stare at'.[22] It was, in other words, a public confession of all the secret repressions, obsessions and desires which he had been unable to express to anyone before. The description of his beating at Dara'a shows an abnormal fascination with physical suffering: his lingering over the colour and texture of his wounds, and the detailed description of the instrument of torture – the Circassian whip – is typical of masochistic reveries, as Lyn Cowan has written: 'in masochistic fantasy the instrument is usually replete with distinctive detail, numinous with beauty and ugliness and fear which create and preserve just the right sensation . . .': 'Even in the barest and most common beating fantasies, we can hear the sharp hymn of the holy thyrsus as it slices down the supplicant's back.'[23] That Lawrence deliberately courted public humiliation is beyond doubt: 'I long for people to look down on me and despise me,' he later wrote; '. . . I want to dirty myself outwardly, so that my person may properly reflect the dirtiness which it conceals . . .'[24] His need to display his suffering is evident in many other passages in the book, and especially in his exaggeration of the number of injuries and bullet-wounds he received. He claimed to have over sixty scars from injuries sustained in Arab service, yet it has been proved conclusively by J. N. Lockman that he had very few scars after the war: to have sustained sixty wounds in a world without antibiotics, anyway, would – as Lockman points out – have required either superhuman powers of resistance or incredible good luck.[25] Lockman has also shown that the testimony of Richard Meinertzhagen, who claimed to have seen scars on Lawrence's back while bathing in 1919, was fabricated. In any case, Lawrence does not state that he was beaten on his *back*, and if his description of the wounds he received is to be believed then he could only have been beaten on his buttocks: it is impossible for a human being to see his back except with the aid of a mirror. Lockman has demonstrated that though Lawrence later had scars on his front and posterior which seem consistent with the Dara'a story, these probably originated in the post-war period and were voluntarily inflicted.[26] We may never know for certain whether or not Lawrence was captured and tortured by the Turks, but the weight of evidence – the missing page, the breakdown in the dating sequence, the long period which he seems to have spent at Azraq, and the lack of relevant scars – suggests, to me anyway, that the Dara'a incident was true only in the sense that it deliberately revealed the unseen Lawrence lurking in the shadows. As the emotional climax of *Seven Pillars*, it was the ultimate expression of his reverse exhibitionism – for as he told Charlotte Shaw coyly: 'I shouldn't tell you, because decent men don't talk about such things. I wanted to put it plain in the book, wrestled for days with my self-respect.'[27] It was, perhaps, his final declaration to the world of his conviction – with him since childhood – that he was 'untouchable' and 'unclean': at last, after years of aloofness, T. E. Lawrence found an opportunity of saying to posterity: 'This is Thomas Lawrence. This is me.'

Once back in Aqaba, Lawrence wrote, he occupied himself mostly with recruiting a personal bodyguard for his protection, suggesting that this was a direct result of his torture at Dara'a. There was a price on his head and he needed 'hard riders and hard livers' who would vow loyalty to himself personally. He wrote that he built up a large private army of ninety men, mercenaries, cut-throats, outlaws and bandits from thirty different clans of every tribe in Syria and north Arabia. Many of them were blood enemies, and there would have been murder among them every day had it not been for Lawrence's restraining hand. Because his rides were so ferocious and painful, every man with him was a picked rider, all mounted upon his own specially chosen camels. They would ride all day and all night at Lawrence's whim, and fought like devils. He paid them £6 a month: this was the standard rate for a man and a camel, but they actually profited far more than other camelry because they did not have to provide their own animals, which would have foundered under Lawrence's hard going. The camels were all provided from Lawrence's own carefully selected stable, and his bodyguard cost three times as much as any unit in the army, but did three times the amount of work. These lads dressed in bright colours deliberately to contrast with the pure white Lawrence himself wore, and had the kind of *esprit* which came from the shared hardship and suffering they endured out of loyalty to him. They took pleasure in subordination, he said, and enjoyed degrading their own bodies so as to throw into relief the freedom of their minds – an emotion suspiciously reminiscent of Lawrence's own masochistic desire for degradation. Of his ninety followers, almost fifty of them 'Agayl, two-thirds died nobly in his service.

There is no more enticing image in *Seven Pillars* than that of Lawrence in his pure white Sharifian robes at the head of his own force of ninety hardened cut-throats, all of whom had sworn to serve him unto death, and many of whom did. Official biographer Jeremy Wilson cites the recruitment of this guard as the single major corroboration of the truth of the Dara'a incident: 'As regards the timing of the incident,' he writes, 'it is worth noting that as soon as he returned to Akaba he recruited a personal bodyguard.'[28] Once again, the evidence – from Lawrence's own records – is against him. In fact, he recruited a bodyguard as early as May 1917, for he apparently told 'Farraj and Da'ud' in June that he did not need servants but fighting men. In October, before the Yarmuk raid, he said, he had decided to give some of the 'old bodyguard' a rest, and recruited six new members: 'Among my own preparations,' he wrote in the Oxford version, 'was the careful picking of my own bodyguard.'[29] He listed the new recruits as Mahmud, 'Aziz, Mustafa, Showak, Salem and Abd ar-Rahman. He dismissed two of the old guard, Mohammad and 'Ali – who had been with him from Wejh – but retained the rest, including 'Farraj and Da'ud' (alias 'Ali and Othman), Ahmad, Kreim, Rahail, Matar, Khidr and Mijbil, a total of fourteen men. At different times he also picked up Awwad and Daher, bringing the total to sixteen. Now, it so happens that Lawrence listed the names of his bodyguard in his pocket-diary in order to keep track of their wages, beginning in March 1918. Though the names and number vary slightly between March and September, there are never more than seventeen names on the list at any one time, and the average over the entire period comes to fourteen – precisely the same number he listed as forming his bodyguard in October 1917, *before* the alleged Dara'a incident. He might, of course, have changed the personnel if not the number, but many of the names recur again and again, and a significant number are traceable to his earlier bodyguard. Ahmad, Rahail, Mahmud, Mustafa, Abd ar-Rahman, Khidr, Mijbil, Salem, Awwad, Daher and Matar all feature in the March–September lists. Conspicuously absent from the lists are 'Ali and Othman, the supposed models for 'Farraj and Da'ud', who were evidently not in Lawrence's service in 1918 at all. It is true, of course, that some of these names are common among the Arabs, but even if the individuals were different, this does not alter the fact that the strength of Lawrence's bodyguard remained essentially unchanged between October 1917 and September 1918, that is before and after the supposed torture at Dara'a – thus proving beyond doubt that it could not have been recruited as a direct result of any incident in November 1917. Certainly, it was not recruited first in January 1917, neither did it ever comprise ninety men, even by aggregation, but consistently averaged about fourteen. Coincidentally, a photograph of 'Lawrence and his bodyguard' taken at Aqaba in the summer of 1918 shows only fifteen men. Hubert Young, an Arabic speaker who served with Lawrence in 1918, noted that the bodyguard comprised 'about 20'.[30] As for the idea that Lawrence's men were a tough crowd of bandits from all the tribes of Syria and Arabia, the provenance of many of them belies this claim. Mahmud, a 'petulant lad' of nineteen, was a peasant from Yarmuk, Matar a 'parasite fellow' of the Bani Hassan, Mijbil an 'insignificant peasant' old enough to be Lawrence's father, Salem a camel-herder of the despised Shararat tribe, 'Abd ar-Rahman a freed slave, 'Aziz a 'shallow, rabbit-mouthed' peasant from Tafas, Mustafa a deaf boy, Zayd an incompetent who was dismissed by Lawrence for failing to saddle a camel properly, and Rahail a Haurani peasant who burst into tears when the going got tough. Only Lawrence's chief, 'Abdallah an-Nahabi ('Abdallah 'the Robber'), appears to meet his claim that his men were outlaws. None belonged to the major Bedu tribes of Arabia (Lawrence told the Sha'alans that he was too humble a man to have Rwalla guards) and few to the 'Agayl – the vast majority were Syrian peasants who, because of old age, infirmity or incompetence, could not get employment elsewhere. As for dying in Lawrence's service, there is hardly a name featuring in March 1918 which does not appear on the list for September. It is just possible that one or two may have been killed, but the number cannot have amounted to sixty – since the sum total of members of the bodyguard was never more than seventeen, and most, if not all, of these survived.

Some stiff claims have been made for the effects of Lawrence's treatment at Dara'a: 'After the homosexual rape . . .' Jeremy Wilson writes, 'the consummation of a marriage would have been utterly abhorrent to him. The incident had left him with an aversion to physical contact, which was noticed by many of his friends.'[31] It has also been said that the horrific experience warped his character for ever, giving him an obsession with cleanliness and bathing, and perhaps turning him into the full-blown masochist he became later. However, all these traits are manifest in Lawrence's early life. He himself wrote that his aversion to physical contact was the result of a struggle he had endured *in his youth* – most probably with his mother. He displayed masochistic behaviour in his self-deprivation at an early age, frequently showed an inordinate concern with cleanliness and bathing in his letters home, and always seems to have preferred men to women. Even a cursory reading of *Seven Pillars* shows an unmistakable approval and acceptance of the idea of homoerotic sex and a rejection and disgust for the heterosexual variety. As early as the second page of the main text, indeed, he commends the youths who reject the 'raddled meat' of women to '[slake] one another's few needs in their own clean bodies – a cold convenience that by comparison seemed sexless and even pure . . .'[32] The ideology is clear. It is very difficult to see how, by any conceivable convolution of logic, the experience of homosexual rape could have created an aversion to heterosexuality and an apparent warm approval of the 'purity' of homosexuality, unless Lawrence had some predisposition to it. As for 'warping him for ever', Lawrence's youngest brother, Arnie, wrote that he 'had always been a person of remarkable control and poise . . . Well, this all went on after the war and in addition he developed a tremendous zest for anything comic. He had obviously gone through tremendous difficulties and done so by seeing the funny side of them.'[33] If this does not sound like a man whose spirit had been shattered by horrific experiences during the war, then neither does the Lawrence who, in December 1917 – a month after the supposed torture at Dara'a – joined Allenby at Jerusalem's Jaffa Gate for his triumphal entry into the old city: 'He was gay that day,' wrote A. P. Wavell, who walked beside him at the procession, 'with jests at his borrowed uniform and at the official appointment that had been loaned him for the ceremony – staff officer to Bertie Clayton. He said as usual little of himself, and barely mentioned that great ride to, and unlucky failure at, the Yarmuk valley bridge, from which he had just returned.'[34]

18. The Most Ghastly Material to Build into a Design

Tafilah and Tel ash-Shahm
January–April 1918

Lawrence had arrived at GHQ expecting some sort of rebuke for his failure to carry the Yarmuk bridge, to find that Allenby had already moved on. The Gaza–Beersheba line had been breached, Jerusalem had fallen, and Sir Edmund's thoughts were already encompassing the Dead Sea. When the EEF had gathered its strength, transport and supplies – by February 1918 – he planned to unleash it on Jericho. The Hashemite base at Aqaba was now behind his own lines. If the Arabs could take Tafilah, in the wheat-growing Belqa uplands on the eastern shore of the Dead Sea, then they could link up again with the British right flank. Lawrence thought they could move even farther – as far as the north end of the Dead Sea – as long as Allenby could supply them through Jericho once it had fallen. The Arab base would then shift from Aqaba to Jericho, which would be defended by the Arab Northern Army under Ja'afar Pasha – now 3,000 strong. Considered indisciplined and inefficient, Ja'afar's regulars had astonished everyone with their tenacity when, in October 1917, the Turks had finally mounted a sledgehammer attack against the Hashemite outpost at Wadi Musa, near Petra, in brigade strength. The regulars had numbered only 350: two companies of camel-corps, and two of mule-mounted infantry under the savagely competent Maulud al-Mukhlis. Yet they had proved once and for all that trained Arab troops could hold a position against superior numbers, and had thrown back the enemy so decisively that the Turks never attacked an entrenched force of Arab regulars again.

The capture of Tafilah did not prove a difficult task. When Sharif Nasir and Auda Abu Tayyi appeared on its doorstep at dawn on 16 January 1918, having ridden all night with some Towayha and Bani Sakhr horsemen, they captured it without difficulty. Their only opposition came, not from the 180-strong Turkish garrison, but from the local Muhaysin peasantry, whose Sheikh was an anti-Hashemite partisan. When Auda rode down to the houses, and declared: 'Dogs! Do you not know Auda Abu Tayyi?' the peasants capitulated at once. By that evening the Arabs had been augmented by a contingent of Auda's rivals, the ibn Jazi Howaytat, who had long since deserted the Turks for the Hashemite cause, and four days later Lawrence arrived with Sharif Zayd, Ja'afar Pasha, Zayd's household 'Agayl, Bishah and 'Utayba, and a small force of regulars with two mountain-guns. They had left their main force at Shobek, where it was stuck for lack of supplies. Auda and his clan were sent back to Jefer to prevent strife between them and the ibn Jazi, who stayed behind under their young chiefs Mata'ab and Annad. In a report written on 22 January, Lawrence wrote that the Hashemites had about 500 men in the town, but that the local peasants were bitterly divided and terrified of each other and of the Hashemite force. That the capture of Tafilah was regarded simply as a stepping-stone to the towns of Moab is indicated by his observation that 'Tafil[ah] will not ease up till we take Kerak, and Kerak till we take Madeba.'[1] Zayd took steps to police the town and appointed a governor, then sent cavalry scouts north along the road to Kerak to probe Turkish strength, with a quick push into Moab in mind. It was in the chasm of Sayl al-Haysa – the great wadi that divides Edom from Moab – that on 23 January his pickets fell foul of a Turkish cavalry screen outriding a force of three infantry battalions with two howitzers. Astonishingly, and against all logic, Lawrence thought, the Turks were coming back.

It was his vexation at this sudden reprise, Lawrence said, that made him determined to break his rule and fight a pitched battle for the first time. According to him, the engagement went off like a travesty of a classic regular battle out of Clausewitz or Foch. First, a tiny unit composed of peasants and Bedu horsemen, with two machine-guns, drove the Turkish vanguard off the plateau to the north of Tafilah and back into Sayl al-Haysa, where they ran slap into the main body of Turkish troops, who had just struck camp, and who opened up immediately with howitzers and machine-guns. The Arabs lost their own gun, and backtracked to the plateau, sheltering behind a four-foot ridge and firing desperately until their ammunition had almost run out, trying to duck the ricocheting spray of bullets from at least fifteen machine-guns directed at them from the Turkish lines. At this point, Lawrence appeared up in the eye of the battle, having strolled unarmed and barefoot across the plateau amid falling shells which the Turkish gunners had as yet failed to range correctly. On the way, he had coolly inspected the skin of an unexploded round to see what calibre of artillery the Turks were using. He saw the position was hopeless, and ordered the Arab riflemen to withdraw to a ridge three kilometres behind them, which he had already manned with twenty 'Agayl of Sharif Zayd's bodyguard. He begged the few horsemen of the ibn Jazi to hang on for ten or fifteen minutes to cover the retreat. He ran back, pacing out the ground, and was soon overtaken by the retreating cavalry, whose leader, Mata'ab, picked him up. Zayd's force now crossed the ravine, and the whole Arab contingent was concentrated on his 'Reserve Ridge', from where they so dominated the terrain with mountain-guns and machine-guns that the Turks were obliged to halt their advance. Lawrence wrote that the battlefield was wedge-shaped with the Reserve Ridge as the flat side, and eastern and western ridges converging on the edge of the Haysa escarpment about three miles before them. The Turkish HQ and reserve lay beyond the apex of the wedge, with infantry and machine-guns deployed along the spines of the ridges to the left and right. For the Arabs, the obvious solution was to slip around the sides, under cover of the ridges, and catch the Turks in a pincer movement. Accordingly, Rasim Sardast, the artillery officer, was sent around the back of the eastern ridge with eighty riders, while Lawrence sent a contingent of new recruits – peasants from a neighbouring village called 'Ayma – to creep round the ridge to the west. Just before four o'clock in the afternoon, the 'Ayma men came over the ridge suddenly, taking the Turkish machine-gun nests from behind. They rushed them from only 200 yards, put them to flight, and captured the guns. On the enemy's left flank, Rasim and his horsemen charged in almost simultaneously, while all the Arabs left behind the Reserve Ridge rushed forwards. The Turks were now streaming off the battlefield, abandoning their machine-guns and howitzers. The Ottoman commander, Hamid Fakhri, who was heard to say that in forty years he had never seen irregulars fight like this, mounted his horse to rally his troops but was struck down by an Arab bullet and mortally wounded. This was the final straw for the demoralized Turks, who withdrew in panic into Sayl al-Haysa, with the Arabs after them. Only about fifty, it was later reported, succeeded in getting back to Kerak. It was a resounding victory: of the 600 Turks who had set out from Kerak two days previously, almost 200 had been killed, including the commander, and 250 taken prisoner. The Arabs had also captured two Skoda mountain howitzers, twenty-seven machine-guns and 200 horses and mules. The official war history, whose account of the battle was – like every other European account – taken directly from Lawrence himself, called it 'a brilliant feat of arms'.[2] Yet Lawrence wrote later that his report on the battle was a deliberate parody whose intention was to mock his superiors' rigid belief in the dicta of military thinkers such as Clausewitz and Foch. The biggest joke of all, he wrote, was that, far from recognizing this mockery, they swallowed it all gravely and awarded him the DSO: 'We should have more bright breasts in the army,' he chuckled, 'if each man was able, without witnesses, to write out his own despatch.'[3] Lawrence claimed in *Seven Pillars* that he, and he alone, had deliberately and voluntarily decided to fight a pitched battle at Tafilah, yet since he also mocked his own account of the engagement, I found myself wondering what part he had really played in its phenomenal success.

I travelled to Tafilah with my ex-Special Forces friend Mohammad al-Hababeh to see the battlefield for myself, and found the town's setting far more lovely than I could have imagined. The old part of Tafilah – the Muhaysin quarter – was a tightly packed neighbourhood of stone houses clustered around a small, square fort, which stood on a panhandle promontory, overlooking the deep rift of the Sayl az-Zarqa. To the south, across the ravine, lay the village of Busayra, and to the north, the great plateau on which the battle itself had been fought. Directly west, looking along the cleft of the Sayl, you could glimpse the gleaming green valley of the Dead Sea.

First, we called in at the Tourist Office. The officer there was very friendly and ordered us tea, but no, he couldn't tell us where the battle of Tafilah had been fought. 'Anyway,' he said, 'Lawrence had nothing to do with the battle. He was just a British spy.' We thanked him, and drove down to the oldest building in the town – the Ottoman fort. This, we decided, was the correct place to start, for it was marked on the plan of the battle I had photocopied from the official war history. From there, I located Lawrence's Reserve Ridge by a simple compass-bearing, and Mohammad drove me around the gorge to the foot of the steep chalky escarpment, where we left the car and climbed up. There were newly planted Aleppo pines and cedars on the terraces, and near the top I saw masonry blocks among the stones which Lawrence had identified as Byzantine – the local name for his 'Reserve Ridge' was Khirbat Nokheh: 'the ruin of the resting-place'. Along the spine of the ridge were pits which might well have been gun-emplacements from the battle itself, and a view across undulating volcanic heath with waving yellow goatgrass and nests of black stones and boulders, but scarcely a single tree. Below me to the left I could clearly see the western ridge on which the Turkish machine-guns had been placed, and which had been taken by the 'Ayma men from the rear. The rest of the battlefield, however, was not as I had expected. From the plan, and from Lawrence's account, I had imagined a triangular plain bounded by ridges on two sides. Instead I saw an undulating hillside of field and stubble tilting up to the right, to the base of a great buttress hogsback along the base of which ran the Kerak–Tafilah road. The far edge of the plateau, where the Turkish HQ had stood, appeared to be in sight from the map, but in practice it was hidden by high ground which lay directly in front of me. The final charge from Reserve Ridge, therefore, had been down a slope into dead ground, and then over another ridge before falling on the Turks – quite a different impression from that given by Lawrence of a charge downhill. Mohammad examined the map carefully and squinted at the ground, then pointed out to me a note stating that the map was based on 'an oblique aerial photograph' – possibly the photo shown in the same report, taken in 1929, which looked at the battlefield from the perspective of the town. In fact the official report had been made in the same year, for I later traced two letters from Lawrence to its author, Major Archibold Becke, dated 1929: 'You want me to check the affair now, on my twelve year old memories,' Lawrence wrote, 'against air-photos of the ground. Isn't that overdoing what was originally meant ... to be a joke? ... The whole thing's absurd.'[4] Although Lawrence subsequently wrote that Becke's map 'squared substantially with his memories', there was plainly some discrepancy between the map and the ground. We began to walk down the hillside, pacing towards the end of the western ridge, where Lawrence had met the Muhaysin and the ibn Jazi and ordered them to withdraw. As I

walked, I had a vivid vision of bullets whining past me, of the boom
and crash of falling shells, the tang of cordite, the rattle of machine-guns.
I was still engrossed in my reverie when a voice said, 'Peace be on
you,' and I saw an old shepherd, a brown-skinned man with a face
like cured vellum, dressed in a dirty sheepskin cloak and a tattered
headcloth, scuffling over a stony fold with about ninety scrawny brown
and white sheep. Mohammad asked him if he knew anything about
Lawrence and the battle of Tafilah. 'No,' the old man said, 'But there
was fighting up here, because we find shells and bullets sometimes.' It
took us almost an hour to reach the far tip of the western ridge where
the Turkish machine-gun battery had supposedly been sited, which
would bear out Lawrence's statement that the distance was roughly
two miles. We climbed to the top through soft ploughed soil, and saw
from there a deep cleft in the ground, cut by water, long ago, which
ran all the way down into the ravine. This, I thought, must have been
the secret path by which the 'Ayma men had sneaked up behind the
Turks, and thus changed the whole course of the battle: 'the main
Turkish effort,' Lawrence wrote to Major Becke, 'was along the ridge
afterwards cleared by the men of ['Ayma].'[5]

The assault of the 'Ayma men was clearly the decisive moment in the
battle, but whether it was Lawrence himself who sent them forward,
as he later told Liddell Hart, is disputable. Another participant in
the battle, Subhi al-Amari, a regular Arab officer commanding a
machine-gun section, recalled that the peasants of 'Ayma had gathered
on a hill called Khirbat as-Saba'ah, about a kilometre to the right of
the Turkish flank. According to Subhi, the Turkish position was out
of range from Reserve Ridge. This is evidently so, for though Lawrence
told Becke that he had to put up the sights of his Vickers to 3,000
yards to spray the retreat, the sights of a Vickers actually only extended
to 2,900 yards, which was the weapon's maximum range. As Richard
Aldington correctly pointed out, a machine-gun duel at 3,000 yards
was unthinkable in that era. Subhi had the sudden idea of moving his
two guns around the western ridge in order to get in range. He and
his men had sprinted across the dead ground and crawled to the base
of the ridge, where they were joined spontaneously by the 'Ayma
peasants. His machine-gunners clambered up the slope and opened
fire on the Turks from point-blank range, and were swiftly followed

by a rush from the 'Ayma men. The Turkish unit nearest the Arabs was badly hit, and the commander ordered his men to turn their line and face the peasants. It was at this point, Subhi wrote, that an unexpected thing happened. When the Turks stood up to change the line, the 'Ayma men thought they were about to retreat and launched an impulsive attack, shouting and cheering. The Turks, taken aback, simply abandoned their guns and ran, and their panic spread to the nearby units, who did the same. Subhi later learned from a prisoner that at this precise moment, most of the Turkish officers had withdrawn from the line to attend an orders-group with the CO, and thus there was no one to rally the Turkish rank and file in their retreat. This was why, when the Turks fell into disorder, Hamid Fakhri had, as Lawrence also recorded, instructed his officers, too late, to take a rifle each and return to the line.

The Arab historian Suleiman Mousa told me that he had spoken with a number of veterans of the battle, most of whom remembered seeing Lawrence on the battlefield, but all of whom confirmed that the engagement was a highly haphazard affair, as Subhi's report suggests. Lawrence himself hinted at this when he told Liddell Hart that as the 'Ayma men had arrived from the west (their village lay a few miles west of the battlefield), 'it is possible that geography had as much part as strategy in deciding the form of their attack'.[6] What of Lawrence's other claims? He wrote that he had decided to fight a pitched battle out of anger at the Turks' stupidity in coming back, sent machine-guns forward to support the peasants, chose the Reserve Ridge as a last defensive line, ordered the spearhead back to the ridge, and urged Zayd to move his main body there. The evidence, though, is that it was neither Lawrence nor Sharif Zayd who decided to confront the Turks on the plateau, but the Muhaysin peasants of Tafilah, who were loath to let them back in their town: the action of a few dozen of them had obliged Lawrence to make a stand. There is no reason to suppose that he did not send the machine-guns to support them on his own initiative, nor that he did not choose the Reserve Ridge, counsel Zayd to move, or order the vanguard to withdraw. Evidently, then, he played a major part in the battle. Why the self-mockery, the peppering of aphorisms from military history in his account? What was the joke? The answer, surely, is that Lawrence realized the impossibility of reducing a series of chance events, by which most military engagements are decided, to some kind of logical pattern, which could be expressed in a brief report: 'Throughout it I was quoting to myself absurd tags of Foch and the other blood fighters,' he wrote to Major Becke in 1929, 'and in every movement I was parodying the sort of thing they recommended, but exaggerating just enough to make it ridiculous. The account I wrote of it afterwards was in the same vein: a parody of a proper despatch. The Palestine staff took it seriously: I hope [you are] not going to follow their mistake.'[7]

A few days after the battle, Lawrence rode down the escarpment to the Dead Sea to urge a force of mounted Bedu from Beersheba, under Sharif 'Abdallah al-Fa'ir, to destroy the Turkish dhows in the harbour at Al-Mezra'a which were lightering supplies to the Turks in Jericho. They attacked on 28 January, burned the supply-sheds and scuttled seven boats, effectively halting traffic on the Dead Sea. Lawrence was thrilled by the yarn-spinning possibilities of such an unusual action. It was, he announced proudly to Robert Graves, 'One of [only] two occasions in military history [when mounted men have fought and sunk a fleet]. I recommended myself, vainly, for a naval DSO after this engagement.'[8] Meanwhile, the Hashemite plan was still to press on north to Kerak and Madeba, and in early February Lawrence rode south to Guweira to collect an extra £30,000 in gold they would need to recruit irregulars for the advance. When he arrived back at Tafilah on 11 February, exhausted after a scramble across the icy hills, he found to his dismay that Zayd had made no preparations for the push into Moab, and that the advantage gained from the battle of Tafilah had been squandered: 'Zayd hummed and hawed,' he wrote in a dispatch to Clayton the next day, 'and threw away his chance of making profit from it. He had the country from Madeba at his feet. These Arabs are the most ghastly material to build into a design.'[9] Indeed, though Lawrence had always tried to remain in the background, he felt increasingly obliged to dictate strategy: 'someday everybody will combine to down me,' he wrote to Clayton. 'It is impossible for a foreigner to run another people of their own free will indefinitely, and my innings has been a fairly long one.'[10] He realized that the Sharif had lost the determination to advance on his own, and decided to ride north to goad various irregular groups into action. The gold would arrive in Tafilah within a few days, and Lawrence felt it would be enough to finance his and the Sharif's immediate needs and support the offensive. He rode off to make a reconnaissance in the Sayl al-Haysa with Lieutenant Alec Kirkbride – a fluent Arabic speaker who had been sent from GHQ Beersheba to report on intelligence possibilities – and after Kirkbride had returned to Palestine, continued with a local Sheikh as far as Kerak and Madeba. The reconnaissance was highly satisfactory, and he arrived back at Tafilah on 18 February to tell Sharif Zayd that the way north was open to them. Zayd argued that this operation would require a great deal of money, and when Lawrence pointed out that he had just had £30,000 in gold sent up, Zayd claimed, to his astonishment, that he had already disbursed the entire amount in payment to the Muhaysin, the 'Ayma men, the ibn Jazi, the Bani Sakhr, and various other groups. Lawrence was shattered: most of these men were peasants centred on Tafilah and could not be used for an advance: the Hashemite system was to enrol men as they moved forward, but the payroll was fictitious, for they could not possibly afford to pay more than a fraction of the men on their books, and would not do so unless there was an emergency in a particular area. Lawrence knew that Zayd was aware of this and realized suddenly that the Sharif was lying to him; the last instalment of the gold had only arrived the previous day, and there were simply not enough clerks to have counted it and disbursed it all within twenty-four hours. Lawrence's intuition that some day the Sharifs would turn against him had all too quickly proved correct. Zayd stuck to his lie, and for once Lawrence lost his cool: 'I am in no way under your orders,' he told the Sharif, 'or responsible to you: rather the contrary. In all respects I expect to have my wishes considered and not acted against without due and previous explanation: and where the British provide through me the whole resources for an operation, it should follow as exactly as possible my instructions.'[11] Zayd would not relent, however, and Lawrence realized the Dead Sea campaign was finished. Once more, he had failed to keep his promise to Allenby. In the morning he sent a note to Zayd asking for the return of the money, and when the Sharif merely sent back a specious account of his expenditure, Lawrence decided to ride to Beersheba, explain to Allenby that he had let him down for a second time due to faulty judgement, and give up for ever his role in the Arab Revolt.

On the very day he arrived at Allenby's GHQ, though, the Turks evacuated Jericho and the campaign in Palestine entered a new phase. The War Office in London was pushing for a final blow to the Turks, and Allenby was already preparing to spring on Damascus and Aleppo. Lawrence's petty squabble with Zayd over £30,000 was forgotten in the new euphoria. Allenby wanted his right flank secured, and the railway cut. He could not afford to have the Medina garrison brought back into play at this crucial stage. He was prepared to send his Egyptian Camel Corps and Australian Light Horse across the Jordan river to take as-Salt, west of Amman, and thus safeguard an Arab assault on Ma'an, the garrison that had proved a constant thorn in the Hashemite side. Lawrence thought that with proper transport, Ja'afar Pasha's 4,000 Arab regulars in Aqaba could be leap-frogged to a point on the railway north of Ma'an and could sit on the line until the Turks marched out to remove them. He now believed the Arab regulars more than a match for Turkish troops in open battle, but doubted they could take Ma'an by frontal assault. To move the regulars, he told Allenby, would require camels, cash and guns. Instantly, the General granted him 700 baggage camels with Egyptian handlers and £300,000 in gold, and promised him artillery and machine-guns. Lawrence moved to Cairo, where, with Pierce Joyce and Lieutenant-Colonel Alan Dawnay – a gifted tactician who had now been assigned as chief of Hedgehog – he planned the advance on Ma'an. The final act of this drama would be an attack on the Mudowwara stretch of the railway to cut off the Medina garrison once and for all.

Sadly, the plans went wrong. The British took as-Salt, but failed to take Amman, and were driven back by a massive Turkish counter-attack, abandoning the town on 2 April. On the same day Lawrence, who knew nothing of the defeat, was riding back to Aba l-Lissan with his bodyguard, when, he wrote, his men urged him to attack an eight-man Turkish patrol on a railway bridge near Faraifra. The attack was undisciplined: Lawrence's servant Othman ('Farraj') rode recklessly ahead of the rest and was cut down by a bullet just as he drew his camel to a halt by the bridge. To Lawrence it seemed that he had deliberately stopped in front of the enemy to draw their fire. When he arrived, 'Farraj' was mortally wounded in the spine, but was 'happy to die', since his partner, 'Ali ('Da'ud'), had perished of cold at Azraq a few weeks previously: 'Farraj' had never smiled again, and had lost the will to go on without his friend. For a second time in his career, Lawrence was obliged to shoot a man in cold blood: 'Farraj' had only hours to live, but could not be left for the Turks, who were already scooting towards them on a railway trolley. He held his pistol low so that the boy would not see it, but 'Farraj' understood his intention and said, 'Da'ud will be angry with you.'

'Salute him from me,' Lawrence said.

'God will give you peace,' the 'Agayli answered. Lawrence shot him in the head.[12]

Lawrence felt responsible for the death of 'Farraj' and if his description of the attack is accurate, rightly so, for his own records show that in April 1918 his bodyguard consisted of only fifteen men, and to have assaulted a Turkish position with so few would have been most unwise. There is no reference to this skirmish in official records, however, and Lawrence makes no note of the deaths of either 'Da'ud' or 'Farraj' ('Ali and Othman) in his diary, nor, as we have seen, are there any records of an 'Ali or an Othman serving in his small bodyguard in April 1918. It is, perhaps, significant that Lawrence uses Farraj's grief at the death of Da'ud as a prime for an essay on the nature of woman in the 'Mediterranean': explaining that while women were only 'machines for muscular exercise' men could really be at one only with each other. It must also be significant that Lawrence felt the need to change their names at all. Since they were both dead when he came to write *Seven Pillars*, and since he took great pains to explain that they were both openly homosexual, and (incorrectly) that no shame was attached, there seems no rationale behind the change of names, unless – as in the case of Hubert Young – Lawrence was 'telling lies about them'. Lawrence's queasiness at letting Robert Graves use the story shows clearly in his note: 'It seems unbearable that you should publish the story of the death of Farraj . . . I suggest that it be cut right out. The narrative was so arranged as not to depend on it . . . You could well say that a week after the Amman visit Farraj himself was dead, being mortally wounded in a mounted raid against a Turkish Railway Patrol and leave it at that. These are private matters.'[13] Yet, as Graves pointed out with amused indignation, Lawrence had already published the story himself in the Oxford version of *Seven Pillars*, which had at that time circulated to thousands of readers. If he had sincerely felt the death of 'Farraj' unbearable, why did he reveal such 'private matters' to the world? Certainly, he had had no such qualms in discussing the literary merits of his 'death scene' with Charlotte Shaw in 1924: 'I have a prejudice against the writer who leaves the reader to make his top scene for him,' he wrote. '*Hounds of Banba* [a novel by Daniel Corkery] does it, in the story of the burning of the village . . . I funked it, in the death of Farraj, my man.'[14] It is interesting to note, too, that Lawrence is here comparing a scene which is supposedly factual to an incident from a novel which is presumably purely fictitious – almost as if he had forgotten that there was a distinction between the two.

The British push across the Jordan failed, and the Arab assault on Ma'an failed also, largely because the Arab officers decided, against Lawrence's advice, on a frontal assault rather than an encircling movement. On 18 April, Lawrence, who had watched the battle and had been impressed, despite its outcome, with the valour of the Arab regulars, rode to Guweira. The same day he commandeered a Ford car and rode to Tel ash-Shahm on the railway, where Dawnay and a mixed force of British, Egyptians and Bedu were concealed in a hollow ready for an attack. The Tel ash-Shahm operation had been planned with textbook precision by Dawnay, but though Lawrence believed him the only high-ranking British officer capable of handling conventional and guerrilla tactics together, he realized that with the heterogeneous medley of troops under his command, things might not turn out quite as predicted. Lawrence volunteered himself for the mission officially as 'interpreter', but actually to keep an eye on relations between the three groups.

This was to be a very different operation from the one Lawrence had led against Mudowwara in the previous year. Besides a squadron of armoured cars and Rolls-Royce tenders, there was a battery of Ford-mounted ten-pounder Talbot guns of the Royal Field Artillery under Lieutenant Samuel Brodie, a flight of aircraft operating from the Ga'a of Rum, a detachment of the Egyptian Camel Corps under Bimbashi Fred Peake, as well as the Bedu irregulars under Sharif Haza'a. At first light on 19 April, the armoured cars slid out of their hollow with their motors churning, crunching across the flint surface, leaving smoke-trails of dust. Lawrence sat in a Rolls-Royce tender on a ridge-top next to Dawnay, who, with a map spread on his knees and a watch in his hand, checked off each movement according to a carefully prepared schedule. Precisely on time, the armoured cars came over the ridge and approached the Turkish entrenchments around Tel ash-Shahm station. Each detail of the scene was accentuated and magnified by long shadows in the crystal-clear light. The Turks, taken by surprise at the sudden appearance of armoured cars, surrendered immediately. Meanwhile two Rolls-Royce tenders under the command of Lieutenant Hornby of the Royal Engineers rumbled down to one of the nearby culverts and blew it spectacularly with a hundredweight of gun-cotton. The blast almost lifted Lawrence and Dawnay out of their seats. The Turks opened fire from behind a thick stone sangar on a steep knoll, and the rat-at-tat of four machine-guns crackled out at once from the armoured-car turrets, their bullets sizzling off the stones. At that moment the Bedu irregulars under Haza'a came from behind a hill, firing raggedly, and charging at the Turkish knoll, capturing it without effort. Lawrence drove down the line in his Rolls-Royce, slapping gun-cotton charges on rails and bridges, covered by the machine-guns in the armoured cars. A chain of explosions rocked the air, and clouds of debris materialized suddenly along the line like dust-devils: fragments of shrapnel and flint bumped and pattered against the steel turrets of the armoured cars. The Bedu rushed the Turkish outpost to the south of the station in a wild flight of camels, streaking up the mound and vaulting the trenches. Meanwhile the Camel Corps under Fred Peake approached the station from the north, working forward more cautiously from ridge to ridge. The Talbot battery opened fire, and shells crumped against the station buildings with ear-splitting impact, and two planes fell suddenly like swallows out of the clear sky to the west and sent a dozen bombs hurtling into the trenches. V-shaped plumes of smoke appeared momentarily around the station, and through the haze and dust the armoured cars edged forwards with their machine-guns spouting drumfire. Peake's camel-corps now threw caution to the wind and broke into a ragged gallop across the plain, and the Bedu, not to be outdone, thundered down from the east, converging on the station, where the Turks threw up their arms in surrender and waved white flags frantically. Lawrence beat them all there in his Rolls-Royce, and while he claimed the brass bell as a memento, Dawnay took the ticket-punch and Rolls, his driver, the rubber stamp. They emerged to find that the Arabs and the Egyptians had gone mad with looting-frenzy, smashing and ransacking the buildings, and rushing about in blind lust for reward. The station store contained hundreds of rifles, thousands of rounds of ammunition, food and clothing, and the factions began shooting at each other in their greed. One camel set off a Turkish trip-mine and was blown over, causing momentary turmoil. Lawrence, who later said that the British officers came within an inch of getting 'scragged', managed to separate the parties, allowing the Egyptian Camel Corps to pick what they wanted first. Afterwards, the Bedu scrabbled for the remainder on the word 'Go!', as Rolls put it, 'like a solid mass of ejected inmates from Bedlam'.[15] They rushed the store-house, leaned on the door until it snapped open, and were so satisfied with their loot that more than three-quarters of them simply loaded their camels and made off into the desert. The attack had been an unqualified success: it was, said Lawrence, 'fighting de luxe'. Dawnay's only reservation was that while he had scheduled the capture of the station for 11.30 precisely, the Turks, out of 'ignorance and haste', had capitulated at 11.20 – ten minutes too soon. This was, Lawrence wrote with tongue coiled in cheek, 'the only blot on a bloodless day'.[16]

The railway-wrecking was not finished, however. One armoured car was sent to clear Ramleh, the next station to the south, while Lawrence, in his Rolls-Royce, and other demolition teams blew bridges and miles of track in between. The culverts were demolished by charges stuffed into their drainage-holes, while Lawrence had developed a more effective method of ruining the metals, planting 'tulip' charges under the sleepers so that they would buckle and warp entire stretches of track. Having satisfied himself that the railway was now effectively out of service between ash-Shahm and Ramleh, Lawrence slept near ash-Shahm, preparing for the attack on Mudowwara scheduled for the following day. The Turks were expecting the assault, however, and threw the combined force back with deadly accurate artillery fire at 7,000 yards. Lawrence took the armoured cars off in an arc to the place in which he had mined his first train, and destroyed the long culvert about 500 yards from the ridge on which he had sited his Stokes and Lewis guns on that day in 1917. Then he retired back to Ramleh to destroy more line. Later, Mohammad adh-Dhaylan and his Howaytat were sent to cripple the railway north of ash-Shahm. By 20 April, the Arabs and the British together had put out of action eighty miles of track, and taken or cut off seven stations. Fakhri Pasha's force in Medina had at long last been neutralized as a potential threat.

19. My Dreams Puffed out Like Candles in the Strong Wind of Success

Dara'a, Tafas and the fall of Damascus
Winter, 1918

Our battered saloon pulled into Tafas just after noon. It seemed a typical Hauran town – a place without a centre, a sprawl of houses constructed haphazardly along a grid of roads amid acres of wheatlands, and desolate red meadows relieved only by poisonous Sodom apple and brakes of eucalypt, cedar and Aleppo pine. In places you could glimpse the village as it had been in 1918 – scattered among the jerry-built breeze-block dwellings were ancient cottages of black basalt. We trawled up and down the main road for a time, then stopped a swarthy man in a black and white headcloth and asked him if he knew where the battle of 1918 had been fought. 'I don't know,' he said. 'But there is an old man in the village who was there. I can take you to him.' I was amazed, and slightly sceptical. All these months I had been pursuing a phantom whom people knew only by hearsay. Was I, finally, to meet someone who had actually *seen* Lawrence with his own eyes? We urged the man into the car, and drove. He stopped us at a modern corner-house set on red earth among Sodom apple bushes. Inside, a spidery old man in a red *kuffiyeh* and a black cloak was sitting on a rug on the floor by a benzene heater, surrounded by half a dozen sons and grandsons. The old man wore thick-rimmed glasses and had a wisp of silver beard. One of his grandsons – a medical student in Aleppo – told me that his grandfather was over ninety years old. We sat down cross-legged on the rug, and after we had answered questions, and sipped the statutory tea, I asked him, with suppressed excitement, if he had ever met Lawrence of Arabia. 'I saw him,' the Sheikh told me in a shaky voice. 'I was just a boy then, of course. I remember seeing the Arab army marching through the village. It was a terrible day. I had been with my parents at another village the night before, and when we arrived here in the morning, we found that the Turks had killed almost everyone. Their bodies were lying about on the road. God have mercy upon them!'

'And what did Lawrence look like?'

'A tall, strong man, with a long beard,' the Arab said.

Later, the grandson took us to see the battlefield, a rolling red meadow, traversed by a stream and full of nests of boulders. It was remarkably close to the village, and seemed unexpectedly small-scale for such a dramatic event. The slaughter of a Turkish column on this very field at Tafas on 27 September 1918, and the subsequent massacre of both Turkish and German prisoners, indeed, were among the most controversial acts of Lawrence's career – convincing some of his critics that he was a bloodthirsty sadist, or alternatively that his torture and rape at Dara'a had permanently unhinged his passions. It was a controversy that Lawrence stoked with customary glee: 'The best of you brings me the most Turkish dead,' he claimed to have told his bodyguard that day, commenting, 'By my order we took no prisoners, for the first time in the war.'[1] This ruthlessness was engendered by fury at the slaughter of non-combatant peasants in Tafas by the retreating Turks, one of the most sickening sights Lawrence had witnessed in the campaign. Not only had they massacred babies, they had also killed and deliberately mutilated women, leaving their corpses spread out obscenely: Lawrence had seen one pregnant woman lying dead with a bayonet thrust between her legs. Talal, a Sheikh of Tafas, with whom Lawrence claimed to have made his fateful reconnaissance of the Hauran the previous November, he wrote, had been so incensed by the slaughter of his people that he died in a suicidal lone charge towards the massed Turkish ranks.

The Tafas massacre was part of the final phase of the campaign that had begun in May 1918, when Lawrence had applied to Allenby for the 2,000 camels made redundant by the disbanding of the Imperial Camel Brigade in Sinai. 'And what do you want them for?' the GOC had asked: 'To put a thousand men into Dara'a any day you please,' Lawrence replied. His plan was to mount a force of Arab regulars on camels and march them north from Waheida, the Arabs' new forward HQ near Ma'an, to Azraq and then to Dara'a with a supply column and artillery, machine-guns, armoured cars and aeroplanes. They would carry all their own supplies, reach Dara'a in only a fortnight, and cut the railway with the aid of Bedu irregulars from the Rwalla, just as the GOC made his autumn offensive into Syria. Allenby pondered the request. Camels were scarce in the Middle East, and his Quartermaster required them urgently for another division. Finally, Lawrence's enthusiasm convinced him. He handed over the camels to the Arab Revolt, and Lawrence rushed to meet Feisal at Aba l-Lissan the following day, certain that they had just been given the means of final victory. Almost at once, he sent home the Egyptian Transport Corps camel-men who were busily but inefficiently shifting supplies from Aqaba to Aba l-Lissan, and replaced them with Arab camel-drivers from Mecca, who would put the animals to better use. The organization of logistics was assigned to Captain Hubert Young, the officer Lawrence had first met at Carchemish before the war. Young had been carefully selected by Lawrence himself as an understudy in case he should be killed: he was a fluent Arabic speaker and a first-class organizer, but he was flawed by an irascibility which made it difficult for him to live peacefully with anyone for very long. Nuri as-Sa'id wrote that Young's temper was his own worst enemy, and recalled once managing to soothe some Arab officers whom Young had upset by telling them: 'Don't worry. He shouts at the British just the same!' Had it not been for this Achilles heel, Young might have been another Lawrence of Arabia. Possibly the most able of all the British officers who served with the Arab forces, his powers of visualizing an operation down to the last camel-load far outweighed those of the mercurial Lawrence, who tended to ride first and consider logistics afterwards. Yet while Lawrence charmed, Young had the manner and appearance of a well-intentioned, highly intelligent, but bad-tempered schoolboy. In February 1918 he had been mysteriously ordered from a posting in India to Cairo: 'It was not until I reported to GHQ at the Savoy . . .' he wrote, 'and the door opened to admit the familiar little figure, that I was enlightened.' 'They asked me to suggest someone who could take my place in case anything happened to me,' said Lawrence, '. . . and I told them no one could. As they pressed me I said I could only think of Gertrude Bell and yourself, and they seemed to think you'd be better for this particular job than she would.'[2] Alan Dawnay, Hedgehog's CO, soon realized that the 'understudy' plan would never work because of Young's abrasiveness, however, and instead assigned him to the Dara'a operation as Quartermaster.

By 22 July, Young had drawn up a detailed logistics scheme for the mission which was approved both by Joyce, commanding Feisal's British staff, and by Feisal himself. Lawrence was then in Cairo, making his own plans for the mission with Dawnay, who suggested that they should utilize the last two companies of the Imperial Camel Corps to complete two jobs which the Bedu had as yet failed to carry off: the destruction of Mudowwara, and the demolition of the viaduct at Qissir, north of Ma'an. Surprisingly perhaps, Lawrence agreed, and they sent a telegram to Joyce in Aqaba instructing him to establish supply dumps for the ICC force at Rum, Jefer and Bair. These instructions were highly unwelcome in Aqaba: Joyce had not been consulted on the question, and both he and Young saw that every load they had to transport for the Camel Corps operation would mean one load less for their 'flying column' to Azraq and Dara'a. 'Joyce and I discussed this telegram with some grinding of teeth,' Young wrote, 'and decided that there was nothing for it but to use some of the priceless camels to put out a dump for [the Mudowwara operation].'³ On 28 July Lawrence arrived in Aqaba, read Young's plan and condemned it at once as unworkable. Allenby was intending to make his final push for Damascus on 19 September, and the Arabs were to lead off not more than four days previously. Timing was crucial: '[Allenby's] words to me,' wrote Lawrence, 'were that three men and a boy with pistols in front of Dara'a on September 16th . . . would be better than thousands a week before or a week after.'⁴ Young's plan, he pointed out, would have the Arabs in Dara'a three weeks too late. He unfolded his own scheme, worked out with Dawnay, for a more limited and more mobile operation against Dara'a. Young lost his temper. Lawrence declared sarcastically that he had executed many such mobile operations success-fully in the past without the help of a Johnny-come-lately-Old Etonian-regular soldier like Young. Young riposted that Lawrence was proposing this time to move regular soldiers, not Bedu – and regulars were quite another thing. Did he expect them to ride two to a camel and live on a roll of apricot paste and a canteen of water for a fortnight? Where did he think the supplies were coming from? And what about the exfiltration? Lawrence's plan allowed no provision for a withdrawal, and if the operation failed, they would starve: '[Lawrence] never knew very much about the regular army,' Young wrote; '. . . he had no sympathy for our transport problems, for he held all military organisations in profound contempt and the letter "Q" so justly and deeply revered by regulars had no place in the Lawrentian alphabet.'[5] This was essentially a conflict between the brilliant professional and the brilliant amateur. Joyce had already complained to Dawnay with some justification that Lawrence tended to bombard GHQ with ambitious and dashing plans but would simply vanish when these 'wildcat schemes' had to be put into practice. The meeting ended inconclusively, and the officers scarcely spoke for three days. Young resented Lawrence's smugness: '. . . the sight of that little man reading *Morte d'Arthur* in a corner of the mess tent with an impish smile on his face was not consoling,' he wrote.[6] Finally Joyce capitulated, and accepted Lawrence's scheme as well as the Camel Corps operation. Young was forced to go along, and employed his genius in ferrying supplies and equipment to Ja'afar Pasha's regulars at Waheida and Aba l-Lissan, an operation in which he succeeded against all odds: '. . . to run a harmonious and orderly train was impossible,' Lawrence grudgingly admitted, 'but Young very nearly did it, in his curious, ungrateful way. Thanks to him the supply problem of the regulars on the plateau was solved.'[7]

On 4 August, Lawrence guided the Camel Corps companies under Buxton to Rum, and, leaving them to attack Mudowwara without him, flew to Jefer to meet Nuri as-Sha'alan of the Rwalla. He was distinctly apprehensive about this meeting. During his secret northern ride from Nabk in 1917, he had assured the Emir that he could trust the most recent of British promises. Nuri now knew the full terms of the Sykes–Picot agreement, and Lawrence thought he might demand fulfilment of the 'dishonourable half-bargain' they had made on that long-ago day in Azraq. What this mysterious 'half-bargain' might have been, Lawrence never revealed, only that, on their meeting at Jefer, the Emir did not claim it, and the encounter ended with Nuri giving his whole-hearted support to the Hashemite cause. A few days later, Lawrence returned to Jefer by car with Joyce to meet the Camel Corps, who had successfully captured Mudowwara station and demolished the water-tower. Lawrence completed a reconnaissance mission to Azraq, while the Camel Corps went for the viaduct at Qissir. The mission was abandoned on 20 August when the column was spotted by German aircraft, and Buxton learned that a hostile Bedu tribe lay encamped between them and their target.

Meanwhile, a crisis was shaping up among the regular Arab officers at Aba l-Lissan, who had read a newspaper report in which King Hussain denied that Ja'afar Pasha had ever been appointed Commander of the Northern Army. This was Hussain's last attempt to assert control over his son Feisal, who had personally promoted Ja'afar Commander-in-Chief in 1917 without consulting his father. Hussain had always been suspicious of the Arab regular officers, fearing that they would 'take over' the Revolt, and it was for this reason he had dismissed Aziz al-Masri, Ja'far's predecessor, who had, long before Lawrence, developed much of the strategy of the Arab campaign. Hussain knew that Feisal was a weak character, easily swayed by his advisers, and he was terrified that the Arab cause would be hijacked by the Allies' territorial ambitions. Though Lawrence put Hussain's reaction down to 'jealousy' and 'lust for power', the fact is that it suited the British and the French to divide the Hashemites, just as it had suited the Turks. Hussain believed that Feisal was opening the doors for French ambitions in Syria, and while Lawrence later claimed that the old man was 'crazy', the Emir was, of course, ultimately proved right.

On reading Hussain's declaration that there was 'no Arab officer higher in rank than captain', Ja'afar Pasha resigned, and was promptly followed by all his staff. Feisal himself resigned in solidarity, which rendered the oaths made to him by the Bedu meaningless. With Feisal's resignation, the chances of massing the great force of Rwalla Lawrence had counted on for a direct assault on Dara'a dissolved. In one fell swoop, the entire Revolt looked ready to collapse, and on 26 August, Lawrence rushed to Aba l-Lissan to deal with the impasse. This was a vital moment in the Dara'a operation. That very day, the first of Young's supply convoys had been about to leave Aqaba, when a cry of '*Tayaara! Tayaara!*' had gone up, and two German aircraft had drummed out of the heat-haze over the Wadi 'Araba and delivered a package of bombs among the caravans. The animals had gone wild, breaking their lead ropes, bucking and scattering their loads across the plain. With silent curses yet infinite attention to detail, Young had rallied the handlers, picked up the baggage, re-packed the camels, re-strung the caravans, and set the train on its way again. At Aba l-Lissan, though, the Arab officers would not shift ground without some conciliatory move from Hussain. On 30 August Lawrence telegraphed

Clayton that the Hedgehog staff were assuming command of the operation, which would go ahead as planned. Lawrence knew that while they might take Dara'a without Feisal, to have marched into Damascus without him would have meant the defeat of everything they had worked for over the past two years. The Arabs would then be without bargaining power, and the Allies would establish a government in Syria. He told Clayton that he could hold things together for only four days – if no solution were found by then, he would have to evacuate the forward posts and abort the Dara'a mission on which the whole future of the Arabs depended. The days clicked by interminably and there was no word from Hussain. At last, on 4 September, a long message arrived from the King consisting of both a lame apology, and a reiteration of the same accusation in a different form. Lawrence brazenly lopped off the offending part of the message, marked it 'most urgent' and sent it to Feisal's tent.

On 3 September, against all odds, an assault caravan of Arab regulars, together with the French-Algerian artillery battery under Captain Pisani on mules, and a supply column, set out for Azraq. Feisal drove out in his Vauxhall car to review them as the camels strutted out across the grassy downs of the Shirah: 'As each section saluted Feisal,' Young wrote, 'I even felt an absurd lump in my bearded throat at the greatness of the sight.'[8] On the 6th, Lawrence drove to Azraq in a Rolls-Royce tender with Sharif Nasir, who was to lead the Bedu in the final stroke, and Lord Winterton, who had just been transferred to Hedgehog from the disbanded Imperial Camel Corps. Over the next week the assault force began to assemble. On 10 September two aircraft of the recently renamed Royal Air Force landed. Joyce and Stirling – another recent recruit to the Arab mission – came in on 11 September with the armoured cars. Feisal arrived on the 12th with Marshall, the medical officer. Behind him came Nuri as-Said with the 450 Arab regulars, Pisani with his Algerian gunners, the baggage convoy of 1,500 camels with Young, a company of trained demolition-men from the Egyptian Camel Corps under Peake, a section of Gurkha camel-men under Scott-Higgins, and Bedu irregulars of the Rwalla under Nuri ash-Sha'alan, of the Howaytat under Auda and Mohammad adh-Dhaylan, the Bani Sakhr under Fahad, clans of the Seridyyeh and Serahiyyin, Druses, Syrian villagers under Talal al-Haraydhin, Lawrence's small bodyguard of Hauran peasants and

Nasir's 'Agayl – a total of almost 1,000 men. As hardware, they had two Bristol aircraft, four quick-firing Napoleon mountain-guns, twenty-four machine-guns, and three armoured cars with their tenders. This was the blade which would carve the victory for which Lawrence had worked so long: the climax of his years of preaching revolt had come. Yet, when the strike force was complete, Lawrence felt despondent. First, he knew that the time of reckoning was near, when the British deception of the Hashemites – and his major role in this charade – would be revealed in all its iniquity. He had raised these 'tides of men', he felt, on a sham promise and brought them to worship an ideal of unity in which he could not believe himself. This conflict between the ideal and the prosaic reflected the inner struggle which had been part of Lawrence since childhood. The Arabs themselves were more practical: Auda Abu Tayyi had corresponded with the Turks when the situation had seemed favourable; the Bedu of the Hejaz had retired from the fighting line when it suited them: even Feisal had made overtures to the Turks. Nuri ash-Sha'alan had remained neutral until it seemed that the Hashemites were on the winning side, while many of the tribes, or sections of tribes, of the Hejaz and even of Syria had never joined the Hashemite cause at all. Certainly, Syrian nationalists like Nasib al-Bakri - upon whom Lawrence poured vitriol – were fighting for liberty, but the Hashemites were fighting largely for family patrimony. On their own, they had proved damp squibs: Zayd had lost the Wadi Safra, 'Ali had almost lost Rabegh. Hussain had sacked his best man, Aziz al-Masri, and almost ruined the final operation by denying that Ja'afar Pasha was his Commander-in-Chief. Zayd had lied to him: 'Abdallah had rejected his advice. At Azraq he felt a sudden surge of loathing for 'these petty incarnate Semites', and for himself who had for two years pretended to be their friend, but had never really become one of them. The terrible fear of being hurt or killed which he had staved off for months, forcing himself to Herculean heights of bravado and self-sacrifice, was reasserting itself with a vengeance. He knew that his nerve was almost at an end, and within a few weeks he must either resign from his position or crack. The old oddness, his sense of inadequacy – absent when he rode with his bodyguard or consorted with Feisal – returned when he found himself among a large crowd. Worst of all, he had heard – perhaps from Syrian recruits – that Dahoum, his pre-war friend, was dead. The boy had been employed as a guard on the Carchemish site until 1916, when almost half the old workforce had perished in a terrible season of sickness and famine. Though Lawrence never mentioned Dahoum by name, he wrote afterwards that one of his main motives in leading the Arabs had been to make a present of freedom to a certain Arab whom he loved. He also wrote that this motive had ceased to exist 'some weeks' before the end of the campaign – referring not to the time of Dahoum's probable death in 1916, but to the moment when he had actually heard of his friend's demise. Later, composing his dedicatory poem 'To SA' while flying between Paris and Lyon in a Handley-Page, he wrote: 'I wrought for him freedom to lighten his sad eyes: but he had died waiting for me. So I threw my gift away and now not anywhere will I find rest and peace.'[9] In sorrow, anger and apprehension, Lawrence shunned the company at Azraq and walked off alone to 'Ain al-Assad, where he had, perhaps, spent idle moments in November 1917 with 'Ali ibn Hussain al-Harithi – another friend he might never see again.

Winterton worried about security: almost as soon as they had arrived at Azraq a Turkish plane had appeared, though it seemed unlikely that they had been spotted. Lawrence knew that the assembly of the raiding force in Azraq could not go unreported to the Turks, but he was confident that the enemy would never venture across the desert to attack them there. Neither could the Turks be sure where they would strike or when it would be. Lawrence had cleverly sent cash to Mithqal of the Bani Sakhr with 'top secret' instructions to buy barley for a combined British and Arab surprise attack on as-Salt and Amman on 18 September. He knew that word would instantly be leaked to the Turks, who would spread their defensive resources thinly from Amman to Dara'a. The idea of a direct attack on Dara'a had been abandoned because of the paucity of Rwalla levies, and replaced by a strategy of encirclement in which the strike force would cut the railway to the north, south and west. Without its railway, the Dara'a garrison – only 500 strong – would choke to death. At dawn on 13 September, Peake and Scott-Higgins mounted their camels and led their combined troops of Egyptian sappers and Gurkhas silently through the maze of basalt boulders and across the glistening slicks of the Gian al-Khunna. Two armoured cars rumbled after them in support. Their task was to demolish the tracks and bridges south of Mafraq – a raid which the

Turks would probably interpret as a prelude to a strike at Amman. The Gurkhas were to assault the station, while Peake's sappers cut the railway, and the entire force was to pull out at first light, covered by the armoured cars.

Next day the main body – almost 1,000 strong – set off into the lava, the camels grumbling and stumbling their way through the stones. Nuri as-Sa'id rode a horse at the head of the Arab regulars, while Joyce commanded the remaining armoured car and tenders which bounced over the *harra* behind. Young, riding a mule, fell into line with Pisani's mule-mounted gunners, whose Napoleons were stripped and lashed to the broad backs of their mounts. 'I tried to forget that we were absolutely in the air,' he wrote, 'with no communications and no possible way of getting back.'[10] Nuri was more at ease, and recalled that Lawrence's 'Plan B' was to hide out in the lava maze of Jabal Druze for the winter if the mission failed, living off the land. A cavalry screen of Nuri ash-Sha'alan's picked riders trotted swiftly about their flanks, and a Bristol fighter flown by Lieutenant Murphy soared out of the clear blue bell of the desert sky, heading for Umm al-Jamal where it later took on a German plane and sent it crashing into the desert in flames. That night they camped amid pickets on the Gian, and the following morning ran into Peake's assault team, returning disconsolately from Mafraq. The railway strike had failed – indeed, it had not been put in at all. Peake's force had run into a band of Bedu whom the Turks paid to defend the railway, and while a political officer might easily have managed to turn them, Lawrence had neglected to attach one to the group. Peake and Scott-Higgins had been chary of fighting Arabs, and had turned back. When Lawrence arrived that morning from Azraq in his Rolls-Royce tender 'Blue Mist', driven by S. C. Rolls, he was absolutely furious that the job had not been completed, and instead of sending Peake back for a second go, decided to take the armoured cars and do it himself.

On the 15th, Lawrence left the main body at Umm Tayeh – a deserted Roman village with a large water-cistern, which was to be the kicking-off point for the operation – and, with Joyce and Winterton, drove off towards the railway at Mafraq with two tenders and two armoured cars. They raced across the Hauran plain and in the early afternoon sighted their target – a four-arched bridge near a fort at Kilometre 149. The two tenders were left with Joyce beyond a ridge.

Winterton's car drove boldly to the fort and opened up on it with burst upon burst of tracer from its heavy Vickers. The place was defended by a handful of men in an entrenchment, and to the surprise of the British crews they suddenly jumped out of their trenches and advanced towards the car in open order: 'Not knowing whether they were expected to run away or surrender,' as Rolls put it, '[they] got up out of their trenches to inquire.'[11] Lawrence surmised later that in fact the cars had appeared so quickly that the Turks believed they belonged to friendly forces. Winterton's gunner mowed them down mercilessly with another stuttering burst, while Lawrence, in the second car, approached the bridge, his Vickers ripping off a drum at its four guards. Two were killed, and the others surrendered. Lawrence took their rifles and sent them up to Joyce on the ridge. Almost at the same moment the fort surrendered to Winterton: the action had lasted five long minutes.

The peace would not last, though, for Joyce and Rolls, on the ridge, had spotted a Turkish camel-mounted patrol closing on them fast. They drove to Lawrence's position with more gun-cotton, and helped him set the charges, running back and forth from the cars to the bridge. They set six charges in the drainage-holes of the spandrils, fired them, and withdrew hastily, before the enemy patrol arrived. In seconds there was a terrific blast, which shattered each of the four arches thoroughly. The cars turned towards their base and sped off with the prisoners thrown on the back, but only 300 yards from the railway Blue Mist shuddered to a halt with a broken spring-bracket. The enemy would be on them within ten minutes. The resourceful Rolls leapt out of the driver's seat and began jacking up the wheel, almost in tears over the potential loss of his beautiful Rolls-Royce. The team was now under fire, and Rolls worked desperately, bathed in sweat. Almost miraculously, he managed to bodge together some lengths of running-board which Lawrence shot off with a pistol and snapped off by hand, and lashed them to the broken spring with telegraph wire. Rolls packed up the jack and tried the suspension cautiously. Incredibly, it held, and as bullets began to ping off the stones around them, Lawrence and Joyce hastily cleared a track, jumped into the car and drove off, jerking and bouncing as fast as Rolls dared, back towards Umm Tayeh. There, they found that Nuri as-Said and the main force had already left for Tel 'Arar. They stayed at Umm Tayeh for the night to repair the tender as well as they could, and on the 17th, confident that the railway had been cut for a week, they set off to catch up with the assault force.

They overtook the main column at eight o'clock in the morning, just as Nuri was deploying the regulars to assault the redoubt at Tel 'Arar, five miles north of Dara'a, which was manned by twenty Turks. A squadron of Rwalla horse under Trad ash-Sha'alan dashed magnificently down to the line and hesitated there, thinking it easily taken. Nuri and Young drove down in a Ford tender, and were just enjoying a snort of whisky to celebrate when a Turkish machine-gun crackled up from the redoubt, and an officer in a nightshirt came charging towards them shouting and waving a sabre, like an apparition. For a moment the two officers looked at him, shocked, then, realizing that the garrison at the fort had merely been asleep, Nuri drew his pistol and shot at their assailant, while Young, who was unarmed, rushed to fetch the French artillery. Pisani's gunners quickly set up their Napoleons and silenced the fort's defenders with a rapid fusillade of shells. Then the Rwalla horse, with the regulars in support, rushed in and captured it. Nuri, Lawrence and Joyce climbed to the crest of a hill to survey the town of Dara'a and the stations of Mezerib and Ghazala to the north and west of it. The next step was to lay 600 charges on the railway, which Lawrence estimated would completely wreck four miles of track and knock traffic out for a week. After breakfast, the Egyptian sappers and the Algerian gunners began to plaster the tracks with tulip mines. As they deployed along the tracks, Lawrence examined Dara'a aerodrome with his binoculars and was disturbed to see that no less than nine aircraft were being hauled out of their hangars by the German teams. Lawrence's men had no air cover: Murphy's Bristol had been badly holed in its clash with a German at Umm al-Jamal, and had retired to Azraq for repair. Lawrence watched Peake's men labouring on the line below, wondering if they could lay their 600 charges before the planes arrived. Suddenly, the first tulip went up with a noise like a thunderclap and a long plume of black smoke. Almost at once, a Pfalz spotter-plane soared over the hill, sending Lawrence and Nuri scrambling for cover. Moments later two big Albatross bombers and four Haberstadt scouts droned out of Dara'a, circling, diving, strafing them with machine-gun fire, and releasing payloads of bombs, which kicked up V-shaped wedges of debris across the plain. In the Arab ranks there was pandemonium: 'we scattered in all directions,' Rolls recalled, 'I hastily crawled beneath my tender . . . bombs crashed down, sending up columns of smoke and earth.'[12] Desperately, Nuri placed his Hotchkiss-gunners in cracks on the hillside and soon patterns of tracer were stitching themselves across the sky, forcing the aircraft higher, out of range. Pisani had his Napoleons swivelled up and blatted shells uselessly at the climbing planes. On the railway, the Egyptian sappers went on laying their charges as methodically as ants, and at that moment the second Bristol fighter from Azraq, flown by Lieutenant Junor, cruised defiantly into the midst of the German planes. The Albatrosses and Halberstadts left off their strafing and bombing, and roared off in pursuit. This gave the Arabs a momentary respite, and Lawrence immediately organized a detachment to ride out and cut the Palestine branch of the railway at Mezerib, to complete the isolation of Dara'a. Half an hour later, just as he and his bodyguard were swinging into the saddle, Junor's Bristol came stuttering back towards them with the Germans buzzing around her like a swarm of bees. Lawrence and Young both realized that she was almost out of fuel. Young yelled to the men to clear a landing-strip. While the others watched impotently, the plane lost height quickly, bounced along the makeshift runway, hit a boulder and pitched heavily over on to her back. Junor leapt out of the crushed cockpit, unhitched his Lewis gun, his Vickers and some drums of tracer, and rushed for the car which Young had considerately driven up to collect him. A second later a Halberstadt came in low and scored a direct hit with a bomb on the wrecked Bristol, which erupted into flames.

At once Lawrence mounted his camel and headed towards Mezerib with Nuri as-Sa'id and his men, leaving only 100 regulars, the Gurkhas, the Rwalla, and the armoured cars with Joyce at Tel 'Arar. He had been hoping that the caravan would look like a troop of Bedu, but very quickly the German planes were out again, sweeping in with exquisite slowness and loosing four bombs in the direction of the running camels. The first three missed, but the fourth struck right into their midst, with an ear-splitting crack, knocking over two of Lawrence's bodyguard and badly mauling their mounts. The two men picked themselves up and swarmed on to their companions' saddles, just as another plane honed in and let fly a brace of bombs, the shock of which spun Lawrence's camel round and almost jerked him out of his saddle. He felt a terrible burning sensation in his elbow, the pain of which brought tears to his eyes. For a horrific moment he thought his arm had been blown clean off, but removing a fold of his cloak, he saw that he had been hit by a shred of shrapnel too small to do any real damage.

Nuri's regulars, with their machine-gunners and artillery, took the first of Mezerib's two stations within half an hour. Young and Lawrence climbed on the roof and cut the telegraph wires: 'Slowly, with cere-mony,' Lawrence wrote, 'to draw out the indignation.'[13] Then, while Nuri's men broached the second station, they turned their attention to the railway. Young began planting tulips along the tracks to the east while Lawrence blew the points in the station itself: 'I had planted a dozen [tulips] when something made me look along the line to Dara'a,' wrote Young, 'and my heart stood still, for a train was crawling slowly out of the town towards Mezerib.'[14] Young's first thought was to warn Lawrence, and he ran back to the station shouting that a train was coming.

'A plane?' Lawrence asked.

'Not a plane, you damned fool,' Young cried. 'A train!'

Lawrence answered calmly that it was time to light the charges, and Young sprinted back towards the oncoming train, fumbled for a taper and found he had none. Instead, he lit a cigarette, quickly ignited the fuses, and finally leapt on to his camel to make his escape, quite forgetting that he had hobbled her. The camel stumbled: Young half fell, half jumped out of the saddle and 'ran like hell'. The tulips puffed smoke, cracked off one by one, and the train immediately reversed gear and pulled back to Dara'a. At sunset, after the Arabs had looted the station thoroughly, Lawrence and Young set fire to the rolling stock and torched two Turkish trucks.

They rested a little while at Mezerib, where thousands of Hauran peasants turned out to join them, and during the night Lawrence and Young marched to within a few hundred yards of the bridge at Tel ash-Shehab, which he had failed to take with Sharif 'Ali earlier in the year. The bridge seemed to be charmed, however, for now it was defended by a German artillery battery, and once again Lawrence was forced to retire. The railway had been wrecked, to the south, east and north of Dara'a, and the Turkish garrison was cut off. The mission had been a success, and all that remained was the exfiltration. In the morning, they caught up with Nuri's party at Ramtha and began to withdraw to Umm Tayeh to rendezvous with Joyce and the armoured cars. The march back proved nerve-racking. The Germans were behind them, and ahead of them, on the railway, they might find reinforcements from Amman. The peasants at Ramtha seemed hostile, and any moment the patrol might be attacked by air. Lawrence cantered ahead with his bodyguard to mine the railway near Nasib, which lay on their line of retreat. Nuri put in a full bombardment on the station there, intending to keep Turkish heads down while the Arabs crossed the metals, and to draw the sentries from the bridge while Lawrence laid on it a whacking charge of 800 pounds of gun-cotton. After dark, the entire detachment crawled across the line unseen, covered by the roar of Pisani's guns. When the artillery had been safely brought across, Lawrence touched off his charge: 'There was a deafening roar,' wrote Young, 'and a blaze which lit up the country for miles. By its light I saw the abutment arch of the bridge sheared clean off and the whole mass of masonry sliding slowly down into the valley below.'[15] Within a mile of the tracks they made camp, but were woken up with a shock at first light by a shell which exploded nearby. In the night, the Turks had cunningly brought up a field-gun mounted on a railway wagon and had ranged it with their spotter plane. The Arabs mounted their camels and trotted quickly out of range. Later the same day they met up with Joyce at Umm Tayeh, and on 19 September Lawrence returned to Azraq by car. The following day he flew to GHQ, now at Ramleh in Palestine, to collect orders and discover the outcome of Allenby's advance.

As Young and Kirkbride were frying sausages for breakfast on 22 September at Umm Surab, just south of Umm Tayeh, Lawrence reappeared with three aircraft, to be followed the same afternoon by a Handley-Page bomber which landed stores, raising Arab morale with its huge dimensions. The news from the Palestine front was electrifying: Nablus, Haifa, Afuleh, Beisan and Samakh had fallen, 22,000 prisoners had been captured, and the Turkish 4th Army from Amman had been ordered to fall back on Dara'a and Damascus. The Turks were on the run, and Lawrence's raiders were to hamper them and cut off the retreat. It would be the most dangerous mission they had undertaken so far. The Turks numbered tens of thousands, were fully equipped with artillery and machine-guns, and were desperate; the Arab force, by comparison, was a flea: 'I noticed with pride,' Winterton wrote, 'but not without apprehension . . . that Lawrence fully intended that we should worry the retreating Turks as mastiffs of old worried a bear in the ring, oblivious of the possible consequences.'[16] Though Lawrence had estimated that the railway would be out for a week, the Turks had managed to get it back into service with astonishing speed. Lawrence was to keep up the pressure on it, to raise the peasant tribes of the northern Hauran at long last. His force would be increased by 3,000 of Nuri ash-Sha'alan's Rwalla camelry who had been waiting in the wings at Azraq. The next day, Nuri as-Sa'id and his regulars, with Young, Stirling and Winterton in the armoured cars, and Nuri ash-Sha'alan at the head of his Rwalla, hit the railway at Kilometre 149, where Lawrence and Joyce had previously destroyed the bridge. They wrecked two-thirds of a mile of line and burned the scaffolding with which the bridge had been repaired. This was the final blow to the Turks' railway efforts, and afterwards they gave up: the Amman garrison began to move to Dara'a on foot with all its artillery and transport. Lawrence did not yet know this, however, and on the 24th he, Winterton and an Arab officer called Jamil set off in the armoured cars to demolish another bridge south of Mafraq. Winterton was reluctant to join the mission, suspecting that it was unnecessary and that Lawrence was now fighting purely for fighting's sake. They came to a bridge and a blockhouse, and when Lawrence went forward in a car to examine the target, a machine-gun and a seven-pound field-gun blasted out at them from the fort. The armoured car commander was wary of challenging artillery, and Lawrence suggested confidently to Winterton that they should each take a Lewis gun out of the cars, creep up on the blockhouse and scourge it with enfilade fire, while the cars opened up from the front. Winterton thought Lawrence had gone crazy: 'How on earth,' he asked, 'are we going to get into range without being killed? . . . They'll spot us and blow us to blazes . . . who ever heard of taking a blockhouse with a Lewis gun?' Lawrence inquired if His Lordship had developed 'cold feet'. 'Certainly not, sir,' Winterton said. 'But all I can say is that if this extraordinary proposal succeeds and we survive we shall both be entitled to the VC.'[17] This gave Lawrence a moment's thought, and he decided to revert to his original plan and rush the fort with the armoured cars, with the intention of getting a car under the bridge, and setting a charge while in its protection. They rolled forward under heavy fire with bullets clattering against their armour, and shells bursting about them, when a Turkish soldier popped up behind Lawrence's car and lobbed a grenade. Lawrence knew the car was vulnerable to grenades and that a direct shot to the gun-cotton in the back would tear them all to pieces. Suddenly Winterton's driver informed him that Lawrence's car was reversing out of action.

'What are your orders, sir?' he asked.

'Get out of range of the enemy as soon as you damned well can!' Winterton replied.

On the way back to the bivouac, Winterton recalled, he tried to run down some gazelles, and Lawrence stopped to tick him off angrily: 'It was typical of him,' he wrote, 'to show one of his rare bursts of anger at the destruction of a gazelle.'[18]

Arriving back at Umm Surab, they found Sharif Nasir about to move to Umm Tayeh, and heard for the first time that the Turkish 4th Army was pouring out of Amman. Lawrence suggested that they should leave the fleeing Turks for the local Bedu to finish off, move to Sheikh Sa'ad, north of Dara'a, and try to force an immediate evacuation of Dara'a from there. The idea was accepted, and it was decided to send the aircraft and armoured cars back to Azraq to await the final move on Damascus. The column left on the afternoon of 25 September, but they had only gone four miles when they sighted clouds of dust on the horizon: 10,000 Turks were retreating towards Dara'a protected by cavalry pickets on their flanks. One of the aircraft sheared back over the caravan and dropped a message that Turkish horsemen were approaching them. It was an inopportune moment. Pisani's guns were in bits on their mules, the armoured cars and the rest of the aircraft had left. Lawrence, Nasir and Nuri decided to pull out the regulars, while the Rwalla horse under Nuri ash-Sha'alan and the Hauran riders under Talal al-Haraydhin went forward to draw Turkish fire. Suddenly, the armoured car squadron, which had spotted the enemy, drove back across the plain trailing scarves of dust and prepared to engage the Turks. As it turned out, though, they were merely a group of stragglers seeking a shortcut: they rode straight into the Arab irregulars, who captured over 100 of them.

That evening they camped at Nuwayma, and Young, whose official post was 'military adviser', came to Lawrence's tent at midnight and suggested that the Arabs had done enough and should now retire to Bosra in the Druse mountains, where the Druses were gathering under Nasib al-Bakri. Here they could wait for the British to take Damascus. Lawrence would not hear of it: Damascus must at all costs be seen to be taken by Arab arms. At first light next day they crossed the railway near Ghazala, and Lawrence laid a charge on the nearest bridge while Auda raced off with his Howaytat riders to capture the station at Khirbat al-Ghazala, where he took 200 prisoners and two mountain-guns. Talal and his fierce Hauranis stormed Izra – which Lawrence claimed was being defended by the traitor 'Abd al-Qadir – drove out its small garrison and took custody of its large grain depot. The Rwalla skittered up the main road towards Dara'a on their camels looking for Turkish stragglers and came back with 400 prisoners, mules and machine-guns. At dawn on 27 September the column had just settled among the olive groves at Sheikh Sa'ad when an RAF plane dropped a message informing them that Allenby's spearhead – the 10th Cavalry Brigade, outriding General Barrow's Indian Division – was already at Ramtha, only fourteen miles away, close on the tail of the fleeing Turks. Two large Turkish columns – 6,000 men from Dara'a, and 2,000 from Mezerib – were converging on the area.

This was the chance they had been waiting for. Lawrence, Nasir and Nuri decided to let the bigger column pass by, to be harried by the Rwalla and Hauran horse, while the regulars would engage the smaller Mezerib column and wipe it out. It was now heading for Tafas, and Talal, a Sheikh of the village, was desperate to get there before the enemy and prevent them from entering it. According to an Arab report, Talal galloped ahead with his Hauranis and attacked the enemy furiously, but was killed by a Turkish grenade. If this is so, he was already dead when Lawrence arrived with Sharif Nasir and Auda, quickly followed by Nuri as-Sa'id and the regulars with Pisani and his guns. When they reached Tafas, Lawrence wrote, the enemy was already in the village, and there was the occasional ominous shot from within, and palls of blue smoke from the houses. Soon the Turks began to march out in ordered fashion, with guards of lancers at the front and rear, infantry in columns with machine-guns on their flanks, and transport – including Jamal Pasha in his motor car – in the centre. As the column came into view from among the houses, Pisani's guns

27. The capture of Aqaba, 6 July 1917, photographed by Lawrence himself. The culmination of a brilliant two-month turning movement through some of the harshest desert in Arabia, Aqaba became the model for all the deep penetration commando raids of the twentieth century.

28. Aqaba fort from inland.

29. The interior of the Aqaba fort. The town was ruined and deserted, smashed to pieces by the shells of British gunships weeks before.

30. Ja'afar Pasha, Feisal and Pierce Joyce at Wadi Quntilla in August 1917. Ja'afar, a former officer in the Turkish army, was the commander of the Arab Regulars, who played an increasingly important part in the Arab campaigns. Lt.-Col. Joyce, Connaught Rangers, was technically Lawrence's commanding officer and was chief of 'Hedgehog' – the British mission to the Arabs.

31. Nuri as-Sa'id, a brilliant young Iraqi artillery officer, was chief of staff to the Arab Regulars under Ja'afar Pasha. He played a distinguished role in the campaign, eventually becoming Prime Minister of Iraq.

32. The gate tower at Azraq, as photographed by Lawrence. In November 1917 he established himself in the southern gate tower for 'a few days' repose'. A year later he assembled a force at Azraq which encircled and isolated the Turks in Dara'a in the last few days of the campaign.

33. Lawrence fought his only pitched battle against the Turks on the plateau of Tafilah in January 1918, when a Turkish column from Kerak was routed and almost wiped out by Arab forces. Afterwards Lawrence photographed these lines of Turkish prisoners near Tafilah fort, which still stands today.

34. Sharif Zayd (*in the centre at the back*) and other Arab leaders with captured Austrian guns at Tafileh.

35. A smiling Lawrence at the army headquarters in Cairo in 1918.

36. General Allenby stepping out of his armoured car, Damascus, 3 October 1918. Allenby, much revered by Lawrence, regarded the Arab forces as a distraction for the Turks rather than major players in the invasion of Palestine and Syria.

37. The Hejaz Camel Corps rounding up Bedouin pillagers after the capture of Damascus, 2 October 1918.

38. Augustus John sketched Lawrence in a couple of minutes during the Paris Peace Conference in 1919.

39. Feisal was photographed at the same time.

40. Gertrude Bell, Sir Herbert Samuel, British High Commissioner in Palestine (in white helmet), Lawrence and Sharif 'Abdallah, photographed in Amman in April 1921.

41. A portrait of Lawrence by William Roberts, autumn 1922. In August that year Lawrence had enlisted as an aircraftman in the RAF under the name John Hume Ross. Lord Trenchard wrote, 'He is taking this step to learn what is the life of an airman,' but Lawrence had other, darker motives for enlistment in the ranks.

42. By 1924 Lawrence had been dismissed from the RAF and had enlisted in the army as Private T. E. Shaw of the Royal Tank Corps, based at Bovington Camp in Dorset.

43. In his later years Lawrence was addicted to speed, and was happiest when riding his 1000 cc Brough Superior motorcycle, one of the most powerful machines of its day. Over the years he owned several of these machines, all of which he nicknamed Boanerges and which were handmade for him by the manufacturer, George Brough.

44. The music room at Clouds Hill, with its large gramophone in the corner. Here Lawrence worked on *The Seven Pillars of Wisdom,* wrote scores of letters to artists, writers, composers and former colleagues, and entertained friends with musical weekends.

45. Lawrence died on 19 May 1935 and his funeral was held two days later at Moreton church in Dorset. The pall-bearers escorting the coffin included Colonel Stewart Newcombe, Sir Ronald Storrs and Eric Kennington, who was later to carve his effigy.

46 (*left and above*). Lawrence's effigy in the old Anglo-Saxon church of St Martin, at Wareham in Dorset, is still visited by thousands of sightseers every year. 'Sunlight was spilling in a cascade of dapples and brindles through the great window, falling on the crusader's effigy of Lawrence in Arab dress, carved by his friend Eric Kennington.'

roared and spat smoke, taking the enemy completely by surprise. According to Lawrence's version, he and Talal then slipped into the streets with a troop of Bedu, only to be met with a nauseating sight. As soon as the Arab battery had opened fire, Lawrence wrote, the Turkish rearguard commander had ordered the massacre of the villagers: they had stabbed and shot to death twenty small children and forty women. As they rode in, a tiny girl – perhaps four years old – tried to run away. Abd al-'Aziz, Lawrence's 'rabbit mouthed' Tafas bodyguard, jumped from his camel and cradled her: she had been wounded in the neck with a lance-thrust, and blood stained her smock. She tried to escape, and screamed, 'Don't hit me, Baba!' then collapsed and died. They rode grimly past the place where the Turks had mutilated the village women and caught up with wounded stragglers who begged for mercy. They shot them down at point-blank range, and Lawrence looked on silently while his bodyguard-lieutenant Ahmad az-Za'aqi pumped three bullets into the chest of a helpless man. As they came within sight of the column, Lawrence wrote, Talal gave a horrible cry: '[he] put spurs to his horse and, rocking in the saddle, galloped at full speed into the midst of the retiring column'.[19] Lawrence moved to join him, but Auda held him back. This was Talal's private appointment with death. According to Lawrence, he charged right into the jaws of the Turkish machine-gun, screaming his battle-cry, 'Talal! Talal!' until, riddled with bullets, he fell from his saddle among the Turkish spears. Lawrence and Auda watched the grim incident from afar, and at last Auda said: 'We will take his price!'

The artillery barrage had shocked the Turks and dispersed them in panic. One section, mostly made up of German and Austrian machine-gunners, grouped themselves tightly round three motor cars, and fought like devils. They proved too strong for the Arabs, who let them go. The other two sections, though, were separated and cut to pieces where they stood: Lawrence ordered 'No prisoners!' and the Arabs charged them again and again, swooping on them like avenging furies, and cutting them down almost to a man. 'In a madness born of the horror of Tafas,' Lawrence wrote, 'we killed and killed, even blowing in the heads of the fallen and of the animals; as if their death and running blood could slake our agony.'[20] Thousands of Hauran villagers gathered like scavengers at the flanks of the beleaguered Turkish column, picking up the rifles of the enemy dead as they fell, and joining their fellow Arabs in the slaughter. By sunset the plain outside Tafas was littered with hundreds of bloody corpses. According to Lawrence, one group of Arabs had not heard his 'no prisoners' order, and had taken 250 of the enemy alive, including a number of Germans and Austrians. As he rode up, Lawrence was shown an Arab named Hassan who had been pinned to the ground with German bayonets, while already wounded. Lawrence had wanted no enemy survivors, and this was the excuse he had been looking for. He told his brother Arnie after the war that he had ordered an Arab crew to turn a Hotchkiss on the prisoners and kill them all. In doing so, he felt, he was avenging not only the children of Tafas, but the numberless generations of Arabs who had been ground down by the tyranny of the hateful Turks.

The picture of Lawrence as a bloodthirsty sadist whose inherent cruelty was finally brought into play by the torture he suffered at Dara'a was much encouraged by David Lean's film *Lawrence of Arabia*, in which Lawrence is seen dripping with blood after the battle at Tafas. How much truth is there in such an image? A close reading of *Seven Pillars* reveals an obsession with cruelty which some have taken to indicate that Lawrence had a sadistic nature. On his very first railway attack near Aba an Na'am, for example, he described how his men captured a shepherd boy whom they kept tied up and threatened to kill, while butchering his goats. There are the beatings which the imaginary 'Farraj and Da'ud' constantly seem to have endured for their pranks, not to mention being made to sit on scorching rocks, and clapped in irons for a week; the Circassian youth, not even a combatant, who was dragged around for an hour by camel, stripped naked and whose feet were then deliberately slit open across the soles – a nauseating and pointless assault; and the even more bizarre incident Lawrence recorded, when his bodyguard picked acacia thorns from a bush and drove them into a man's body for some unexplained crime. The more sadistic of these punishments are nowhere recorded as customary among the Arabs by the great Arabian travellers, and seem alien to Bedu culture. Wilfred Thesiger, indeed, wrote that the Bedu were so mindful of the dignity of others that they would prefer to kill a man rather than humiliate him. Some of the accounts may be imaginary – an expression of masochistic rather than sadistic fantasy: Lawrence's constant concern with his own pain and suffering makes it clear that it was not with the perpetrators but with the victims of these imaginary punishments that he identified. While a masochistic tendency is clearly observable throughout his life, a sadistic stratum is not. Lawrence was by nature gentle, highly sensitive and compassionate: '. . . they say his mouth suggests cruelty,' wrote his friend Vyvyan Richards; '. . . is there any trace of that in his nature? I have found none in all the thirty years I have known him . . . his campaign shows only strong justice where patience and mercy would have been a greater evil.'[21] Alec Kirkbride, who was with Lawrence at the very end of the Syrian campaign, wrote: 'it is complete nonsense to describe him as having been either sadistic or fond of killing . . . He once told me that his ideal of waging war was based on the professional condottieri of medieval Italy. That is to say, to gain one's objectives with a minimum of casualties on both sides.'[22]

Lawrence makes two related claims in *Seven Pillars* regarding Tafas: first, that he gave the Arabs the order to take no prisoners, and secondly, that the Arab regulars machine-gunned a host of prisoners with his approval. He does not state specifically that he himself ordered the prisoners shot: this claim only appears after the war in conversation with his brother Arnie. Unlike most events in Lawrence's career, though, there were other witnesses at the battle of Tafas. Fred Peake, who arrived there soon after Lawrence, and who saw the atrocities for himself, wrote to Arnie Lawrence years later that his brother had actually tried to halt the killing of wounded Turks. The Arabs had gone berserk, Peake said, and when he turned up with his Camel Corps detachment, Lawrence had asked him to restore order. Peake had dismounted 100 troopers and marched them into Tafas with fixed bayonets. The Arabs had given way, stopped killing the wounded, and had ridden after the retreating column, finishing off a few strays but withdrawing quickly when they saw that the Turks meant to fight. It is hardly surprising that Lawrence should have failed to mention this, for among the berserk Arabs were members of his own bodyguard over whom he claimed to have an almost hypnotic control.[23] As for the 'no prisoners' command, Peake recalled that Lawrence had ordered him personally to ensure the safety of Turkish prisoners – proof, he said, that there was never any such thing. Moreover there is a discrepancy in Lawrence's two accounts of the massacre, for while in his official dispatch he wrote 'we' ordered 'no prisoners', in *Seven Pillars* the 'we' has become 'I'. There were several senior figures present by the time Lawrence arrived at Tafas: Sharif Nasir, who was in command of the irregulars, and Nuri as-Sa'id, in charge of the trained troops. Auda Abu Tayyi was also present, and was said by Lawrence himself to have taken command of the last phase of the attack. Is it likely, therefore, that Lawrence, who claimed to work through the Arabs' own leaders rather than taking the foreground himself, should have been in a position to order the entire Arab force to take no prisoners? Both Peake and biographer John Mack agreed that the 'we' was a 'commander's we' – that is, not a personal order, but an assumption of responsibility. Young, who was not present at Tafas, heard from an Arab officer named 'Ali Jaudet that he and Lawrence had desperately tried to prevent the killing of prisoners after the battle, but to no avail. 'I am certain,' Peake wrote, 'that Lawrence did all he could to stop the massacre but he would have been quite unable to do anything as any human mob that has lost its head is beyond control.'[24] According to Nuri as-Sa'id, however, many Turkish prisoners who fell into Arab hands had actually survived.[25] Why should Lawrence claim falsely to have committed an act which he knew was against military convention, not to mention morally reprehensible, especially when he was known as a man of great compassion – who had, indeed, only weeks before, spared an unarmed Turkish soldier he had come across on the railway, and who had written to Edward Leeds that the 'killing and killing' of Turks sickened him? There are resonances here of the tale of Hamad the Moor's execution – the alleged incident which forms the overture to his arrival in the desert battle-zone. On the one hand such apparent acts depict Lawrence as a strong and ruthless man capable of righteous anger, on the other they show an apparent burden of guilt which he delighted in displaying to the world. Arnie Lawrence himself suggested to John Mack that he had doubts about the veracity of his brother's claim, and Alec Kirkbride believed that Lawrence had a horror of bloodshed: '. . . it is because of this,' he wrote, 'that he tends to pile on the agony in the passages of *Seven Pillars*, dealing with death and wounds . . . however, I suspected him of liking to suffer himself.'[26] Indeed, there is a sense in which Lawrence, the masochist, liked to absorb the sin and suffering of the world: the duplicity of the British he bore on his shoulders, together with the inconstancy, cruelty and barbarousness of the Arabs. There is, as we have already seen, a Christ-like leitmotif in Lawrence's story – especially in his betrayal, torture and humiliation at Dara'a and his 'resurrection' afterwards. Lawrence was perfectly aware of this messianic strand: just as Christ died for the sins of the world, Lawrence's penchant for sacrifice may have obliged him to assume responsibility for savage acts in which he personally had played no part.[27]

At sunset, Trad ash-Sha'alan's horsemen reached Dara'a and captured the Turkish rearguard of 500 soldiers. Lawrence arrived at first light. There was no time to linger, however, for British cavalry pickets were already in sight, and, ignorant of the fact that the town had fallen, were actually starting to engage Arab troops. General Barrow, commanding the British spearhead, had been ordered by Allenby to capture Dara'a and was intent on launching a full-scale assault. Only fast work would avert a disaster. Lawrence and his bodyguard rode out to meet Barrow through British lines – a hazardous undertaking, for he was dressed as an Arab and the British cavalrymen, trigger-happy and flushed with fight, could not distinguish between Hashemite Bedu and Arab irregulars in Turkish pay. George Staples, who was leading a troop of the Middlesex Yeomanry, claimed that he had almost given the order to shoot Lawrence: '. . . it was a blistering hot day,' he told a Toronto newspaper, 'and we were all edgy, when around a sand dune came about ten Arabs on camels . . . They came straight at us and our horses . . . started to shy. We thought they were the enemy and took aim at the leading Arab. Just as we were about to fire the Arabs stopped and out of the flowing robes came an Oxford accent. He said, "I'm Lawrence. Where's Barrow?" He acted as if the whole world should know who he was and he was terribly self-opinioned . . . I had quite a shock, I don't mind telling you when I realized I might have given the order to shoot him down – he was a thin little chap, about my size, five foot five . . .'[28] Lawrence, however, recalled only being 'captured' by an Indian machine-gun post, and that while he was being held up he had watched British aircraft bombing Nuri's regulars on the Dara'a road, having mistaken them for Turks. His task became urgent, and he managed to speak to a British officer who directed him to General Barrow. He found the General uncompromising: Allenby had given him no instructions as to the status of the

Arabs, and Clayton had not intervened, believing that the Hashemites deserved only what they could keep. For a moment the Arab efforts – and Lawrence's miseries – of two years hung in the balance: '. . . my head was working full speed,' he wrote, '. . . to prevent the fatal first steps by which the unimaginative British . . . created a situation which called for years of agitation . . . to mend.'[29] Barrow announced his intention of posting sentries to control the inhabitants of the town: Lawrence countered that the Arabs were already in control: the General said that his sappers would inspect the wells: Lawrence said they were welcome, but that the Arabs had already started the pump engines. Barrow snorted that the Arabs seemed to have made themselves at home and said that he would take charge of the railway station: Lawrence pointed out that the Arabs were already working the railway, and asked politely that British sentries should not interfere. Once again, it was Lawrence's rhetoric which saved the Hashemites: so persuasive was he, indeed, that Barrow not only accepted that the Arabs were in possession of Dara'a, but, on entering the town, actually made them the thrilling compliment of saluting the Hashemite flag fluttering from the ruined *serail*.

The British remained in Dara'a one night, and on the 29th marched north for Damascus, with the Arabs under Nasir now holding their right flank. Lawrence waited for Feisal, who arrived in his Vauxhall car from Azraq, followed closely by Frank Stirling and the armoured cars. That night, however, he could not sleep, and before light he and Stirling climbed into Blue Mist and set off for Damascus, driving along the track of the disused French railway. They caught up with Barrow, watering his horses at a stream, and Lawrence borrowed a camel and rode up to him. The General, not realizing that Lawrence had come most of the way by car, was dumbfounded to hear that he had left Dara'a only that morning.

'And where will you spend the night?' Barrow inquired.

'In Damascus!' Lawrence answered, and rode away.[30]

Soon, he and Stirling in Blue Mist had caught up with the Hashemite cavalry under Nasir and the Rwalla under Nuri ash-Sha'alan. The Rwalla had never ceased their harassment of the larger Turkish column, which their attrition had now reduced to half its original strength. Auda was in the country beyond, gathering the local Bedu for an ambush. Lawrence asked them to hold the Turks for an hour. Nasir selected a lonely farmstead on a distant ridge, and posted Nuri and his Rwalla there to slow down the enemy, while Lawrence and Stirling drove back to the British lines to get the Middlesex Yeomanry and horse artillery to attack the Turkish rear. With the Arabs in front and the British behind them, the Turkish column began to break up and, abandoning their guns and transport, fled in straggling groups into the hills to the east, where Auda's hyenas were waiting: 'In the night of his last battle,' Lawrence wrote, 'the old man killed and killed, plundered and captured, till dawn showed him the end. There passed the Fourth Army, our stumbling block for two years.'[31]

Lawrence and Stirling slept by the Rolls-Royce on a ridge above Damascus. It was a cold, windless night, and Stirling recalled seeing flashes of light from the direction of the hills, where Auda's men were cutting up the remnants of the Turks. Damascus, the final prize, was hidden in darkness below them, but in the early hours of the morning they were woken up by a series of explosions from inside. 'Good God!' Lawrence said. 'They are burning the town!' They discovered later that the German troops had destroyed their ammunition dumps before pulling out. Lawrence told Stirling that he had already sent thousands of Rwalla horse into Damascus ahead of the British forces, in search of 'Ali Ridha ar-Rikabi, the Governor of the town, whom Lawrence had met on his perilous journey north, more than a year previously. The Rwalla carried instructions from Sharif Nasir that 'Ali Ridha or his assistant Shukri al-Ayyubi should form a government at once in the name of the Hashemites. Actually, the work had already been done: although 'Ali Ridha was no longer in Damascus, Shukri had been supported by Lawrence's old enemies, the brothers 'Abd al-Qadir and Mohammad as-Sa'id, whose Algerian bodyguard had hoisted the Hashemite flag before the last Turks had even left the town.

In the morning – 30 October – Lawrence and Stirling managed to escape some over-zealous Bengal Lancers who 'captured' them, and entered Damascus in Blue Mist just after sun-up, to be greeted by a galloping horseman who held out to them a bunch of yellow dates: 'Good news: Damascus salutes you,' he said.[32] According to Lawrence, the streets along the Barada were packed with thousands of chanting people – women threw flowers and splashed scent, men hurled their hats in the air, roaring: 'Feisal! Nasir! Shukri! Urens!' 'There were dervishes dancing in front of the [car],' Stirling recalled, 'fierce Bedu in their flowing robes, their horses mad with excitement at the noise and shouting of the townsfolk who were hysterical in their joy – as we drove through the streets with their overhanging houses the women . . . leaned out from their windows crying, laughing, sobbing with joy and excitement.'[33] Later, though, in a letter to Stirling, Lawrence remembered quite a different scene: 'my memory of the entry into Damascus was of quietness and emptiness of street,' he wrote, 'and of myself crying like a baby with eventual thankfulness in the Blue Mist by your side. It seemed to me that the frenzy of welcome came later.'[34] Stirling remembered that Lawrence had not been happy: 'His mind was too complex,' he wrote, 'to permit of satisfaction for an achievement successfully carried out . . . his moment of triumph was embittered by his knowledge that the government wouldn't keep their promises to the Arabs.'[35] They arrived at the Town Hall, which was tightly packed with people, and Lawrence pushed his way through to find Auda Abu Tayyi in the centre of it all wrestling savagely with the Druse leader, Sultan al-'Atrash. It took Lawrence, Za'al, Mohammad adh-Dhaylan and two others to drag him off and prevent him from murdering the Druse before their eyes. Nasir, the senior Hashemite, was not present, and Lawrence learned that he was with 'Abd al-Qadir and his brother. He went off looking for them in Blue Mist, only to meet up with General Chauvel entering the town at the head of the British troops. Lawrence impressed upon him that the Arabs were in possession of Damascus, and urged him, unsuccessfully, to emulate Barrow's action at Dara'a and salute the Hashemite flag as a gesture of good will. Lawrence returned to the Town Hall and summoned 'Abd al-Qadir and his brother, who marched into his presence with their bodyguard. Lawrence had Nuri ash-Sha'alan's Rwalla around him, and Nuri as-Sa'id's regulars mustered in the square outside. He told the Algerians that as Feisal's representative he was abolishing the government they had formed the previous day and named Shukri al-Ayyubi as Acting Military Governor with Nuri as-Sa'id as Commander of Troops. 'Abd al-Qadir leapt up and drew his dagger intending to kill Lawrence, cursing him as a Christian and an Englishman, but in a flash Auda threw his weight on him and wrestled the blade from his grasp. Nuri ash-Sha'alan announced quietly that Lawrence had the support of the Rwalla. As the Algerians swept out in high dudgeon, someone suggested that they should be taken out and shot. Lawrence was inclined to agree, but desisted. By the next day they were brewing unrest again, however, and had gained some support from the Druses who had not fought at all in the Revolt, and who had been refused any reward by Lawrence. Now itching to shoot them, Lawrence sent a section of regulars to arrest the brothers: Mohammad as-Sa'id was taken: 'Abd al-Qadir escaped. Lawrence had the Druses expelled, and established himself, until the arrival of Feisal, as the effective Governor of the city.

There was much work to be done: the police to be appointed, the water supply to be attended to, electrical power to be restored, sanitation to be established, starving people to be fed. In fact, within a few days Lawrence had set running a system which endured for the next two years. An Australian doctor asked him to attend to the Turkish barracks, which was now a makeshift hospital without a single medical orderly, and packed with dead and dying men. Lawrence realized that it had been forgotten, went to inspect it himself, and was appalled. The floor was littered with dozens of bloated, putrefying corpses, lying in stinking pools of blood and excrement. Many of them were only freshly dead, and most had been gnawed by rats. Hearing a faint sighing, Lawrence lifted his robe and walked through the bodies to find a ward full of dying men who implored him for mercy. Quickly he commandeered some Turkish prisoners, who went about burying the dead in a common grave in the nearby garden. That night he started out of sleep, sweating and trembling with the memory of the dead bodies, and the following day he returned to the hospital to find things a little better: one room had been cleaned and disinfected ready to house the most serious cases, and there were medical orderlies present. Suddenly he was confronted by a British major of the Medical Corps, who asked if he was in charge. 'In a way, I suppose I am,' Lawrence replied.

'Scandalous, disgraceful, outrageous,' the Major said. 'You ought to be shot!'

Lawrence cackled with laughter, wondering what the officer would have thought had he been present the previous day. The Major muttered, 'Bloody brute,' smacked Lawrence across the face, and stalked off. All the fear, loathing and hypocrisy that Lawrence had borne for two years seemed to be expressed in those words 'Bloody brute' – 'in my heart I felt he was right,' he wrote, 'and that everyone who pushed through to success a rebellion of the weak against their masters must come out of it so stained in estimation that afterward nothing in the world could make him feel clean.'[36]

Lawrence returned to the Victoria Hotel to find that Allenby had arrived. He was closely followed by Feisal, who had ridden into the city at the gallop to a tumultuous welcome. It was at the hotel that the Sharif and the General met for the first time, with Lawrence as their interpreter – precisely the role he had created and envisaged for himself over the past eighteen months. Allenby explained to Feisal that he was to have control of Syria, with the exception of Palestine and the Lebanon, but only under the guidance of the French. He informed him that he would continue to work with Lawrence as liaison, but that he would shortly be given a French liaison officer in addition. Feisal objected in no uncertain terms: he would not accept a French liaison officer, would not accept French guidance, and did not recognize French authority in the Lebanon. He also said that Allenby's liaison officer – Lawrence – had informed him that the Arabs were to have all of Syria apart from Palestine. Allenby, astonished, inquired whether Lawrence had outlined to the Sharif the French claim to the Lebanon. Lawrence replied untruthfully that he had not. Allenby concluded that since Feisal was a Lieutenant-General under his command, he must obey orders at least for the time being.

Feisal departed as abruptly as he had come, but now in little mood for jubilation. As soon as he was gone, Lawrence told his chief that he could not work with a French liaison officer, and asked for leave to return to England. His war was over and he could do more for the Arabs behind the scenes at home. He was dog-tired, but like many men who had fought and longed for the war's end, he found in it the ultimate anticlimax. The misery he had suffered over two years was either forgotten or had already become enshrined in legend. Now his mind was blank. An Arab army had entered Damascus, and after five centuries the conquest of Selim the Grim had been avenged. If it had not been for European ambitions, Lawrence believed, then the Arabs might have gone on to take Anatolia, Baghdad and even the Yemen, and established a new Arab empire in the East. But European greed had brought the movement to a halt in its finest hour, and Lawrence's illusions had been shattered: '. . . my dreams puffed out like candles,' he wrote, 'in the strong wind of success.'[37]

PART THREE

THE MAGICIAN
1918–1935

20. Colonel Lawrence Still Goes On; Only I Have Stepped Out of the Way

The Peace Conference and the Colonial Office
1918–22

Lawrence arrived back in England a full colonel with a DSO, a CB, and a recommendation from Allenby himself that he be granted a knighthood. Only a few days after his arrival he was invited to Buckingham Palace for a private investiture by King George V, but to the consternation of everyone present politely refused both his knighthood and his medals to the King personally. He told His Majesty that the British government were about to let the Arabs down over the Sykes–Picot treaty: that he had pledged his word to Feisal that he would support him come what may, and that he might be obliged to fight Britain's French allies for the Hashemite cause in Syria. Curiously, though, the man who refused to become a British knight also told the King that he was an 'Emir' (Prince) among the Arabs – a title which he is nowhere recorded as having been granted officially. And while he refused his British medals, he accepted the Croix de Guerre from the French: the very nation whom he told George V he regarded as being his enemies. These inconsistencies suggest that there was, as usual, a darker level to Lawrence's actions: after all, knighthoods and DSOs were almost ten-a-penny among those who had fought in the Arab campaign (though Croix de Guerre were more exotic). As Lawrence had told Hubert Young (who would himself later be knighted) in 1918, 'there is plenty of honour and glory to be picked up without any great difficulty'.[1] Like the woman who wore ordinary clothes at the opera while everyone else wore evening-dress, Lawrence automatically became distinct, not through his acquisition of honours but by his conspicuous rejection of them. Even his admirer Liddell Hart was shrewd enough to observe that for Lawrence 'self-deprecation, like his rejection of distinction, was a kind of vanity – his wisdom led him to see the absurdity of acclamation, then found himself liking it, then

343

despised himself for liking it'.² The rejection of honours by the war's most famous hero, the man whom, by 1919, the press were already calling 'the most interesting Briton alive',³ of course, immediately devalued such distinctions. Not surprisingly, many who had fought four hard years, some of them in conditions far more appalling than those Lawrence had seen, who had survived terrible hardships, perhaps performed great feats of personal bravery, and justifiably felt themselves deserving of recognition, were incensed by his apparent mockery.

Lawrence's commitment to the Hashemites was, however, also very real. He was determined to vindicate the promises he had made to Feisal during the war, and to rescue his own sense of honour. Within days of arriving back he was bombarding War Office and Foreign Office officials with his views, and on 29 October – the day on which he met the King – he also appeared in front of the Eastern Committee of the War Cabinet. The meeting opened with a eulogy by Lord Curzon, acting Foreign Secretary, on Lawrence's achievements, upon which Lawrence ungraciously blurted out: 'Let's get to business. You people don't understand the hole you have put us all into!' – causing the volatile Curzon to burst into tears. Lawrence's views were uncompromising, but they did not encompass the single Arab state Hussain had demanded from McMahon in 1916. Mesopotamia, he said, should be divided into two, with Sharif Zayd in Baghdad, presiding over the northern part, and Sharif 'Abdallah, in Basra, supervising the southern. Feisal, in Damascus, should rule the whole of Syria, with the exception of the Lebanon, which should go to the French, and the Alexandretta district, which should be jointly run by the Allies. In Palestine, the Arabs would accept Jewish immigration as outlined in the Balfour Declaration in 1917, but would resist any attempt to establish a Jewish state there. A single British authority, based in Egypt, should watch over the fledgling Arab states, which would effectively cut out Anglo-Indian interference. Lawrence already knew that British hands were tied by Sykes–Picot: Mosul, in Mesopotamia, had been allocated to the French, while Palestine had been assigned to international administration. If Britain opposed French aspirations both in Palestine and Mesopotamia, which she coveted for her own sphere of influence, she would find it most difficult to oppose French claims in Syria too.

The armistice was signed on 11 November 1918, and the Peace Conference began at the Quai d'Orsay in Paris in January the following year. Here, Lawrence drew great attention to himself by his flamboyant adoption of Arab headdress, his fluent Arabic and his obvious devotion to Feisal. Acting as Feisal's interpreter, he laid out the Hashemite proposals on 6 February. The French had been determined from the beginning that there would be no concessions over Syria, and demanded that both littoral and inland Syria should be governed by a single authority. These demands were supported by a vigorous campaign in the French press. Lawrence and Feisal had two strong cards, however: first the backing of the American President, Woodrow Wilson, who proposed a policy of self-determination for Syria, and second, General Allenby's army, which was still actually deployed in the country, and which the British Prime Minister, Lloyd George, refused to withdraw until the conference had made a decision. No such decision was ever reached, however. President Wilson stood by his belief that an inquiry should be set up to ascertain the will of the people, and in June the King–Crane commission arrived in Palestine. The commissioners probed deeply and made extensive inquiries, and in August reported to Wilson in Washington in favour of a temporary system of Mandates, proposing the United States as mandatory power for Syria, Great Britain for Iraq, and excluding France entirely on the grounds that a French Mandate in Syria would lead to war with the Arabs. The commissioners also recommended abandoning the idea of creating in Palestine a Jewish Commonwealth, which they believed could not be established without force. The King–Crane report was a remarkable and prophetic document, but predictably it was ignored by France and Britain. By the time it was released, Wilson himself was ill, and without his impetus the European Allies simply decided to make a settlement of their own. In September Lloyd George informed French Prime Minister Clemenceau that he was pulling British troops out of Syria and Cilicia on 1 November. The British garrisons in Cilicia – west of the line drawn by Sykes–Picot – would be replaced by French troops, while those in Syria proper would be replaced by an Arab force. British troops would, however, remain in Palestine and Mesopotamia. At first Lawrence regarded this as a victory, and he wrote personally to Lloyd George, thanking him for the decision: '. . . you have kept all our promises,' he wrote, '. . . and my relief at getting out of the affair with clean hands is very great.'[4] He returned to England and on 1 September, with as little ceremony as had attended his commission in the army in 1914, he demobilized himself from it forthwith.

Lawrence's gratitude was premature. Even if he did not grasp that Britain's withdrawal would leave Syria wide open to French aggression, Feisal certainly did. In September the Sharif arrived in London and complained bitterly that the Arabs were now at the mercy of the French in the Lebanon. The British cabinet advised him coldly that he must negotiate with France alone, however, effectively washing their hands of the Arabs. Lawrence, whose machinations at the Peace Conference had made him *persona non grata* in France, was no longer in a position to help his friend, and fell into deep depression. The consequences were unhappy ones for Feisal. He was obliged to come to a provisional understanding with Clemenceau, but on returning to Syria in January 1920 was promptly accused of 'selling out' by the Nationalists, and obliged to abandon it. In March 1920, the General Syrian Congress proclaimed him king of an independent Syria which theoretically included the Lebanon, northern Mesopotamia and Palestine. This angered both the French, who were already in control of the Lebanon, and the British, who were seeking control of the other two regions. Only a month later, an Allied conference at San Remo decided that Britain should have a mandate for influence in Mesopotamia and Palestine, while the French should be the mandatory power in all of Syria. The Arabs saw, finally, that they had been abused and cheated by Britain and France, and from that moment lost faith in the European powers. The upshot was inevitable: using the excuse of attacks on French personnel and property, French forces moved into Syria in July 1920, swatted aside a force of 2,000 regulars and irregulars which prepared to defend Damascus, and drove Feisal into exile. The Nationalists were suppressed as fiercely as they had been under the Turks; the press was muzzled; French was substituted for Arabic in law courts and schools. The situation which both Lawrence and Feisal had most dreaded during the hard years of fighting had ultimately come to pass.

Lawrence never fulfilled his threat to fight against the French. By early 1919 other developments were taking place in his life. First, he had long wished to turn his experiences into a book, and had begun to draft out *Seven Pillars* during the Peace Conference. The first few chapters were written purely from memory, but in May he was flown to Cairo in one of the Handley-Page bombers being transferred to help put down the anti-British insurrections there – to pick up his Arab Bureau files. On the way, his aircraft made a bad landing at Centocelle in Italy, killing the pilot, fatally injuring the co-pilot, and leaving Lawrence himself with a fractured collar-bone. He completed his journey only a few days later, however, continuing to work on his book in the aircraft. In September he was back in Britain, where his growing fame as a media personality had led to his being elected to a Research Fellowship at All Souls College, Oxford – the same institution by which, as an unknown postgraduate scholar, he had been rejected in 1910. The Fellowship was worth £200 a year, and enabled Lawrence to continue with his work on *Seven Pillars*. However, in December the manuscript was stolen at Reading station while he was changing trains, obliging him to begin all over again. In January 1920 he moved to London, and began work on the new text in a flat in Barton Street, borrowed from his friend Sir Henry Baker, where he wrote more than 400,000 words in three months, during marathon sittings. This was not quite the superhuman effort it appears, for most of the new text was lifted directly from Lawrence's wartime dispatches and reports in the *Arab Bulletin* which he had with him in London, checked against the dates in his two skeleton diaries. Any discrepancies between *Seven Pillars* and the official reports, therefore, cannot be explained by faulty memory: in any case, Lawrence's memory was superb: he once told Clare Sydney Smith he could remember everything he ever read in a book, and never forgot a date.[5] Lawrence's documents were extraordinarily well written, but once they had been strung together, he realized, they did not make a book – at least, not the work of art he had craved to write. The book had no personality, no dramatic structure of its own, and – more important – no great emotional climax of a personal nature: a story must have a clearly identifiable hero who was seen to overcome great obstacles and to evolve spiritually in response to his experience. This was to be his *magnum opus*, his definitive statement of himself to the world. He had performed heroic deeds, certainly: he had saved the life of Gasim, had made a reckless ride of 560 miles through enemy-held territory alone, had devised a brilliant guerrilla strategy, had fought scores of actions against the Turks. These incidents were admirable, but they were not sufficient to lend the book the dramatic edge Lawrence required. He solved the problem by inventing a series of personal incidents which would give fire to the story – none of these can have been taken from his dispatches or diaries, because none of them is mentioned therein. He had not been sent to Arabia on an intelligence-gathering mission by the Arab Bureau, he wrote, but had gone there of his own initiative because his inspiration told him that the Revolt lacked leadership – a leadership which he alone could provide. He had adopted Arab ways as if born to them, as if he were fulfilling some messianic prophecy. On his first journey in the Hejaz, he had witnessed a charade by two Arab Sharifs which defined the cruelty and inter-tribal hatred inherent there: the petty hatreds which could only be overridden by his own advocacy of a romantic and abstract idea. He had been obliged on his first major operation to shoot a man in cold blood; he had performed camel-journeys impossible for normal human beings, and, like Jesus Christ, he had been betrayed, horribly tortured and humiliated, but had risen again to bring his struggles to full fruition, now so brutalized that he had ordered the massacre of helpless prisoners. The addition of these nuances and others, a careful 'elaboration' on the mundane details, pushed what might have been no more than a well-written memoir into the realms of Malory and Homer, full of larger-than-life incidents, and larger-than-life characters: the noble prince Feisal, the brave veteran warrior Auda, the despicable traitor 'Abd al-Qadir, the heroic knights Sharif 'Ali, Sharif Shakir, Za'al Abu Tayyi and Talal al-Haraydhin, the indolent Sharif 'Abdallah, the 'rat' Nasib al-Bakri, the 'clowns' 'Farraj and Da'ud', the paternal Allenby, the gallant but rigidly hidebound British regulars Young, Joyce, Dawnay, Newcombe, Garland (all of whom are sniped at surreptitiously under the cloak of high praise), and above all the elvish Bedu against the goblin Turks, with Lawrence, the 'Prince of Mecca', the Merlin–King Arthur figure rolled into one, with his 'Round Table Knights' – ninety hardened Bedu warriors sworn to protect him unto death. Under Lawrence's fluent pen, *Seven Pillars* grew from a series of dispatches into an epic of the calibre of *Lord of the Rings*: in 1928 he wrote Jim Ede: '[in my book] I was trying very hard to do a thing for which I am totally unfitted by nature: – to produce a work of creative imagination . . .'[6]

The text also had an ideological purpose, however. Almost simultaneously, Lawrence was fighting a campaign in the press in support of the Hashemites, and the secondary objective of *Seven Pillars* was to provide a glowing encomium on Feisal and his Arabs by painting the story of their heroic struggle in the Pre-Raphaelite hues of Burne-Jones. Many Arabs resented this view. As historian George Antonius wrote, it was not that Lawrence lacked perception or intelligence, but simply that, like everyone else, his intellect was subordinate to a set of schemata which were defined by his culture. He could not help seeing the Arabs through the romantic images he had learned as a youth: the Bedu, the Ashraf, the self-sufficient peasants of the Euphrates – these were 'noble' Arabs. The townsmen, the 'craven' villagers of the sown, were not. The paradox was, of course, that it was within the ranks of precisely these townsmen and villagers that the spirit of Arab Nationalism burned most fiercely. Paradoxically, and unintentionally, Lawrence's pro-Bedu, pro-Ashraf stance amounted to an anti-Arab policy in many people's eyes. Lawrence's official biographer Jeremy Wilson writes: '*Seven Pillars* often tells less than the whole truth, concealing politically damaging matters . . . Lawrence also plays down the enormous contribution to the Revolt made by non-Arab personnel . . . This emphasis cannot be excused by the claim that [he] was writing about only his experience of the war.'[7]

Lawrence knew that the book was unique – no one else had experienced the Arab Revolt as he had, and for the first 'heroic' era of the struggle there was no other European witness to gainsay him. All his life he had practised the arts of intrigue and mystification, and he knew perfectly well that the best way to arouse interest in his work was to conceal what lay in it for as long, and from as many people, as possible. Though he had originally thought to make money out of *Seven Pillars* – for he had revived the idea of building a medieval hall with Vyvyan Richards and starting a printing-press at Pole Hill near Chingford – the finished version was not to be published until after his death in 1935. A limited subscribers edition (the Oxford version) was completed in 1922, but not issued until 1926, at £30 per copy. Predictably, perhaps, Lawrence refused to reveal how many copies had been printed. In the same year, an abridged version of the book entitled *Revolt in the Desert* – from which most of the personal and controversial matter had been expurgated – was published to enormous popular success, but was quickly withdrawn as soon as Lawrence thought it had earned enough money, making himself, as George Bernard Shaw commented later, 'the talk of the town',[8] and adding a further impetus to public interest.

Winston Churchill wrote that *Seven Pillars* ranked with the greatest books ever written in the English language and called it 'an epic, a prodigy, a tale of torment'.[9] The book also received high praise from distinguished figures such as George Bernard Shaw, Siegfried Sassoon, Thomas Hardy, H. G. Wells and many others. Lawrence wrote Vyvyan Richards in 1923 that he was aware that it was 'a good book' but added that it 'was not as good as it should have been'[10] – that is, it was not as good, he felt, as *Moby Dick* or *War and Peace*. It was an aspect of Lawrence's competitive nature that he should aspire to equal the works of Tolstoy, Melville and others, and it was also typical that he should feel that he had fallen short. Indeed, he seemed to grow less and less satisfied with *Seven Pillars* over the years, frequently referring to it as 'my shit'. He was convinced that it was a failure, and would accept no praise for it, dismissing any approving comments as flattery, and considering them a tribute to the legend he had become. He was partly, but not entirely correct in this. *Seven Pillars* is a masterpiece of technical ability: it displays a wit and a mastery of language which is far out of the ordinary. Yet it has its faults. Lawrence himself commented that it had no unity, was too discursive, dispersed, heterogeneous: 'I've shot into it,' he wrote, 'as a builder into his yard, all the odds and ends of ideas which came to me during those years.'[11] Lawrence was a superb descriptive writer, but the narrative of *Seven Pillars* is occasionally so oppressively overwhelmed with detail that the story itself is obscured: 'the paint,' as St John Philby observed, 'is too thick on the canvas.'[12] Lawrence's passion for concealment and whimsicality is counter-productive, because writing is about the clear communication of ideas, whereas some of his passages are opaque. The book's greatest fault, however, is its lack of spontaneity: Lawrence's emotions seem artificial – there is no ecstasy, little real passion: there are likes and dislikes, but little genuine love or hate. Lawrence has often been called 'a poet', yet he wrote almost no poems. He became a 'man of letters' after the war, but he was never a 'writer' in the sense that his friends Forster, Hardy, Sassoon, Graves, Shaw and others were writers. If he had not been 'Lawrence of Arabia', *Seven Pillars* would have remained a remarkable book, but it certainly would not have had the same impact on the world: *The Mint*, his second book, might not have been published at all. He himself suspected this: when he tried to submit articles to various newspapers and magazines later under an assumed name, they were rejected. Lawrence was a famous man who had one magnificent story to tell, who told it magnificently. He found himself a niche among the great artists and writers of the age, but was never quite certain that he belonged there.

Indeed, Lawrence's post-war career is in many senses an essay in the exigencies of fame – a phenomenon which was perhaps less well known or understood in his era than it is today, in the age of television. At the end of the millennium we are familiar with personalities who are 'famous for being famous', as the saying goes, and we are aware that fame obscures all truth and rides in an ethereal dimension of self-perpetuating fantasy. We know now that fame need have little connection with talent or accomplishment, and can often be entirely the result of presentation. Other than stars of the screen, Lawrence was perhaps the first international megastar of the century, and 'Lawrence of Arabia' was created by its first major publicity campaign. Lawrence's fame began almost as soon as he arrived back in Britain after the war, when he was interviewed by newspaper correspondents who found him surprisingly 'unassuming' for a hero. They did not know, of course, that this apparently guileless exterior had been carefully cultivated by Lawrence from childhood and, coupled with a sense that there was more concealed which he was too modest to reveal, was guaranteed to pique their interest – as, by Lawrence's own admission, it was fully intended to do. Even at school this quality had been noticed by his teachers: time and time again it had worked to Lawrence's advantage: with Hogarth, with Feisal, with Allenby, and now with the press. Predictably, they became avid for more and more about the strange 'Colonel Lawrence'. It was in 1919, though, when the American journalist Lowell Thomas opened at the Royal Opera House, Covent Garden, with an illustrated lecture, eventually entitled 'With Allenby in Palestine and Lawrence in Arabia', that the myth of 'Lawrence of Arabia' was firmly established.

In 1918, Thomas had been commissioned by the American government to produce material which would generate enthusiasm for the war among the American people. Finding that the Western Front, with its dirt, disease and monotonous stalemate, presented no image worth carrying home, Thomas had been steered by John Buchan, Britain's propaganda chief, to the more photogenic Eastern front.

In March 1918 Thomas had met Lawrence in Jerusalem, and the arch-propagandist in Lawrence had immediately recognized the efficacy of publicity. He had arranged for Thomas to visit him in Aqaba, where he had not only posed for him happily in Arab costume, but had succeeded in getting him permission to film the Bedu. Thomas wrote later that it was not Lawrence himself, but his fellow British officers who tended to be camera-shy. Although Thomas returned to the United States too late for his material to perform its original function, his post-war presentation in London was a phenomenal success. It quickly boosted Lawrence to superstar status: in Britain alone it was watched by more than a million people, including the King – who asked for a private showing. It succeeded by harnessing a series of heroic archetypes which appealed deeply to the subliminal consciousness of a people whose nation had just survived a devastating war. In a very real sense, 'Colonel Lawrence' redeemed the souls and the seemingly pointless deaths of thousands of Britain's young men. Thomas claimed that Lawrence had been regarded by the Arabs as 'a sort of supernatural being' who had been sent from heaven to deliver them from their oppressors; he declared that Lawrence had done more to unify the Arabs than anyone since the age of the 'Great Caliphs'. Lawrence had achieved this, he said, by 'transforming himself into an Arab' and wandering around the Arabian deserts with only two companions, persuading individual tribesmen to join the revolt by pure rhetoric. This 'youth' had, he said, become virtually the ruler of the Holy Land of the Arabs and the commander-in-chief of thousands of Bedu. It was a compelling picture: the messianic nature of the story was just what the audience wanted to hear. It also expressed precisely the kind of mythological, archetypal images in which Lawrence himself had always liked to deal. In early 1920 he wrote to Sir Archibald Murray, his former Chief in Cairo, who objected to certain comments Thomas had made about him in the lecture, noting that he himself had to 'sit still' while Thomas called him 'Prince of Mecca' and 'other beastly things',[13] yet a year earlier Lawrence had announced to the King of England that he was 'a prince among the Arabs' and even used the title 'Prince of Mecca' deliberately in the 1922 edition of *Who's Who*. The truth was that Lawrence loved Thomas's lecture, was fascinated by it, went to see it several times, and hated himself for loving it. Lawrence called the publicity 'rank', yet when Thomas asked him what his attitude to mis-statements would be, he answered that he would neither confirm nor deny them. Thomas, who, unlike Lawrence's later biographers, had actually met Lawrence during the campaign, wrote that he revelled in being the leader of an army, a strategist, and a maker of history: 'he got a real thrill,' he wrote, 'out of the kudos that accrued from his success.'[14]

Thomas's presentation was an exercise in mass manipulation, and its effects were staggering: within weeks many who had opposed or criticized Lawrence were praising him unreservedly, realizing that they, too, were accessories in the heroic story. So powerful did the mythical image become that in the ensuing years it was almost impossible for anyone to make a balanced statement about Lawrence: all but the most iconoclastic felt that it was expected of them to pay lip-service to the official version, and to oppose it became almost tantamount to treason. Lawrence's fame opened every door: prominent writers, artists, poets – many of those who might be thought of as capable of individual and independent views – simply accepted passively the verdict of the crowd. (There were some exceptions: neither Kipling nor Doughty joined in the popular circus.) Such is the overwhelming power of fame: not that Lawrence did not deserve to be famous, but that the fame itself became a fantastic entity quite out of proportion to the reality, bathing everything Lawrence did or touched in a gaudy, neon glow. Lawrence became a 'hero', that is, not a creature of flesh and blood living in the real world, but a composite character inhabiting what today we might call 'cyberspace' – the collective consciousness – an imaginary focus of human aspirations and desires. He became so bound up with many people's concept of what it was to be British that any criticism of Lawrence came to be seen in some quarters as an attack on the British themselves. It was not until the 1960s – long after Lawrence's death – that a writer named Richard Aldington had the courage to stand up and point out the absurdity of the worship of Lawrence as a secular saint – and Aldington's 'debunking' was made with such ill-conceived sarcasm and vitriol that he virtually demolished his own case.

What part did Lawrence himself play in the creation of this legend? There can be no doubt that his sensitivity and his tendency to project the mundane into the mythological played a major role. Mythogeny – the creation of myth – is a two-way process. The hero-in-the-making

353

must have a feeling for the myth he is in – the capacity to reflect what is projected upon him by others – to provide, as it were, the raw material upon which the legend can be built. Lowell Thomas revealed later that Lawrence had actually visited him at Richmond regularly and had consulted with him. Thomas wrote that he had often asked Lawrence if certain anecdotes were true, upon which Lawrence would giggle and reply: 'History is not made up of the truth anyway, so why worry?'[15] Yet Lawrence's masochistic nature prevented him from simply accepting the adulation of others. He was not vain: his exhibitionism was, as can be frequently observed throughout his life, not of the narcissistic kind. He felt himself to be fundamentally 'unclean' and needed to show this to the world also. His life thus became a ceaseless dialectic between his exultation in his success and his instinctive need for self-degradation. Thomas recognized that Lawrence loved fame, but wanted at the same time to flee from it: 'He would protest that he wanted to be left alone by the world,' Thomas wrote, '. . . but at heart he loved it all.'[16] It was Thomas himself who wrote the famous line about Lawrence having a talent for 'backing into the limelight',[17] and George Bernard Shaw – no doubt one of the most perceptive men of his day – who called him a born actor, writing: 'when he was in the middle of the stage, with ten limelights blazing on him, everyone pointed at him and said: "See! He is hiding. He hates publicity."'[18] Lawrence pre-empted all these comments, though, when he admitted that he had 'a craving to be famous; and a horror of being known to like being known'.[19] His predicament was remarkably like that of J. M. Barrie's rascally old Etonian, Captain Hook, whose 'vitals were tortured' by the reflection that it was 'bad form' to think about having 'good form', and that one could only truly have 'good form' without knowing it. As Lyn Cowan has commented, such a trait is perfectly consistent with masochism: 'the masochist reveals that he is a forceful actor,' she has written. 'He must act, and lives to act, and hates to act. So great is his inner torment that it must hide behind curtains and burst forth on to centre stage.'[20] Lawrence both helped to create and then tried to deny the myth, telling Joseph Conrad that the 'Lawrence of Arabia' legend was all untrue: that his success had been exaggerated out of all proportion: 'You see I know how false the praise is,' he wrote later, 'how little the reality compared with the legend: how much luck: how little merit.'[21] Yet he acknowledged that the legend had a life of its own, when he announced: 'Colonel Lawrence still goes on; only I have stepped out of the way.'

At almost the moment when 'Colonel Lawrence' was being born, however, Lawrence discovered that he was not 'T. E. Lawrence' at all. In April 1919 his father died of influenza, and he flew back from the Peace Conference for the funeral to discover his true identity. Thomas had inherited the Chapman baronetcy from his uncle in 1914, although, of course, he had never used the title. Lawrence now discovered that he was the son of Sir Thomas Chapman, who was the heir to vast estates in Ireland. His reaction to this revelation is difficult to gauge. From an early age, he had sensed that there was something strange about his parents' relationship. It cannot have escaped his notice, for instance, that while other children had cousins, grandparents, aunts and uncles, he seemed to have no relatives at all. He claimed to have known that he was illegitimate before he was ten, but according to notes taken down by Charles Bell of the Ashmolean from David Hogarth, he knew only a garbled version of the story. He believed that Thomas was not his real father, but had married his mother – a servant in another man's house – after she had acquired some or all of her sons. Lawrence maintained that he had not 'given a straw' about his illegitimacy: it had not affected his childhood, and it certainly had not affected his success. Arnie Lawrence, who himself had burst into raucous laughter when Ned first told him the truth, said that his brother felt no bitterness about his inheritance: 'He cannot possibly have felt any grievance . . .' Arnie wrote, 'because the money had actually come to his father, and why should he regret Bob's exclusion from the landed estate (but he did once remark how funny it would be if Bob had been able to become Sir Montague)?'[22] Moreover, since Lawrence frequently wrote to acquaintances informing them that his name was 'not really' Lawrence, he cannot have felt a great sense of shame. Lawrence's biographers have frequently attempted to turn his story into a tale of existential guilt over his family circumstances. Apart from some play over his name, and an assertion of his 'Irishness' which was new, though, the revelation came too late either to mould his character or to affect his career: when he learned the truth in 1919, he was already on the way to becoming a national hero.

*

355

Lawrence was not satisfied that the Hashemites had been fairly treated by the Allies. The Allied victory over the Turks, whose prospects had appeared so rosy in October 1918, indeed, had very quickly dissolved into chaos. Anti-British uprisings under Zaghlul Pasha and his Wafd party in Egypt had been suppressed with great violence in 1919, when British troops had opened fire on rioting crowds, RAF aircraft had bombed and strafed civilians, ring-leaders had been arrested and tortured. In Kurdistan, a nationalist movement had been nipped in the bud by a British column. In Mesopotamia, there was a savage rebellion against the British Mandate, only stamped out by 40,000 troops at a cost of £40 million – three times the total amount spent during the Arab Revolt. There were as many as 10,000 casualties, including 400 British soldiers. In Palestine there was growing tension between Arabs and Jews, and in Syria Feisal's displaced tribesmen were eyeing their French conquerors malevolently from the wings. In short, as Winston Churchill put it: 'the whole of the Middle East presented a most melancholy and alarming picture'.[23]

In February 1921, Churchill took over as Colonial Secretary and decided that the situation must be redressed. He gathered around him a team of experts, including Lawrence, who agreed, less reluctantly than many had expected, to become his adviser on Arab Affairs. Though Churchill came from a far more privileged background, he and Lawrence were made of similar stuff. Both were intuitive, both romantic, both had suffered childhood traumas (Churchill had been emotionally neglected by his promiscuous mother), neither was physically impressive, but both had overcome physical limitations by tremendous willpower and courage, both were rhetoricians, master propagandists and master wordsmiths. Their admiration was mutual. It was Churchill's intention to hold a conference in Cairo calling together all the parties concerned with policy in the Near East and hammer out a settlement once and for all. The conference met at the Mena House hotel in Cairo, under the shadow of the pyramids, in March 1921 and included almost every British soldier and administrator concerned in the Middle East question. The decision, which had been made previously in consultation with Feisal in London, was to revoke the British Mandate in Iraq and hand the administration over to an Arab government, with the recommendation that Feisal should be king subject to a general plebiscite. Britain would then enter an alliance with Feisal, and withdraw British troops in favour of Lord Trenchard's RAF bombers. In April Lawrence and Churchill travelled to Jerusalem to confer with Sharif 'Abdallah, who the previous year had arrived at Ma'an with a force of tribesmen ready to attack the French in Syria. 'Abdallah proposed that he should govern a single state consisting of Trans-Jordan and Palestine, but this plan was rejected due to Britain's promises to the Jews. Instead, 'Abdallah was confirmed as provisional governor of Trans-Jordan, and Lawrence remained in the country as British representative until December, when he returned to Britain, satisfied that he had done his best to fulfil his wartime pledges to the Hashemites: '[Churchill] made straight all the tangle,' Lawrence wrote, 'finding solutions fulfilling (I think) our promises in letter and spirit (where humanly possible) without sacrificing any interest of our Empire or any interest of the people concerned. So we were quit of our war-time Eastern adventure, with clean hands, but three years too late to earn the gratitude which peoples, if not states, can pay.'[24]

It was, said Arab historian George Antonius, a statement 'so palpably untenable as to cast serious doubts on Lawrence's understanding of the issues involved'.[25] In fact, the Cairo Conference heralded a period of unrest in the Middle East which had scarcely been surpassed even under Ottoman rule. Iraq failed to enjoy a single year of peace until the end of the Second World War, and remains in dire straits today. The same can obviously be said for Palestine. In Syria, the French met with severe opposition until they finally accepted an Arab administration in 1936. Only in Trans-Jordan, a relatively poor country, mostly desert, was some semblance of balance maintained by the Arab Legion under the gifted administrator John Bagot Glubb. King Hussain, the fox who had conspired from his youth to create an independent Hejaz, was driven from his own country in 1924 by 'Abdal Azziz ibn Sa'ud, the desert puritan who was the real victor of the Arab Revolt. The 'war-time Eastern adventure' is still with us, and we are not quit of it with clean hands yet.

Lawrence was never to return to Arabia, however. He had done what he could for the Arabs, had, rightly or wrongly, emerged as the greatest hero of history's most devastating war, and was obliged to carry the fantastic 'Lawrence of Arabia' with him for the rest of his life. He might have named his job – it was even rumoured (by Lawrence himself) that Churchill had offered him the post of High Commissioner in Egypt, in the footsteps of Kitchener, McMahon and Allenby. But Lawrence had no taste for high office. The reward he chose for his wartime service was the most curious one imaginable: he chose to join the armed services as a private soldier, thus bringing to full circle the ambition he had nurtured when, at the age of seventeen, he had run away from home.

21. *In Speed We Hurl Ourselves Beyond the Body*

The RAF, RTC and death
1922–35

On 30 August 1922, a small, ragged-looking man named John Hume Ross hovered shakily outside the RAF recruiting-office in Henrietta Street, central London, wondering whether or not to enter. Finally, after rushing to a public lavatory to ease the 'melting of his bowels' from fright, he resolved to walk in. He was confronted by a stern-looking Warrant Officer, Sergeant-Major McGee, who thought him suspicious-looking, and called his officer, Captain W. E. Johns, an aspiring author who would later entertain the boys of the world with his 'Biggles' books. McGee made a signal to Johns, indicating that Ross might be a crook, for he had no identity-papers or references with him. Johns sent Ross away to get references and his birth certificate, and while he was gone contacted the registry of births at Somerset House, ascertaining that there was no 'John Hume Ross' born on the date the man had given. When 'Ross' returned with references which were obviously forged, the Sergeant-Major showed him out.

To Johns's astonishment, however, the little man was back within the hour, in the company of an official messenger from the Air Ministry who carried a message signed by the Chief of Air Staff, Lord Trenchard, that Ross was to be enlisted as an Aircraftman Second Class. However, there was still the medical examination to contend with, and the two RAF doctors found that Ross not only bore signs of voluntarily inflicted beating,[1] but was also severely malnourished. The doctors rejected him as unfit. Johns took the case to his Commanding Officer, who telephoned the Air Ministry. When he had finished, he put the phone down and said: 'Watch your step. This man is Lawrence of Arabia. Get him in, or you'll get your bowler hat!'[2] Johns returned to the doctors with this sensational news, but they adamantly refused to sign.

359

Johns was obliged to bring in a civilian doctor to get Lawrence of Arabia enlisted as a private in the RAF.

It is not given to every man to realize his life's fantasy, but then the fantasies of many men revolve around dreams of grandeur, wealth and success. Lawrence's curious psychology – the 'reverse exhibitionism' which was the social expression of his masochism – made sure that his fantasies always extended in the opposite direction – towards degradation, poverty, self-denial and enslavement. Short of being an actual slave or a prisoner in jail, the situation which best allowed Lawrence to experience such degradation was in the ranks of the armed forces. He later said that it had been his wartime experience with army and RAF personnel which had encouraged him to join the ranks: 'These friendly outings with the armoured car and Air Force fellows were what persuaded me that my best future, if I survived the war, was to enlist,' he wrote.[3] In January 1922, though, while still working for the Colonial Office, he had written to Trenchard, Chief of the Air Staff – whom he had met at the Cairo Conference in 1921 – that he would like to join the RAF 'in the ranks, of course'. He told Trenchard that his reason for enlisting was to obtain material for a book about the Royal Air Force 'from the ground'. When Trenchard – with Churchill's agreement – finally issued the order that 'John Hume Ross' should be admitted to the RAF as 'AC2' (Aircraftman 2nd Class) No. 352087 on 16 August, he wrote, 'He is taking this step to learn what is the life of an airman.'[4] He later wrote to an acquaintance that he had joined up because he had found himself destitute, and enlisting in the ranks was a quick and easy way of staying alive.

None of these explanations was the complete truth, as Lawrence himself admitted: 'Honestly I couldn't tell you exactly why I joined up,' he wrote Robert Graves; '. . . it was a necessary step, forced on me by an inclination towards ground level: by a despairing hope that I'd find myself on common ground with men: by a little wish to become a little more human . . .'[5] If Lawrence's enlistment in the ranks seems perverse, then it must be remembered that he had run away from home to do exactly that at seventeen, and had fantasized about serving in the ranks, or being a deserter from them, all his life. He inhabited a masochistic world of reverse values – for him pain was pleasure, servitude freedom, and self-denial orgiastic self-indulgence: as he was to tell Charlotte Shaw later, '*Il faut souffrir pour etre content*.'[6] His service in the ranks of first the RAF, then the army, then the RAF again, which extended for most of the rest of his life, was for Lawrence not a penance but the ultimate reward for his struggles and achievements. The 'official' explanation – that Lawrence joined the forces for 'security' – will not wash: he would have had far more financial security as an officer or an official of the Colonial Office, without the constant hardships and threat of violence he experienced in his first years in the ranks. In one sense his enlistment allowed him to avoid the responsibility which international notoriety had given him. It removed from him the burden of playing the hero, and yet, in itself, made him far more remarkable than those 'ordinary' war heroes who did the 'vulgar things expected of them' such as accepting knighthoods, awards and high office. There was also a more positive side to his enlistment, however: Lawrence had long ago sensed in himself a powerful competitive force, and during the occupation of Damascus, when he had been briefly *de facto* ruler of the city, had seen clearly that if given opportunity the dragon within would emerge as a fully-fledged tyrant. Any high post would have provided such an opportunity, and in order to prevent the 'beast' from emerging Lawrence felt the need to be physically shackled and confined. Service in the ranks would allow him to exert moral power through his influential friends, without the inevitable corruption of spirit that material wealth and physical power would bring. If there had ever been any danger that 'Lawrence of Arabia' might be forgotten, his enlistment in the ranks made certain that he would not – paradoxically, it was the ultimate self-advertisement. On another level, though, his years of military service may be seen as a self-prescribed 'cure' for his paraphilia – an attempt to 'balance' whatever it was he felt was out of kilter in his psyche, and to make himself whole again: 'partly,' he wrote Robert Graves in 1923, 'I came in here to eat dirt until it's normal to me.'[7] 'It's going to be a brain sleep, and I'll come out of it less odd than I went in: or at least less odd in other men's eyes.'[8]

Great secrecy and a conspiratorial air accompanied his enlistment, but it is clear that he took few pains to conceal his true identity. Before he had left the recruitment office that first day, Johns already knew who he was: 'Lawrence knew that I knew,' said Johns, 'because I had a long talk with him while he was waiting for the train to take him to

Uxbridge.'[9] Johns had also telephoned through to the Recruit Depot at Uxbridge to warn his opposite number there, Flight-Lieutenant Nelson, that Lawrence of Arabia was on the way *incognito*, so his 'secret' was well known from the moment he arrived at the Depot, to almost everyone except the ordinary Aircraftmen and NCOs with whom he shared his life. Lawrence spent two months at Uxbridge and found the life one of drudgery, alternating between kitchen fatigues, drill and PT. In an exhausted and malnourished state when he joined up, he was also deeply depressed and drained of energy after writing *Seven Pillars*, and hoped the RAF would help bring him out. He was older than most of the recruits and physically debilitated. He could not keep up with them during PT, fumbled his drill, and was victimized by the Adjutant, 'Stiffy' Breese, to whom he had unfortunately had the cheek to apply for a private room in which to pursue his writing – a clear indication that he had not yet wholeheartedly adopted his role of ordinary airman – almost, perhaps, a deliberate attempt to bait authority. Breese wrote later that 'Ross' had been constantly 'up' for dirtiness, insubordination, refusing to obey direct orders, and being late on parade. Breese recalled that in his defence 'Ross' had simply remarked with Oxford hauteur that 'he had always felt a little tired in the early morning'.[10] His fellow Aircraftmen thought him 'a queer sort of bloke': '. . . the erks (Aircraftmen) found him useful,' one of his room-mates recalled; '. . . he was always good for half-crowns, books, technical advice etc.'[11] Although, on one level, Lawrence sought acceptance by the 'erks', he also purposely retained his oddness, writing to Edward Garnett that in the barrack-room he was 'apart' and felt like a 'dragon-fly among wasps' or a 'wasp among dragon-flies'.[12] His old propensity for fitting into a community without belonging to it quickly reasserted itself.

If Lawrence had really desired anonymity, he could have found it. If he had really meant to leave 'Colonel Lawrence' behind and find the shape of the 'worm inside the caddis shell', as he put it, it would have been possible. As Bernard Shaw so acutely observed, though, Lawrence sought to hide always in full spotlight on mid-stage. Anonymity was not really his objective: his purpose in joining up was to abase himself and be seen to abase himself: to suffer and be seen to suffer. Just as his night expeditions to dive through the ice on the Cherwell in his college days had been made with the object of shocking 'orthodox folk', so his service as a 'beast' in the ranks had to be communicated to the exalted personages among whom Lawrence would otherwise have lived. They must be enjoined to share in his degradation. It had been his own choice to join the RAF as a ranker: indeed, most of his acquaintances including Winston Churchill and Lord Trenchard had tried to dissuade him from it. Yet once he had chosen his path, he proceeded to write sheaves of letters to the great and powerful of the land, wallowing in the self-abasement he had opted for voluntarily. Lawrence's desire to exhibit the disgusting conditions of his life can be felt almost palpably in his letter to Bernard Shaw: 'You ask for details of what I'm doing in the RAF,' he wrote. 'Today I scrubbed the kitchen out in the morning . . . Yesterday I washed up the dishes in the sergeants' mess in the morning (messy feeders, sergeants: plates were all butter and tomato sauce, and the washing water was cold) . . . I've been dustman, and clerk, and pig-stye cleaner, and housemaid and scullion . . . but the life isn't so bad . . .'[13] There is a curious parallel between Lawrence's service life and his attitude to *Seven Pillars*, which he was revising during his first weeks in the RAF. Once again, it was a book no one had obliged him to write, revealing 'secrets' and 'private matters' no one had asked him to reveal: yet once it was completed and coyly passed around his inner circle, he continually bemoaned and bewailed its inadequacy: 'if you say it's rot,' he wrote Shaw, who had received one of the original bound copies, 'I'll agree with you and cackle with pleasure at finding my judgement doubled.'[14] 'I wish the beastly book had never been written,' he wrote Edward Garnett, almost as though he had had no hand in it.[15] Lawrence's attitude to the publication of *Seven Pillars* is also a perfect showcase of his personality – the personality Liddell Hart described as that of 'a woman wearing a veil while exposing the bosom'. The book was completed in 1922, and Lawrence might well have published it then and simply forgotten about it. Instead, he proceeded to waft it enticingly under the noses of the public for the rest of his life – first releasing eight copies to privileged friends, then, four years later, a limited edition for subscribers and an abridged version with most of the controversial material removed. He continued to rework the text for years, thus ensuring that interest in the book and consequently in himself, the author, was never allowed to subside. This is not the behaviour of someone who genuinely seeks anonymity.

If he had really wished his identity to remain secret, he need not have befriended George Bernard Shaw – one of Britain's most famous writers – nor any of the other powerful souls he corresponded with, including Churchill, Lord Trenchard, Leo Amery – First Lord of the Admiralty – and even the former Prime Minister, Lloyd George. The humble Aircraftman, fresh from his pig-swilling and scrubbing, would inform the hero of his youth, Charles Doughty – with just a soupçon of patronage – that of the current Ministry (of Defence), 'three or four are Fellows of All Souls, and most of the others are friends of mine. The Duke of Devonshire, & Lord Salisbury, & Amery and Wood and three or four others.'[16] What Doughty thought of this is not recorded: he appreciated Lawrence's attempts to help him re-issue his book *Arabia Deserta*, and to obtain a civil-list pension for him, but he returned *Seven Pillars* without comment: this, perhaps, was comment enough. Lawrence also pestered Air Vice-Marshal Sir Oliver Swann, the RAF Chief of Personnel and Training, whom Trenchard had ordered to arrange his enlistment, but who had strongly disapproved of the matter. Since Lawrence was now on the lowest rung of the RAF ladder, it must have given him exquisite delight to address the Air Vice-Marshal as 'Swann', knowing that, lowly as he was, he had the backing of the highest in the land. Although Lawrence claimed to have left 'Colonel Lawrence' behind, the contrast between his two identities 'Lawrence of Arabia – national hero' and 'Aircraftman Class 2 Ross' was an endless source of pleasure and amusement to him. It made a travesty of the social hierarchy – the class snobbery which had marred the lives of his parents – and became a hugely enjoyable game. Just as 'Lawrence of Arabia' had been able to flit from 'Prince of Mecca' to 'British Intelligence Officer', so Ross could now navigate in the course of a day from 'pig-stye keeper' to international diplomat: 'In case I'm wanted by the Colonial Office,' AC2 Ross wrote the glowering Air Vice-Marshal, casually, 'I'll send you a note as often as I change station.'[17] Swann was not amused, and sensed, perhaps, that he was a pawn in Lawrence's private games: 'One would think from the letters, that I was a close correspondent of [his],' he wrote, 'possibly even a friend of his' . . . 'But as a matter of fact . . . I disliked the whole business . . . I discouraged communication with him . . . his eventual discovery at Farnborough was solely due to carelessness at the Colonial Office and Lawrence's unfortunate love of drawing a veil of mystery about himself.'[18]

The end began in November, when Lawrence was moved suddenly from Uxbridge to the RAF School of Photography at Farnborough. At first he was delighted, and wrote to Swann that he had 'almost burned down the camp with joy' when the news of his transfer had arrived. When he reached his new posting, however, his mood quickly changed, for he discovered that the current photography course was already under way and that he would have to wait until January for the next one. He complained to Swann, making it clear that unless he could begin training as a photographer at once, he wished to be posted elsewhere. He confessed that he was glad to get away from Uxbridge because the physical side of the training had been knocking him up, but though Farnborough was by comparison 'a jolly rest cure' it was not the kind of RAF he wanted to write about, and without the photographic training he would simply be bored. For ten days he filled in as orderly in the Adjutant's office, until an order came down from the Air Chief Marshal that AC2 Ross must be put on the current course at once. By this time many of the staff of the School of Photography were aware of Ross's 'secret identity', and the presence of an international celebrity posing rather half-heartedly in their midst as a lowly private naturally disturbed the officers, who suspected that he had been planted as some kind of Air Ministry spy. Lawrence continued to exhibit his self-imposed suffering to the gallery of high society, writing to E. M. Forster, for instance, that he 'hated' the 'dirty living' of the barrack-room, and could not bear to think of the years of poverty which stretched endlessly before him. He confessed that he was physically afraid of his colleagues, hated their noise and 'animal spirits', but insisted – as if begging contradiction – that he was exactly like them, declaring that he would not leave the RAF for any other job. The effect was rather like that of a man locking himself in a filthy prison-cell and crying through the bars that the conditions were terrible, but that this was where he really belonged and that he would do anything rather than come out. It is clear, however, that Lawrence was not as committed to remaining in the ranks as he maintained. Indeed, at Farnborough he started to become openly provocative with his officers – once, when a young subaltern criticized his turn-out, replying to him in Arabic or ancient Greek, making him a laughing, stock in front of the men. While Lawrence later claimed to have been 'sold out' to the press by one of his officers, it is much more likely that he deliberately exposed himself. In fact, he had begun giving away his pseudonym and address quite freely, and had even, in a fit of unadulterated self-destructiveness, written to R. D. Blumenfeld, editor of the *Daily Express*, giving full details of his enlistment and beseeching him not to reveal it to the public. This was asking too much of a professional newspaperman, and Blumenfeld may have realized that Lawrence was flashing a subliminal green light. He probably gave a tip-off to one of his reporters, for on 27 December 1922 the *Express* printed on its front page a story entitled *Uncrowned King as Private Soldier*, revealing Lawrence's 'hiding place' to the world and making it impossible for him to continue in the RAF. In January 1923 – much to his apparent chagrin – he was obliged to leave. By this time, however, his disappointment was genuine, for in the meantime he had become romantically attached to an attractive blond-haired young airman named R. A. M. Guy, whose radiant good looks were likened by one of his colleagues to those of a 'Greek god'. Lawrence himself called Guy 'angelic' but noted snobbishly that his beauty was marred by his 'vile' Brummie accent – as if Greek gods had naturally spoken Oxford English. Just as Lawrence had seen his attachment to the Arab cause partly as an expression of his relationship with the 'noble' Dahoum, so his admiration for the air force as an organization began to grow through his idealization of Guy. He thought Guy embodied all that was best in its ranks, and was soon waxing enthusiastic about the infinite superiority of the young men in the RAF to those in the army. Though his relationship with Guy was probably as platonic as his association with Dahoum, they were becoming emotionally intimate when they were forced to split up: 'You and me, we're very un-matched,' Lawrence wrote to Guy later, 'and it took some process as slow and kindly and persistent as the barrack-room communism to weld us comfortably together. People aren't friends till they have said all they can say, and are able to sit together, at work or rest, hour-long without speaking . . . We never got quite to that, but we were nearer it daily . . . and since S.A. died I haven't experienced any risk of that happening.'[19]

Lawrence appealed for reinstatement to Trenchard and Minister of Air Sam Hoare, but his credit had expired. His status-games were fun for him, but detrimental to the good order of the RAF, and Trenchard would reconsider only if he agreed to take a commission, which for

Lawrence would have spoiled the effect completely. By February, however, he had succeeded in pulling strings at the War Office, and with the help of Alan Dawnay, his wartime colleague from Hedgehog, and General Sir Philip Chetwode, who had commanded the Desert Column in Palestine, managed to enlist again, this time as a private in the Royal Tank Corps. In March, Lawrence signed on in the army for seven years at Bovington Camp, Dorset, under yet another pseudonym: T. E. Shaw. This time, however, he did not enter the ranks alone, for when he walked into the guard-room at Bovington he was escorted by a tall, tough-looking young Scotsman named John Bruce, who had joined the army with him to act as his personal minder.

Lawrence had met Bruce in London in 1922, while still working for the Colonial Office, at the Mayfair flat of a man called Edward Murray, who was considering the eighteen-year-old Scotsman for a job. On their second meeting, Lawrence told Bruce who he was, and informed him that he was looking for someone who was young, strong and alert, who could be trusted with highly confidential personal matters. Bruce thought him a crank, and protested that he was not qualified, but he was desperately in need of a job, and Lawrence offered him a generous salary of £3 a month as a retainer. On subsequent meetings Lawrence swore Bruce to the utmost confidence, and began to unfold a long and complicated fantasy, claiming to be in the power of a relative he referred to as the 'Old Man'. The story went that he was in debt and, under pressure from his bank, had decided to write a book, hoping that it would make enough money to allow him to pay off his debt and retire to the country. He had applied to a merchant bank for the money to live on while the book was being written, and the bank had asked for the copyright of the book, and requested a guarantor. He said that when his father had died in 1919, the Old Man had inherited his money, and Lawrence had asked him to act as his guarantor. At first he had agreed, but when he discovered that Lawrence had quit his job with the Colonial Office, he had changed his mind, called Lawrence a 'bastard' and accused him of a plethora of sins, including insulting King George at Buckingham Palace, ruining the career of Lord Curzon, turning his back on God, and dragging the family name through the gutter. The Old Man, said Lawrence, had agreed to take over his financial affairs and handle his debts, but only on the understanding that all 'disciplinary matters' were to be placed in his hands: if he did not agree the Old Man would expose the circumstances of his birth. His life was to be strictly curtailed: he was to enlist in the army or the RAF as a private, and spend his time either writing or soldiering. The only friends he was to be allowed in the 'upper bracket' were people connected with his writing. Lawrence told Bruce that he had sworn on the Bible to respect the Old Man's every wish, and mentioned that corporal punishment might be involved.[20] Bruce was suspicious, not because he disbelieved the story, but because he and Lawrence were poles apart socially and he wondered why Lawrence had chosen him for this particular job. Lawrence explained that most of his 'friends' couldn't be trusted, and the few who could were 'too big'. They would be willing to help only for personal gain: 'you don't know what is to be gained,' Lawrence told him, 'and wouldn't be disappointed if you gained nothing.'[21] He sent Bruce back to Aberdeen, telling him that he would be called for when needed.

While Lawrence was at Uxbridge and Farnborough, he corresponded with Bruce occasionally, telling him how much he loathed the RAF, but hinting that the Old Man thought the life too soft: he had no right to be there at all, he wrote, since the Old Man had arranged for him to join the army. In November Lawrence asked Bruce to come to Farnborough, and when they met informed him that 'a birch had arrived' and that the Old Man wanted him to 'take a few over the buttocks' as a penalty for having 'cheated him' in joining the RAF instead of the army. Before the 'punishment' could be carried out, however, Lawrence was exposed by the press in his guise of 'Ross' and obliged to leave. He told Bruce that the Old Man had paid an officer at Farnborough £30 to give the story to the *Express*. Bruce temporarily lost touch with him, but in January 1923 he moved to London and managed to get a job as a bouncer in a Paddington nightclub, leaving a message for Lawrence at his borrowed Barton Street flat. A few days later Lawrence came to see him, looking dirty, ragged, sick and exhausted, telling him he had been sleeping rough for several nights (in fact he had been sleeping in the sidecar of the motorcycle he had acquired while in the RAF). Lawrence told Bruce that the Old Man was now forcing him to join the Royal Tank Corps. According to Bruce, he then volunteered to join the army with Lawrence.

*

It seems likely that someone in the military authorities knew of the association between Lawrence and Bruce, for Bruce recounted that his recruitment in Aberdeen had been pre-arranged. Lawrence told him that his offer had pleased the Old Man, who would be writing to him directly once they had enlisted. At Bovington they were given consecutive serial numbers, and adjoining beds in the same hut. They were issued with ill-fitting uniforms, and assigned to a squad of twenty-two recruits, for the duration of their sixteen weeks' training: 'we had everyone in the hut sized up,' Bruce wrote. 'It was the bad ones I had to keep my eyes on, especially the drinkers, who were continually touching Lawrence for money . . . I came into the hut and heard a fellow giving Lawrence a mouthful of filth because he refused to give him a pound. I jumped him there and then and one hell of a fight took place . . .'[22] Shortly afterwards, Lawrence rented Clouds Hill, a cottage which stood close to the camp, as a refuge from the almost intolerable life of the barrack-room, and it was here, in 1923, that Bruce gave Lawrence a birching for the first time. The beating was arranged with the precision of a ritual. First, Lawrence told Bruce that the Old Man had decided he must be punished, and had sentenced him to twelve strokes of the birch. He then handed Bruce a typed letter, purporting to be from the Old Man, which informed him that he was to pick up a birch from the local railway-station and administer the punishment, afterwards reporting to him in writing that he had done so, and describing how Lawrence had conducted himself throughout the beating. At first, Bruce declared that he would have nothing to do with it, but Lawrence insisted that it had to be done. Since Lawrence seemed to be willing, Bruce finally agreed, and carried out the 'sentence' the same afternoon. However, since Lawrence kept his trousers on during the birching – which consisted of twelve strokes to the buttocks – the Old Man was not appeased, and the thrashing had to be repeated later, on Lawrence's bare behind: 'After I had given him the twelve, he said: "Give me another one for luck," ' Bruce remembered. 'It is nasty. The prongs go into the skin and break the blood vessels and it bleeds. He just lay there and gritted his teeth. He never moved.'[23] Whether this was the first such birching Lawrence had ever received is open to question. Curiously, Bruce stated that he saw 'no other scars', though W. E. Johns claimed to have seen 'a mass of recent scars' on Lawrence's back at the recruiting office less than a year earlier. Bruce also said that he was not the only man to have beaten Lawrence in this manner – indeed, some time later he discovered birch-marks on Lawrence's legs while they were working out in a gymnasium in Bournemouth, and Lawrence told him they had been inflicted by 'an employee of the Old Man'.[24] Between 1923 and 1935, Bruce birched Lawrence on nine occasions, at Clouds Hill, at Barton Street, at his home in Aberdeen and at other places in Scotland, and on at least one occasion another witness was present. Moreover, Philip Knightley and Colin Simpson, the *Sunday Times* reporters to whom Bruce told his story, revealed in their 1968 article that they knew of two other men who had been employed to thrash Lawrence, though whether before, after, or concurrently with Bruce is unknown. If Johns did see 'recent' scars on Lawrence's back in 1922, then it may be that Lawrence's flagellation disorder had begun before he met Bruce earlier that year. However, it is likely that Johns's statement was spurious: Bruce's beatings were always administered to the buttocks rather than the back, suggesting a sexual element which some biographers have tried to suppress, and which was confirmed by Bruce's admission that Lawrence sometimes experienced orgasm as a result of the floggings. The attempt of some biographers to 'sanctify' Lawrence's masochism by suggesting that he tried to emulate the practices of medieval saints also falls down on this point – for medieval flagellants were invariably whipped on the back rather than the buttocks.

Some have maintained that this disorder was created by Lawrence's experience at Dara'a. However, while we have no corroborating evidence that Lawrence was captured and beaten by the Turks in 1917, we do know for certain that he was beaten severely on the buttocks by Sarah as a child, and that he showed distinct masochistic tendencies as a youth. The flagellation disorder, indeed, was the culmination of a life which was dominated by masochistic and self-degrading fantasies both social and physical, and its foundations lie not in Dara'a – whatever did or did not happen there – but in Lawrence's relationship with his mother during his earliest years. Dara'a – fantasy or reality – is simply one expression of a process which may be traced directly from Polstead Road in the 1890s to Clouds Hill in 1923. What is interesting about the Bruce story, however, is the light it sheds on some other aspects of Lawrence's character. The edifice of fantasy he told Bruce was a calculated lie from beginning to end, yet he unfolded it in astonishing and consistent detail. He invented the 'Old Man' and had him 'corresponding' with Bruce, sending him dozens of letters which he had actually written himself. Bruce liked and admired Lawrence and was proud to have been able to help him. Even after Lawrence's death the Scotsman refused to believe that he had ever told him a deliberate lie, and remained convinced, fifty years later, that the Old Man had actually existed. He was perhaps naïve and inexperienced, bemused by Lawrence's rhetoric and dazzled by his intellect, but he was not stupid. It is a superlative comment on Lawrence's powers of invention, manipulation and persuasion that he was able to convince another human being of the actual existence of a character he had simply made up, and maintain the fantasy over a period of thirteen years without once giving himself away. Of his 'Old Man' story, Arnie wrote to John Mack: 'From my slight experience of psychological warfare (of which T.E. had plenty) an elaborate fiction is more plausible the nearer it comes to fact, although the fact is unknowable to the audience; hence he [Lawrence] gives his lies a garbled foundation of fact . . .'[25] It does not seem to have occurred either to Arnie or to his correspondent Mack that Lawrence may have told lies based on garbled fact at other times in his life too – for instance when describing the alleged Dara'a incident. Neither did it occur to Arnie that in this case Lawrence was not fighting the Turks, but taking in a good-natured and trusting young man, who believed him to be honest and devoted a major part of his life to helping him. Though, throughout these years, Lawrence had conspicuous, high-profile 'friendships' with famous men such as Thomas Hardy, Bernard Shaw, E. M. Forster, Robert Graves and many others, it was John Bruce, an uneducated young Scotsman, with whom he felt truly 'safe'. Bruce remained close to Lawrence for the rest of his life, but after his death was sneered at by Arnie and Bob, and treated as if it was he who had victimized Lawrence. Even Charlotte Shaw joined in the conspiracy and tried to silence him: 'they were prepared to go to any lengths,' Bruce wrote, 'to see that the reason for our association did not become public property . . . They were so impressed with their own importance, that they thought I was going to be an easy nut to crack . . . Had they been successful then this story would never have been told.'[26]

Bruce was unhappy in the army and soon left, though he and Lawrence were to meet at intervals thereafter. Lawrence himself could not settle down in the Tanks, and pined for the RAF. He wrote letters to Trenchard and Hoare whose tone became increasingly strident, until he began to mention suicide. Once, while a guest at Trenchard's house during his time in the Tank Corps, he threatened to 'end it all' there and then, upon which Trenchard smiled and asked him if he wouldn't mind doing it in the garden as he did not want his carpets ruined. On another occasion at Clouds Hill, Bruce had to jerk a pistol out of Lawrence's hand by banging it repeatedly against the wall, when he declared his intention to shoot himself. Afterwards, Bruce recalled, Lawrence burst into tears. His discontent was not with the army, but with himself, and his need always to 'seek his pleasures downwards'. Nevertheless, he had his sights set on the RAF again, and in June 1925 he wrote to Edward Garnett: 'I'm no bloody good on earth. So I'm going to quit: but in my usual comic fashion . . . I will bequeath you my notes on life in the recruits' camp of the RAF. They will disappoint you.'[27] Garnett was alarmed and wrote to Bernard Shaw, who sent on the letter to the Prime Minister, Stanley Baldwin, with his card, suggesting that Lawrence's suicide would create a scandal, especially since Lowell Thomas's book *With Lawrence in Arabia* had just appeared to popular acclaim. He was supported by John Buchan, whom Lawrence had once buttonholed in the street and asked for help. Baldwin intervened personally, and in early July Trenchard sent for Lawrence and informed him that he was to be transferred back to the RAF.

Lawrence felt that he now had all that he had ever wanted. He knuckled down to becoming 'ordinary' and stuck it out more or less faithfully for the next ten years. He was posted to the RAF Cadet College at Cranwell in Lincolnshire – one of the most comfortable postings available – and continued to work on *Seven Pillars* and *Revolt in the Desert* and continuously revised his notes on the life of a recruit in the RAF which would eventually be published as *The Mint*. In 1926, he was transferred to Karachi in India at his own request, to avoid the publicity which would accompany the appearance of *Revolt in the Desert* and the subscribers' edition of *Seven Pillars*. Although the books were a financial success, Lawrence had by now decided that he should not profit from the Arab Revolt, and donated the money to the RAF Memorial Fund. In November 1927 he was posted to a small hill station at Miranshah, near the border with Afghanistan. Unfortunately, however, there was a rebellion in Afghanistan during 1927–8, and a British newspaper, the *Empire News*, implicated him, stating that he was operating as British pro-consul in Afghanistan disguised as a holy man. The article was reprinted in India, and led to disturbances in which a genuine holy man was beaten almost to death under suspicion of being Lawrence. The situation had become embarrassing for the British government, and on 8 January 1929 he was flown back to Karachi and a few days later put aboard the S.S. *Rajputana*, bound for Plymouth. Lawrence's homecoming from India was a matter of public knowledge: he was hounded by reporters from the moment he arrived back in Britain, and the fact that 'Lawrence of Arabia' was serving in the RAF remained well known for the rest of his service. Lawrence was aware that any further sensations in the press would be likely to scupper his career in the ranks for ever, and for a time made an attempt to lie low. Like many public personalities of the twentieth century, he detested the press only when he could not control it – as a gifted propagandist he had been aware of its power from an early age, and in 1911 had been quite happy to use *The Times* to manipulate public opinion, and incidentally to get himself a good job. In the immediate post-war period he had fought an energetic campaign in the newspapers to gain support for his views on the Middle East question. Following the débâcle in India, though, he began to see it as the double-edged blade it really was.

Lawrence's last six years in the RAF were in many ways the most contented period of his life. He was now middle-aged, and had grown thick-set: there was no longer any trace of 'girlishness' about him. He continued to veer between elation and depression, continued to commute between the barrack-room and his rich, powerful and famous friends, continued to seek anonymity and yet make certain he was clearly seen hiding. In his more balanced moods, he felt that he had come to terms with the world: 'I measure myself against the fellows I meet and work with,' he wrote, 'and find myself ordinary company, but bright and sensible. Almost, I would say, popular!'[28] He had, at least in part, found a sense of community, a sense of belonging among 'ordinary mortals'. He no longer felt out of his depth with other men. He told an American correspondent that there were no real heroes in the world, and that instead of distinctions between human beings, he was coming to see only similarities. The man who had always been

373

ashamed of his appearance now admitted that the difference between a 'very big man' and a 'very small man' was only a matter of a few inches, and this difference only appeared important to human beings.

He was posted first to RAF Cattewater on Plymouth Sound, where he developed a genuine friendship with his commanding officer, Wing Commander Sydney Smith, and his wife Clare. Later, after witnessing the crash of an Iris flying-boat in which nine air-crew were killed, he threw himself enthusiastically into a programme of improving fast rescue-boats. He found that he had a special talent for mechanics, which was complemented by his passion for speed – a passion pursued avidly at sea in his private motor-launch *Biscuit*, and on land on his 1000cc Brough Superior motorcycle, Boanerges. Over the years, Lawrence got through seven Brough motorcycles, which were among the most powerful machines of their day. Speed became one of the few luxuries he indulged in to excess, and only at speed did he seem to recapture that intense feeling of connection with the cosmos which he had felt during the war: 'When I open out . . . at 80 or so,' he told Robert Graves, 'I feel the earth moulding herself under me . . . Almost the earth comes alive, heaving and tossing on each side like a sea . . . It is the reward of speed . . . I could write you pages and pages on the lustfulness of moving swiftly.'[29] At speed, the body – the part of himself which he had always despised and tried to subdue – was transcended: 'In speed we hurl ourselves beyond the body,' he wrote, in one of his few attempts at verse. 'Our bodies cannot scale the heavens except in a fume of petrol . . . Bones. Blood. Flesh. All pressed inward together.'[30]

He continued to meet Bruce on occasions, and entertained former colleagues from the RAF and the Tank Corps for musical weekends at Clouds Hill. He wrote scores of letters to artists, writers, composers and former colleagues. He made new friends among the powerful, including the local MP for Plymouth, Nancy Astor, and the Labour MP for Shoreditch, Ernest Thurtle. He became a sort of surrogate son to Bernard Shaw and kept up a lively literary dialogue in hundreds of letters to his wife Charlotte. He undertook reviews and introductions. He started work on a translation of the *Odyssey* from ancient Greek for an American publisher, insisted on publishing it anonymously in Britain, revealed to the literary establishment that he was working on it, and threatened to stop work when the fact was inevitably leaked to the press. Although he occasionally had ideas for books, there was nothing new after *The Mint*, which Trenchard felt was damaging to the RAF and had asked him not to publish until after his death. He authorized two biographies of himself, by Robert Graves and Basil Liddell Hart, vetted virtually every word, asked both to publish notes declaring he had had nothing to do with the books, and then complained to acquaintances that the authors had availed themselves of too much 'artistic licence'. He criticized Hart, his sincere admirer, in particular, for having succumbed to his charm and failed to take an objective view, and disdained his biography as 'Panegyric III'. He also began to realize that while he had thought of himself as a writer, he actually lacked the creative urge: he had all the tricks of writing, he knew, but he had nothing further to say. Occasionally this knowledge led him to fits of melancholy and despair: 'Life isn't very gay, I fancy,' he wrote, 'and I shouldn't like to feel that I'd brought anyone into the world to have such times as I've had and still have . . . I have found nothing to justify my staying on, and yet one can't go – it's a sad state.'[31] The RAF station had now become his world and at times his prison: he felt afraid and hesitant when outside it. He told a new friend, writer Henry Williamson, that he felt like a clock whose spring had run down. He knew, ultimately, that he was a misfit who had found his proper niche only in the extraordinary circumstances of the Arab Revolt. He had been the perfect man in the right place at the right time, had won the war in the desert, had restored a kind of freedom to the Arabs after 500 years, had written a wonderful book about that experience which nobody would ever forget, and had become the most famous man of his era. He was a phenomenon, but unlike the artists, writers and poets he envied so much, his was a one-time accomplishment which could never be repeated or improved: 'You have a lifetime of achievement,' he wrote to Sir Edward Elgar, sadly, in 1932, 'but I was a flash in the pan.'[32]

Lawrence left the RAF on 25 February 1935, and drove his Brough from his last posting at Bridlington in Lincolnshire to Clouds Hill: 'My losing the RAF numbs me,' he wrote, 'so I haven't much feeling to spare for a while. In fact I find myself wishing all the time that my own curtain would fall. It seems as if I had finished now.'[33] However, the press had got wind of his retirement and hounded him for the next month, making his life a misery until he came to an arrangement with various newspaper proprietors, and the reporters began to drift away.

By April he was alone, and he began to settle in and plan a motorcycle journey around Britain for the summer. He considered writing a biography of the Irish patriot Sir Roger Casement, and began inviting friends to the cottage. Nancy Astor wrote to him, hinting that there might be a possibility of government work – even reorganizing British defence forces. He wrote back that wild horses would not drag him away from Clouds Hill: his will was gone, he told her: 'there is something broken in the works.'[34]

On 11 May 1935, Lawrence kick-started his motorcycle, Boanerges, and set off to Bovington village, about a mile and a half from Clouds Hill, to send a parcel of books and to dispatch a telegram to Henry Williamson inviting him to lunch the following Tuesday. This was to be Lawrence of Arabia's last ride. At about 11.20 he drove back to his cottage. The road between Bovington and Clouds Hill was straight, but marked by a series of three dips, and concealed behind one of them were two boy cyclists, Frank Fletcher and Bertie Hargreaves, who were pedalling in the same direction. Lawrence changed down twice to take the dips, and Pat Knowles, his friend and neighbour, who was working in his garden opposite Clouds Hill, heard the crisp changes of gear. Precisely what happened in the next moments is, like so much of Lawrence's life, a mystery. The boys claimed to have heard the motorcycle coming and moved into single file. Corporal Ernest Catchpole, of the Royal Army Ordnance Corps, who was walking his dog in the waste land to the west of the road, later told the inquest that Lawrence passed a black car coming in the opposite direction, though the boys stated there was no car, and no such vehicle was ever traced. It seems unlikely that Lawrence was travelling at more than forty miles an hour, for Knowles heard the gear changes clearly, and the motorcycle was later found to be stuck in second gear, in which its top speed was thirty-eight miles an hour. Whether his concentration momentarily deserted him, or whether the boys were actually riding abreast, will never be known for certain: what seems to have happened is that Lawrence clipped Bertie Hargreaves's back wheel, knocking the boy off his bicycle, and swerving to avoid further damage was thrown over the handlebars of his motorcycle and pitched head first on to the road five yards away. The motorcycle twisted and turned and finally lay still. It was over in seconds. Lawrence lay in the road quivering, with his head a mass of blood. Shortly, Corporal Catchpole ran up and tried to wipe away the blood with a handkerchief. At this moment an army lorry came along, and Catchpole stopped it. Lawrence's body was placed on a stretcher and taken to Wool Hospital. He had suffered severe brain damage, and never recovered consciousness. At last, the rider had hurled himself beyond the body, beyond the point of no return. Six days later, on 19 May, he was dead.

I visited Lawrence's grave in a corner of Moreton cemetery, marked by a stone bearing the same Latin inscription which decorated the façade of his school: *Dominus Illumunatio Mea* – an affirmation of the God in which he had long ago ceased to believe. A more impressive monument, however, lies in St Martin's Church at Wareham – the medieval hall which Lawrence had always dreamed of acquiring, but in life never did. St Martin's – one of the oldest Anglo-Saxon churches in Dorset – has precisely the naked simplicity that Lawrence loved. When I visited the church on a warm day at the end of all my travels, sunlight was spilling in a cascade of dapples and brindles through the great window, falling on the crusader's effigy of Lawrence in Arab dress, carved by his friend Eric Kennington. As I gazed at his serene face, rendered in stone for posterity, I realized that I had in some measure answered the question that I had asked myself on that day at the spring in Wadi Rum. I had discovered that Lawrence, like each one of us, was unique. His unique blend of qualities was exactly that required at a certain moment in history to save the Arab Revolt from oblivion and bring it to success. Lawrence was not a hero of the dragonslayer order – superhumanly strong in body and spirit, unfailingly courageous, immaculately honourable, perfectly truthful – the white knight that Sarah Lawrence tried to create. Such beings, as Lawrence himself knew, exist only in the imagination. On the contrary, he was a man whose physical weakness, bizarre sexuality, unimpressive appearance and abnormal fear of pain led him to develop an extraordinary capacity for determination, courage, compassion and sympathy. He was no authoritarian, but a man whose sensitivity lent him the ability to empathize with men – and women – of all classes, races and creeds; whose inner lack of strong identity allowed him to be anything and anyone he felt others needed him to be. Lawrence was not an imaginary hero, but a real man with a real blend of strengths and weaknesses: a leader, a strategist, a motivator, a thinker, a doer, a

377

romancer, an elaborator, a manipulator of myth. Millions of words have been written in tribute to him, but to me those which serve as his most fitting epitaph are the ones he himself wrote to a friend some years before his death: 'I am human. There ain't no such supercreatures as you would fain see. Or if there are I haven't met one [yet].'[35]

ACKNOWLEDGEMENTS

I am especially grateful for the advice and suggestions of John Lockman alias Jon Loken of the USA and Marten Schild of Holland – two contemporary Lawrence scholars who have managed in their different ways to examine the Lawrence myth in an original and relatively unprejudiced light.

I much appreciate the assistance of the Trustees of the T. E. Lawrence Estate for permission to see the embargoed material in the Bodleian Library, Oxford. I am grateful for the help of Jack Flavell and the staff of the Bodleian Library, and that of the staff of the British Library, Manuscripts Reading Room, the Imperial War Museum, of John Fisher and the staff of the Public Record Office, Kew, the National Library of Scotland, the Liddell Hart Centre for Military Archives, King's College, London.

I am also most grateful to the following previous biographers of Lawrence: Jeremy Wilson, Malcolm Brown, Lawrence James, Suleiman Mousa and John Mack. I much appreciate the assistance of Colin Wallace, and of Richard Belfield of Fulcrum Productions Ltd and his staff, Charles Furneaux of Channel 4, and the help and suggestions of Stephen White, Gerry Pinches and the rest of the film team which accompanied my journeys to Mudowwara and in Sinai. I would also very much like to thank Bertram Zank of Edinburgh, Sheikh Zaki M. Farsi of Jeddah, Tony Howard and Diane Taylor, Sabah Mohammad, Mifleh, Dakhillalah, Salem 'Iid and the late Salem Abu Auda and their families of the Wadi Rum, Jibrin and Mohammad Hababeh of Aqaba, 'Iid Swaylim of Nuwayba', Sinai, and his family, Ronan and Leslie O'Donnell, my agent Anthony Goff of David Higham Associates, and Eleo Gordon and Lucy Capon of Penguin Books. I would like to express a special thanks to Dr Basil Hatim of the School of Arabic Translation and Interpreting, Heriot-Watt University, Edinburgh, for his help in authenticating Lawrence's letter in Arabic.

I would also like to thank my parents-in-law, General and Prof. Peru, for the use of their houses in Sardinia, and lastly my wife, Mariantonietta, and my son, Burton, without whom this book would not have been possible.

MICHAEL ASHER
Frazione Agnata, Sardinia, and Nairobi, Kenya

NOTES ON THE TEXT

Key

Brown Letters	*The Letters of T. E. Lawrence*, ed. Malcolm Brown, Oxford, 1991
Garnett Letters	*The Letters of T. E. Lawrence*, ed. David Garnett, London, 1938
HL	*The Home Letters of T. E. Lawrence and His Brothers*, ed. M. R. Lawrence, Oxford, 1954
MS. Res.	Reserve Manuscripts Collection: Bodleian Library, Oxford
SPW, Oxford text	*The Seven Pillars of Wisdom*, Oxford text (limited edn), London, 1926
SPW, 1935	T. E. Lawrence, *The Seven Pillars of Wisdom*, London, 1935
LH	*T. E. Lawrence to His Biographer Liddell Hart*, London, 1938
RG	*T. E. Lawrence to His Biographer Robert Graves*, London, 1938
Friends	A. W. Lawrence (ed.), *T. E. Lawrence by His Friends*, London, 1938
Leeds Letters	T. E. Lawrence, *Letters to E.T. Leeds*, ed. J. Wilson, London, 1988
Wilson	Jeremy Wilson, *Lawrence of Arabia. The Authorised Biography of T. E. Lawrence*, London, 1989
Mack, *Prince*	John Mack: *A Prince of Our Disorder – the Life of T. E. Lawrence*, London, 1976

Introduction: The Valley of the Moon

1. *SPW*, 1935, p. 363.

1. *Apparent Queen Unveiled Her Peerless Light*

1. Celandine Kennington, MS. Res., c. 228.
2. François Bedarida, *A Social History of England*, London, 1979, p. 162.
3. *RG*.
4. John Betjeman, *Victorian and Edwardian Oxford*, Oxford, 1971.
5. Celandine Kennington, MS. Res., c. 228.
6. ibid.
7. ibid.
8. ibid.
9. Mack, *Prince*.
10. Celandine Kennington, MS. Res., c. 228.
11. *Brown Letters*, p. 325.
12. ibid., p. 326.
13. Mack, *Prince*, p. 7.
14. MS. Res., c. 228.
15. Proverbs 13:12.
16. Marten Schild, '*The Immaculate Hero and His Imperfect Shadow*', unpublished MS: I am most grateful to Marten Schild for the inspiration of several of the ideas on this page.
17. MS. Res., c. 228.
18. British Library, Add. MSS. 45903, Charlotte Shaw Letters.
19. ibid.
20. Mack, *Prince*.
21. MS. Res., c. 228.
22. British Library, Add. MSS. 45903, Charlotte Shaw Letters.
23. *SPW*, 1935, p. 446.
24. See Arnie Lawrence in a letter to Miss Early, 17 December 1963. 'TE had a more than customary fear of pain . . . nor was he a natural hero or naturally brave.' MS. Res., b. 56.
25. *Friends*, p. 37.
26. ibid.
27. British Library, Add. MSS. 45903, Charlotte Shaw Letters.
28. *Friends*, p. 31.
29. Sir Harold Nicolson, MS. Res., 55/2.
30. *SPW*, Oxford text, 1926, p. 262.
31. MS. Res., 55/2.
32. *SPW*, 1935, p. 584.

2. Dominus Illuminatio Mea

1. Jan Morris, *Oxford*, Oxford, 1978, p. 30.
2. *SPW*, Oxford text, 1926.
3. *LH*, p. 79.
4. T. E. Lawrence, *The Mint*, London (1936), 1973, p. 175.
5. *Friends*, p. 314.
6. Bedarida, *Social History of England*, p. 72.
7. *HL*, p. 35.
8. *Garnett Letters*, p. 78.
9. *LH*.
10. *Friends*, p. 591.
11. Lawrence James, *The Golden Warrior: The Life and Legend of Lawrence of Arabia*, London, 1995.
12. MS. Res., b. 56.
13. *RG*.
14. *Clare Sydney Smith, The Golden Reign. The Story of My Friendship with Lawrence of Arabia*, London, 1940, p. 8.
15. ibid., p. 37.
16. *Friends*, p. 53.
17. *SPW*, 1935, p. 57.
18. Mack, *Prince*, p. 21.
19. MS. Res., 55/2.
20. *Friends*, p. 62.
21. *Friends*, p. 31.
22. A. W. Lawrence, letter to Jim Ede, 1937.
23. *Brown Letters*, p. 305.

3. Nothing Which Qualified Him to be an Ordinary Member of Society

1. *SPW*, 1935, p. 581.
2. *Brown Letters*, p. 67.
3. ibid., p. 45.
4. *HL*, p. 198.
5. Suleiman Mousa, *T. E. Lawrence: An Arab View*, London, 1966, p. 78.
6. *SPW*, 1935, p. 569.
7. Ronald Storrs, *Daily Telegraph*, in MS. Res. 55/2.
8. *Garnett Letters*, p. 553.
9. ibid.
10. *Friends*, p. 246.

11. Harold Orlans (ed.), *Lawrence of Arabia – the Literary Criticism and Correspondence of T. E. Lawrence*, London, 1993, pp. 29–30.
12. *HL*, p. 18.
13. Lawrence, *The Mint*, p. 102.
14. *HL*, p. 31.
15. Orlans, *Lawrence of Arabia*, p. 32.
16. *HL*, p. 24.
17. ibid., p. 52.
18. Wilson, *Authorised*, p. 143.
19. ibid.
20. Vyvyan Richards, *Portrait of T. E. Lawrence, The Lawrence of the Seven Pillars of Wisdom*, London, 1936, p. 21.
21. ibid.
22. *SPW*, 1935, p. 547.
23. *Brown Letters*, p. 36.
24. ibid., p. 33.
25. *Friends*, p. 588.
26. *Brown Letters*, p. 29.
27. Richards, *A Portrait of T. E. Lawrence*.
28. Orlans, *Lawrence of Arabia*, p. 239.
29. Richards, *A Portrait of T. E. Lawrence*, p. 45.
30. *Friends*, p. 48.
31. *HL*, p. 61.

4. *The Sultan Drank Tea as Usual*

1. *HL*, p. 62.
2. Randall Baker, *King Hussain and the Kingdom of the Hejaz*, Cambridge, 1979, p. 10.

5. *A Rather Remarkable Young Man*

1. *Friends*, p. 55.
2. *HL*, p. 81.
3. ibid.
4. *SPW*, 1935, p. 36.
5. *Brown Letters*, p. 325.
6. ibid., p. 305.
7. Lawrence, *The Mint*.
8. Mack, *Prince*, p. 69.
9. George Lloyd, *Blackwood's Magazine*.

10. Wilson, *Authorised*, p. 53.
11. *RG*, p. 67.
12. *HL*, p. 31.
13. Philip Knightley and Colin Simpson, *The Secret Lives of Lawrence of Arabia*, London, 1969, p. 20.
14. *Brown Letters*, p. 359.
15. ibid., p. 531.
16. *Garnett Letters*, p. 62.
17. *HL*, p. 98.
18. *Garnett Letters*, p. 63.
19. *HL*, p. 74.
20. ibid.
21. ibid., p. 97.
22. ibid.
23. ibid., p. 103.
24. ibid.
25. ibid., p. 104.
26. T. E. Lawrence, *Crusader Castles*, London, 1936, p. 95.
27. *HL*, p. 106.
28. ibid.
29. *Friends*, p. 77.
30. ibid.
31. *Leeds Letters*, p. 8.

6. Mr Hogarth is Going Digging

1. Mack, *Prince*, p. 66.
2. After the war, Lawrence gave a sum of money to Janet Laurie – this was part of Will's inheritance from his father, which Lawrence received after Will's death. This money would have come to Janet had she married Will, that is, if he had not been killed in the war, so Lawrence considered it rightfully hers. This gift was a sign of generosity and a sense of duty, but not evidence of personal attraction.
3. *Brown Letters*, p. 117.
4. *HL*, p. 208.
5. *Leeds Letters*, p. 10.
6. Lawrence, *The Mint*, p. 82.
7. *Leeds Letters*, p. 25.
8. ibid., p. 13.
9. *HL*, p. 144.
10. *Friends*, p. 115.

11. ibid.
12. *HL*, p. 141.
13. *Friends*, p. 87.
14. *HL*, p. 169.
15. ibid., p. 170.
16. ibid., p. 115.
17. ibid., p. 170.
18. *Friends*, p. 92. Neither Woolley nor Lawrence ever confirmed that Dahoum's name was Salim Ahmad. This idea came from Tom Beaumont, who served with Lawrence as a machine-gunner in the Syrian campaign and whose testimony is dubious. However, whether or not Dahoum was actually called Salim Ahmad or Sheikh Ahmad he seems to be the best candidate for the subject of 'To SA' – Lawrence frequently changed names when it suited him.
19. C. Leonard Woolley, *Dead Towns and Living Men, being Pages from an Antiquary's Notebook*, London, 1932, pp. 24–5, 18.
20. *HL*, p. 114.
21. ibid., p. 172.
22. *Brown Letters*, p. 40.
23. ibid.
24. *SPW*, 1935, p. 354.
25. ibid.
26. *Friends*, p. 92.
27. *HL*, p. 161.
28. ibid., p. 162.
29. ibid., p. 161.
30. Bell, Lady, *The Letters of Gertrude Bell*, London, 1927.
31. T. E. Lawrence, *1911 Diary*, London, 1939, p. 31.
32. *HL*, p. 161.

7. *The Baron in the Feudal System*

1. *HL*, p. 181.
2. *LH*, p. 54.
3. *HL*, p. 190.
4. ibid., p. 195.
5. Woolley, *Dead Towns*, p. 152.
6. ibid., p. 156.
7. ibid.
8. *Leeds Letters*, p. 137.
9. *Garnett Letters*, p. 161.

10. *Friends*, p. 91.
11. *Leeds Letters*, p. 137.
12. *HL*, p. 218.
13. Woolley, *Dead Towns*, p. 171.
14. *Leeds Lottery*, p. 43.
15. Woolley, *Dead Towns*, p. 172.
16. ibid., p. 129.
17. *HL*, p. 125.
18. ibid., p. 229.
19. ibid.
20. ibid., p. 232.

8. Peace in Mesopotamia Such as Has Not Been Seen for Generations

1. *Garnett Letters*, p. 152.
2. *Brown Letters*, p. 51.
3. ibid.
4. *RG*, p. 67.
5. *Leeds Letters*, p. 76.
6. *HL*, p. 442.
7. ibid., p. 443.
8. *Garnett Letters*, p. 155.
9. *SPW*, 1935, p. 96.
10. *Friends*, p. 96.
11. ibid., p. 80.
12. *Garnett Letters*, p. 161.

9. The Insurance People Have Nailed Me Down

1. *Friends*, p. 105.
2. *HL*, p. 285.
3. *Garnett Letters*, p. 167.
4. *Leeds Letters*, p. 99.
5. *Garnett Letters*, p. 161.
6. *Leeds Letters*, pp. 102–3.
7. *Garnett Letters*, p. 185.
8. ibid., pp. 185–6.
9. ibid. p. 187.
10. *RG*, p. 81.
11. Richard Aldington, *Lawrence of Arabia: A Biographical Enquiry*, 1955, p. 124.

12. Baker, *King Hussain and the Kingdom of the Hejaz*, p. 43.
13. ibid.

10. Cairo is Unutterable Things

1. Mack, *Prince*, p. 132.
2. *Friends*, p. 160.
3. *HL*, p. 305.
4. *Friends*, p. 138.
5. *Brown Letters*, p. 72.
6. John Buchan, *Greenmantle*, p. 24.
7. *HL*, p. 302.
8. *Brown Letters*, p. 72.
9. *SPW*, 1935, p. 56.
10. Ronald Storrs, *Orientations*, London, 1944, p. 224.
11. ibid., p. 219.
12. *Garnett Letters*, p. 196.
13. George Antonius, *The Arab Awakening*, London, 1938, p. 158.
14. *Garnett Letters*, p. 196.
15. ibid., p. 197.
16. ibid.
17. James Morris, *Farewell the Trumpets: An Imperial Retreat*, London, 1978, p. 191.
18. *Garnett Letters*, p. 199.
19. *Brown Letters*, p. 72.
20. Lawrence, *The Mint*, p. 35.
21. MS. Res., 55/2.
22. James, *The Golden Warrior*, p. 198.
23. *Garnett Letters*, p. 198.
24. ibid., p. 197.
25. Elie Kedourie, *In the Anglo-Arabian Labyrinth – the McMahon–Husayn Correspondence and Its Interpretations 1914–1939*, Cambridge, 1976, p. 67.
26. ibid.
27. *HL*, p. 308.
28. ibid.
29. *Brown Letters*, pp. 78–9.
30. Antonius, *The Arab Awakening*, p. 175.
31. Wilson, *Authorised*, p. 259.
32. *Friends*, p. 123.
33. Sulayman Fayzi, interviewed by Suleiman Mousa, in MS. Res., c. 569.
34. ibid.

35. *RG*, p. 81.
36. From Wilfred Owen, 'Anthem for Doomed Youth', *Poems*, 1918.
37. Eric Linklater, *A Highland Regiment*.
38. *SPW*, 1935, Introduction.
39. ibid., p. 58.
40. *Garnett Letters*.

11. The Biggest Thing in the Near East Since 1550

1. David Hogarth, 'War and Discovery in Arabia', *Geographical Journal*, March 1920.
2. Antonius, *The Arab Awakening*, p. 196.
3. Baker, *King Hussain and the Kingdom of the Hejaz*, p. 102.
4. Abdallah, King of Jordan, *Memoirs*, ed. Philip Graves, 1950, p. 147.

12. Fallen Like a Sword into Their Midst

1. Robertson–Murray Correspondence, British Librrary, 1 October 1916.
2. ibid., 17 October 1916.
3. Storrs, *Orientations*, p. 203.
4. *SPW*, 1935, p. 67.
5. James, *The Golden Warrior*, p. 175.
6. Wilson, *Authorised*, p. 302.
7. *SPW*, 1935, p. 446.
8. ibid. p. 92.
9. ibid.
10. *LH*, p. 188.
11. ibid., p. 189.
12. T. E. Lawrence, *Secret Despatches from Arabia*, ed. Malcolm Brown, London, 1991, p. 70.
13. Pierce Joyce Papers, King's College, London, 27 September 1917.
14. *LH*, p. 189.
15. *SPW*, 1935, p. 63.
16. *RG*, p. 51.
17. J. L. Burckhardt, *Notes on the Bedouins and Wahhabys*, 2 vols., London, 1830, p. 133.
18. ibid., p. 134.
19. C. S. Jarvis, *Yesterday and Today in Sinai*, London, 1941, p. 18.
20. Pierce Joyce Papers, King's College, London, 18 November 1917.
21. Alec Kirkbride, BBC interview, December 1962, in MS. Res., 55/2.
22. *SPW*, 1935, p. 64.

13. *Not an Army But a World is Moving upon Wejh*

1. T. E. Lawrence, 'Evolution of a Revolt' in *Evolution of a Revolt: Early Postwar Writings of T. E. lawrence*, ed. S. and R. Weintraub, Pennsylvania, 1968, p. 106.
2. Wilson, *Authorised*, p. 320.
3. Lawrence to Clayton, 5 December 1916, PRO FO, 882.
4. ibid.
5. ibid.
6. Wilson, *Authorised*, p. 342.
7. Wilson to Clayton, 7 December 1916, PRO FO, 882.
8. ibid.
9. *SPW*, 1935, p. 134.
10. PRO FO, 686.
11. N. N. E. Bray, *Shifting Sands*, London, 1934, p. 133.

14. *I Do Not Suppose Any Englishman Before Ever Had Such a Place*

1. Literally 'Father of the Ostrich'.
2. *SPW*, 1935, p. 187.
3. Wilson, *Authorised*, p. 358.
4. PRO FO, 88/6 196.
5. *Brown Letters*, p. 103.
6. Richards, *A Portrait of T. E. Lawrence*, p. 97.
7. *Friends*, p. 87.
8. Joyce, BBC interview, 14 June 1941 and 30 April 1939, in MS. Res., 55/2.
9. British Library, Add. Mss. 45915.
10. Mack, *Prince*, p. 239.
11. *SPW*, 1935, p. 193.
12. ibid., p. 198.
13. Mousa, *T. E. Lawrence: An Arab View*, p. 56.
14. Lawrence to Joyce, PRO FO, 686/6.
15. British Library, Add. Mss., 45983a.
16. *SPW*, 1935, p. 216.
17. PRO FO, 686/6, 24 April 1917.
18. ibid.
19. PRO FO, 686/6, 150.

15. *It is Not Known What are the Present Whereabouts of Captain Lawrence*

1. Auda was a great tale-teller, and the stories of his eating the hearts of his victims, as well as the toll of his killings, could well be exaggerated. J. N. Lockman has suggested that Auda's tendency to elaborate might well have influenced Lawrence – in particular, Auda was so certain of his own fame that he would even tell stories against himself – perhaps giving Lawrence a precedent for the Dara'a fantasy – if fantasy it was (see J. N. L. Lockman, *Scattered Tracks*, p. 133). It is, however, by no means impossible that Auda had killed seventy-five men: even at the end of the twentieth century there exist men such as the Sardinian bandit Francesco Messina, who was convicted of killing fifty men in a family blood-feud.
2. Murray–Robertson correspondence, British Library.
3. Vickery to Clayton, PRO FO, 686/6 47.
4. Clayton to Vickery, PRO FO, 686/6 46.
5. Clayton, PRO FO, 882/6.
6. Lawrence's 'shopping list' for the Aqaba mission, handwritten in his skeleton diary, includes a Lewis gun, but this is not referred to at all in his reports and dispatches.
7. Wilson to Clayton, PRO FO, 882, 351.
8. British Library, Add. Mss., 45983a (Skeleton Diaries).
9. ibid.
10. British Library, Add. Mss., 45915 (War Diary).
11. Richards, *A Portrait of T. E. Lawrence*, p. 95.
12. *SPW*, 1935, p. 28.
13. British Library, Add. Mss., 45915 (War Diary).
14. *SPW*, Oxford text, 1926, p. 45.
15. *SPW*, 1935, p. 382. J. N. Lockman has claimed that this 'Shimt' is actually Gasim Abu Dumayk, the volatile Sheikh of the Dumaniyya Howaytat. This seems unlikely, for though the Dumaniyya fought at Aba l-Lissan, they were not at Mudowwara: Lawrence clearly states that he had banned them from accompanying this raid.
16. British Library, Add. Mss. 45983a (Skeleton Diaries).
17. British Library, Add. Mss. 45915 (War Diary).
18. Lowell Thomas, MS. Res., 55/2.
19. Lyn Cowan, *Masochism: A Jungian View*, Texas, 1982, p. 124.
20. British Library, Add. Mss., 45915 (War Diary).
21. *SPW*, Oxford text, 1926.
22. Wilson, *Authorised*, p. 410.
23. British Library, Add. Mss. 45915 (War Diary).
24. *SPW*, 1935, p. 284.

25. Mousa, *T. E. Lawrence: An Arab View*, p. 175.

26. *RG*, pp. 88–90.

27. *Brown Letters*, p. 408.

28. ibid., p. 274.

29. British Library, Add. Mss, 45915 (War Diary).

30. *SPW*, 1935, p. 325.

31. Lawrence does not mention *Slieve Foy* in the 1935 text. He told Liddell Hart that the ship had actually been put in place to support the Arab attack on Aqaba: this does not square with the idea that the mission was unauthorized.

16. An Amateurish, Buffalo-Billy Sort of Performance

1. Lawrence, 'Evolution of a Revolt', p. 45.

2. W. F. Stirling, 'Tales of Lawrence of Arabia', *Cornhill Magazine*, 74 (1933), pp. 494ff.

3. *SPW*, 1935, p. 324.

4. ibid.

5. Lawrence, *Secret Dispatches*.

6. *Garnett Letters*, p. 228.

7. After writing this, I discovered that both Richard Aldington and J. N. Lockman had discovered the discrepancy. All credit must go to both of them for coming across this fact before myself.

8. *SPW*, Oxford text, 1926, p. 262.

9. Clayton to CIGS, PRO FO, 882/6.

10. *SPW*, 1935, p. 330.

11. ibid., p. 582.

12. PRO FO, 882, 12/13.

13. *SPW*, 1935, p. 395.

14. Clayton to Joyce, 18 September 1917, PRO FO, 882/7.

15. ibid.

16. *SPW*, 1935, p. 360.

17. *Friends*, p. 167.

18. ibid.

19. 13 September 1917, PRO FO, 882/4.

20. *SPW*, 1935, p. 369.

21. PRO FO, 882.

22. *Brown Letters*, p. 126.

23. *Garnett Letters*, p. 238.

17. Ahmad ibn Baqr, a Circassian from Qunaytra

1. *SPW*, 1935, p. 253.
2. Philip Graves later asserted that Lawrence could himself perform this act. It is picture which smacks more of red Indians or the heroic world of Malory than of *Arabia Deserta*. The average camel stands about six feet at the shoulder, and perhaps nine feet at the withers. For a man to 'leap into the saddle' one-handed would require something more than the ability of an Olympic high-jump champion. More probably, 'Ali mounted his camel by stepping on the animal's neck and swarming on to its withers – a customary way of mounting, yet one so ungainly and vulnerable in its lack of control as to be scarcely worthy of the expression 'leaping into the saddle'.
3. *SPW*, 1935, p. 397.
4. ibid., p. 415.
5. *Garnett Letters*, p. 239.
6. *SPW*, 1935, p. 545.
7. ibid.
8. ibid.
9. *SPW*, 1935, p. 454.
10. ibid., p. 456.
11. ibid.
12. *Brown Letters*, p. 166.
13. *Friends*, p. 124.
14. *SPW*, 1935, pp. 445–8.
15. *Brown Letters*, p, 132.
16. Mack, *Prince*, p. 233.
17. Wilson, *Authorised*, p. 1084.
18. *Friends*, p. 124.
19. It is, of course, possible, that both the Artillery and Khalfati incidents were mere figments of Lawrence's masochistic fantasy also – no independent corroboration exists for either.
20. *SPW*, Oxford text, p. 38.
21. British Library, Add MSS., 45903, Charlotte Shaw Letters.
22. *SPW*, 1935, p. 581.
23. Cowan, *Masochism*, p. 248.
24. *Brown Letters*, p. 299.
25. See Lockman, *Scattered Tracks*, pp. 139ff.
26. ibid.
27. H. Montgomery-Hyde, *Solitary in the Ranks – Lawrence of Arabia as Airman and Private Soldier*, London, 1977, p. 40.

28. Wilson, *Authorised*, p. 1084.
29. *SPW*, Oxford text, 1926, p. 78.
30. Winterton recalled that Lawrence's bodyguard consisted of about sixty men during the Dara'a operation, but it may be that Lawrence's own guard was combined with Sharif Nasir's larger 'Agayl bodyguard at this point, or that Winterton's memory was influenced by *SPW*. In any case, if Lawrence's bodyguard exceeded the fifteen or so listed in his diary as having been paid, presumably the extra hands worked for him for nothing!
31. Wilson, *Authorised*, p. 1084.
32. *SPW*, 1935, p. 28.
33. MS. Res., 55/2.
34. *Friends*, p. 147.

18. The Most Ghastly Material to Build into a Design

1. PRO, 882/4 251.
2. Falls, Cyril, *et al.*, *Military Operations in Egypt and Palestine*, Vol. 1, 1928, Parts 1 and 2 (Official War History), p. 404.
3. *SPW*, 1935, p. 492.
4. *Brown Letters*, p. 434.
5. ibid., p. 435.
6. *LH*, p. 105.
7. ibid.
8. *RG*, p. 97.
9. *Brown Letters*, p. 434.
10. PRO FO, 882/4.
11. *SPW*, Oxford text, 1926, p. 99.
12. S. C. Rolls, *Steel Chariots in the Desert*, London, 1937, p. 221.
13. *SPW*, 1935, p. 535.
14. *Brown Letters*, p. 260.
15. Rolls, *Steel Chariots*, p. 230.
16. *SPW*, 1935, p. 499.

19. My Dreams Puffed out Like Candles in the Strong Wind of Success

1. *SPW*, 1935, p. 653.
2. Hubert Young, *The Independent Arab*, London, 1933, p. 142.
3. ibid., p. 203.
4. *SPW*, 1935, p. 555.
5. Young, *The Independent Arab*, p. 199.
6. ibid.

7. *SPW*, 1935, p. 543.
8. Young, *The Independent Arab*, p. 211.
9. Knightley and Simpson, *Secret Lives*, p. 162.
10. Young, *The Independent Arab*, p. 219.
11. Rolls, *Steel Chariots in the Desert*, p. 264.
12. ibid., p. 288.
13. *SPW*, 1935, p. 620.
14. Young, *The Independent Arab*, p. 228.
15. *SPW*, 1935, p. 620.
16. Lord Winterton, 'Arabian Nights and Days', *Blackwood's Magazine*, 207 (1920), p. 754.
17. Lord Winterton, *Fifty Tumultuous Years*, 1955, p. 70.
18. ibid.
19. *SPW*, 1935, p. 653.
20. ibid., p. 654.
21. Richards, *A Portrait of T. E. Lawrence*, p. 97.
22. Mack, *Prince*, p. 239.
23. Peake evidently believed, probably incorrectly, that all these Bedu belonged to Lawrence's bodyguard. (See ch. 17, n. 30.)
24. ibid.
25. Lord Birdwood, *Nuri As Said. A Study in Arab Leadership*, London, 1959, p. 199.
26. Kirkbride to Liddell Hart, 8 November 1962 in MS. Res., b. 56.
27. Mack, *Prince*, p. 239.
28. George Staples, interviewed in the *Toronto Telegraph*, 31 January 1963. Staples's testimony has been challenged. Lawrence himself says that he rode in search of Barrow with only his lieutenant Ahmad az-Za'aqi.
29. *SPW*, 1935, p. 657.
30. *SPW*, 1935, p. 660.
31. *SPW*, 1935, p. 662.
32. ibid., p. 666.
33. W. F. Stirling, 'Tales of Lawrence of Arabia', pp. 494ff.
34. *Brown Letters*, p. 275.
35. ibid.
36. *SPW*, 1935, p. 682.
37. ibid., p. 659.

20. *Colonel Lawrence Still Goes On; Only I Have Stepped Out of the Way*

1. Young, *The Independent Arab*, p. 142.
2. *LH*, 20 May 1935.
3. Wilson, *Authorised*, p. 603.

4. Wilson, *Authorised*, p. 620.
5. *RG*, p. 36.
6. *Brown Letters*, p. 332.
7. Wilson, *Authorised*, p. 630.
8. *Friends*, p. 245.
9. ibid., p. 199.
10. *Brown Letters*, p. 223.
11. ibid., p. 219.
12. Orlans, *Lawrence of Arabia*, p. 26.
13. *Brown Letters*, p. 172.
14. *Friends*, p. 208.
15. ibid., p. 214.
16. ibid.
17. ibid.
18. Aldington, *Lawrence of Arabia*.
19. *SPW*, 1935, p. 580.
20. Cowan, *Masochism*, p. 124.
21. *RG*, p. 20.
22. Mack, *Prince*, p. 525.
23. *Friends*, p. 197.
24. *SPW*, 1935, p. 276.
25. Antonius, *The Arab Awakening*, p. 319.

21. *In Speed We Hurl Ourselves Beyond the Body*

1. J. N. Lockman reports having read Lawrence's RAF medical record, and though this was not available for publication concludes that the evidence suggests his scars were voluntarily acquired after the war. Lockman discounts Johns's later testimony to the *Sunday Times*, 1968. See Lockman, *Scattered Tracks*, pp. 139ff.
2. Montgomery-Hyde, *Solitary in the Ranks*, p. 52.
3. *RG*, p. 97.
4. Montgomery-Hyde, *Solitary in the Ranks*, p. 48.
5. *Garnett Letters*, p. 379.
6. British Library, Add. Mss. 45903, Charlotte Shaw Letters.
7. *Brown Letters*, p. 221.
8. *Garnett Letters*, p. 379.
9. *Friends*, p. 379.
10. *Brown Letters*, p. 210.
11. ibid., p. 216.
12. ibid., p. 215.

396

13. Wilson, *Authorised*, p. 687.
14. *Garnett Letters*, p. 375.
15. *Brown Letters*, p. 209.
16. Montgomery-Hyde, *Solitary in the Ranks*, p. 48.
17. John Bruce, sworn testimony, Knightley and Simpson Papers, Imperial War Museum, p. 17.
18. ibid.
19. Wilson, *Authorised*, p. 704.
20. Bruce, sworn testimony, p. 17.
21. Knightley and Simpson, *Secret Lives*, p. 193.
22. ibid., p. 194.
23. Mack, *Prince*, p. 525.
24. John Bruce, sworn testimony, p. 74.
25. Mack, *Prince*, p. 525.
26. Bruce, sworn testimony.
27. *Brown Letters*, p. 488.
28. ibid., p. 462.
29. ibid., p. 468.
30. Wilson, *Authorised*, p. 928.
31. *Brown Letters*, p. 408.
32. ibid., p. 486.
33. *Brown Letters*, p. 526.
34. ibid., p. 537.
35. ibid., p. 486.

BIBLIOGRAPHY

Archives

The Bodleian Library, Oxford: Reserve Manuscript Collection (embargoed material on T. E. Lawrence).
The National Library of Scotland, Manuscripts Collection: Various files, rare books and manuscripts.
The Public Record Office, Kew: Foreign Office and War Office Files; Arab Bureau Files; Intelligence Files.
The British Library Additional Manuscripts Collection: Robertson–McMahon Correspondence; T. E. Lawrence – Letters to Charlotte Shaw; T. E. Lawrence – War Diaries and Pocket Diaries.
King's College, University of London, Basil Liddell Hart Centre for Military Archives: Joyce Pierce Akaba Papers.
Imperial War Museum, London: Knightley and Simpson Papers.

Books and Journals

Abdallah, King of Jordan, *Memoirs*, ed. Philip Graves, London, 1950.
Admiralty War Staff – Intelligence Division, *A Handbook of Arabia*, Vol. 1, London, 1916.
Aldington, Richard, *Lawrence of Arabia: A Biographical Enquiry*, London, 1955.
Andrews, P., and Brunner, E., *The Life of Lord Nuffield*, London, 1955.
Antonius, George, *The Arab Awakening*, London, 1938.
Baker, Randall, *King Hussain and the Kingdom of the Hejaz*, Cambridge, 1979.
Barbor, Patricia, *Desert Treks from Jeddah*, London, 1996.
Barker, A. J., *The Neglected War: Mesopotamia 1915–1916*, London, 1967.
Bedarida, François, *A Social History of England 1851–1975*, London, 1979.
Bell, Lady (ed.), *The Letters of Gertrude Bell*, 2 vols., London, 1927.
Ben Yusuf, Ofer, and Khazanov, Anatoly, *Pastoralism in the Levant*, 1992.
Berne, Eric, *Games People Play – The Psychology of Human Relationships*, New York, 1964.
Betjeman, John, and Vaisey, D., *Victorian and Edwardian Oxford*, Oxford, 1971.

Birdwood, Lord, *Nuri As Said. A Study in Arab Leadership*, London, 1959.

Blackmore, Charles, *In the Footsteps of Lawrence of Arabia*, London, 1986.

Blunt, Lady Anne, *Bedouin Tribes of the Euphrates*, 2 vols., London, 1879.

Bray, N. N. E., *Shifting Sands*, London, 1934.

Brill, E. J., *Mecca and the Tribes of Arabia – Some Notes on Their Relations* in *Society and Religion from Jahiliyya to Islam*, ed. M. J. Kister, London, 1990.

Brown, Malcolm, *A Touch of Genius – the Life of T. E. Lawrence*, Oxford, 1988.

Bullock, David L., *Allenby's War – The Palestinian–Arabian Campaign 1916–18*, London, 1987.

Burbidge, W. F., *The Mysterious A C2 – A Biographical Sketch of Lawrence of Arabia*, London, 1943.

Burckhardt, J. L., *Notes on the Bedouins and Wahhabys*, 2 vols, London, 1830.

Candler, E., 'Lawrence in the Hedjaz', *Blackwood's*, 243 (December 1925).

Charmley, John, *Lord Lloyd and the Decline of the British Empire*, London, 1987.

Clayton, Gilbert, *An Arabian Diary*, London, 1969.

Cowan, Lyn, *New Ways in Psychoanalysis*, New York, 1966.

Cowan, Lyn, *Masochism – A Jungian View*, Texas, 1982.

Djemal, A., *Memories of a Turkish Statesman 1915–1919*, London, 1922.

Donner, Fred McGraw, *The Early Islamic Conquests*, Princeton, 1981.

Doughty, Charles M., *Travels in Arabia Deserta*, 2 vols., Cambridge, 1888.

Ellis, Havelock, *Psychology of Sex*, New York, 1933.

Eph'al, Israel, *The Ancient Arabs – Nomads on the Borders of the Fertile Crescent 9th–5th Centuries BC*, London, 1982.

Facey, William, and Grant, Gillian, *Saudi-Arabia – The First Photographers*, London, 1996.

Falls, Cyril, *et al.*, *Military Operations in Egypt and Palestine*, Vol. 1, 1928, Parts 1 and 2 (Official War History).

Foucault, Michel, *History of Sexuality*, London, 1975.

Glen, Douglas, *In the Steps of T. E. Lawrence*, London, 1934.

Glubb, John Bagot, *The Great Arab Conquests*, London, 1963.

Graves, Robert, *Lawrence and the Arabs*, London, 1927.

Graves, Robert, *T. E. Lawrence to His Biographer Robert Graves*, London, 1938.

Gurney, O. R., *The Hittites*, London, 1972.

Herbert A., *Mons, Anzac and Kut*, London, 1919.

Hitti, Philip, *A History of the Arabs*, New York, 1937.

Hogarth, David G., 'War and Discovery in Arabia', *Geographical Journal*, March 1920.

James, Lawrence, *Imperial Warrior – Life and Times of Sir Edmund Allenby*, London, 1993.

James, Lawrence, *The Golden Warrior – The Life and Legend of Lawrence of Arabia*, revised edn, London, 1995.

Jarvis, C. S., *Yesterday and Today in Sinai*, London, 1941.

Kedourie, Elie, *In the Anglo-Arabian Labyrinth – the McMahon–Husayn Correspondence and Its Interpretations 1914–1939*, Cambridge, 1976.

Kirkbride, Alec, *A Crackle of Thorns*, London, 1956.

Kirkbride, Alec, *An Awakening*, London, 1971.

Knightley, Philip, and Simpson, Colin, *The Secret Lives of Lawrence of Arabia*, London, 1969.

Knowles, Pat, *A Handful with Quietness*, London, 1992.

Kressenstein, K. von, 'The Campaign in Palestine from the Enemy Side', *Journal of the Royal Society Institute*, Vol. 67, 1922.

Lancaster, William, *The Rwala Bedouin Today*, Cambridge, 1981.

Lawrence, A. W. (ed.), *T. E. Lawrence by His Friends*, London, 1938.

Lawrence, T. E., *The Seven Pillars of Wisdom*, Oxford text (limited edition), London, 1926.

Lawrence, T. E., *The Seven Pillars of Wisdom*, London, 1935.

Lawrence, T. E., *Crusader Castles*, London, 1936.

Lawrence, T. E., *The Mint*, London, 1936.

Lawrence, T. E., *The Letters of T. E. Lawrence*, ed. Edward Garnett, London, 1938.

Lawrence, T. E., *et al.*, *The Home Letters of T. E. Lawrence and his Brothers*, ed. M. R. Lawrence, Oxford, 1954.

Lawrence, T. E., *Fifty Letters 1920–1935*, Texas, 1962.

Lawrence, T. E., *Letters to E. T. Leeds*, ed. Jeremy Wilson, London, 1988.

Lawrence, T. E., *The Letters of T. E. Lawrence*, ed. Malcolm Brown, Oxford, 1991.

Lawrence, T. E., *Secret Despatches from Arabia*, ed. Malcolm Brown, London, 1991.

Lawrence, T. E., and Woolley, L., *The Wilderness of Zinn*, London, 1915.

Layard, Austin, *Nineveh and Its Remains*, London, 1848–9.

Layard, Austin, *The Ruins of Nineveh and Babylon*, London, 1853.

Lewis, Norman N., *Nomads and Settlers in Syria and Jordan 1800–1980*, Cambridge, 1987.

Lewis, R., *Everyday Life in Ottoman Turkey*, London, 1971.

Liddell Hart, Basil, *T. E. Lawrence: in Arabia and After*, London, 1934.

Liddell Hart, Basil, *T. E. Lawrence to His Biographer Liddell Hart*, London, 1938.

Lockman, J. N., *Scattered Tracks on the Lawrence Trail – 12 Essays on T. E. Lawrence*, Michigan, 1996.

Lonnroth, Eric, *Lawrence of Arabia, An Historical Appreciation*, London, 1956.

Lowe, Gordon R., *The Growth of Personality*, London, 1972.

Mack, John, *A Prince of Our Disorder – The Life of T. E. Lawrence*, London, 1976.

Marriot, Paul, *The Young Lawrence of Arabia 1888–1910*, Oxford, 1977.

Marriot, Paul, and Argent, Yvonne, *The Last Days of T. E. Lawrence*, London, 1996.

Mauger, Thierry, *The Bedouins of Arabia*, London, 1988.

McCarthy, Fiona, *William Morris – A Life for Our Times*, London, 1991.

Meeker, Michael, *Literature and Violence in North Arabia*, Cambridge, 1979.

Meinerzhagen, Richard, *Middle East Diary 1917–1956*, London, 1959.

Meyers, Jeffrey, 'T. E. Lawrence and *Seven Pillars of Wisdom*' in *Homosexuality in Literature 1890–1930*, New York, 1987.

Meyers, Jeffrey, *The Wounded Spirit – T. E. Lawrence's Seven Pillars of Wisdom*, New York, 1989.

Meyers, Jeffrey (ed.), *T. E. Lawrence: Soldier, Writer, Legend*, London, 1989.

Miller, James, *The Passion of Michel Foucault*, New York, 1993.

Montgomery-Hyde, H., *Solitary in the Ranks – Lawrence of Arabia as Airman and Private Soldier*, London, 1977.

Morris, James, *The Hashemite Kings*, London, 1959.

Morris, James, *Farewell The Trumpets – An Imperial Retreat*, London, 1978.

Morris, Jan, *Oxford*, London, 1965; Oxford 1978.

Mousa, Suleiman, *T. E. Lawrence – An Arab View*, trans. Albert Butros, London, 1966.

Musil, Alois, *The North of Hegaz – A Preliminary Report of the Exploring Expedition of 1910*, PRO FO 882/1–3, 1916.

Musil, Alois, *The Northern Hegaz*, New York, 1926.

Musil, Alois, *The Manners and Customs of the Rwala Bedouins*, New York, 1928.

Neville, R. G., and Sloggett, T., *Oxford as it Was*, Oxford, 1979.

Nicolle, D., *Lawrence and the Arab Revolts – Warfare and Soldiers of the Middle East, 1914–18*, London, 1989.

O'Brien, Philip, *T. E. Lawrence: a Bibliography*, London, 1988.

Ocampo, Victoria, *338171 'T.E.'*, ed. D. Garnett, London, 1963.

Orlans, Harold (ed.), *Lawrence of Arabia, Strange Man of Letters – the Literary Criticism and Correspondence of T. E. Lawrence*, London, 1993.

Park, James, *Sons, Mothers and Other Lovers*, London, 1995.

Payne, Robert, *Lawrence of Arabia: a Triumph*, London, 1966.

Pearson, E., *Awakening the Hero Within*, New York, 1991.

Pratten, Dr John, *Social Stratification in Edwardian England*, London, 1985.

Randell, John, *Sexual Variations*, London, 1973.

Reik, Theodor, *Of Love and Lust: A Study of Human Sexual Emotions*, London, 1954.

Reynolds, J. J., *Canon Christopher of St. Aldates*, London, 1967.

Richards, Vyvyan, *Portrait of T. E. Lawrence, The Lawrence of the Seven Pillars of Wisdom*, London, 1936.

Rolls, S. C., *Steel Chariots in the Desert*, London, 1937.

Sachar, H., *The Emergence of the Middle East 1914–1924*, New York, 1969.

Said, Edward, *Orientalism*, London, 1978.

Schild, Marten, *Lawrence and Arabia and T. E. Lawrence: Essays on the Private Life of an Immaculate Hero and His Imperfect Shadow* (draft MS, unpublished).

Seymour-Smith, Martin, *Robert Graves*, London, 1982.

Sherwood, John, *No Golden Journey – A Biography of James Elroy Flecker*, 1973.

Stewart, Desmond, *T. E. Lawrence*, London, 1977.

Stirling, W. F., 'Tales of Lawrence of Arabia', *Cornhill Magazine*, 74 (1933).

Stirling, W. F., *Safety Last*, London, 1953.

Storr, Anthony, *Sexual Deviations*, London, 1973.

Storrs, Ronald, *Orientations*, London, 1944.

Sugarman, Sidney, *A Garland of Legends: Lawrence of Arabia and the Arab Revolt*, Worcester, 1992.

Sweet, Louise E., 'Camel Raiding of the North Arabian Bedouin: a Mechanism of Ecological Adaptation', *American Anthropologist*, 67 (1965).

Sydney Smith, Clare, *The Golden Reign – The Story of My Friendship with Lawrence of Arabia*, London, 1940.

Tabachnick, S. E., and Matheson, R., *Images of Lawrence*, 1988.

Thesiger, Wilfred, *Arabian Sands*, London, 1959.

Thomas, Edward, *Oxford*, 1903.

Thomas, Lowell, *With Lawrence in Arabia*, London, 1924.

Turner, Adam, *The Making of David Lean's Lawrence of Arabia*, London, 1994.

Weintraub, Stanley, *Private Shaw and Public Shaw – A Dual Portrait of Lawrence of Arabia and GBS*, London, 1963.

Weintraub, Stanley and Rodelle (eds.), *Evolution of a Revolt: Early Postwar Writings of T. E. Lawrence*, Pennsylvania, 1968.

Williamson, Henry, *Genius of Friendship 'T. E. Lawrence'*, London, 1936.

Wilson, Colin, *The Outsider*, London, 1956.

Wilson, Jeremy, *T. E. Lawrence – Lawrence of Arabia. National Portrait Gallery Catalogue of the T. E. Lawrence Exhibition*, 1988.

Wilson, Jeremy, *Lawrence of Arabia. The Authorised Biography of T. E. Lawrence*, London, 1989.

Winstone, H. R. V., *The Illicit Adventure*, 1987.

Winterton, Lord, *Fifty Tumultuous Years*, London, 1955.

Winterton, Lord, 'Arabian Nights and Days', *Blackwood's Magazine*, 207 (May 1920).

Woolley, C. Leonard, *Dead Towns and Living Men, being Pages from an Antiquary's Notebook*, London, 1932.

Yardley, Michael, *Backing into the Limelight*, London, 1985.

Young, Hubert, *The Independent Arabs*, London, 1933.

INDEX

Proper names are indexed alphabetically according to the commonly used element in the names, and where they are prefixed with *ad, adh, al, an, ar, as, ash, bin,* or *ibn* these words remain as prefixes but are ignored for purposes of alphabetization. Thus *ibn Hamza* is indexed under H.

Names beginning with *Abu* and *Umm* are indexed under A and U respectively.

Sub-entries are arranged in page order so that they reflect, on the whole, the historical sequence of events.